OPPOSING THE RULE OF LAW

The rule of law is a political ideal today endorsed and promoted worldwide. Or is it? In a major contribution to the field, Nick Cheesman argues that Myanmar is a country in which the rule of law is 'lexically present but semantically absent'. Charting ideas and practices from British colonial rule through military dictatorship to the present day, Cheesman calls upon political and legal theory to explain how and why institutions animated by a concern for law and order oppose the rule of law. Empirically grounded in both Burmese and English sources, including criminal trial records and wide ranging official documents, *Opposing the Rule of Law* offers the first significant study of courts in contemporary Myanmar. It sheds new light on the politics of courts during dark times and sharply illuminates the tension between the demand for law and the imperatives of order.

NICK CHEESMAN is a Research Fellow in the Department of Political and Social Change at the Australian National University.

CAMBRIDGE STUDIES IN LAW AND SOCIETY

Cambridge Studies in Law and Society aims to publish the best scholarly work on legal discourse and practice in its social and institutional contexts, combining theoretical insights and empirical research.

The fields that it covers are studies of law in action; the sociology of law; the anthropology of law; cultural studies of law, including the role of legal discourses in social formations; law and economics; law and politics; and studies of governance. The books consider all forms of legal discourse across societies, rather than being limited to lawyers' discourses alone.

The series editors come from a range of disciplines: academic law, socio-legal studies, sociology, and anthropology. All have been actively involved in teaching and writing about law in context.

A list of books in the series can be found at the back of this book.

OPPOSING THE RULE OF LAW

How Myanmar's courts make law and order

Nick Cheesman
Australian National University

CAMBRIDGE
UNIVERSITY PRESS

CAMBRIDGE
UNIVERSITY PRESS

University Printing House, Cambridge CB2 8BS, United Kingdom

Cambridge University Press is part of the University of Cambridge.

It furthers the University's mission by disseminating knowledge in the pursuit of education, learning and research at the highest international levels of excellence.

www.cambridge.org
Information on this title: www.cambridge.org/9781107083189

First published 2015

A catalogue record for this publication is available from the British Library

Library of Congress Cataloguing in Publication data
Cheesman, Nick, author.
Opposing the rule of law : how Myanmar's courts make law and order / Nick Cheesman, Australian National University.
pages cm. – (Cambridge studies in law and society)
Includes bibliographical references and index.
ISBN 978-1-107-08318-9 (hardback)
1. Criminal justice, Administration of – Burma. 2. Rule of law – Burma. I. Title.
KNL3411.C48 2015
347.591'01–dc23
2014050254

ISBN 978-1-107-08318-9 Hardback

In memory of Phyo Wai Aung

CONTENTS

ACKNOWLEDGEMENTS

This book began in 2003. I had been working with the Asian Legal Resource Centre (ALRC) in Hong Kong for over a year and had gone to Thailand to renew old acquaintances and make new ones. In Mae Sot, I met Min Lwin Oo. We sat and talked on the veranda of the Burma Lawyers' Council office. Leafing through the records of criminal cases brought across the border from Myanmar, we selected one. A court had wrongly convicted a teenage boy for allegedly throwing rocks at policemen. Back in Hong Kong, I wrote up the case, and publicised it. Radio stations picked it up and contacted the boy's family. His mother spoke out fearlessly. People in Myanmar and abroad expressed their support. Something happened that I had not expected. Within days, a government minister ordered the boy's release. It got me thinking.

Over the coming years, Min Lwin and I collaborated on many more cases. Now and then we had successes. More often we did not. But I learned a great deal along the way. And I had the opportunity to work closely with Basil Fernando, director of the ALRC and its sister organisation, the Asian Human Rights Commission. Basil pushed my thought from individual narratives to larger questions of politics, power, and violence. He posed questions both intuitively and intellectually. His lived experiences affected how he communicated. Although my experiences are not his, I hope a little of Basil's voice has carried onto the pages that follow.

I researched and wrote the book at the Australian National University (ANU). From first steps as a doctoral candidate until putting the finishing touches on the manuscript, I got all the support I needed. To my supervisors, Hilary Charlesworth, Robert Cribb, and one external supervisor, Myint Zan, I owe a lasting debt of gratitude. Above all, I am grateful to Ed Aspinall for chairing my panel. Ed did not know a great deal about Myanmar or the politics of courts, but he knew everything about how to guide a student to successful submission of a thesis. His advice was unfailingly reliable, his friendship and good humour, irreplaceable.

For much of my time studying at the ANU, Ed headed the Department of Political and Social Change, in the College of Asia and the Pacific. Three other heads of this department helped the book to fruition. Ben Kerkvliet left just as I arrived, yet stayed in touch and always responded generously when I contacted him. Paul Hutchcroft – initially in the department and then as head of the School of International, Political and Strategic Studies, where the department is located – gave strong backing throughout. And as a research fellow I have had the pleasure of working with Greg Fealy, whose unreserved support has made all the difference to the book's timely completion.

Among fellow travellers in the department, Tyrell Haberkorn and Jacqui Baker have provoked me to think about my research critically, and have been generous with the contents of their bookshelves. Other colleagues who have set examples for me as a scholar include Marcus Mietzner, Sally Sargeson, Tamara Jacka, Luigi Tomba, Paul Kenny, and Andrew Walker. Eve Warburton and Sheryn Lee taught undergraduate classes with me while I was revising the manuscript, and did so brilliantly. Julie Fitzgibbon and Helen McMartin steered all of us through the paperwork and peculiarities of university administration.

With Trevor Wilson, Monique Skidmore, and Nicholas Farrelly, I have convened a number of the Myanmar/Burma Update conferences. These events have been tremendously nourishing intellectually, and Trevor's tireless advocacy for research on Myanmar at the ANU has been greatly encouraging.

None of my work at the ANU would have been possible without a Vice Chancellor's Scholarship for doctoral study, supplemented along the way by funding to do fieldwork and attend local and international conferences obtained from my department, school, college, the Research School of Asia and the Pacific, and the Vice Chancellor's office. For all this funding I am truly appreciative.

To my pleasant surprise, as my research progressed other people whose writing I admire started to take an interest. Craig Reynolds read various drafts and listened patiently to good ideas and bad. Frank Munger gave me confidence during early stages of research. As it neared completion, Martin Krygier gave me much more. Both Frank and Martin have welcomed me into their homes with friendship, food, and conversation full of good ideas and advice, as have Jim Scott and Dan Slater. Discussions with Eve Darian-Smith, Terry

Halliday, Mary Callahan, and Dany Celermajer have been stimulating and too short.

Sophie Viravong, head librarian of the Mainland Southeast Asia collection at the National Library of Australia, helped me to obtain many materials used for this research. The library is an exemplary public institution thanks to the commitment and enthusiasm of Sophie and her colleagues. While on cataloguing stints there, I habitually snuck away to meet Andrew Selth. I am indebted to him for all his assistance, and eagerly await his next book. At the other end of the library's line, thank you to the ever-resourceful Thant Thaw Kaung, and the ever-gracious Ma Win Win at the Myanmar Book Centre.

My Burmese-language instructor, Daw Mar Lay, would have preferred a student of sociolinguistics or stone inscriptions. To her credit, she took me in as a pupil and as one of the family, even after she knew that those topics were not mine. My other instructor and lunchtime companion U Kyaw Nyunt has over the years become a dear friend. Without him my knowledge of Burmese would be far more rudimentary than it is today, and the lunches would have been less appetising.

Among the many courageous and resilient people in Myanmar whom I have had the honour of getting to know are U Aung Thane and fellow lawyers at his inconspicuous yet indefatigable firm, Ko Min Min and colleagues at Olive Branch, Kyaw Min San and everyone at Justice For All, Than Myint Aung, Law Dan Zau and family, U Tin Aung Htun, and U Myint Aye and team at Human Rights Defenders and Promoters – more strength to them all. Thanks to Eugene Quah for breakfast discussions. Thank you also, with great respect, to Htet Wai Aung, Nandar, U Kyaw Min, and Wai Wai Nu. Above all, I am grateful to everyone who has taken the time to meet me and speak about courts, police, and criminal cases in Myanmar.

As Myanmar has entered a period of political change, so too has scholarship on the country. A new and exciting intellectual community is emerging. Among its members, thanks in particular to Dom Nardi and Melissa Crouch for comments and questions about my work. I look forward to continued discussions, and to reading what these scholars publish in coming years.

Other people whose insights and friendship have helped me along the way include Moon Jeong Ho, Sanjeewa Weerawickrama, Danilo Reyes, Baseer Naveed, Bijo Francis, Md. Ashrafuzzaman, Philip and Irene Setunga, Angkhana Neelaphaijit, Kishali Pinto-Jayawardena,

Wong Kai Shing, Kim Soo A, Michael Anthony, Nilantha Ilangamuwa, Purdey Mak, Norman Voss, Meryam Dabhoiwala, Louise Sun, Amy Mak, Hazel Le, Linda Lai, Lao Mong Hay, Mark Tamthai, Jack Clancey, Sor Rattanamanee Polkla, Preeda Tongchumnum, Pornpen Khongkachonkiet, Supinya Klangnarong, Puttanee Kangkun, Kyaw Htet, Aye Aye Mar, Kirity Roy, Shiv Prasad Singh, Shiv Karan Singh, Mandira Sharma, and Chris Cusano. Thank you also to Sieglinde and Robert, Bianca and Carl.

At Cambridge University Press, Lucy Rhymer guided the manuscript smoothly from proposal to publication. I am appreciative of her, Amanda George, and their colleagues for their professionalism and expertise, as well as the two reviewers of the manuscript. In Australia, Matt Fenwick gave valuable writing advice. Belinda Henwood edited and Sherrey Quinn indexed the final text. Sarah Bishop and Chit Win double-checked the citations. Allison Ley proofread an earlier draft. In Yangon, 'Boothee' Thaik Htun went on assignment for the cover photograph.

My wife Saranyaphak monitored the drafting and revising of this book in all its iterations. More than anyone else, she will be happy to see it in print at last. As it is mine, so it is hers.

Back in the mid-1980s, my family moved to the Philippines. At the time, my parents might have wondered if they were doing the right thing for their two teenage boys. They were. In Manila, our family grew from four to five. There they awakened in their three children a lifelong love of inquiry, an enthusiasm for meaningful work, and a lasting interest in Southeast Asia: Jeremy for a time in Vietnam and Cambodia, Emily back in the Philippines. Thanks to Wendy and John, we lost any inhibitions we might have had to seek out and explore the unfamiliar. They opened the door; we walked through it. What more could we have wanted?

Copyright acknowledgements are as follows. Chapter 1 builds on 'Law and Order as Asymmetrical Opposite to the Rule of Law', *Hague Journal on the Rule of Law* 6.1 (2014): 96–114; Chapters 2 and 3 contain parts taken from 'Rule-of-law Lineages in Colonial and Early Postcolonial Burma', *Modern Asian Studies* (2015): forthcoming; Chapter 2 also draws on a section of 'Bodies on the Line in Burma's Criminal Law Reports, 1892–1922', *Law, Society and Transition in Myanmar*, eds. Melissa Crouch and Tim Lindsey (Oxford: Hart, 2014) 77–94; Chapter 6 is taken in part from 'Myanmar's Courts and the Sounds Money Makes', *Myanmar's Transition: Openings, Obstacles and Opportunities*, eds. Nick Cheesman, Monique Skidmore, and Trevor Wilson (Singapore: ISEAS, 2010) 231–48, reproduced here with the kind permission of the publisher, Institute of Southeast Asian Studies, Singapore http://bookshop.iseas.edu.sg; Chapter 8 intersects with the contents of 'Not Just Defending; Advocating for Law in Myanmar', *Wisconsin International Law Journal* 31.3 (2014): 702–33 (with Kyaw Min San); and, 'What Does the Rule of Law Have to Do with Democratisation (in Myanmar)?' *South East Asia Research* 22.2 (2014): 213–32 (copyright © 2014 SOAS. Used by Permission of IP Publishing Ltd). Thank you to Ronald Janse, Claire Weatherhead, Ng Kok Kiong, Kim Hardtke, John Edmondson, and Sue Allerton for giving or arranging for permission to republish material from these pieces.

NOTE ON BURMESE USAGE

Throughout this book I have used the BGN/PCGN 1970 Romanisation System for Burmese where transliterating Burmese words into italicised text. For capitalised proper nouns, I have Romanised place names as per official standard conventions for the relevant period, hence 'Rangoon' and 'Burma' up to and including 1988 and 'Yangon' and 'Myanmar' thereafter. I have transliterated the new capital's name as Naypyidaw rather than Nay Pyi Taw to be consistent with other place names, which I have also transliterated as single words, hyphenated where necessary to distinguish closing and opening vowels and consonants. Personal names I have spelled, wherever possible, as the person named prefers, even where these spellings are uncommon, hence 'U Aung Thane' rather than 'U Aung Thein'. Otherwise, I have followed common usage. After the first reference to a person, subsequent references omit honorific prefixes. Hence, for older women, 'Daw Aung San Suu Kyi' is followed with 'Aung San Suu Kyi'; for younger women, 'Ma Hnin Sanda' is followed with 'Hnin Sanda'; for older men, 'U Nu' is followed with 'Nu'; and, for younger men 'Maung Chan Kun' is followed with 'Chan Kun', and 'Ko Aung Hlaing Win' with 'Aung Hlaing Win', except where 'Maung' or 'Ko' are part of the man's name. All translations of materials from Burmese are my own unless otherwise indicated.

INTRODUCTION

In early June 2012, a group of people in the west of Myanmar stopped a bus carrying Muslim pilgrims. They beat ten passengers to death and torched the vehicle. According to news reports, they killed in reprisal for the rape and murder of a young Buddhist woman a few days earlier, allegedly by three Muslims. Not long after the attack, demonstrators gathered outside a mosque in the centre of Yangon, the country's former capital. Speakers called for justice. Some carried photographs of the bus passengers' mutilated bodies, along with placards bearing the term in Burmese for 'the rule of law', *taya-ubade-somoye*.

In the following days, violence spread and worsened. Meantime, Daw Aung San Suu Kyi, symbol of political resistance to the previous two decades of dictatorship, went on her first major overseas tour since her release from house arrest in 2010. While abroad, she referred to the rule of law as a prerequisite to address the violence. 'We have said again and again rule of law is essential. ... Without rule of law, such communal strife will only continue,' she told a gathering in Geneva.[1] In Oslo, London, and Paris, she emphasised that her country's future prospects would depend on the rule of law. She mentioned it so often that one commentator quipped the trip should have been called the Rule of Law Tour.[2]

Nor did the tour end in Europe. In September, it continued in the United States. At Yale University, Aung San Suu Kyi said that her

[1] *CNN* 14 June (2012), 15 Nov. 2012 www.cnn.com.
[2] *Asia Sentinel* 26 June (2012), 25 Nov. 2012 www.asiasentinel.com.

National League for Democracy had put the rule of law at the top of the party platform, ahead of resolving ethnic conflict, because 'we can't put an end to ethnic conflict unless there is rule of law'.[3] In San Francisco, she again spoke to its importance. The calibre of judges and lawyers in Myanmar had fallen, she said, and to create a culture of rights the country would 'have to start from scratch'.[4]

Returning home from her European trip, Aung San Suu Kyi accepted an offer from the national legislature, to which she had been elected in May, to head a new committee on the rule of law and tranquility. The first item on its mandate was 'alerting, urging and enabling' of legislators, prosecutors, civil servants, the government, media, and other people and institutions to obey the law.[5] At its inaugural meeting in September, Aung San Suu Kyi articulated a vision for the rule of law that went well beyond the narrow confines of the committee's mandate:

> For the rule of law it is insufficient merely to have laws. It is insufficient that the laws are just. How the designs of laws are realised is also important. To put it simply, our view is that in a society bound by the rule of law everybody has faith that the law will protect one's individual security and liberty, that the law is capable of protecting every citizen's freedoms and security, and that it does so. Where it can do so and where confidence in it exists, we can say that a society is bound by the rule of law.[6]

Given that army officers arbitrarily confined her to her house for over a decade, Aung San Suu Kyi's stress on the rule of law is understandable. In one classic formulation, the rule of law is nothing if not a bulwark against arbitrary exercise of authority to deny people their individual liberties.[7] Its bottom line is its capacity to prevent the sort of detention Aung San Suu Kyi endured. Yet the rule of law apparently means more to Aung San Suu Kyi than just this. Her rule of law also helps put an end to communal conflict, and to ethnic warfare. It bolsters democracy. It has a big agenda.

[3] *Yale News* 27 Sept. (2012), 25 Nov. 2012 http://news.yale.edu.
[4] *KQED* 28 Sept. (2012), 8 Dec. 2012 http://blogs.kqed.org.
[5] Pyithu Hluttaw, 'Rule of Law and Tranquility Committee', 2012, www.pyithuhluttaw.gov.mm, 25 Nov. 2012 (in Burmese).
[6] *Weekly Eleven* 19 Sept. 2012: 3.
[7] Albert V. Dicey, *Introduction to the Study of the Law of the Constitution*, 8th ed. (Indianapolis, IN: Liberty Fund, 1982) 110–22.

Aung San Suu Kyi's invocations of the rule of law, like countless others in Myanmar following the country's return to electoral politics after more than twenty years of unmediated military rule, could be evidence of the ideal's continued ascent worldwide.[8] A decade and a half after one expert pronounced that the concept was 'suddenly everywhere – a venerable part of Western political philosophy enjoying a new run as a rising imperative of the era of globalization', its run shows no sign of coming to an end.[9] To the contrary, as another long-time observer of the concept has noted, 'Once a quasi-technical term of interest only to lawyers and legal philosophers, [the rule of law] appears all over the globe these days, at ease in the company of such unassailably Good Things as democracy, equality, and justice . . . an international hurrah term, on the lips of every development agency, offered as a support for economic growth, democracy, human rights, and much else.'[10]

Aung San Suu Kyi's faith that the rule of law is the solution to her country's troubles evidently rests on the belief that not only does it belong in the company of these unassailably Good Things, but that it will help to deliver them as well. Nor is she alone in this belief. Practically every development worker and government official in Myanmar seems to share it, as do noodle vendors, bus conductors, and schoolteachers. But is this Southeast Asian country just the latest corner of the globe where the rule of law has suddenly appeared with a hurrah, or is there more to it than that? And why does the rule of law matter to Myanmar, or Myanmar matter for study of the rule of law?

HURRAH FOR THE RULE OF LAW . . . IN MYANMAR?

Well might we cry, 'Hurrah for Myanmar!' Over six decades since wresting political independence from British colonial rule, its roughly fifty-two million occupants situated between China and India have enjoyed neither the growing prosperity of one nor the personal

[8] As discussed in Nick Cheesman, 'What Does the Rule of Law Have to Do with Democratisation (in Myanmar)?' *South East Asia Research* 22.2 (2014): 217–21.

[9] Thomas Carothers, 'The Rule of Law Revival', *Foreign Affairs* 77.2 (1998): 95.

[10] Martin Krygier, 'Four Puzzles About the Rule of Law: Why, What, Where? And Who Cares?' *Getting to the Rule of Law*, ed. James E. Fleming, vol. V, Nomos (New York and London: New York University Press, 2011) 64.

freedoms of the other.[11] Stymied from the beginning by economic devastation and war, mired in civil conflict, and thwarted by successive military despots, their achievements have been despite the work of government, not because of it.

But impressive advances beyond army-dominated politics notwithstanding, we ought to be wary of crying 'hurrah' for the rule of law in Myanmar. Television or newspaper reports might give the impression that people there had just heard of 'the rule of law' when Aung San Suu Kyi began uttering the term following her release from house arrest. We need not look far for evidence to the contrary. 'The rule of law' is no stranger to Myanmar. It has long been a part of the Burmese political lexicon, common to the language of democrats and dictators alike.

For decades, soldiers, bureaucrats, and politicians in Myanmar have professed concern for the rule of law. Parliamentarians in the 1950s invoked it to justify emergency regulations to combat insurgency.[12] Ten years after the country's independence, the military ran an interim government under the banner, 'Peace and the rule of law first'.[13] In 1974, a one-party government cited the rule of law when it imposed military administration on the capital city following widespread anti-government protests.[14] Four years later, the government portrayed violence that accompanied its attempt to expel tens of thousands of alleged foreigners to Bangladesh as wanton illegality in the face of legitimate efforts to enforce the law.[15] Decrying news reports abroad about the persecution of Muslims, an editorialist in the state press wrote, 'The sense of justice and fairness which governs our relations with other nations extends to a sense of justice in our internal affairs with the Rule of Law a principal criterion in our human relations, economic affairs and in all other fields of human endeavour.'[16]

[11] Population estimates vary. In 2014 the government undertook a census and released provisional results in August; however, exact numbers will remain elusive for a host of political and procedural reasons discussed in Mary Callahan, Christoph LeFranc, and Nancy Stiegler, Documentation of Risk Mitigation Report: 2013 Pilot Census, Myanmar (n.p.: UNFPA, 2013). See also TNI/BCN, *Ethnicity without Meaning, Data without Context: The 2014 Census, Identity and Citizenship in Burma/Myanmar* (Amsterdam: Transnational Institute and Burma Centrum Nederland, February 2014).

[12] Maung Maung, *Law and Custom in Burma and the Burmese Family* (The Hague: Martinus Nijhoff, 1963) 25.

[13] Revolutionary Council, *Burma: Administrative and Social Affairs, 1962–63* (Rangoon: Office of the Director of Information, 1965) 34 (in Burmese).

[14] Govt. of the Socialist Republic of the Union of Burma, *Digest of Undertakings of the First Pyithu Hluttaw* (Rangoon: Office of the Pyithu Hluttaw, n.d.), 278 (in Burmese).

[15] *Botataung* 30 Apr. 1978: 1–2, 7; 7 May 1978: 1–3.

[16] *Working People's Daily* (*WPD*) 12 May 1978: 4.

In 1988, a new junta that described itself as a council for law and order stated in its first announcement that the rule of law was topmost among its major tasks.[17] It referred to the rule of law when it imposed martial law countrywide in 1989.[18] Its members lost few opportunities over the next two decades to reiterate their concern for the rule of law. Among them was General Thein Sein, who as prime minister in 2009 said that 'constant measures are to be taken to ensure the rule of law in order to thwart any disturbances' to the state.[19] In his inaugural speech as president in 2011, having retired from his military commission, Thein Sein again stressed that the government had to ensure the rule of law so as to build a modern, developed, and democratic nation.[20] In 2013, the same topics came up for discussion at the White House during his trip to the United States.[21]

Given the frequency that successive governments in Myanmar have linked state stability to the rule of law, it is not surprising that when in 2012 people on the western seaboard went out armed with knives and sticks Thein Sein concurred with Aung San Suu Kyi that the violence was in one way or another a problem of the rule of law.[22] Establishing a commission to investigate, he declared, 'There occurred unrests [*sic*] and killings in Rakhine State in May and June 2012, which undermined peace and stability and rule of law.'[23] In a broadcast, he urged the public to obey the law, so the rule of law could be maintained.[24] Hundreds of women marched in the capital city of Rakhine State to demand the Citizenship Law specifically be obeyed, so as to get rid of 'Bengali illegals'.[25] The commission of inquiry for its part found the rule of law had declined to a point where not only had alleged illegals successfully infiltrated the country in large numbers, but also that some had succeeded in infiltrating the new legislature as elected members.[26]

In sum, the language of the rule of law is not new to Myanmar. It is language with precedent. Far from having arrived with a hurrah and a mood for democratisation, the rule of law is a fixture of the political

[17] State Law and Order Restoration Council (SLORC) Announcement 1/88, 18 Sept. 1988.
[18] SLORC Order 3/89, 27 June 1989. [19] *New Light of Myanmar* (*NLM*) 15 Sept. 2009: 1, 6.
[20] *NLM* 1 Apr. 2011: 7–8. [21] *Voice of America* (*VOA*), 21 May 2013.
[22] On rule-of-law language in response to the violence, see Cheesman, 'What Does the Rule of Law Have to Do with Democratisation?' 225–31.
[23] Office of the President, Notification 58/2012, 17 Aug. 2012. [24] *NLM* 11 June 2012: 8.
[25] *Biweekly Eleven* 12 Oct. 2012: Supp. C1.
[26] ICSVRS, *Report of the Inquiry Commission on the Sectarian Violence in Rakhine State* (Naypyidaw: Republic of the Union of Myanmar, 2013) 80 (in Burmese).

lexicon to which everyone has had recourse at one time or another. Its tone is precautionary rather than triumphant: look what happens without the rule of law.

Obviously, what happens without the rule of law depends on what one means by it. Like other political concepts its meaning changes as it moves around.[27] It obtains political 'logics' from specific contexts, and by actions learned, reproduced, and repeated over time.[28] And like other political concepts, it resonates in peculiar ways, conveying different things to different people, and different audiences. As Daniel Lev once said of Indonesia, the rule of law there may well have had its origins in a continental European idea, but it took on new meanings when imported to a Southeast Asian archipelago.[29] The idea changed through the political actions and usages of Indonesians.

Writers who talk up the rule of law as a global political ideal tend to play down how its meaning changes across time and space. Of course, nobody fails to acknowledge that its meaning is contested – perhaps essentially contested.[30] But the tendency is to assume, or insist, that everyone must be talking about basically the same thing. Introducing a well-known study on the rule of law's history and modern relevance, for instance, Brian Tamanaha has described it as '*the* preeminent legitimating political ideal in the world today, without agreement upon precisely what it means'.[31] For Tamanaha, the rule of law might be a contested concept, but it is still *the* concept with which modern political discourse is concerned.

This book challenges such assertions. It rejects the assumption that because people use the rule-of-law nomenclature, they are referring to approximately the same thing. Not only might they be referring to

[27] Carol Gluck, Introduction, *Words in Motion: Towards a Global Lexicon*, eds. Carol Gluck and Anna Lowenhaupt Tsing (Durham, NC, and London: Duke University Press, 2009) 5. See also Frederic C. Schaffer, *Democracy in Translation: Understanding Politics in an Unfamiliar Culture* (Ithaca, NY, and London: Cornell University Press, 1998) ch. 1.

[28] Lisa Wedeen, *Peripheral Visions: Publics, Power, and Performance in Yemen* (Chicago: University of Chicago Press, 2008) 15.

[29] Daniel S. Lev, 'Between State and Society: Professional Lawyers and Reform in Indonesia', *Making Indonesia*, eds. Daniel S. Lev and Ruth T. McVey (Ithaca, NY: Cornell University Press, 1996) 148.

[30] See, for example, Jeremy Waldron, 'Is the Rule of Law an Essentially Contested Concept (in Florida)?' *Law and Philosophy* 21.2 (2002): 137–64; David Collier, Fernando Daniel Hidalgo, and Andra Olivia Maciuceanu, 'Essentially Contested Concepts: Debates and Applications', *Journal of Political Ideologies* 11.3 (2006): 211–46.

[31] Brian Z. Tamanaha, *On the Rule of Law: History, Politics, Theory* (Cambridge: Cambridge University Press, 2004) 4.

different versions of the same concept, they might be referring to different concepts: even opposing concepts. The 'apparent unanimity in support of the rule of law' is neither as apparent nor as unanimous as Tamanaha makes it out to be.[32]

PURPOSE, ARGUMENT, AND SCOPE

The purpose of this book is to bring opposing ideas to the rule of law back to the study of politics: to challenge the monism dominating contemporary literature on the concept, by reintroducing one of the rule of law's opposites to the debate.

Opposing ideas enrich the study of politics. They expand the corpus of concepts used to explore and analyse what happens, and why. They deepen our analysis of specific places, institutions, and events. They also cast light on the ideas they oppose, sharpening analytical distinctions between antithetical concepts, offering clarity not attained by studying concepts in isolation. Thus, Judith Shklar chose to examine liberalism through the study of injustice.[33] When Shklar talks about injustice, she does not mean simply the absence of justice, positively defined. Her concern is with varieties of injustice as wickedness, each with distinctive contents, with unique animating ideas. For Shklar, justice only makes sense if understood through study of how people and institutions can act cruelly. Similarly, when Avishai Margalit asked what a decent society is, he answered the question not by exploring the notion of decency, but rather, the notion of humiliation.[34] Philip Pettit argued that to grasp the concept of liberty requires an appreciation of what it means to be dominated.[35] And Hannah Arendt in her study of violence opposed it with power, with which, she said, it is wrongly likened: 'it is not correct to think of the opposite of violence as nonviolence; to speak of non-violent power is actually redundant', she wrote.[36]

Each of these authors recognised that if they were to get at the political idea mattering most for them, they had to do more than just single it out for study. Nor could they simply contrast it with conditions

[32] Tamanaha, *On the Rule of Law* 3.

[33] Judith N. Shklar, *The Faces of Injustice* (New Haven: Yale University Press, 1990).

[34] Avishai Margalit, *The Decent Society* (Cambridge and London: Harvard University Press, 1996).

[35] Philip Pettit, *Republicanism: A Theory of Freedom and Government* (Oxford and New York: Oxford University Press, 1997).

[36] Hannah Arendt, *On Violence* (New York: Harcourt, 1969) 56.

where it is absent. Each tackled the idea through other ideas, including rival concepts. Likewise, I contend that to get at the rule-of-law idea scholars sometimes need to come at it through opposing ideas. To take the rule-of-law ideal seriously, there must be genuine concern not only for how it is embodied in action, as Philip Selznick would have it, but also for how opposing ideals are likewise embodied.[37] We need to take seriously places where the rule of law is in practice and *in principle* denied, and treat them not as rule-of-law negatives, or caricatures, but as places animated by different ideas, perhaps opposing ones, to the rule of law.

Often, the rule of law is not studied in relation to its rivals because it is conflated with them. Conflation of opposing concepts constitutes a peculiar problem for the study of politics, one different from study of the gap between principle and practice, between the rule of law present and the rule of law absent. Where the problem consists of the denial in practice of a principle to which political institutions subscribe, something may be learned from study of the gap between aspiration and reality. Where principles are conflated, the problem goes beyond the contrast between life with the rule of law and life without it. The question is not just, as Martin Krygier has posed it, 'What can one learn about the rule of law from its absence?'[38] The absence of the rule of law is not a vacuum. It is not a negative, not un–rule of law.[39] It is a space that competing ideas about political organisation occupy. To appreciate how the rule-of-law ideal animates politics we must also consider how its opposites animate politics.

Studies of the rule of law in context tend to concentrate on countries associated with strong rule-of-law traditions. This book comes at the concept from another direction so as to explicate opposing ideas and practices, and through them, to understand better the rule-of-law ideal

[37] Philip Selznick, *TVA and the Grass Roots: A Study in Politics and Organization* (New Orleans: Quid Pro, 2011) viii.

[38] Martin Krygier, 'Marxism and the Rule of Law: Reflections after the Collapse of Communism', *Law and Social Inquiry* 15.4 (1990): 640.

[39] Previously, I explored and used the 'un–rule of law' idea, drawing on work by the then United Nations Special Rapporteur on human rights in Myanmar, Paulo Pinheiro. Nick Cheesman, 'Thin Rule of Law or Un–Rule of Law in Myanmar?' *Pacific Affairs* 82.4 (2009): 597–613. See also Juan Méndez, Paulo Sergio Pinheiro, and Guillermo O'Donnell, *The (Un)Rule of Law and New Democracies in Latin America* (Notre Dame, IN: University of Notre Dame Press, 1998). I became dissatisfied with this approach for reasons set out in this book. For a short critique identifying a number of weaknesses in my earlier argument, see Wilson Tay Tze Vern, 'The Rule of Law in Myanmar: A Response to Professor [*sic*] Cheesman', *Comparative and Non-US Constitutional Law eJournal* 8.82 (2013), 10 Oct. 2013.

itself. It does so via research into a country where ideas opposed to the rule of law have animated political practices for much of its modern history: Myanmar, or Burma.[40]

If cruelty opposes justice, humiliation opposes decency, and domination opposes freedom, what concept in Myanmar opposes the rule of law? My answer is that the political ideal opposed to the rule of law in Myanmar is law and order: in Burmese, *ngyeinwut-pibyaye*. But if ideas and practices of law and order in Myanmar oppose the rule of law, they are also conflated with it. In this respect, Myanmar has wider relevance. Had successive governments pronounced unambiguously a commitment to law and order, excluding the rule of law, then the country would be much less interesting to scholars of these ideas. Instead, just as law and order has become a synonym for the rule of law worldwide, in Myanmar too it has semantically occupied its antonym, albeit in distinctive ways. Much of this book is concerned with how these two concepts are conflated.

While my purpose in writing the book is to interrogate the rule-of-law idea through an opposing concept, it is also to make Myanmar's courts central to analysis of its politics and to bring Myanmar into the burgeoning comparative literature on the politics of courts. However, I do not intend to privilege courts and, much less, judges. Courts matter to me not because they occupy a special place in legal imagination, but because they transmit and realise political ideas through what Lisa Wedeen calls 'performative practices' – actions learned and repeated over time that produce particular kinds of social beings.[41]

Other studies of courts in politically repressive settings concentrate on the role of the judge.[42] This book tells a story not of adjudication

[40] On 'Myanmar' versus 'Burma', see Gustaaf Houtman, *Mental Culture in Burmese Crisis Politics: Aung San Suu Kyi and the National League for Democracy* (Tokyo: Tokyo University of Foreign Studies, 1999) 43–54; Ian Holliday, *Burma Redux: Global Justice and the Quest for Political Reform in Myanmar* (New York: Columbia University Press, 2011) 4–10.

[41] Lisa Wedeen, 'Ethnography as Interpretive Enterprise', *Political Ethnography: What Immersion Contributes to the Study of Power*, ed. Edward Schatz (Chicago and London: University of Chicago Press, 2009) 87–88.

[42] See, for example, David Dyzenhaus, *Hard Cases in Wicked Legal Systems: South African Law in the Perspective of Legal Philosophy* (Oxford: Clarendon, 1991); Gretchen Helmke, *Courts under Constraints: Judges, Generals, and Presidents in Argentina* (Cambridge: Cambridge University Press, 2005); Lisa Hilbink, *Judges Beyond Politics in Democracy and Dictatorship: Lessons from Chile* (Cambridge and New York: Cambridge University Press, 2007); Mark J. Osiel, 'Dialogue with Dictators: Judicial Resistance in Argentina and Brazil', *Law and Social Inquiry* 20.2 (1995): 481–560; Anthony W. Pereira, *Political (In)Justice: Authoritarianism and the Rule of Law in Brazil, Chile, and Argentina* (Pittsburgh, PA: University of Pittsburgh Press, 2005); Sebastiaan Pompe,

but of interaction. It tells a story of policemen, prosecutors, lawyers, complainants, and defendants. As such, it is emphatically not a book about *the* courts, or the judiciary as a distinctive institution. Nor is it about the judicialisation of politics in Asia.[43] Rather, it is a study of courts' personae, of courts' representations of a larger political order, and of courts as spaces for political language and practice.[44] It is a study of how the texts that move into, through, around, and out from courts construct and reconstruct the idea of the state, and of a particular bureaucratic vision, or visions, of society.[45]

Official texts studied with a 'distorting mirror' reveal political ideas and practices they are supposed to conceal.[46] Their contents at once disaggregate the political ideas and institutions they are constructing. Agreeing with Mary Callahan that researchers of Myanmar have tended to 'overstate the logic, unity, and integrity' of the state, I use court records to disassemble the supposedly coherent entity that is the judiciary reified by diagrammatic schema.[47] Heeding Philip Abrams' call for demystification of the state by 'attending to the senses in which the state does not exist rather than to those in which it does', I attend to courts *both* in the senses in which they exist, as well as in the senses they do

The Indonesian Supreme Court: A Study of Institutional Collapse (Ithaca, NY: Southeast Asia Program, Cornell University, 2005).

43 See, for example, Björn Dressel, 'Governance, Courts and Politics in Asia', *Journal of Contemporary Asia* 44.2 (2014): 259–78; Shoaib A. Ghias, 'Miscarriage of Chief Justice: Judicial Power and the Legal Complex in Pakistan under Musharraf', *Law and Social Inquiry* 35.4 (2010): 985–1022; Tom Ginsburg, 'The Constitutional Court and the Judicialization of Korean Politics', *New Courts in Asia*, eds. Andrew Harding and Penelope Nicholson (London and New York: Routledge, 2010) 145–57; Hootan Shambayati, 'Courts in Semi-Democratic/Authoritarian Regimes: The Judicialization of Turkish (and Iranian) Politics', *Rule by Law: The Politics of Courts in Authoritarian Regimes*, eds. Tom Ginsburg and Tamir Moustafa (Cambridge and New York: Cambridge University Press, 2008) 283–303.

44 In this sense the study also departs from the literature on juridification, in which political contests brought within the domain of the courts are depoliticised under the rule-of-law rubric. See Julia Eckert et al., Introduction, *Law Against the State: Ethnographic Forays into Law's Transformations*, eds. Julia Eckert et al. (Cambridge: Cambridge University Press, 2012) 4–7.

45 Pierre Bourdieu, 'Rethinking the State: Genesis and Structure of the Bureaucratic Field', trans. Loïc J. D. Wacquant and Samar Farage, *State/Culture: State-Formation after the Cultural Turn*, ed. George Steinmetz (Ithaca, NY, and London: Cornell University Press, 1999) 55.

46 Ranajit Guha, *Elementary Aspects of Peasant Insurgency in Colonial India* (Durham, NC, and London: Duke University Press, 1999) 333.

47 Mary P. Callahan, *Making Enemies: War and State Building in Burma* (Ithaca, NY, and London: Cornell University Press, 2003) xii.

not.[48] Recognising the empirical facts of Myanmar's courts, as well as their imaginary qualities, I decline to reify law and its institutions, although I do acknowledge their potency. Instead, I concentrate on courts as sites of political activity and interaction, on their institutional features not found in organisational charts and directives, and on the underlying implications of law and order as an animating principle.

Because of this book's preoccupation with politics, it concentrates on criminal cases. In a politically repressive setting, criminal cases are the representative mode of legal authority.[49] In the exercise of control over the body of an accused we find the basic elements for the exercise of control over the body politic. By telling the previously untold story of the politics of criminal cases in Myanmar, this book also tells the untold story of the part Myanmar's courts have played in the country's politics.

Ultimately, my aim is to give the rule-of-law idea more traction by demonstrating how its global idiom is instantiated locally in unexpected and sometimes counterintuitive ways; how it is 'thickly shaped by local institutions and structures'.[50] If scholars of law in society are to come to terms with the rule of law's significance as supposedly the preeminent political ideal in the world today, we need to move away from the parochialism of conventional European and American literature.[51] We need to locate and explain this phenomenon through study of ideas and practices in other places, out of which we can develop new vocabulary and analytical tools to ensure the rule of law's continued salience.

CHAPTERS AND SOURCES

The book consists of nine chapters. Chapter 1 sets out the conceptual relation of law and order to the rule of law. It closes by bringing the discussion back to Myanmar, and the country's relevance to the larger

[48] Philip Abrams, 'Notes on the Difficulty of Studying the State (1977)', *Journal of Historical Sociology* 1.1 (1988): 82.

[49] Philippe Nonet and Philip Selznick, *Law and Society in Transition: Toward Responsive Law* (New Brunswick, NJ, and London: Transaction, 2001) 35.

[50] Sally Engle Merry, 'Transnational Human Rights and Local Activism: Mapping the Middle', *American Anthropologist* 108.1 (2006): 48.

[51] As discussed in Eve Darian-Smith, *Laws and Societies in Global Contexts: Contemporary Approaches* (New York: Cambridge University Press, 2013) ch. 1.

debate, through an excursus on the interplay between the two concepts in the Burmese lexicon. Chapters 2 and 3 track the lineages of law and order and the rule of law from British Burma to militarised Myanmar. The remaining chapters explore paradigmatic features of courts in Myanmar as institutions enthralled with the law-and-order ideal.

Chapter 4 focuses on the prosecution of public enemies and the exercise of sovereign power through courts. Chapter 5 concerns confession obtained through judicial torture. Chapter 6 discusses how institutions evocative of law and order can accommodate practices antithetical to the rule of law, in particular, money making through case outcomes. Chapter 7 shows how law-and-order imperatives enable wholesale departures from law in the interests of order, through a case study of the response to antigovernment protests in 2007. Chapter 8 concludes the book's empirical contents on an optimistic note, with observations on how Myanmar's citizens are mobilising through the legal idiom to advance the rule-of-law ideal.

Chapter 9 brings the book's findings back to the discussion of opposing ideas, and argues for situated, informed debate on the rule of law that recognises how local political struggles shape and alter the concept's normative contents.

Because this book constitutes the first serious attempt for half a century to situate Myanmar's courts in its politics, it contains details from a wide range of primary sources that other authors writing on the country have not used, or have used scarcely. In the book's appendix, I explain the strategies I adopted for reading and citing these sources, and provide details of the types of published and unpublished sources used. Here I restrict my remarks to their elementary features.

Records pertaining to 393 criminal cases in 86 courts at all levels from across Myanmar are at the book's core. The cases span over a decade, from 2000 to 2013. Most are from 2006 onwards. Around half are from Yangon and vicinity. The records vary from case to case. They include police officers' letters to initiate criminal proceedings; private citizens' letters of complaint; first information reports about alleged offences, registered at police stations; search-and-seizure forms; arrest sheets; charge sheets; court daily diaries, where judges document their activities; courtroom testimonies; verdicts; and appeal submissions. Various supplementary sources amplify, confirm, or cast doubt on the case records. Those sources include interviews with and notes from lawyers, journalists, human rights defenders, and others familiar with cases, and media reports from inside and outside the country.

Aside from the records and supplementary materials on cases, the book also draws on an abundance of primary and secondary material from published and classified sources, most of which authors writing in English have rarely or never used.[52] These sources include the law reports from 1892 to 2012; the annual volumes of statutes, rules, and official notifications from 1989 to 2009; the fortnightly *Supreme Court Gazette*, and internal records, from 1994 to 2010; the weekly government gazette; irregularly published volumes of notifications, directives, and circulars; periodicals of the Supreme Court and the Office of the Attorney General, as well as irregularly published academic legal journals.

Reference books consulted include bilingual editions of the core criminal codes; volumes of collected miscellaneous statutes; the Police Manual, which sets out the official structure and routine operations of the police force – both the revised Burmese-language edition of 2000 as well as the superseded version of 1985; the bilingual Courts Manual, 1999 edition; and Burmese-language handbooks for discipline of civil servants and lawyers.

A range of monographs and periodicals offered further insights. Among them are records of seminars and congresses of the Burma Socialist Programme Party, and volumes of collected articles on party ideology and policy; handbooks for courts and offices; university textbooks and syllabi; judicial officers' promotion exam papers; official and semi-official histories; a variety of books on law, most written by lawyers and judicial bureaucrats; and some biographies and bibliographies. News media sources include the state-run newspapers from the 1960s onwards, and the domestic private print media since the mid-2000s, both electronic and on paper; as well as the Burmese-language broadcasts of the British Broadcasting Corporation, Democratic Voice of Burma, Radio Free Asia, and Voice of America.

Clearly, the book relies heavily on written sources. This emphasis is deliberate. Writing is not merely a by-product of state activity. Modern bureaucratic states are constituted through writing.[53] Even more than edifices of stone, accumulations of paper assert the

[52] For further discussion of resources see Melissa Crouch and Nick Cheesman, 'A Short Guide to Resources on Myanmar Law', *Law, Society and Transition in Myanmar*, eds. Melissa Crouch and Tim Lindsey (Oxford: Hart, 2014) 21–32.

[53] Jack Goody, *The Logic of Writing and the Organization of Society* (Cambridge: Cambridge University Press, 1986) 89–90. Akhil Gupta, *Red Tape: Bureaucracy, Structural Violence, and Poverty in India* (Durham, NC, and London: Duke University Press, 2012) 142–43.

know-how of rule.[54] And perhaps to a greater degree than in any other areas of state activity, juridical practices bind their subjects, and one another, through written record keeping. Each moment in a juridical or administrative process brings forward a document or form for someone to complete and place on file. These forms are the materials of procedure, the records of sequential events. But they are also expressions of power. Mastery of the written text enables control of its subjects. When an official removes a document for completion from his cardboard folder, when a policeman pulls a notebook and click-pen from his shirt pocket, he opens up another world: a world of documentation that the object of record keeping may understand little, and can control even less. Out of these commonplace events come the materials with which Myanmar's courts make law and order.

[54] 'Accumulations of paper and edifices of stone were both monuments to the asserted know-how of rule, artifacts of bureaucratic labor duly performed, artifices of a colonial state declared to be in efficient operation.' Ann Laura Stoler, *Along the Archival Grain: Epistemic Anxieties and Colonial Common Sense* (Princeton and Oxford: Princeton University Press, 2009) 2.

1

HOW LAW AND ORDER OPPOSES THE RULE OF LAW

Law and order is often conjoined with the rule of law. The two are conflated in popular culture, such as when the president in an American television series stresses that in invading a make-believe part of Africa 'our priority is to maintain order in the streets. People need to see that their country is being governed under the rule of law.'[1] In this statement, fiction does resemble fact. Law and order is among the rule-of-law types active in the United Nations.[2] The mandates of international missions tend to link the rule of law with law and order, despite one often running contrary to the goals of the other.[3]

Scholarly and professional research also brackets law and order with the rule of law. Indicators for the rule of law associate the quality of legal systems with the level of order in society.[4] In at least one instance, researchers rebadged an indicator for 'law and order tradition' as 'rule of law'.[5] Some studies equate the restoration of law and order after conflict

[1] Episode 1, *24*, dir. John Cassar, perf. Kiefer Sutherland, Twentieth Century Fox, 2009.

[2] Jeremy Matam Farrall, *United Nations Sanctions and the Rule of Law* (Cambridge: Cambridge University Press, 2007) 33. Richard Zajac Sannerholm, 'Looking Back, Moving Forward: UN Peace Operations and Rule of Law Assistance in Africa, 1989–2010', *Hague Journal on the Rule of Law* 4.2 (2012): 359–73.

[3] Per Bergling, Erik Wennerström, and Richard Zajac Sannerholm, 'Rule of Law and Security Sector Reform: Casual Assumptions, Unintended Risks and the Need for Norms', *Hague Journal on the Rule of Law* 4.1 (2012): 111. Stephen Humphreys, *Theatre of the Rule of Law: Transnational Legal Intervention in Theory and Practice* (Cambridge: Cambridge University Press, 2010) 165.

[4] Svend-Erik Skaaning, 'Measuring the Rule of Law', *Political Concepts*, 29, Working Paper Series (Mexico City: Committee on Concepts and Methods, 2009).

[5] John K. M. Ohnesorge, 'The Rule of Law', *Annual Review of Law and Social Science* 3 (2007): 108–09.

and internal security with the rule of law.[6] Graduate students at Princeton University link the establishment of public order and the rule of law to projects dealing with criminality, terrorism, and institutional underdevelopment.[7] The list goes on and on: drug eradication efforts, arming of police officers, programmes to combat human trafficking, and a myriad of other activities all fall under the rubric of the rule of law as law and order.

The conflation of the rule of law with law and order is not new; however, it has become common for at least two reasons. One is, as the rule of law has become an international hurrah term, it has eclipsed other political ideals like human rights. Another is that as its stature has grown, it has also subsumed other concepts. The rule of law looks less like a singular essentially contested concept and more like a package of goods, along with others such as equality before the law, government bound by law, human rights, and, of course, law and order.[8]

If, like Lawrence Solum, we propose to think about the rule of law not as a single essentially contested concept but as a 'set of ideals connected more by family resemblance than by a unifying conceptual structure', we may not be too worried by this semantic bundling up of other concepts under the rule of law.[9] But I think we ought to be at least a little concerned, because as the rule of law has grown in stature, its family resemblances too have multiplied and diversified. Some concepts claiming to be part of the family deserve no part in it. And law and order, I argue, is one of them.

This chapter establishes the conceptual parameters of the relation between law and order and the rule of law that are relevant to the discussion of Myanmar that follows. It begins by advocating for study of the rule of law through opposing concepts. It then rejects 'rule by law' as an alternative concept for study of the rule of law, because rule by law empties the rule of law of its normative contents while

6 See, for example, Seth G. Jones, Jeremy M. Wilson, Andrew Rathmell, and K. Jack Riley, *Establishing Law and Order after Conflict* (Santa Monica, CA: RAND, 2005); Stephan Haggard and Lydia Tiede, 'The Revival of the Rule of Law in the Wake of Civil War', *Hague Journal on the Rule of Law* 4.1 (2012): 120–34.

7 Cited in Whit Mason, 'Axioms and Unknowns', *The Rule of Law in Afghanistan: Missing in Inaction*, ed. Whit Mason (New York: Cambridge University Press, 2011) 319.

8 Markus Schultze-Kraft, 'Security and the Rule of Law in Colombia and Guatemala: Priorities, Trade-Offs and Interdependencies', *Hague Journal on the Rule of Law* 4.1 (2012): 136.

9 Lawrence B. Solum, 'Equity and the Rule of Law', *The Rule of Law*, ed. Ian Shapiro, vol. XXXVI, Nomos (New York and London: New York University Press, 1994) 121.

remaining referential to them. It reduces rule-of-law questions to empirical accounts of how law serves instrumental ends. By contrast, law and order *is* a political ideal opposed to the rule of law. It has its own contents, which are asymmetrical to the rule of law. Its asymmetry makes it a useful concept for study of the rule of law through juxtaposition.

To be clear, this chapter concerns how the rule of law relates to, and is different from, other political concepts. Its problem is one of *relation*, not *definition*. Admittedly, problems of relation and definition cannot be isolated from one another. As a concession to readers accustomed to having terms defined, the chapter closes with a working conception of law and order as an asymmetrical opposite to the rule of law, by situating their opposition in the Burmese lexicon. This conception is contingent. I do not intend it to capture the essence of 'law and order' in all times and places.

Lastly, the chapter omits a section on the wider literature about the rule-of-law concept, eliding debates about its substantive or formal, thin or thick types. The omission is not an oversight. Readers interested to pursue that line of inquiry have many publications already available to them.[10] The chapter's purpose is not to review the gamut of existing literature but to advocate for study of the rule of law through conceptual opposition.

[10] In addition to Brian Z. Tamanaha, *On the Rule of Law: History, Politics, Theory* (Cambridge: Cambridge University Press, 2004), see, for example, Nicholas W. Barber, 'Must Legalistic Conceptions of the Rule of Law Have a Social Dimension?' *Ratio Juris* 17.4 (2004): 474–88; Adriaan Bedner, 'An Elementary Approach to the Rule of Law', *Hague Journal on the Rule of Law* 2.1 (2010): 48–74; Tom Bingham, *The Rule of Law* (London: Penguin, 2010); Rosa Brooks, 'The New Imperialism: Violence, Norms, and the "Rule of Law"', *Michigan Law Review* 101.7 (2003): 2275–340; David Dyzenhaus, 'Recrafting the Rule of Law', *Recrafting the Rule of Law: The Limits of Legal Order*, ed. David Dyzenhaus (Oxford and Portland, OR: Hart, 1999) 1–12; Paul Horwitz, 'Democracy as the Rule of Law', *When Governments Break the Law: The Rule of Law and the Prosecution of the Bush Administration*, eds. Austin Sarat and Nasser Hussain (New York and London: New York University Press, 2010) 153–81; Andrei Marmor, 'The Rule of Law and Its Limits', *Law and Philosophy* 23.1 (2004): 1–43; Guillermo O'Donnell, 'Why the Rule of Law Matters', *Journal of Democracy* 15.4 (2004): 32–46; Philip Selznick, 'Legal Cultures and the Rule of Law', *The Rule of Law after Communism*, eds. Martin Krygier and Adam Czarnota (Dartmouth: Ashgate, 1999) 21–38; Michael Sevel, 'Legal Positivism and the Rule of Law', *Australian Journal of Legal Philosophy* 34 (2009): 53–68; Robert Stein, 'Rule of Law: What Does It Mean?' *Minnesota Journal of International Law* 18.2 (2009): 293–303; Cameron Stewart, 'The Rule of Law and the Tinkerbell Effect: Theoretical Considerations, Criticisms and Justifications for the Rule of Law', *Macquarie Law Journal* 4 (2004): 135–64.

A CASE FOR OPPOSING CONCEPTS

Carl Schmitt wrote that the rule of law is conceptually empty 'if it does not receive its actual sense through a certain opposition'.[11] He believed the rule of law had to be juxtaposed with some other political idea to have a meaning of its own.[12] His observation points to a lacuna in contemporary work on the rule of law motivating my own work, namely, the lack of attention paid to opposing concepts: not concepts on the same scale of practices, different in degree, but concepts different in kind.

While agreeing with Schmitt that the rule of law should obtain its actual sense through a 'certain opposition', I am not being so crude as to imply that a wide range of ideas and practices cannot conceivably be brought under its rubric. Nor do I want to suggest that the rule of law can be made intelligible only through opposing concepts. Gottfried Dietze once observed that the struggle for law is not reducible to absolute values.[13] He wanted to traverse and map out the distance between two different conceptions of the rule of law in an era dominated by ideological clashes. But if in his time the ground between concepts needed to be opened up and explored, today the challenges are different. The rule of law suffers from too much 'conceptual stretching'.[14] Put another way, whereas Gary Goertz emphasises the need for students of concepts to study the grey zone between their opposing poles, I think that debate about the rule of law in our time suffers from lack of concern for what constitutes 'black' on its scale, as well as for other colours on a wider spectrum of political concepts.[15]

[11] Carl Schmitt, *Constitutional Theory*, trans. Jeffrey Seitzer (Durham, NC, and London: Duke University Press, 2008) 181.

[12] Schmitt was not writing about the rule of law in the Anglo-American tradition but about its continental counterpart. Scholars differ on the extent that the two traditions share features. The debate is beyond the scope of this book. The two have in common certain core concerns with non-arbitrariness and predictability of state action, which distinguish both from the concept of law and order. See Nicholas W. Barber, 'The *Rechtsstaat* and the Rule of Law', *University of Toronto Law Journal* 53.4 (2003): 443–54; Martin Krygier, 'Rule of Law (and Rechtsstaat)', *International Encyclopedia of the Social and Behavioural Sciences*, 2nd edn. (Elsevier, 2015), forthcoming; Gianluigi Palombella, 'The Rule of Law as an Institutional Ideal', *Rule of Law and Democracy: Inquiries into Internal and External Issues*, eds. Leonardo Morlino and Gianluigi Palombella (Leiden and Boston: Brill, 2010) 11–26.

[13] Gottfried Dietze, *Two Concepts of the Rule of Law* (Indianapolis, IN: Liberty Fund, 1973) 12.

[14] Giovanni Sartori, 'Concept Misinformation in Comparative Politics', *American Political Science Review* 64.4 (1970): 1034.

[15] Gary Goertz, *Social Science Concepts: A User's Guide* (Princeton and Oxford: Princeton University Press, 2006) 33–35.

Opposing concepts to solve this problem involves more than just contrasting a political ideal with conditions of its absence. It requires scholars to think of opposing concepts *asymmetrically*, as ideas with their own distinctive contents.[16] We can, for instance, oppose the concept of war with the concept of peace. In its opposition to war, peace does not entail the absence of armed conflict alone. It is asymmetrical in its opposition. It entails more than non-war. Non-war and peace have different membership functions: a case may meet the necessary and sufficient conditions for the former, but not the latter.

By way of a specific example from contemporary scholarship, Milan Svolik has argued that research on dictatorship tends to treat it as a less-perfect form of government to democracy, when the difference between the two should be 'thought of first as one of kind and only then as one of degree'.[17] And, when Hannah Arendt studied totalitarianism, she did not propose to examine it as a more severe form of old-fashioned absolutism, at the opposite end of a numerical scale from democracy.[18] She studied it on its own terms, and said it was a novel form of government. Whether or not one is convinced by her argument, or Svolik's on authoritarianism, the point is that in examining politically repressive forms of government both declined to reduce their subject matter to the residue of politics left behind after the last vestiges of democracy had drained away. Instead both looked at their subject matter asymmetrically, as a form of government fundamentally unlike its democratic counterpart, having its own contents, its own logics.

Asymmetrically related concepts are also, as I conceive them, multifaceted. Unlike symmetrical concepts situated along a scale, each can have more than one opposite. The claim that war opposes peace is not exclusive. It invites the possibility that other concepts oppose it too, in dissimilar ways. Likewise, we can accept that cruelty opposes justice, or humiliation opposes decency, without having to refute claims to other oppositions. And we might oppose them with other concepts having symmetrical relations – injustice, indecency – but in so

[16] Gary Goertz and James Mahoney, *A Tale of Two Cultures: Qualitative and Quantitative Research in the Social Sciences* (Princeton: Princeton University Press, 2012) 161–65.

[17] Milan W. Svolik, *The Politics of Authoritarian Rule* (New York: Cambridge University Press, 2012) 20.

[18] Hannah Arendt, *The Origins of Totalitarianism*, 3rd edn. (London: George Allen & Unwin, 1966) pt. 3.

doing we would be embarking on a project with different aims, design, and outcomes from what they would be if we concentrate on problems of asymmetry.

Therefore, to posit that a concept is asymmetrically opposed to the rule of law is not to prohibit it from having oppositional relations with other concepts. However, in considering the relation of the rule of law with other concepts, and in particular, with opposing concepts, scholars need to be attentive to whether the relation is asymmetrical or symmetrical. Does the problem concern qualitatively distinct concepts, or, as Joseph Raz would have it, the greater or lesser degree to which a legal system possesses or lacks the rule of law?[19]

Traditionally, the rule of law has stood in opposition to the rule of persons, or rule of men; a shorthand designation for a condition of government absent of law, where men rule according to their fancies, not according to general rules.[20] Reuban Balasubramaniam calls this condition tyranny.[21] Friedrich Hayek, building on Henry Maine, spoke of the rule of status, whereby people who rule accrue special legal privileges.[22] In both cases, the relation implies the superiority of one concept over the other. At the high end of the scale is the rule of law, at the low end, rule of men or its analogues. The high end gets most attention, while the low end tends to be mentioned in passing, usually in preliminary comments setting the scene for the task that follows: study of the rule of law. Rule of men serves as the opposition one has when one has no particular interest in thinking through the characteristics and implications of opposing concepts.

In a paper on the rule-of-law ideal, Gianluigi Palombella has paid more attention to rule of men than most authors. He proposes that as law is always written, enacted, and enforced by men – or, nowadays, men

[19] Joseph Raz, 'The Rule of Law and Its Virtue', *The Authority of Law: Essays on Law and Morality* (Oxford: Clarendon, 1979) 211.

[20] As for example in Richard H. Fallon, '"The Rule of Law" as a Concept in Constitutional Discourse', *Columbia Law Review* 97.1 (1997): 2–3; Kanishka Jayasuriya, 'Franz Neumann on the Rule of Law and Capitalism: The East Asian Case', *Journal of the Asia Pacific Economy* 2.3 (1997): 361, 370; Margaret Jane Radin, 'Reconsidering the Rule of Law', *Boston University Law Review* 69.4 (1989): 781; Frank Upham, 'Mythmaking in the Rule of Law Orthodoxy', 30, *Carnegie Endowment Working Papers* (Washington, DC: Carnegie, 2002) 10–11.

[21] Ratna Reuban Balasubramaniam, 'Indefinite Detention: Rule by Law or Rule of Law?' *Emergencies and the Limits of Legality*, ed. Victor V. Ramraj (Cambridge: Cambridge University Press, 2008) 133.

[22] Friedrich A. Hayek, *The Constitution of Liberty* (Chicago: University of Chicago Press, 1960) 154; *The Road to Serfdom* (Chicago: University of Chicago Press, 1994) 87. Henry Maine, *Ancient Law*, 10th edn. (New York: Henry Holt, 1906) 165.

and women – rule of men is in all settings an empirical fact, which if legally channelled to prevent domination can in abstract terms satisfy the rule-of-law ideal.[23] Palombella shifts rule of men from its oppositional relation with the rule of law to one where, in its plain sense, rule of men is a necessary but not sufficient condition for the rule of law. Even then, the relation between rule of men and the rule of law is symmetrical, as in the traditional use. It is just no longer oppositional.

Schmitt, who held the rule-of-law ideal in contempt, addressed the problem of its conceptual opposition roughly as follows. The distinction between the rule of law and its other is the distinction between the norm and the command. Whereas the rule of law has a general, normative character, against it stands a political concept of law, which consists of concrete will.[24] Schmitt concluded that the political quality of law must be independent from the rule-of-law idea, insisting that the latter represses politics through normative frameworks aimed at limiting political action.[25] And, since the form of the state rested on the political concept of law, through this artifice he could assert that this concept of law was superior to the rule of law.[26]

Schmitt's distinction is valuable, even if his formulation aimed at denigrating the rule of law and promoting an opposing concept with atrocious implications. The value in the distinction lies in Schmitt's concern to contrast the rule of law not with a symmetrical, negative concept, but with an asymmetrical one. In other words, he distinguished between the *principle* of the rule of law as normatively binding and delimiting of political action, versus what he identified as *another principle* of government residing in the power of the sovereign to decide on a case-by-case basis. The latter was an essentially pragmatic political principle, separated from the rule-of-law ideal not by degrees but by kind: different in its strategies and also in its orientation.

This insight is key to how I differentiate between the concepts of the rule of law and law and order later in this chapter. I preface that part of the discussion with a critique of the relation between the rule of law and rule *by* law, since it helps to sharpen the distinction between symmetrical and asymmetrical approaches to study of the rule of law, and its relations with other concepts. Through this critique, I also aim to show

23 Palombella, 'The Rule of Law as an Institutional Ideal' 10.
24 Schmitt, *Constitutional Theory* 187. 25 Schmitt, *Constitutional Theory* 93.
26 Schmitt, *Constitutional Theory* 238–39.

that in contrast to law and order, rule by law has limited analytical utility for study of the rule of law.

RULE BY LAW

Rule by law is not a new concept. Scholars once dismissed it as a rhetorical flourish by which the excesses of repressive states could be justified in the name of law – a designation of what Lon Fuller referred to as the inveterate confusion between deference for authority and fidelity to law.[27] Others have referred to it as just another way of describing a morally empty rule-of-law idea, because rule by law says nothing about how laws are made or the substantive purposes they pursue.[28] Taken in this sense, rule by law is just an iteration of the rule of law.

Despite a lacklustre career, rule by law has made a bit of a comeback. Social scientists rummaging about for old terms to articulate the difference between the rule of law and new or emergent types of authoritarian legality have rediscovered and to an extent rehabilitated the concept. Some scholarship treats rule by law as a poor man's rule of law, a step up from rule by man. So conceived, rule by law is a worthwhile practice for rulers who cannot or do not want to commit themselves to the variety of practices in the substantive rule-of-law package – those practices associated with human rights, social welfare, and political equality.[29] This rule by law is a better-than-nothing option. It is premised on an assumption that whatever the contents of law, any attempt to rule by it must be superior to the alternatives – even if the alternatives are unknown.[30]

In a volume of essays on rule by law, Tom Ginsburg and co-editor Tamir Moustafa associate the concept with authoritarian governments that provide courts latitude to help maintain social control, obtain political legitimacy, manage administrative agencies, advance their economic interests, and deal with controversial

[27] Lon L. Fuller, *The Morality of Law* (New Haven and London: Yale University Press, 1969) 160.

[28] See for example, Robert Barros, 'Dictatorship and the Rule of Law: Rules and Military Power in Pinochet's Chile', *Democracy and the Rule of Law*, eds. José María Maravall and Adam Przeworski (New York: Cambridge University Press, 2003) 189–90; Tamanaha, *On the Rule of Law* 92–93; Kenneth Winston, 'The Internal Morality of Chinese Legalism', *Singapore Journal of Legal Studies* (2005): 318–19.

[29] Bedner, 'An Elementary Approach to the Rule of Law' 57–58.

[30] Marmor, 'The Rule of Law and Its Limits' 4.

decisions.[31] Balasubramaniam observes that despite the book's title, its authors fail to distinguish clearly between the rule of law and rule by law.[32] He describes rule by law as 'a scenario where a ruling regime tries to project a veneer of legal and political legitimacy for arbitrary power by exploiting the legal form'.[33] For him, rule by law is 'pathological of the rule of law'. It undermines the rule of law by straining the limits of legitimate legal order to serve illegitimate goals. Similarly, Jothie Rajah writes that rule by law 'signifies "law" which, in content and institutional execution, is susceptible to power such that the rights content of "law", and restraints on and scrutiny of state power, are undermined'.[34] Mark Massoud characterises it as 'a kind of state-led abuse of the rule of law'.[35] Rule by law is what happens when rulers make use of law for their own ends, rather than for higher-order goals. It is essentially instrumental and ultimately damaging to the rule of law.

Whether used to describe some kind of minimal rule of law, or a political arrangement in which rulers treat law as an instrument for control, rule by law is like rule of men symmetrical to the rule of law. However, conceptually it is more ambiguous than the traditional opposition to the rule of law. Rule by law is based on an assumption that all political arrangements can be made legible by comparing criteria for the rule of law along a 'continuum of legality'.[36] Unlike the traditional relation between the former two concepts, it concerns the grey zone between the rule-of-law ideal and the other end of the continuum. Because it has no immanent contents of its own, rule by law cannot function as an 'other' of the rule of law, except insofar as it designates some other part of the continuum. Rule by law is either what you get because institutions are not working well enough to

[31] Tamir Moustafa and Tom Ginsburg, Introduction, *Rule by Law: The Politics of Courts in Authoritarian Regimes*, eds. Tom Ginsburg and Tamir Moustafa (Cambridge and New York: Cambridge University Press, 2008) 1–22. See also Tamir Moustafa, 'Law and Courts in Authoritarian Regimes', *Annual Review of Law and Social Science* 10 (2014): 281–99.

[32] Ratna Reuban Balasubramaniam, 'Judicial Politics in Authoritarian Regimes', *University of Toronto Law Journal* 59.3 (2009): 412.

[33] Ratna Reuban Balasubramaniam, 'Rule by Law as Juridical Pathology', unpublished paper (2009), 1.

[34] Jothie Rajah, *Authoritarian Rule of Law: Legislation, Discourse and Legitimacy in Singapore* (New York: Cambridge University Press, 2012) 4.

[35] Mark Fathi Massoud, *Law's Fragile State: Colonial, Authoritarian, and Humanitarian Legacies in Sudan* (New York: Cambridge University Press, 2013) 23.

[36] Ratna Reuban Balasubramaniam, 'Has Rule by Law Killed the Rule of Law in Malaysia?' *Oxford University Commonwealth Law Journal* 8.2 (2008): 225.

produce anything better but, thankfully, well enough that a type of 'law' prevails, or because powerful people are manipulating laws and institutions for their own ends. In either case, the rule-by-law problem is empirical. Rule by law is what *is*, the rule of law is what *ought to be*.

The literature on rule by law remains referential to the rule-of-law ideal, even though it describes conditions that depart from core values associated with the ideal, in particular, those opposed to the arbitrary exercise of power.[37] Any theoretical explanation for rule by law must be in symmetry with theories concerning the rule of law. In particular, it must relate to formal conceptions of the rule of law, which in their contents are closest to the rule-by-law concept.[38] Yet, current literature on rule by law is imprecise about the relation between the two and, in particular, about where the rule of law ends and rule by law begins. It is even less coherent about where rule by law ends and what lies beyond it, because the literature is oriented towards the rule-of-law ideal, not towards whatever lies at the opposite end of the scale. As David Dyzenhaus has noted, at some stage on the continuum 'not only does the rule of law disappear entirely but even the claim that there is rule by law starts to seem implausible'.[39] We slide down from the rule of law, to rule by law, and then apparently to no rule by law either, but where is the other end? What is zero rule of law? The literature has had little to say about the point at which the rule of law is absent.

One other problem remains with the literature on rule by law. Because this concept sits on a continuum from the rule-of-law ideal, but is also instrumental and lacks any immanent goals or contents, it reduces the rule-of-law problem to questions of empirical measurement. Stephen Holmes offers the clearest exposition of this approach. He argues that the rule of law and rule by law are not mutually exclusive, because all real-life situations are at best approximations of the rule-of-law ideal.[40] Where political power and wealth are highly dispersed,

[37] As discussed in Martin Krygier, 'Still a Rule of Law Guy', *Recht der Werkelijkheid* 34.1 (2013): 47, 49–50.

[38] See Balasubramaniam, 'Judicial Politics in Authoritarian Regimes' 413. See also Paul P. Craig, 'Formal and Substantive Conceptions of the Rule of Law: An Analytical Framework', *Public Law* (1997): 467–87; Tamanaha, *On the Rule of Law* 91–101.

[39] David Dyzenhaus, *The Constitution of Law: Legality in a Time of Emergency* (Cambridge: Cambridge University Press, 2006) 7.

[40] Stephen Holmes, 'Lineages of the Rule of Law', *Democracy and the Rule of Law*, eds. José María Maravall and Adam Przeworski (New York: Cambridge University Press, 2003) 49.

society reaches its closest approximation of the rule of law.[41] If we accept Holmes's account of rule by law as coterminous with the rule of law – as I think we must, since rule by law, being symmetrical to the rule of law, has no contents of its own – then the very idea of the rule of law is put in jeopardy. By this account, law is deployed incrementally in all circumstances to achieve outcomes that serve the interests of specific groups: those with more power and money than others. The difference between the rule of law and rule by law lies in how these commodities are distributed. Norms do not come into it. Rule by law reduces questions about the rule of law to matters of instrumentality, of empirical degree, of gradation along a sliding scale of practices.

In response to Holmes, Palombella proposes to treat rule by law as a concept contrasted with the rule of law, precisely because it abandons the inherent value associated with the latter.[42] Even then, rule by law remains symmetrical in its relation to the rule of law. It does not inhere in any other principle or principles of government. It is still derivative of the rule of law, but occupies a position closer to rule of men, rather than one proximate to formal conceptions of the rule of law.

And so, dissatisfied with the analytic limitations of the rule-by-law concept, I turn to the next part of the argument, that unlike rule by law, law and order is a concept asymmetrically opposed to the rule of law, with its own distinctive contents.

LAW AND ORDER

I began this chapter by illustrating how the rule of law corresponds with law and order in popular and scholarly parlance, and suggested rather innocent reasons for their conflation. But the reasons for their intertwining today may also be to conceal their antagonistic qualities. The lexicon of law and order in many settings around the world has an undignified past.[43] Repackaged under the rule-of-law label, it carries a 'legitimating cachet' that it would not have otherwise.[44] Far from happening innocently, the two concepts' conjoining seems to have involved some amount of 'professional distortion'.[45]

[41] Holmes, 'Lineages of the Rule of Law' 50–51.
[42] Palombella, 'The Rule of Law as an Institutional Ideal' 6–8.
[43] Humphreys, *Theatre of the Rule of Law* 171. [44] Ohnesorge, 'The Rule of Law' 109.
[45] Alexander Passerin d'Entrèves, *The Notion of the State: An Introduction to Political Theory* (Oxford: Oxford University Press, 1967) 153.

Of course, the rule of law's conflation with law and order did not just happen in the last couple of decades, even if today the imperative for conflation is perhaps greater than in earlier periods. The two are intertwined in history, as well as in current usage. Rachel Kleinfeld Belton attributes what she calls the poor-cousin status of law and order to the way in which it became an attribute of the rule of law 'through the back door'.[46] Law and order, she observes, was 'never part of the philosophical basis of the rule of law but emerged from the way in which Enlightenment thinkers groped toward their political ideals. Although it pervades the common use of the term, it elided with the rule of law rather than finding a comfortable situation within Western jurisprudential definitions.'[47]

Michel Foucault says that the conciliation of law with order, and hence, of the rule of law with law and order, is an impossible dream because law 'is always referred to a juridical system, and order is referred to an administrative system, to a state's specific order'.[48] He explains that this specific order pertains to 'the conjunctural, temporary, local, and individual decisions' of public authorities, versus the 'general and permanent prescriptions' of law.[49] Foucault associates the former with the police model of government and the latter with the rule-of-law state. This association offers a convenient starting point for the conceptual distinction I make between law and order and the rule of law. Therefore, I will briefly discuss it before summarising the differences between the two and setting out the grounds for their antagonism.

The police state was not an organisation or activity akin to the uniformed constabularies of the present day. Police was a concern to maintain order, to abolish disorder, through good use of the state's forces. In its philosophy, this notion of the state was concerned with the means to oversee and administer all aspects of civil life, including internal administration, public welfare, and surveillance.[50] In its

[46] Rachel Kleinfeld Belton, 'Competing Definitions of the Rule of Law: Implications for Practitioners', 55, *Carnegie Endowment Working Papers* (Washington, DC: Carnegie, 2005) 11.

[47] Belton, 'Competing Definitions of the Rule of Law' 11.

[48] Michel Foucault, 'The Political Technology of Individuals', *Technologies of the Self*, eds. Luther H. Martin, Huck Gutman, and Patrick H. Hutton (Amherst: University of Massachusetts Press, 1988) 162.

[49] Michel Foucault, *The Birth of Biopolitics: Lectures at the Collège de France, 1978–1979*, trans. Graham Burchell, ed. Arnold I. Davidson (New York: Picador, 2008) 168.

[50] Mark Neocleous, 'Policing and Pin-Making: Adam Smith, Police and the State of Prosperity', *Policing and Society* 8.4 (1998): 431–32.

management, police connoted administration in its broadest sense, in its institutional and procedural means to secure order among a given people within a given territory.[51]

Police began at the municipal level, but over time became a matter of central government, encompassing all parts of administration, embracing society in all its aspects: monitoring public morals and decency, preventing robberies and fires, maintaining public health, regulating weights and measures, ensuring the supply of food to towns and cities, and providing welfare for the needy.[52] It did so not through law, but through specific and permanent interventions into the lives of subjects.[53] According to Foucault, the police state established 'a continuum between every possible form of injunction made by the public authorities, whatever the origin of their coercive character'.[54] Whether a rule was general and permanent or contingent and temporal mattered little to police. What mattered was the coercive force of injunctions. And in contradistinction to rule-of-law models in which arbitrary forms of interference in daily life were minimised, the police state used a range of methods to submit society to an ever-expanding array of habitual interference.[55]

In this sense, the police state was, according to Michael Oakeshott, a political idea consisting of a 'comprehensive and designed denial of the notion of a state as an association in terms of the rule of law'.[56] This comprehensive denial of the rule of law did not mean the police state was devoid of law. Rather, it meant that the political relations of the police state were ultimately not determined legally, but administratively. Police did not designate association through law, but through a form of benign custodianship. It was not absent of political values. Its political values just lay elsewhere from those of the rule of law.

In its politics, police was conservative, aimed at restoring order to whatever its administrators identified as disorderly.[57] Above all, it was preoccupied with maintaining authority over the poor through

[51] Marc Raeff, *The Well-Ordered Police State: Social and Institutional Change through Law in the Germanies and Russia, 1600–1800* (New Haven and London: Yale University Press, 1983) 5.

[52] Leonard J. Hume, *Bentham and Bureaucracy* (Cambridge: Cambridge University Press, 1981) 34–35.

[53] Foucault, 'The Political Technology of Individuals' 159.

[54] Foucault, *The Birth of Biopolitics* 169. [55] Raeff, *The Well-Ordered Police State* 4.

[56] Michael Oakeshott, 'The Rule of Law', *On History, and Other Essays* (Indianapolis, IN: Liberty Fund, 1999) 167.

[57] Neocleous, 'Policing and Pin-Making' 435.

measures for coercion and relief, and with preventing lower classes from threatening established order. Built into it was an inherent relationship of paternalistic domination: what Hayek described as an exogenously imposed order, one emanating from the will of a superior authority.[58]

Since the subjects of the state were the source of disorder – or latent source of disorder – people holding positions of authority were engaged in a permanent programme of suppression. But these people did not include judicial officers. Police was not the domain of courts.[59] Police, like the rule of law, was concerned with heterogeneous practices and conveyed a range of meanings; however, questions of justice and eliminating of arbitrariness through general rules were not among its chief concerns. Police existed so people might conduct themselves 'in an orderly, modest, courteous, and respectable fashion wherever human life was organised communally'.[60] Or, as William Blackstone put it, police was 'the due regulation and domestic order of the kingdom: whereby the individuals of the state, like members of a well governed family, are bound to conform their general behaviour to the rules of propriety ... and to be decent, industrious, and inoffensive in their respective stations'.[61]

Law and order naturalises a similar kind of order to police: not one with autonomous citizens bound together through the regulatory force of law, but one with an emphasis on exogenously imposed discipline.[62] Discipline is achieved through the good use of the state's forces and through the concomitant compliance of the target population. It serves, like the discipline associated with police, as a source of efficiency and productivity.[63] It concerns the institutions of the administrator: departments of home affairs and local government, police forces and prisons.

The type of discipline imbued through law and order is unlike the type associated with the rule-of-law ideal, which is obtained through the coordinating power of law. Some kind of subordination is implicit in law and order. Discipline does not happen of its own accord. Power

[58] Friedrich A. Hayek, *Law, Legislation and Liberty* (London and New York: Routledge, 1982) 35–36.
[59] Franz-Ludwig Knemeyer, 'Polizei', *Economy and Society* 9.2 (1980): 178–79.
[60] Knemeyer, 'Polizei' 174.
[61] William Blackstone, *Commentaries on the Laws of England*, vol. IV, 4 vols. (New York: Legal Classics Library, 1983) 162.
[62] Humphreys, *Theatre of the Rule of Law* 168.
[63] Humphreys, *Theatre of the Rule of Law* 170–71.

holders impose it. Well-trained officials ably assist them. These groups must dominate legal subjects, since legal subjects are the source of disorder that officials are empowered to resolve.[64] Law and order is a condition of supervision, instruction, prescription, and notification. Furthermore, it is a condition in which these arrangements are valued.

In contrast to the rule-of-law ideal, this mode of association is not determined through shared recognition of the superiority of law. Binding of citizens to rules of propriety is opposite to the notion that the state's power to coerce its subjects must be strictly delimited through the exercise of law. The concept of law and order cannot entertain the latter idea, because people in superordinate positions are entitled to intervene to maintain order through mechanisms to discipline others. In this arrangement, arbitrariness might be minimised through professional practice and effective supervision, but no principle requires it be so.

EXCURSUS ON LANGUAGE

Evidently, the uneasy elision of law and order with the rule of law is partly to do with language. The linking of law with order in English enables their conflation. The relation between law and order and the rule of law is confused because 'law' attaches lexically to both. But whereas for law and order conformity to law is just one factor among many to consider, for the rule of law such conformity is essential. Its effectiveness is predicated on it.

The asymmetry both between law and order and the rule of law and also within 'law and order' itself causes difficulty for scholars who are uncomfortable at how law has been conflated with order, but are perhaps unsure of how to overcome the conventions that pull the two together in English. Some disassociate the two by describing conditions where law partners with *dis*order.[65] But this disassociation is, like the relation of rule of men to the rule of law, symmetrical. We move from law with order to law without it. The opposite of law and order is, well, the absence of order.

[64] Ratna Reuban Balasubramaniam, 'Hobbism and the Problem of Authoritarian Rule in Malaysia', *Hague Journal on the Rule of Law* 4.2 (2012): 216–17.

[65] See, for example, John L. Comaroff and Jean Comaroff, Introduction, *Law and Disorder in the Postcolony*, eds. John L. Comaroff and Jean Comaroff (Chicago and London: University of Chicago Press, 2006) 1–56; Jonathan Saha, *Law, Disorder and the Colonial State: Corruption in Burma, c. 1900* (Basingstoke and New York: Palgrave Macmillan, 2013).

Unlike English, the Burmese language has no semantic overlap to facilitate the conflation of law and order with the rule of law. The lexical contrast in Burmese between the two conveys a distinctive, asymmetrical relation. 'The rule of law', *taya-ubade-somoye*, connotes its English equivalent, where *taya-ubade* is a couplet for 'law' and *somoye* is 'rule'. The couplet consists of a formal conception of law, *ubade*, and a substantive conception, *taya*. Both words have Indic origins. *Taya* is the Burmese lexical equivalent of *dhamma*, or dharma: loosely, the law of nature, or universal law. *Ubade* derives from *ubadesa*, meaning a directive or instruction. Whereas *ubade* signals positive law – statutory law – *taya* is natural law. *Ubade* approximates the Latin *lex*, *taya* is close to *jus*. *Taya* is fairness; *taya* is justice. *Taya* represents the normative contents of the rule of law. Therefore, *taya-ubade-somoye* cannot be misunderstood as meaning merely the rule of whatever law is written. Nor can it be mistaken for rule *by* law, absent of normative contents. Without *taya*, law does not rule.

The contrast with the Burmese for 'law and order', *ngyeinwut-pibyaye*, could not be sharper. In this law and order, neither *taya* nor *ubade* is anywhere to be found. Law and order does not inhere in any type of law at all. It is a compound describing 'stillness', *ngyeinwut (-ye)*, and 'calmness' or 'demureness', *pibya(-ye)*. The couplets can be broken down: *ngyein* is a condition of being still, static, quiet and *wut* is crouched, prostrated, or stilled; *pi* means pressed and *pya* (*bya* in the compound) is flattened.[66]

Ngyeinwut-pibyaye is a condition where the state's forces bind people's general activity, to ensure they remain decent and inoffensive, quiet and unassuming. In the first authoritative Burmese-English dictionary, an illustration for the condition of *ngyeinwut* is that 'owing to thieves, dacoits [armed robbers], bad characters and opium-smokers being scarce, towns and villages' are peaceful.[67] The binding is implicit: the state's forces have successfully driven off anyone who would cause harm to law and order. The people remaining conform to the rules laid down for decency and propriety.

Ngyeinwut-pibyaye requires the presence of a superior who determines when and how to secure and maintain order. In official parlance,

[66] In both this term and *taya-ubade-somoye* the suffix –*ye* closes the compound to form an abstract noun.

[67] Robert C. Stevenson, *Judson's Burmese-English Dictionary*, rev. edn. (Rangoon: Govt. Printing, 1893) 354.

ngyeinwut-pibyaye opposes anarchy, *minmè-zayaik*, literally, a condition of being kingless. The dictionary cited above denotes the compound *ngyeinwut-pibya* as being 'in frequent use in Upper Burma to express the tranquil and peaceful state of a country, *usually* implying that such state has succeeded one of anarchy and disorder'.[68] Without a monarchical figure, lawlessness and disorder ensues. With one, people reside in peaceable conditions, guided by a suitably endowed and enlightened superior.

Therefore, in Burmese law and order is a concept that reinforces existing political relations through exogenously imposed order. It is hierarchical, because it presumes that certain people or groups occupy positions of authority that entitle them to decide when order is lost, and when the state's forces should restore it. The concept corresponds with Ranajit Guha's description of law and order as 'the most formal expression of the culture of a ruling class'.[69] Law and order always entails an impulse towards unequal political relations, imbued with the moral right of the superior class to impose its conception of order on others.

This lexical contrast establishes an imperative to conflate the two concepts if (law) and order is to inhere in *law*. In English, 'law' has already secured its place alongside 'order'. In Burmese, *ngyeinwut-pibyaye* can find a place in *taya-ubade* only if the two are interchanged so frequently as to blot out their contrast through dint of repetition: the subsuming of the rule of law to law and order, the semantic occupancy of the former by the latter, is manifestly not a meeting of analogous concepts, but of antithetical ones.

In practice, interchange occurs at a variety of levels, and in a variety of texts, including in codified laws, in criminal cases, and in bureaucratic sanctions. Among statutes, the 2004 Electronic Transactions Law, for instance, criminalises use of electronic communications to do 'any act damaging to state security, the rule of law [*taya-ubade-somoye*], community peace and tranquility, national races' solidarity, the state economy or national culture'.[70] The Office of Attorney General rendered *taya-ubade-somoye* in the statute's English version as 'prevalence of law and order'. Cases brought under the statute have cited causing

[68] Stevenson, *Judson's Burmese-English Dictionary* 689. Here the compound is reversed, *pibya-ngyeinwut*, and is suffixed with another term used commonly in political parlance today to signify tranquility, *thaya*.

[69] Ranajit Guha, 'On Torture and Culture', *Frontier* 23 Jan. 1971: 15.

[70] Electronic Transactions Law, 5/2004, sec. 33(a).

damage to the rule of law as an element in the offence. One case against an accused person involved in antigovernment protests described him as having 'damaged state security, the rule of law and community peace and tranquility by sending [news and] photographs of a demonstration march' via the Internet.[71]

The conflation of law and order with the rule of law in some statutes flows over into cases brought under laws that mention neither concept. Police officers accused fourteen persons of having endangered life as a result of their roles in protests during 2007 because they upset state security and the rule of law, even though neither was an element of their alleged offences.[72] A court convicted another man involved in the same events for having allegedly exhorted demonstrators to upset the rule of law, community peace, and the state administration.[73] The statute under which he was jailed did not refer to the rule of law but did list among its offences disruption of law and order.[74] The officials handling this case read 'law and order' as 'the rule of law' and transposed the two. A restraining order brought against another demonstrator stipulates that she participated in activities to 'destabilise community peace and the rule of law'.[75] And an administrator who in 2012 issued a notice under the Criminal Procedure Code prohibiting demonstrators from entering confiscated farmland did so out of concern 'for the rule of law and law and order'.[76]

Unauthorised demonstrators are not the only offenders against the rule of law – read as law and order. Assorted troublemakers can come within its ambit. A 2009 court order against an elderly man who had repeatedly complained about poor electricity supply held that his persistent annoyance of public officials could lead to unruliness

71 *Pol. Maj. Ye Nyunt* v. *Win Maw* (a) *Mawgyi* (a) *Japangyi*, 2009 Criminal Case 30, Yangon Eastern District Court, 5 Mar. 2009. All unreported cases cited are translated from Burmese. Where '(a)' appears between names in criminal cases, it stands for 'alias'. People in Myanmar commonly use more than one name. Hence many case records refer to aliases. Some prosecuting police officers also take advantage of this custom to assign accused persons aliases.

72 *Pol. Capt. Myint Aung* v. *Kyaw Win and 13*, 2008 Criminal Case 265, Yankin Township Court, 24 Nov. 2008.

73 *Sub Inspector San Shwe Thein* v. *Min Aung*, 2007 Criminal Case 29, Thandwe District Court, 17 Oct. 2007.

74 Organisation Law, 6/88, sec. 5(b)(c). The Organisation Law was repealed via section 43 of the Law on Registration of Organisations, 31/2014, which in sections 8(a) and 17(a) provides for registration of organisations that 'do not disturb the state's rule of law and security'.

75 *Inspector Win Lwin* v. *Naw Ohn Hla*, 2007 Misdemeanour Case 157, Hmawbi Township Court, 12 Oct. 2007.

76 Salingyi Township General Administration Dept. Order 15/2012, 1 Sept. 2012.

among the local populace, which would disturb the rule of law.[77] At the end of 2012, a court in the country's west sentenced a community leader to prison for purportedly 'creating conflict among Rakhine national races and Muslim ethnicities in order to destroy state peace and the rule of law' as well as to 'undermine security and law and order'.[78] And an appellate court ruling against two men convicted in 2010 for contacting insurgents described them as having acted to undermine state security and the rule of law.[79] The court convicted them under a colonial-era statute whereby an offence is committed if someone assists an association designated as unlawful because it 'has for its object interference . . . with the maintenance of law and order, or that it constitutes a danger to the public peace'.[80] The court in this case also read *ngyeinwut-pibyaye*, law and order, as a synonym for the rule of law.

Officials who fail to take the narrative on the rule of law seriously can be reproached. The Supreme Court chastises judges for failing to uphold the rule of law when they do not impose sufficiently harsh jail terms. In 2008, it reprimanded an appellate judge who reduced a sentence for a defendant found guilty of causing grievous hurt, because his lenient verdict could undermine the rule of law.[81] It has rebuked others for turning a blind eye to instructions for exemplary sentencing in cases that can damage the rule of law and community tranquility.[82] Senior policemen issue similar complaints. A high-level officer investigating subordinates for drug and arms running in 2013, for instance, described their actions as 'weakening the rule of law'.[83]

The remainder of this book tracks the movement of the rule-of-law idea through texts like these into the practices of courts in Myanmar. But before proceeding, I draw together my reading of the conceptual literature with the insights offered by Burmese lexicon to formulate a working conception of law and order.

[77] *Inspector Htun Htun Win* v. *Khin Maung Kyi*, 2009 Misc. Criminal Case 143, Hlaing Township Court, 3 Nov. 2009.

[78] *Inspector Aung Naing* v. *Nurul Haque* (a) *Dr. Tun Aung*, 2012 Criminal Case 58, Sittwe District Court, 21 Nov. 2012: 3, 5.

[79] *U Maung Thein and Another* v. *The State*, 2010 Criminal Appeal 10, Thaton District Court, 15 Nov. 2010.

[80] Unlawful Associations Act, India Act 14/08, sec. 16.

[81] Supreme Court (SC) Order 48/2008, 16 Sept. 2008. All Supreme Court orders and letters cited are in Burmese, as are all internal documents of government agencies after 1962.

[82] SC Order 32/94, 27 Apr. 1994. [83] VOA 20 June 2013.

CONCLUSION

In sum, the relation of law and order to the rule of law has the following features. The rule of law relies on general rules to maintain order, whereas law and order rests on particularistic commands and directives, in response to exigencies. The former emphasises the role of juridical institutions, whereas the latter privileges administrative ones. Under the rule-of-law ideal, public adjudication according to general rules guides conduct so that people can make decisions of their own accord. To maintain law and order, authoritative institutions act on specific injunctions to intervene directly in people's lives. Lastly, law and order entails the exogenous imposition of discipline, which requires a superordinate-subordinate political relationship, whereas under the rule of law, discipline is an endogenous feature of political relations: it is characteristic of those relations, not imposed on them.

The two concepts are asymmetrically opposed because law and order is not a negative of the rule of law, the way that rule of men is. Law and order has its own virtues, its own contents that are disagreeable to the rule-of-law ideal. While both envisage conditions of order, they are characterised by dissimilar types of order. For law and order, although restlessness might be eliminated through non-arbitrary methods, it need not be the case. By contrast, the rule of law does not aim to eliminate disorder, least of all through whatever means are necessary to achieve this end. It does not purposefully design and pursue activities to maintain order. But neither is it disorderly. An inherent type of order characterises it.[84] Law and order *makes* orderliness; the rule of law *is* orderly.

The rule of law doubtless implies a commitment to rule-ordered behaviour. However, 'law' is hostile to the notion that absolutely anything can be done to maintain order. The normative contents of the rule of law prohibit the type of expediency that the concept of law and order allows. The rule of law is also inimical to certain values associated with the exogenously imposed order of law and order. Consequently, the rule of law cannot be reconciled with the concept of law and order without casting doubt on its meaning as a political ideal, and perhaps, on the idea of law itself.

Whereas the rule of law is concerned with minimising arbitrariness, law and order has different goals, and different methods for their

[84] Oakeshott, 'The Rule of Law' 175.

realisation. The unessential quality of law to the law-and-order ideal does not imply its absence, only that it does not go to the essence of the ideal in the same way that it goes to the heart of the rule of law. Law and order is not premised on a condition of non-arbitrariness, but on a condition of non-restlessness. It entails a mode of association whereby people are subdued so that they might be protected. Put another way, the political ideal of law and order has *quietude* as its telos, realised through instruments of *immobilisation*. Law and order as an ideal recognisable through political lexicon and praxis in Myanmar conceives of a mode of association whereby essentially administrative immobilising mechanisms quieten people.

We must immediately distinguish immobilisation from some of its synonyms. Mechanisms for immobilisation do not prohibit all movement. They do not aim to create inertia or inactivity. Law and order's subjects are busy, but harmless to themselves and others; they are unthreatening because they occupy postures that ensure they are incapable of posing a danger to the body politic.

Some kind of subordination is implicit in this idealised conception of law and order. Quietude does not happen of its own accord. Somebody is immobilised, and somebody else immobilises. But the practices of immobilisation are not merely instrumental. They are bound to law and order as a matter of principle. In contrast to the rule-of-law ideal, this mode of association is not determined through shared recognition of the superiority of law. The law-and-order ideal cannot entertain this form of recognition, because it would jeopardise the relationship of subordination, whereby people in superordinate positions are entitled to intervene to maintain order through mechanisms for the immobilisation of others.

Schmitt put it this way: 'The endeavour of a normal state consists above all in assuring total peace within the state and its territory. To create tranquillity, security, and order and thereby establish the normal situation is the prerequisite for legal norms to be valid.'[85] The law-and-order ideal is 'total peace': the elimination of any activity that the sovereign designates hostile. Coupled to the ideal is the necessity that a process to establish order precede legal norms for them to be valid.

The problem with this formulation, which this book explores through study of Myanmar's courts, is that when nominally legal

[85] Carl Schmitt, *The Concept of the Political*, trans. George Schwab (Chicago and London: University of Chicago Press, 2007) 46.

institutions function as administrative mechanisms for immobilisation, they become participants in a project to maintain law and order. Furthermore, that project becomes permanent. Like the rule-of-law ideal, the goal of total peace is nowhere fully achievable. The law-and-order project is unending.

2

ORDERING LAW IN THE COLONY

Writing on Africa, Martin Chanock has described the legacy of justice bequeathed to colonised peoples as 'one of the most stubborn fantasies about British colonialism'.[1] For Chanock, the legacy of the rule of law is a myth belied by the insistent concern of the British to dominate politically through judicial, or juridical, means. Similarly, Ranajit Guha has railed against scholars who 'go on talking about a rule of law in colonial India when the facts of colonialist practice did nothing to support such assertion'.[2] He points to the despotic qualities of colonial government, preponderance of executive orders and concentrating of power in an executive head, and patent inequality of colonisers and colonised before the law as evidence for the case against the rule of law.

If the legacy is a myth, then it is truly a stubborn one. It persists not just in postcolonies with relatively developed courts, but also in other places where law matters far less. In Sudan, for instance, despite a perception among Sudanese and foreigners alike that the country lacks any semblance of law, lawyers retain a firm belief in the independence and integrity of the colonial judiciary.[3] Their counterparts in Myanmar, too, nurture hopes that if they can regain the lost legacy of colonial legality, then they will somehow set the country on a path

1 Martin Chanock, *Law, Custom and Social Order: The Colonial Experience in Malawi and Zambia* (Cambridge: Cambridge University Press, 1985) 5.

2 Ranajit Guha, *Dominance without Hegemony: History and Power in Colonial India* (Cambridge and London: Harvard University Press, 1997) 67.

3 Mark Fathi Massoud, *Law's Fragile State: Colonial, Authoritarian, and Humanitarian Legacies in Sudan* (New York: Cambridge University Press, 2013) 1, 64.

towards peace and prosperity. Nor are lawyers the only people to hark back to the colonial period. Politicians speak fondly of imagined days when people respected law and courts were strong. And even the Office of the Attorney General describes its country's legal system favourably, albeit misleadingly, as a 'near replica' of its English counterpart.[4]

If the rule-of-law legacy is myth, why is it so stubborn? Guha attributes its persistence to the 'hallucinatory effects' of the ideology of law in English political thought.[5] Other scholars have emphasised the curious ambiguity of European law in colonisation.[6] Colonised people moved into the legal regimes of colonisers neither through brute force nor simple persuasion, but through, as Lauren Benton has written, 'a series of contests over the structure of the legal order that shaped a juridical space for the state and brought participants into a single discourse about law'.[7] The British as colonisers used law to dominate colonised people and extract resources from their lands. But they also provided the colonised with spaces where they could mobilise the ideology of law to protect at least some of their interests. Colonised people recognised the advantages of engaging with legal institutions and using them for various purposes. Some, like the political elite in Egypt, embraced European legal models in order to advance their own state-building plans.[8] Others, like villagers in Sri Lanka, found pliable resources in colonial courts that they adapted to fit with local norms for resolving conflict.[9]

This chapter explores the dissonances that the ambiguity of British law created abroad, through study of the ideas that animated courts in colonial Burma. With the next chapter it aims to 'counter the ahistorical construction of the rule of law' by 'recovering and reattaching historical context to otherwise sterilised legal processes and precedents', as Eve Darian-Smith has put it.[10] The

[4] Office of the Attorney General, 'The Role of the Office of the Attorney General' (Union of Myanmar, 2005) 2.

[5] Guha, *Dominance without Hegemony* 67.

[6] Sally Engle Merry, 'Law and Colonialism', *Law and Society Review* 25.4 (1991): 891.

[7] Lauren A. Benton, *Law and Colonial Cultures: Legal Regimes in World History, 1400–1900* (Cambridge: Cambridge University Press 2002) 261.

[8] Nathan J. Brown, 'Law and Imperialism: Egypt in Comparative Perspective', *Law and Society Review* 29.1 (1995): 116–18.

[9] John D. Rogers, *Crime, Justice and Society in Colonial Sri Lanka* (London: Curzon, 1987) 40.

[10] Eve Darian-Smith, 'Precedents of Injustice: Thinking About History in Law and Society Scholarship', *Studies in Law, Politics, and Society* 41 (2008): 62. On the problem of ahistoricism in analysis of contemporary Myanmar politics, see Ian Brown, *Burma's Economy in the Twentieth Century* (Cambridge: Cambridge University Press, 2013) 4–5.

chapter begins in India, with the project to codify criminal offences. It then concentrates on courts in occupied Burma. Through study of reported trial records, it considers how the codes and courts permitted some colonial subjects to pass through procedural interstices so as to protect themselves, while closing off opportunities for others.

CODIFICATION AND ORDER

A fellow of the Royal Geographic Society publishing in 1907 wrote that, 'Practically, the whole criminal law of Burma is contained in the Indian Penal Code'.[11] He may have exaggerated the code's significance, but not grossly. A government administrator writing a couple of decades later estimated that in his district around 60 percent of criminal cases fell under the code.[12] Another put the figure at around half in his locality.[13] Although the numbers varied from time to time and place to place, the Penal Code and its procedural legs, the Criminal Procedure Code and Evidence Act, were the centrepieces of criminal law in colonial Burma.

And so they remain. Around Myanmar, numerals designating criminal offences and injunctions from colonial-era statutes resonate throughout public life. They tumble from the mouths of police officers and lawyers in radio broadcasts, as interviewers interrupt the steady flow of numbers to insert explanatory references for those listeners not already familiar with what they designate. They feature in official notices on government premises and roadside signboards. Teashop conversations buzz with them.[14]

Where did the codes come from? What was their rationale? How have they endured? And what do they have to do with the conceptual relation of law and order to the rule of law?

[11] Alleyne Ireland, *The Province of Burma*, vol. I, 2 vols. (Boston and New York: Houghton Mifflin, 1907) 173.

[12] A. Williamson, 'Shwebo District', *Burma Gazetter* (Rangoon: Govt. Printing, 1929) 170.

[13] F. C. Owens, 'Pakokku District', *Burma Gazetter* (Rangoon: Govt. Printing, 1913) 88.

[14] In one such conversation on an early trip to the country in the 1990s, a friend who doubted my explanation for something replied 'four-twenty'. When I asked him what he meant, he said I was bluffing him. Only later did I learn he was referring to section 420 of the Penal Code: the offence of cheating. Indian and Pakistani colleagues say that they have also heard the number used in this sense.

Codification was closely associated with the police state in Europe.[15] Central authorities needed codified law to establish legal supremacy over the multiplicity of local customs and regulations. It also strengthened the hand of the sovereign power over the judiciary, reducing the judge's task from interpreting to applying law.[16] The sheer convenience of codification, its reassuring framework for political control, and its effectiveness in defining and managing crime, as well as in shaping economies and cultures, strongly recommended it to the administrators of colonies. Codification gave law a feeling of solidity and regularity. It engendered thinking and practices that were oriented towards efficient enforcement of rules – towards a conception of justice suited to despotic government that desired to appear powerful but fair.[17]

The Indian Penal Code's ideological seeds lie in the work of Jeremy Bentham. In India, Bentham found a territory where the use of law to shape society could be profitably discussed because the place was in every respect so different from England, and also because the issues of law were not hypothetical. Bentham said he could write legislation for India just as well as he could for his own parish.[18] Since his jurisprudence was supposed to be scientific and universal, he was confident of his ability to legislate for Indians and English alike. In the end, his concern was not in a remote place of which he had no direct experience or special interest, but in the possibilities that legislating for India opened up for reform in the metropole. 'I would venture to lay down', he wrote,

> 1st, that the English law is a great part of it of such a nature, as to be bad every where: 2d, but that it would not only be, but appear worse in Bengal than in England: 3d, that a system might be devised, which, while it would be better for Bengal, would also be better even for England.[19]

[15] Marc Raeff, *The Well-Ordered Police State: Social and Institutional Change through Law in the Germanies and Russia, 1600–1800* (New Haven and London: Yale University Press, 1983) 151.

[16] Leonard J. Hume, *Bentham and Bureaucracy* (Cambridge: Cambridge University Press, 1981) 37–39.

[17] Taylor C. Sherman, *State Violence and Punishment in India* (London and New York: Routledge, 2010) 7.

[18] Jennifer Pitts, 'Jeremy Bentham: Legislator of the World?' *Utilitarianism and Empire*, eds. Bart Schultz and Georgios Varouxakis (Lanham, MD: Lexington, 2005) 69.

[19] Jeremy Bentham, *The Works of Jeremy Bentham*, vol. I, 11 vols. (Edinburgh and London: William Tait; Simpkin, Marshall, 1968) 185.

The ultimate and persistent aim of legal reform in the colony was to agitate for change at home.[20] The Benthamites fell short of this aim, and Bentham never had the opportunity to legislate for India, but a number of men influenced by his ideas did have a profound and lasting effect on the criminal law of the colonies. Among them was James Mill.

Beginning as an administrator of India in London, Mill argued for a single comprehensive set of legal codes in the colony, managed by skilful, disinterested officials, freed from the 'unintelligible, tedious, and expensive' common law.[21] If custom – be it English or Indian – was the problem, then the solution was statutory. And the solution lay not in the writing down of custom, but in its writing out. Custom could be eliminated through the written word: not the word of God, as in the past, but the word of jurisprudential science.

In 1832, Mill spoke before a parliamentary committee that led to the setting up of the first law commission for the whole of India. With other Benthamites he succeeded in getting a small, expert commission established to draft the subcontinent's new statutes, consistent with principles set out in Bentham's Codification Proposal.[22]

Thomas Macaulay chaired the law commission. Macaulay had criticised parts of Mill's work, but he respected Bentham, and spoke before parliament in favour of codified law for India. 'We know that India cannot have a free Government,' he wrote in 1836, 'But she may have the next best thing – a firm and impartial despotism.'[23] Macaulay's interest in Bentham's model lay not in what it offered of universal value, but in the advantages it afforded for a type of paternalistic, cheap absolutism – yet one unlike the allegedly arbitrary despotism of earlier periods. Codification would give the legislative council authority, he wrote, to reserve 'the power in great emergencies of legislating with the utmost promptitude, and yet to put this power under such checks as may render it very difficult for ourselves or our successors to abuse it'.[24] A more precise summation of the British legal enterprise in India would be hard to find.

[20] James A. Colaiaco, *James Fitzjames Stephen and the Crisis of Victorian Thought* (London and Basingstoke: Macmillan, 1983) 92.

[21] Cited in Javed Majeed, *Ungoverned Imaginings: James Mill's 'The History of British India' and Orientalism* (Oxford: Clarendon, 1992) 132.

[22] Eric Stokes, *The English Utilitarians and India* (Oxford: Clarendon, 1959) 177–79. See also Bentham, *The Works of Jeremy Bentham*, vol. IV, 554–59.

[23] In C. D. Dharker, ed., *Lord Macaulay's Legislative Minutes* (London: Oxford University Press, 1946) 180.

[24] In Dharker, ed., *Lord Macaulay's Legislative Minutes* 150.

Macaulay's task may have been modest in comparison to many of Bentham's ideas, but it was still breathtaking in its audacity. Macaulay claimed that unlike earlier efforts to codify law for India he was not consolidating or rearranging existing law but writing something new.[25] The Penal Code was not supposed to be a digest of what already existed: it would reflect the universality of jurisprudential science. Scholars have since countered that Macaulay and his proponents exaggerated his claims to the code's originality.[26] Nevertheless, the drafting and introducing of the code to India was a more radical undertaking than anything that could have been attempted in England. Macaulay recognised as much when he concluded that codified law was 'almost the only blessing – perhaps it is the only blessing – which absolute governments are better fitted to confer on a nation than popular governments'.[27] If despots could not hope to govern with consent, they might at least govern with certainty and efficiency.

As the question of codified law passed from theory into practice, Macaulay became bogged down in the politics and bureaucracy of empire. By the time he had drafted the Penal Code, legal reform was no longer a priority in India. The draft gathered dust for a quarter century, until a new wave of political and legal reform followed the uprising of 1857–1858. Barry Wright has written about how the code then 'became a legislative priority ... to enhance the rule of law and minimise the future need to resort to arbitrary emergency measures or military intervention'.[28] Despite the long delay in enactment, the Indian Penal Code, Act 45 of 1860, was the first British criminal

[25] The trend in Bengal, to which Burma was annexed, had been towards codification since the 1790s. However, the earlier efforts to codify lacked the later universalizing impulse, and were grounded in a 'desire to construct a "fixed system of jurisprudence" in textual form' in 'response to officials' failure to develop stable hermeneutic practices in court'. Jon E. Wilson, *The Domination of Strangers: Modern Governance in Eastern India, 1780–1835* (Basingstoke and New York: Palgrave Macmillan, 2010) 97.

[26] Nasser Hussain, *The Jurisprudence of Emergency: Colonialism and the Rule of Law* (Ann Arbor: University of Michigan Press, 2003) 63. Kunal M. Parker, 'The Historiography of Difference', *Law and History Review* 23.3 (2005): 692. David Skuy, 'Macaulay and the Indian Penal Code of 1862: The Myth of the Inherent Superiority and Modernity of the English Legal System Compared to India's Legal System in the Nineteenth Century', *Modern Asian Studies* 32.3 (1998): 539–44.

[27] Cited in Stokes, *The English Utilitarians and India* 219.

[28] Barry Wright, 'Macaulay's Indian Penal Code: Historical Context and Originating Principles', *Codification, Macaulay and the Indian Penal Code: The Legacies and Modern Challenges of Criminal Law Reform*, eds. Wing-cheong Chan, Barry Wright, and Stanley Yeo (Surrey and Burlington, VT: Ashgate, 2011) 21–22.

code. In divergent amended versions, it affects the lives of about one in six of the world's occupants today, including hundreds of millions in India, Pakistan, and Bangladesh, as well as in Myanmar.

But Bentham's vision was not for a solitary code. It was for a compendium of statutory law, which he called a 'pannomion'. The pannomion was to be for criminalisation what the panopticon, which Michel Foucault has made famous to contemporary audiences, was to be for punishment: a design for the efficient, homogeneous, and automatic functioning of power.[29] If for Foucault the panopticon was a paradigm for social relations, the pannomion was a schema that would literally bring order to all of society.

While Macaulay's draft criminal code sat on the shelf, his successors in the second law commission of 1853 drafted a uniform Criminal Procedure Code to accompany it. This code lacked the ideological flavour of the Penal Code. Far from having universal pretensions, it contained measures to protect Europeans and mollify British who were opposed to the same law governing them and colonised peoples.[30] It was further amended before becoming Act 5 of 1898, which has remained the basis for criminal procedure in Myanmar's courts over more than a century.

James Stephen, another admirer of Bentham, helped to amend the procedural code. He also codified Act 1 of 1872, the Evidence Act, which is the other integral statute in the pannomion of criminal law. Like Macaulay, Stephen was keen to promote the value of an orderly empire built through codification. But while Macaulay aimed for a despotism that, in his own mind at least, would be the next best thing to free government, Stephen was unashamedly concerned with enforcing order as cheaply, clearly and efficiently as possible. He admired the Penal Code and its accessories because it was 'eminently well calculated to protect peaceable men and to beat down wrongdoers, to extort respect, and to enforce obedience'.[31]

Stephen added new sections to the Penal Code emphasising the need to maintain order, *ngyeinwut-ye*, over aspirations for justice.[32] A raft of

[29] Michel Foucault, *Discipline and Punish: The Birth of the Prison*, trans. Alan Sheridan (London: Allen Lane, 1977) 201–02.

[30] Elizabeth Kolsky, *Colonial Justice in British India* (Cambridge: Cambridge University Press, 2010) 78–86.

[31] James Fitzjames Stephen, *A History of the Criminal Law of England*, vol. III, 3 vols. (London: Macmillan, 1883) 345.

[32] Wright, 'Macaulay's Indian Penal Code' 46–47.

measures targeted political offenders with crimes such as treason, sedition, and conspiracy. On reading the section of the code concerning sedition, a judge in Burma observed wryly that it had apparently been drafted 'to cover any eventuality' and make something out of 'almost any disagreeable remark aimed at the Government'.[33] Stephen might well have replied, *and why not?* After all, he had once pointed out matter of factly that British government in India was 'essentially an absolute government, founded, not on consent, but on conquest ... having no justification for its existence except that superiority' of the conqueror.[34] Penal law aimed to keep things that way.

The Benthamites fancied that their genius lay in devising a scientific and comprehensive system of law that could fundamentally alter how the colonised lived. With codification, they aimed to penetrate and shape society while resisting attempts to penetrate and change law. Stripped of technicality, their jurisprudence would allow a few well-trained, enlightened administrators to issue commonsense orders on the basis of a handful of statutes, free from the legal game-playing that bedevilled the courts of England. Stephen gushed that the Penal Code contained 'no obscurity or ambiguity worth speaking of'.[35] Codification would eliminate blank spaces from the pages of law.[36] In so doing, it would eliminate blank spaces from society. Everything would become visible and legible when illuminated under its bright light. Zones of darkness, zones of disorder, would cease to exist.[37]

Reading the Benthamites' statements on their undertaking, as well as their codes, I agree with Foucault that we ought to treat utilitarianism not merely as an ideology but as a technology of government 'permeated with philosophical, theoretical, and juridical elements'.[38] The technology represented something altogether different from what had existed in India under the mercantile, pragmatic form of government that preceded it. Law, not religion, was the justification for the new British colonial despotism; or rather, law as religion, since the

[33] Maurice Collis, *Trials in Burma* (London: Faber & Faber, 1953) 88, 121.

[34] Cited in Thomas R. Metcalf, *Ideologies of the Raj*, New Cambridge History of India, ed. Gordon Johnson, vol. III.4 (Cambridge: Cambridge University Press, 1994) 210.

[35] Stephen, *History of the Criminal Law*, vol. III, 303.

[36] Gerald J. Postema, *Bentham and the Common Law Tradition* (Oxford: Clarendon, 1986) 424.

[37] Michel Foucault, *Power/Knowledge: Selected Interviews and Other Writings 1972–1977*, trans. Colin Gordon, Leo Marshall, John Mepham, and Kate Soper (Hemel Hempstead, Hertfordshire: Harvester, 1980) 152.

[38] Michel Foucault, *The Birth of Biopolitics: Lectures at the Collège de France, 1978–1979*, trans. Graham Burchell, ed. Arnold I. Davidson (New York: Picador, 2008) 41.

technology's designers also represented it as something transcendental, rising above the usual fray of competing interests.[39] Stephen described codified law as 'a compulsory gospel which admits no dissent and no disobedience', 'the sum and substance' of what the colonisers had to teach the colonised.[40] With good reason one historian has characterised the invasion of Burma that brought forth this gospel as 'a Benthamite *jihad*'.[41]

DISTRICT OFFICERS AND BAYONETS

The British invaded Burma in three phases over the nineteenth century.[42] In 1824–1826 they occupied Arakan, on the western seaboard, today neighbouring Bangladesh, and Tenasserim, adjacent to Siam, now Thailand; as well as Assam, which they incorporated into India. In 1852–1853 they seized what became Lower Burma, including the town that became the new capital, Rangoon. In November 1885 they took Mandalay, in Upper Burma, and exiled King Thibaw and his family to India, provoking a protracted insurgency, which spread across the north of the territory and also into parts of Lower Burma. Through a provisional reign of terror, the colonial government succeeded by the early 1890s in 'dealing with the universal disorder which prevailed and could not be suppressed by the ordinary law even when backed by overwhelming military force'.[43] Thus, the British achieved victory in Burma in an especially unmediated and coercion-intensive manner.[44]

During the early years after 1826, before codification and rationalisation of government and courts in India, the colonialists improvised. Officials administered the two newly occupied territories separately, making choices based on expediency and personal inclination, or as

[39] Eve Darian-Smith, *Religion, Race, Rights: Landmarks in the History of Modern Anglo-American Law* (Oxford and Portland, OR: Hart, 2010) 160.

[40] Cited in Stokes, *The English Utilitarians and India* 302.

[41] Andrew Huxley, 'Positivists and Buddhists: The Rise and Fall of Anglo-Burmese Ecclesiastical Law', *Law and Social Inquiry* 26.1 (2001): 139.

[42] For an overview of the phases of invasion, occupation, and colonial administration, see Neil A. Englehart, 'Liberal Leviathan or Imperial Outpost? J. S. Furnivall on Colonial Rule in Burma', *Modern Asian Studies* 45.4 (2011): 769–82. On the political territoriality of 'Burma' prior to colonial invasion and mapmaking, see James C. Scott, *The Art of Not Being Governed: An Anarchist History of Upland Southeast Asia* (Singapore: National University of Singapore Press, 2010) 50–62.

[43] Charles Crosthwaite, cited in Ireland, *Province of Burma*, vol. I, 713.

[44] Mary P. Callahan, 'State Formation in the Shadow of the Raj: Violence, Warfare and Politics in Colonial Burma', *Southeast Asian Studies* 39.4 (2002): 513–15.

two officials later expressed it, based on 'broad principles of equity and common sense rather than nicely determined points of law'.[45] The first British administrator in the town of Mergui, in Tenasserim, sentenced a man suspected of sexual relations with his niece to 'have his face blackened and to be led in that state round the town, his crime at the same time being proclaimed by beat of gong'.[46] In Sandoway, a district of Arakan, administrators from India adopted Persian as the official court language.[47] After 1834, both territories were brought under the administration at Calcutta. More personnel came to oversee local affairs, and their numbers increased after 1853. When the criminal codes rolled out across India, formally they took force contiguously in the newly occupied territory. In Upper Burma, the indigenous administration introduced a penal code modelled after the utilitarian archetype.[48] But the kingdom's days were numbered, and its innovations were too little, too late.

When the imperial army entered Mandalay and shipped the last king and his family off to India, its northward march coincided with the high point of British interest and effectiveness in imposing a preconceived model of legal authority on colonised societies. At the time, a senior officer wrote, 'Our annexation must be followed by a rain of district officers all over the country, civilians whose courts must be hedged in by British bayonets for a long time to come.'[49] The army was only one of the empire's two arms. The other, the judiciary, was also reaching into Burma.

Yet this judiciary was unlike its counterpart in England. District officers were not judicial personnel but civil servants who took on judicial functions. From the early days of colonial rule in Lower Burma, district officers had run the subordinate courts, and their executive head – a commissioner, later a chief commissioner of British Burma – had his own court of final appeal. In 1872, a judicial commissioner began work in Rangoon, and from 1875 he served as the appellate official for all courts under British dominion in Burma. From 1892,

45 John S. Furnivall and W. S. Morrison, 'Insein District', *Burma Gazetter* (Rangoon: Govt. Printing, 1914) 114.

46 Departmental letter cited in John S. Furnivall, 'The Fashioning of Leviathan: The Beginnings of British Rule in Burma', *Journal of the Burma Research Society* 29.1 (1939): 19.

47 W. B. Tydd, 'Sandoway District', *Burma Gazetter* (Rangoon: Govt. Printing, 1912) 54.

48 U Aung Than Tun, *History of Myanmar Dhammasats*, vol. II, 3 vols. (Yangon: Sarpay Beikman, 2007) 298–302 (in Burmese).

49 Brigadier General George White cited in Thant Myint-U, *The Making of Modern Burma* (Cambridge: Cambridge University Press, 2001) 196.

another judicial commissioner took the post in Mandalay, for Upper Burma. This non-separation of powers was partly due to the pull of circumstances.[50] But it was also consonant with utilitarian ideas. Bentham had himself described the separation of powers as anarchic.[51] Colonial officials in Bengal also claimed that the division of power between administrative and legal officers had failed them empirically.[52] Administrators were not just the only men available to serve as magistrates: they were the best men to serve as magistrates, both in principle and in practice.

By the turn of the century the trend across the empire favoured autonomous judicial services. From 1900, the peak court in Lower Burma was comprised of civil servants and barristers. In 1905, the colonial government formally separated the day-to-day operations of the senior judiciary from the executive. However, judges remained answerable to the governor, and district officials continued to handle criminal cases. By this time, the lower professional judiciary in Burma included large numbers of men from the local population. Nonetheless, as late as the eve of the Japanese interregnum, in 1942, Burmese personnel still numbered just 40 percent.[53] Europeans and Anglo-Burmese dominated the upper courts until independence in 1948.

In December 1922 with the devolution of powers from India under diarchy, a High Court began operating in Rangoon, presiding over the whole territory of Burma. In 1937, Burma became a fully autonomous colony. This change in government did not significantly alter the work of the courts. War did. The judiciary continued to function under Japanese occupation, but it was peripheral to the politics of the period. In the aftermath of the Second World War, it kept exercising authority during a time of political uncertainty and economic hardship, up to independence at the start of 1948.

The remainder of this chapter is based on a reading of criminal cases in the law reports issued by these commissioners and courts from 1892 to 1947. It covers four sets of reports. From 1892 to 1922 and 1900 to 1922, they consist of the Upper Burma Rulings of the judicial commissioner's court in Mandalay, and the Lower Burma Rulings of the Chief

[50] Hugh Tinker, 'Structure of the British Imperial Heritage', *Asian Bureaucratic Systems Emergent from the British Imperial Tradition*, ed. Ralph Braibanti (Durham, NC: Duke University Press, 1966) 49.

[51] Bentham, *The Works of Jeremy Bentham*, vol. I, 570–71.

[52] Wilson, *The Domination of Strangers* 133–34.

[53] James F. Guyot, 'Bureaucratic Transformation in Burma', Braibanti, *Asian Bureaucratic Systems* 377.

Court at Rangoon respectively. From 1923 to March 1937, the High Court in Rangoon published the Indian Law Reports – Rangoon Series. It issued the Rangoon Law Reports from 1937 to 1942 and again after the Second World War from 1946 to 1947.[54] From 1948, the High Court continued functioning under a new Supreme Court at the apex. The next chapter draws on the reports of those courts.

The reports are a rich source of historical material, yet researchers of Burma have neglected them.[55] As records of colonial thought and practice, they provide, as Elizabeth Kolsky has put it, 'a unique opportunity to simultaneously comprehend the workings of the colonial state alongside the rhythms of everyday life'.[56] Read with 'a constructive attitude of critical engagement' with the forms of knowledge they produce, they speak to the rule-of-law idea and to its 'material force', its 'potential to act upon the world'.[57] Together, they constitute an historical artefact that demands attention to its peculiar historical specificity and biographical identity.[58]

The law reports of Burma for this period are also of special relevance because they reflect the British colonial legal enterprise at its zenith. The utilitarian experiment in India had run its course. The pannomion now served as positive law for hundreds of millions of people. At the turn of the twentieth century, colonial law was at the height of its power and furthermost in its reach. Burma's court records from this era reveal the tension between normatively grounded claims referential to the rule of law, and the pragmatic law-and-order objectives of the colonial state. They are the products of contestation

[54] In citations the four sets of reports are abbreviated as UBR, LBR, Ran., and RLR respectively.

[55] Only one other author writing in English has used law reports extensively. See Myint Zan, 'Two Divergent Burmese Rulings on Criminal Defendants' Confessions: An "Ideological Analysis"', *University of Tasmania Law Review* 19.2 (2000): 335–53; 'Of Consummation, Matrimonial Promises, Fault, and Parallel Wives: The Role of Original Texts, Interpretation, Ideology and Policy in Pre- and Post-1962 Burmese Case Law', *Columbia Journal of Asian Law* 14.1 (2000): 153–212; 'A Comparison of the First and Fiftieth Year of Independent Burma's Law Reports', *Victoria University of Wellington Law Review* 35.2 (2004): 385–426. More recently, see Dominic Nardi and Lwin Moe, 'Understanding the Myanmar Supreme Court's Docket: An Analysis of Case Topics from 2007 to 2011', *Law, Society and Transition in Myanmar*, eds. Melissa Crouch and Tim Lindsey (Oxford: Hart, 2014) 95–116.

[56] Elizabeth Kolsky, 'A Note on the Study of Indian Legal History', *Law and History Review* 23.3 (2005): 705–06.

[57] Ricardo Roque and Kim A. Wagner, Introduction, *Engaging Colonial Knowledge: Reading European Archives in World History*, eds. Ricardo Roque and Kim A. Wagner (Basingstoke and New York: Palgrave Macmillan, 2012) 4, 5.

[58] Roque and Wagner, Introduction, *Engaging Colonial Knowledge* 14.

not only over the facts of a case, but also over the opposing political ideals at issue in this book.

THE SPIRIT OF PROCEDURE

The purportedly scientific, procedurally exact form of law the British introduced to Burma and India distinguished them sharply, or so they imagined, from their predecessors. As Nasser Hussain has explained,

> Legal procedure was to be the ultimate answer to the question of what it meant to bring law to India. It was to be the form of a civilized despotism, for it would both declare to subjects that their identity, their offenses, their grievances, all began and ended in the authority of the law, and would reflect the morality of publicity and process lacking in the authority of a native despotism. Procedure was not substance but spirit, and in its exactitude it covered all law, English or Indian, statutory or customary, insisting that no authority preceded law, or more specifically, the workings of law, and that these workings created and reflected their own authority.[59]

The Benthamites wanted clear, concise, and predictable law. Judges would not have to cast about for answers. Everything they needed would be in a few bound volumes on the bench before them. John Stuart Mill, son of James, wrote that the Penal Code had been designed to 'contain in itself all the law that is necessary, all that the judge requires to enable him to execute the will of the legislator when he knows the facts of the particular case'.[60] At each point in a case, a procedure would indicate to functionaries what to do. However, procedures should not serve to delay or obstruct justice. Superficially, these ends appear consonant. In fact, they conceal a contradiction in the technology: procedure must be followed, but not to follow procedure is not wrong, provided it does not cause injustice.

The contradiction between adherence to procedure and fairness of outcome is not peculiar to the utilitarian model. In any relationship of contest before an adjudicator, a tension always exists between adherence to procedure on one hand and substantive notions of right and

[59] Hussain, *The Jurisprudence of Emergency* 65.

[60] John Stuart Mill, 'Penal Code for India', *Writings on India*, eds. John M. Robson, Martin Moir, and Zawahir Moir, vol. XXX (Toronto and Buffalo: University of Toronto Press, 1990) 19.

wrong on the other.[61] The contradiction that codified law in India presented was not unique, but because of the stress placed on procedure, it loomed large over trial proceedings, giving rise to 'tediously legalistic, semantic debates' about the terms of law.[62] Although they may have been tedious and legalistic, these debates mattered a great deal to anyone who was caught up in criminal cases heard in Burma's courts, for reasons set out in the remainder of this chapter.

Section 537 of the Criminal Procedure Code directed judges in Burma to ensure that minor procedural errors would not invalidate their verdicts, as it still does today. A reasonable and just decision could not be disturbed merely because of a flaw in procedure.[63] The thinking behind the section is straightforward, but the problem of whether an error was a mere technical flaw or an illegality depends upon the circumstances of a case. Consequently, questions over the distinction between procedural flaws and illegalities gave rise to extensive litigation.

Many rulings on procedural questions fell against appellants. A magistrate's use of an incorrect term, for example, was not fatal to the ruling if other officials could still easily infer its meaning.[64] Failure to read depositions aloud back to witnesses was not sufficient cause for retrial.[65] The neglect of a court to give formal notice to an accused of a case against him was not an illegality.[66] Failure of a judge to ask an accused if he wanted witnesses called did not necessarily prejudice the proceedings.[67] Non-compliance with the provisions in the Criminal Procedure Code for examination of an accused did not constitute sufficient grounds to overturn a conviction.[68] An unsigned confession was still valid if a higher court believed it was genuine.[69] Similarly, an unsigned judgement constituted a minor error that fell under section 537.[70] If a magistrate had not recorded his reasons for thinking that a dispute would lead to a breach of the peace, his order stood

[61] Mirjan R. Damaška, *The Faces of Justice and State Authority: A Comparative Approach to the Legal Process* (New Haven and London: Yale University Press, 1986) 101.

[62] Jonathan Saha, 'Colonization, Criminalization and Complicity: Policing Gambling in Burma c. 1880–1920', *South East Asia Research* 21.4 (2013): 662.

[63] *King-Emperor* v. *Nga Po Min*, 10 Ran. 511 FB. [64] *King-Emperor* v. *Nga Po*, 5 LBR 72 FB.

[65] *E. E. Mayeth* v. *King-Emperor*, 3 Ran. 612; *Abdul Rahman* v. *King-Emperor*, 5 Ran. 53 PC.

[66] *Nga Po Gaung* v. *King-Emperor*, (1897–1901) 1 UBR 96.

[67] *Nga Po Tein* v. *King-Emperor*, (1910–13) UBR 149.

[68] *U Ba Thein and Another* v. *King-Emperor*, 8 Ran. 372.

[69] *Ba Yin and One* v. *King-Emperor*, 7 Ran. 759.

[70] *Mohamed Hayet Mulla* v. *King-Emperor*, 7 Ran. 370.

so long as he did have a reason and could articulate it when examined before a superior judge.[71] Where he recalled prosecution witnesses and did not then re-examine the accused, the error did not vitiate the trial.[72] Nor did the failure of a court to indicate the duration of a restraining order render it void.[73]

But colonial-era judges in other cases ruled that procedural flaws did cause failures that undermined case outcomes. Statements made to the police were inadmissible, and judges had no authority to consult police records unless an accused requested they do so.[74] Where the accused had been unable to enter a defence, he had to be retried.[75] A retrial was invalid when the court did not re-examine defence witnesses but merely had their earlier statements read back to them.[76] The evidence of a single witness was not ordinarily enough for a court to convict, especially if it was from an approver (an accomplice who had turned witness for the prosecutor).[77] Where a magistrate chose not to hear defence witnesses, he had to record the reason for not doing so and demonstrate that the purpose of the defence in calling the witnesses had been to vex or delay justice.[78] If, in a committal hearing, a subordinate court had not considered the defence's evidence, it amounted to an illegality.[79] A *prima facie* case had to be established at committal before ordering a trial.[80] Even where convinced that a case existed, a judge could not dispense with procedure and fail to complete the hearing as statute required.[81] A retrial was unavoidable where a judge had not actually examined a defendant.[82] Likewise, where a court took evidence not in the presence of the accused or his lawyer, the conviction of the accused was invalid.[83] Failure to read a deposition back to a witnesses or his lawyer might not invalidate the trial, but it did

[71] *Maung Pu* v. *Maung Chit Pyu*, 5 Ran. 129.
[72] *Nga Hla U* v. *King-Emperor*, 3 Ran. 139; *K. M. Subbaya Naidu* v. *King-Emperor*, 7 Ran. 470.
[73] *Maung Thwe* v. *King-Emperor*, 3 Ran. 74.
[74] *Nga Po Chon* v. *King-Emperor*, 4 Ran. 356; *Nga U Khine and Others* v. *King-Emperor*, 13 Ran. 1; *King-Emperor* v. *Nga Lun Thuong*, 13 Ran. 570 FB.
[75] *Nga Thet U* v. *King-Emperor*, 2 LBR 115.
[76] *Hnin Yin (King-Emperor)* v. *Than Pe*, 9 LBR 92.
[77] *Nga Po Thet* v. *Queen-Empress*, 1 LBR 29; *Tha Hmu* v. *King-Emperor*, 2 LBR 206.
[78] *Shwe Bwin* v. *King-Emperor*, 2 LBR 270.
[79] *King-Emperor* v. *Nga Khaing and One*, 6 Ran. 531.
[80] *Tambi* v. *Appalsawmy (King-Emperor)*, 9 LBR 208.
[81] *King-Emperor* v. *Channing Arnold*, 6 LBR 129 FB.
[82] *King-Emperor* v. *Kyan Baw*, 2 LBR 239.
[83] *Nga Po Shein and 2* v. *King-Emperor*, (1910–13) UBR 152.

make the evidence inadmissible.[84] A court could not try the accused in two different cases together.[85] Nor could a single accused have two alternative charges combined and brought against him simultaneously.[86] And a judge violated the law when he passed an order on the basis of evidence that his predecessors had collected, without personally hearing from the accused.[87]

The superior courts frequently heard appeals in cases where a man's liberty was under question. In many, they ruled in favour of the detainee because of the authorities' failures to comply with procedure. Where a man successfully escaped from a wrongly issued arrest order, for instance, the escape was not illegal. Only escape from lawful custody could be penalised.[88] Likewise, resistance to illegal arrest could not constitute an offence.[89] A magistrate's order imprisoning a convicted person at a police lockup was also illegal, because a lockup did not constitute a jail under the terms of the Criminal Procedure Code.[90] And where a police officer was acting on orders of a superior to make an arrest, the orders had to be in writing.[91]

Detainees brought cases complaining about the abuse of security bonds as a means of imprisoning them without charge or trial. The notion of habitual criminality had taken hold in the British-ruled colonies and in the metropole.[92] In Burma, authorities routinely misused statutes for dealing with habitual criminals, detaining people against whom they had no proof of criminality who could not produce money for bonds. Superior courts complained about how lower courts interpreted general repute of habitual criminality when issuing bonds, and criticised the 'overzeal' of executive authorities in their pursuit and imprisonment of innocent people.[93] In an early expression of concern to protect civil rights through adherence to procedure, a judge warned that law 'must not be strained in order to secure even a public advantage. It is better that one dangerous man should be at large, than that a precedent should be established which would jeopardise the liberties of an indefinite number of citizens.'[94] Another

[84] *Nga San Myin* v. *King-Emperor*, (1910–13) UBR 123.
[85] *H. M. Eusoof and Abdul Khudus* v. *King-Emperor*, 11 LBR 73.
[86] *King-Emperor* v. *Po Thin Gyi*, 7 Ran. 96. [87] *King-Emperor* v. *Myat Aung*, 4 LBR 135.
[88] *King-Emperor* v. *Ramara*, 4 LBR 103.
[89] *King-Emperor* v. *Taik Pyu and Nga Thaik*, 5 LBR 21. [90] *King-Emperor* v. *Po Thin*, 7 LBR 62.
[91] *Mohamed Ismail* v. *King-Emperor*, 13 Ran. 754. [92] Metcalf, *Ideologies of the Raj* 124–25.
[93] *Nga Shwe Ywe* v. *Crown*, 1 LBR 71, 75. See also *Crown* v. *Nga Nyein*, 1 LBR 90.
[94] *Nga Po Nyun* v. *King-Emperor*, 2 LBR 76, 79.

court warned that the mere fact of someone's being a prior offender did not justify classing him as habitually criminal.[95] Despite such warnings, one retired official estimated that in the 1910s and early 1920s officials in the delta alone jailed some ten thousand people for failure to pay bonds.[96]

Courts also censured defects due to sloppy policing and prosecuting. Where police officers failed to obtain a properly issued search warrant, they had wrongly imprisoned an accused.[97] When evidence was uncovered that would 'throw an entirely new aspect' on a case, the judge refused to entertain the prosecutor's appeal for a retrial because of the earlier 'gross negligence on the part of those whose duty it was to investigate the case and put it before the Court'.[98] Likewise, after a pardoned approver absconded and a prosecution case collapsed, the officials involved could not go after the approver instead.[99] Where police officers had only generally recorded how they got information that two persons had murdered a third, the court refused to accept their account and acquitted the accused.[100] When the police and a magistrate had incorrectly issued summons, warrants of arrest, and proclamations of the accused as fugitives for not appearing at court, the appellate judge recommended dropping the matter and went on to say that in all cases some proof of an offence had to precede the giving of an order.[101] The failure of a magistrate and higher court judge to examine a case properly and put its substance in writing rendered their orders invalid.[102] And, a district police superintendent who busted a gambling den saw his case thrown out because he conducted the search improperly, exceeded his authority, acted illegally in delaying prosecution, submitted a report that was inadmissible as evidence, and ordered an announcement that implied he had authorised certain types of gambling in certain premises.[103] Not satisfied with having chastised the police, the court continued that for his part the magistrate had tried the case wrongly and had failed to record the charge and his findings as the Criminal Procedure Code required.

95 *Nga Po Than* v. *King-Emperor*, 3 Ran. 156.
96 R. Grant Brown, *Burma as I Saw It, 1889–1917* (London: Methuen, 1926) 84–85.
97 *Crown* v. *Majun and 12*, 1 LBR 120. 98 *King-Emperor* v. *Po Gyi*, 3 LBR 114, 115–16.
99 *Po Hla* v. *King-Emperor*, 8 LBR 357.
100 *Kha Hlaw and Poo Sa* v. *King-Emperor*, 4 LBR 116.
101 *King-Emperor* v. *Po Ni and Others*, 3 LBR 116. 102 *Crown* v. *Nga Kyauk Lon*, 1 LBR 75.
103 *King-Emperor* v. *Maung Cho and Others*, 2 LBR 43. But illegal items uncovered in an improper search could still be used to frame a charge. *Maung San Myin* v. *King-Emperor*, 7 Ran. 771; *Chwa Hum Htive and Another* v. *King-Emperor*, 11 Ran. 107.

Judges did express some concern to rein in police officers seeking to exceed their authority or interpret sections of the pannomion to their advantage. For instance, under the Criminal Procedure Code, when the police search premises they must have two witnesses in attendance who sign the search-and-seizure form. Use of 'professional' witnesses or people intimate with police officers came in for criticism early on. The apex court in one case noted that an excise officer had had the same witness to his searches 'some 8, 9 or 10 times'.[104] It overturned the sentencing of twenty-three persons convicted for illegal gambling because two ward headmen witnessed the search. It remarked that even though the code did not state it explicitly, its requirement was for witnesses 'unconnected in any way with the Government and officialdom', or else 'a police officer might call in two other police officers to witness the search, and might say with truth that the search had been witnessed by two respectable inhabitants of the locality'.[105]

The Chief Court in another case warned of the 'harassing and oppressing [of] persons on charges of gambling', encouraging magistrates to 'be careful to see that precautions are used to avoid unnecessary hardship, and to follow strictly the procedure laid down by law'.[106] Its counterpart in Upper Burma convicted a police sergeant for falsifying official records.[107] Overturning a lower court's sentence of one month's imprisonment for resisting arrest, an appellate judge castigated the magistrate for assuming that an arrest should involve handcuffing, even when an accused resisted a police officer.[108] A search warrant issued to go 'fishing for evidence' in the general contents of an office was unlawful, and the evidence obtained as a result of the search inadmissible.[109] A person's refusal to answer the questions of an investigating officer did not constitute a criminal offence.[110]

The small spaces that enabled victories for individual defendants in certain types of cases are what Larry May has described, borrowing from

[104] *Mi Hauk* v. *King-Emperor*, 4 LBR 121, 122.

[105] *Ah Shee and 22* v. *King-Emperor*, 3 LBR 229, 231, followed in *King-Emperor* v. *Kwe Haw and 16*, 4 LBR 213 FB. But *Kwe Haw* was later overturned in *Ti Ya and* 6 v. *King-Emperor*, 8 LBR 38 FB, where the full bench decided that the earlier verdict had had the effect of improving the code rather than interpreting it, and that there was nothing to prohibit village headmen from being witnesses.

[106] *Queen-Empress* v. *Nga Lu Gyi and 7*, 1 LBR 49, 50.

[107] *Nga Po Hmi* v. *Queen-Empress*, (1897–1901) 1 UBR 29.

[108] *Tan Sein* (a) *Maung Saing* v. *Crown*, 1 LBR 173.

[109] *V. S. M. Moideen Brothers* v. *Eng Thaung and Co.*, 9 LBR 45, 47.

[110] *Mawzanagyi* v. *King-Emperor*, 8 Ran. 511.

Henry Maine, as the 'interstices of procedure'.[111] May argues that in Europe, early procedural guarantees opened the door for courts to protect a body of substantive rights that emerged later. People expressed these rights normatively, in bills and declarations. Where procedural guarantees are operative, he posits, they introduce minimal fairness that makes the exercise of other rights possible. As Edward Thompson famously contended, they make other rights conceivable, even if they are not yet achievable.[112] They smuggle in substantive rights, such as the right not to be deprived of liberty arbitrarily or secretly, which invite people to imagine themselves and politics differently.

If a claim can be made for the rule of law in Burma during the colonial period, its grounds are in these procedural interstices and the checks on arbitrariness they contained. It is a claim corresponding with Friedrich Hayek's well-known formal conception of the rule of law as 'government in all its actions [which] is bound by rules fixed and announced beforehand – rules which make it possible to foresee with fair certainty how the authority will use its coercive powers in given circumstances, and to plan one's individual affairs on the basis of this knowledge'.[113] This rule of law is minimal. It consists of little more than a guarantee against arbitrariness of the sort associated with rule by man, which the colonialists identified with their indigenous antecedents.[114] It is a claim for the rule of law through an assertion of lawfulness absent of any commitment to the self-determination of those subject to the law.[115] The utilitarian technology contained technical forms designed to mitigate the worst excesses of despotism, while ensuring its continuance. The technology was meticulous in its oppressiveness, but equally it left a good deal of room for argument – too much in the eyes of some administrators, men of action like Godfrey Harvey, who grumbled that many a criminal accused in Burma 'who would have been seen through at a glance by his own [Burmese] rulers now went scot free after a

[111] Larry May, *Global Justice and Due Process* (Cambridge: Cambridge University Press, 2011) ch. 2. See Henry Maine, *Dissertations on Early Law and Custom* (London: John Murray, 1883) 389.

[112] Edward P. Thompson, *Whigs and Hunters: The Origin of the Black Act* (London: Allen Lane, 1975) 258–69.

[113] Friedrich A. Hayek, *The Road to Serfdom* (Chicago: University of Chicago Press, 1994) 80.

[114] A survey of precolonial law in Burma is beyond the scope of this book. For an overview, see Andrew Huxley, 'Pre-Colonial Burmese Law: Conical Hat and Shoulder Bag', *IIAS Newsletter Online* 25 (2001), 23 July 2008 www.iias.nl/iiasn.

[115] Hussain, *The Jurisprudence of Emergency* 134.

patient trial before an English judge'.[116] As competition and conflict seeped into courts, people in Burma, like their counterparts in India and elsewhere in the British Empire, learned how to use procedural interstices to talk back to power.

It is not surprising that the complaints of administrators about superfluous technicalities and legal niceties in Burma corresponded with the complaints of counterparts in India.[117] The two shared the same corpus of codified law, and many officials made their way to Burma from India. But the fact that the same types of complaints were heard in Egypt or Algeria suggests something more significant about the opportunities that colonial legal technology afforded colonised people. A concern to prevent inefficient abuses of power through the mechanical responses of procedures was inscribed within the pannomion. Once colonial subjects learned how to negotiate their way through procedure's interstices, bureaucrats found that, like Thompson's eighteenth-century Whigs, having 'played the games of power according to rules which suited them ... they could not break those rules' – or not all of them – 'or the whole game would be thrown away'.[118] Over time, courts became sites of contest not only over the crimes of accused persons, but also over the ideas that colonial government represented. To some extent, the empire's servants became prisoners of their rule-of-law rhetoric.

INTERSTICES' LIMITS

At the start of this chapter, I implied that the rule-of-law project in the British colony was more than just myth or fantasy. So far I have set out some evidence in support of that inference. Yet, compelling evidence exists against colonial claims to have established the rule of law. Much of it comes from the same sources. Therefore, before ending the chapter, I qualify the preceding observations with remarks on the limits of procedural interstices in the colony.

In his classic study of policing in colonial India, David Arnold posited that the 'order' police imposed did not necessarily square with 'law'.[119] Authorities gave the police a great deal of leeway to operate

[116] Godfrey E. Harvey, *British Rule in Burma, 1824–1942* (London: Faber & Faber, 1946) 34.

[117] Martin J. Wiener, *An Empire on Trial: Race, Murder, and Justice under British Rule, 1870–1935* (Cambridge: Cambridge University Press, 2009) 150–51.

[118] Thompson, *Whigs and Hunters* 263.

[119] David Arnold, *Police Power and Colonial Rule: Madras 1859–1947* (Delhi: Oxford University Press, 1986) 3.

outside the terms formally laid down for them. Jonathan Saha has reached a similar finding in his study of official misconduct in the Burma delta. Saha says that the relationship between state power and illegality was more ambivalent than historians of Burma have acknowledged.[120] Publicly, judges might have chided wayward officials. Privately, they tolerated disorder in the police ranks and among other personnel as necessary to maintain a semblance of orderliness. Police officers adept at malfeasance learned how to engage with courts and turn the Benthamite technology to their advantage. The violence of police officers and other officials enabled and eluded the control of colonial government.[121]

Here we encounter some of the empirical limits to the argument advanced in the preceding section that procedural interstices enable the rule of law. In colonial Burma, things did not always turn out that way. Instead, the regime of procedural law also restricted and delimited avenues for certain types of complainants. While allowing some claimants to seek remedies within its confines, it routinely and consistently denied access to others. Among the latter categories, I will concentrate the remaining remarks for this chapter on just one: women.

I have two reasons for this concentration. First, many studies have already examined the differential treatment of racially classed subject peoples.[122] But differential treatment in colonial law took many forms, including gendered differentiation, which arguably has received less attention. Second, the law reports contain a rich vein of material involving women as victims and as criminal accused through which to explore this issue.[123]

Legal procedure in the colonial period acted to deny rather than protect victims of sexual violence. In her study of rape cases reported in high court decisions across India during colonial rule, Kolsky cites the 1926 *Maung Ba Tin* case, where the High Court in Rangoon ruled that a woman's testimony of rape would be notoriously unreliable for a

[120] Saha, *Law, Disorder and the Colonial State* 4.

[121] Sherman, *State Violence and Punishment in India* 6.

[122] See Darian-Smith, *Religion, Race, Rights;* Kolsky, *Colonial Justice in British India;* Philippa Levine, *Prostitution, Race, and Politics: Policing Venereal Disease in the British Empire* (New York and London: Routledge, 2003); Saha, *Law, Disorder and the Colonial State*, ch. 3; Wiener, *An Empire on Trial.*

[123] As discussed further in Nick Cheesman, 'Bodies on the Line in Burma's Criminal Law Reports, 1892–1922', Crouch and Lindsey, *Law, Society and Transition* 77–94.

court to accept.[124] She neglects to mention the most remarkable aspect of the ruling – that it was practically the only published superior court judgment on a charge of rape in Burma over sixty-five years, from 1872, when a judicial commissioner began work in Lower Burma, to 1937, when the territory separated from India.[125] Where it did get reported rape was sometimes incidental to technical issues of law.[126] Sometimes it was downgraded to 'assault with intent to outrage modesty'.[127] However, rape rarely appears in the reports as an explicitly sexual offence. A few cases, such as the public gang rape of a Burmese woman by a group of British soldiers in Rangoon, gained notoriety.[128] Notwithstanding, the message coming loud and clear from the law reports is that the codes' purpose was to protect peaceable *men*. The procedural interstices were male spaces, just as the state itself was masculine.[129]

In all types of assault on women – not just sexual assault – judges found grounds to justify crimes, and reduce sentences. A man who stabbed a woman to death escaped a charge of homicide because the judge concluded it was natural for him to lash out with a knife when she squeezed his testicles.[130] In two cases where relatives beat women to death while supposedly attempting to cast out evil spirits, the judges appear to show more empathy for the perpetrators than the victims. One ruling repeatedly implies that had the beating been less aggressive, the accused might have escaped with a lesser penalty.[131] A judge in another case states that the act of striking a girl more than a hundred times was not unlawful, and had it been done 'with the proper care and

[124] Elizabeth Kolsky, '"The Body Evidencing the Crime": Rape on Trial in Colonial India, 1860–1947', *Gender and History* 22.1 (2010): 116.

[125] Published, since the case appeared in the *Burma Law Journal* of the same year, and in a subsequent digest of rulings, but not officially reported.

[126] As in *Queen-Empress* v. *Nga Han Shin*, (1892–96) 1 UBR 50; *King-Emperor* v. *Po Ba*, 8 LBR 143; *King-Emperor* v. *Mi Wa*, 8 LBR 534; G. C. *Siricar* v. *King-Emperor*, 3 Ran. 68.

[127] As in *Nga Aung Dwe* v. *Queen-Empress*, (1892–96) 1 UBR 229; *Queen-Empress* v. *Nga Chit Kyu*, (1897–1901) 1 UBR 325.

[128] Kolsky, *Colonial Justice in British India* 199–202; Jeremy Neill, '"This Is a Most Disgusting Case": Imperial Policy, Class and Gender in the "Rangoon Outrage" of 1899', *Journal of Colonialism and Colonial History* 12.1 (2011), 18 Aug. 2011 http://muse.jhu.edu/journals/journal_of_colonialism_and_colonial_history.

[129] As discussed in Jonathan Saha, 'The Male State: Colonialism, Corruption and Rape Investigations in the Irrawaddy Delta c. 1900', *Indian Economic and Social History Review* 47.3 (2010): 343–76.

[130] *Po Gyi*. [131] *Nga Po Tha and 2* v. *King-Emperor*, (1917–20) UBR 54.

attention' no offence of any sort would have been committed: the girl would not have died.[132]

Procedure here worked systematically against complainants or victims. Defendants, lawyers, and judges could in practically every case cast sufficient doubt on an allegation so as to dismiss it as unreliable, as in the *Maung Ba Tin* case. In one trial, a judge overturned a prior conviction on the grounds that the woman had consented to adulterous sex, and he did not believe her allegations.[133] He quotes the judgment of the lower court to support his finding, that,

> The important point for consideration . . . is the possibility or probability that the complainant and her witnesses, knowing in their own hearts of the adultery, determined to make up the story of rape and tell it to the husband on his return and so save [the] complainant's face and leave him to report the rape.[134]

The belief among British men that women alleging sexual abuse were liars was not peculiar to Burma. Men back in the metropole shared it. But in the colony officials also assigned attributes to Burmese women that further disadvantaged them in court: that they were assertive and domineering, and more inclined to make unfounded allegations than men.[135] These views were pervasive not only among government bureaucrats but also among missionaries, members of the indigenous elite, and representatives of women's groups at home and abroad.[136] Whereas among suffragettes and nationalists such attributes might have been a cause for celebration, for colonial officials they were cause for concern.

Courts treated women who were parties to criminal cases with suspicion. In the abovementioned case, the judge went on to conclude that the story of rape was false because, 'Knowing the independent character of Burmese women, there is no necessity whatsoever . . . to wait till the husband's return. If the case were a true one, she would have gone off and complained at once'.[137] Attributing a general purported quality of Burmese womanhood to the woman in a specific case, the judge concluded she was untrustworthy. A general attribute once

[132] *Nga Po Kyaw and 3* v. *King-Emperor*, (1902–03) 1 UBR Pen. Co. 1, 2.

[133] *Nga Po Thaw* v. *King-Emperor*, (1910–13) UBR 155. [134] *Nga Po Thaw*, 155.

[135] Saha, *Law, Disorder and the Colonial State* 117–18.

[136] Chie Ikeya, *Refiguring Women, Colonialism, and Modernity in Burma* (Honolulu: University of Hawai'i Press, 2011) 47.

[137] *Nga Po Thaw*, 155–56.

applied could be extended across practically all cases in the same category to reach the same kind of outcome.

Men's testimonies could also be untrustworthy, but the reports implicitly distinguish the untrustworthiness of the man from the untrustworthiness of the woman. In finding that a farmer who alleged policemen assaulted him to force him to confess to a crime was lying, a judge said the farmer probably confessed out of ignorance, since 'uncivilized cultivators are not likely to be aware of the cautious measures which the law prescribes before any man can be deprived of his liberty when he does not admit his guilt'.[138] The man who lies in order to escape punishment does so because he is unknowing of the highly refined technology designed to test the truth or falsity of his claims. The woman does so because she is duplicitous and scheming. The falsehood of the man is determined case by case, subject to availability of evidence; the falsehood of the woman precedes her testimony in the courtroom.

Behind the gendered stereotypes prevalent in rape and abduction cases, something else also seems to have been at work. Women and girls lacked the protections afforded peaceable men because the crimes against them were crimes occupying liminal, concealed spaces. The illuminating light of codification was not cast directly on these crimes. They were necessarily kept in the darkness. Crimes upon women's bodies had to be policed, not adjudicated. Policing is about concealment, about keeping under the covers those things that are likely to cause disturbance. Adjudication is about making things public, about putting on display through performance. Policing suppresses vice. But to suppress is not to eliminate. It is to secrete, to cover up. For this reason, crimes against women could be regulated, and documented accordingly, but not tried. By their nature, they were matters for law and order, not the rule of law.

CONCLUSION

The British colonial government claimed to distinguish itself from its predecessors through an insistence on firm, albeit oppressive, legality. An abundance of scholarship since its time has described the tensions in this legality. Some scholars, like Sandria Freitag, have argued that the tension lay between different formulations of crime for individuals

[138] *Chit Tun and 4* v. *Crown*, 1 LBR 238, 248.

and groups – the former in a rule-of-law framework, the latter outside it.[139] Other writers have taken an interest in the tension between ordinary and extraordinary moments, like the late colonial period in Burma, when the emergency paradigm all but overwhelmed the utilitarian technology.[140]

But as Terrence Halliday and Lucien Karpik have noted, the internal contradiction to the British colonial enterprise went beyond the use of emergency regulations 'as a pretext for escaping the constraints of the rule of law'.[141] They point to two qualifications to the universalising discourse of the rule of law, one based on threats to public order, the other on the lines drawn between colonisers and the colonised. They refer to the former as the law of exception and the latter, the rule of difference – what Kolsky has more precisely designated the rule of colonial difference through codification.[142]

The difficulty with this reading of colonial governmentality is that it still imputes the existence of a singular normative framework for the rule of law to which certain reservations attached discursively in response to contingencies. By starting with the rule-of-law ideal and then moving into the realm of practices, it pushes analysis back onto the sliding scale from the rule of law to rule by law and other derivatives. Measures to address threats to public order, or to differentiate between people categorically, again become problems of the gap between norm and reality, between ideal and necessity, between teleology and instrumentality.

But the procedural interstices that worked to the advantage of some colonial subjects and to the disadvantage of others did not meet this problem. Nothing about the procedural model for the rule of law was inherently incompatible with the rule of colonial difference. The one could accommodate the other precisely because British colonial

[139] Sandria B. Freitag, 'Crime in the Social Order of Colonial North India', *Modern Asian Studies* 25.2 (1991): 260.

[140] Maitrii Aung-Thwin, 'Discourses of Emergency in Colonial and Postcolonial Burma', *Emergency Powers in Asia: Exploring the Limits of Legality*, eds. Victor V. Ramraj and Arun K. Thiruvengadam (Cambridge: Cambridge University Press, 2010) 187–212.

[141] Terence C. Halliday and Lucien Karpik, 'Political Liberalism in the British Post-Colony: A Theme with Three Variations', *Fates of Political Liberalism in the British Post-Colony: The Politics of the Legal Complex*, eds. Terence C. Halliday, Lucien Karpik, and Malcolm M. Feeley (New York: Cambridge University Press, 2012) 4, 12–13.

[142] Elizabeth Kolsky, 'Codification and the Rule of Colonial Difference: Criminal Procedure in British India', *Law and History Review* 23.3 (2005): 631–83. See also Partha Chatterjee, *The Nation and Its Fragments: Colonial and Postcolonial Histories* (Princeton: Princeton University Press, 1993) 16–18.

law created categories of people from whom ordinarily available protections could be withdrawn via the mechanical application of procedure. The rule of colonial difference through codified procedure was an altogether different matter from the use of emergency decrees and other extraordinary measures to combat perceived threats to the political order. The differential treatment of colonial subjects via the procedural interstices was not exceptional, but mundane. Courts maintained the rule of colonial difference through their everyday routines.

Beginning with the ideas underpinning the technology of law that the British brought to Burma, in this chapter I have sought to show that the problem for colonial courts was not how to escape the constraints of the rule of law but how to reconcile practices annexed to *competing ideals* – one, the rule of law, the other, law and order – which ran throughout colonial administration. The tension was not just between ideas and practices, between ideals and reservations, but also between entirely different, opposing ideas, and the practices associated with each. It was not that in its colonies the British rule of law encountered the limits of its application because government was despotic. Rather, as Eric Stokes has pointed out, in India 'the paradox in utilitarianism between the principle of liberty and the principle of authority' was most clearly exposed.[143] The inherent contradictions with which colonial bureaucrats, police, judges, and prosecutors struggled, and of which many took advantage, were internal to the utilitarian technology. In moments when administrators gave up on the technology and resorted to openly coercive measures, they were not escaping the constraints of the rule of law; they were declining any longer to struggle with the opposing principles on which the pannomion rested. At those moments, they abandoned generality as a principle of government and proposed to maintain order without attempting to conciliate it with law. They resolved the hostility between the rule of law and law and order by forsaking the former in favour of the latter.

143 Stokes, *The English Utilitarians and India* viii.

3

REORDERING LAW IN THE POSTCOLONY

In February 1950, two years after the end of colonial rule, the new Supreme Court of Burma ruled on a petition for release of a prominent anticolonial leader accused of plotting against the government. Lawyers seeking his release argued that the statute used to detain him was unconstitutional, because it was not in accordance with natural law. Acting Chief Justice E Maung considered the history of codified law making in Burma since the British invasion, finding that,

> Customary laws, the Common Law of England and the principles of justice, equity and good conscience were not applied by their inherent force but were made applicable by enactment. It is by people who had lived or who had been trained under this system that the Constitution of the Union of Burma was drawn up and enacted and it is therefore reasonable to conclude that when the Constitution speaks of 'law' it speaks of the will of the legislature enacted in due form, provided that such enactment is within the competence of the legislature.[1]

Burma was free from colonial rule, but, the court made clear, the pannomion, the Benthamite technology, and the colonial-style courts were there to stay.[2] This continuity was unremarkable. Colonial-era law and judiciaries persisted throughout Asia as an inevitable

[1] *Tinsa Maw Naing* v. *Commissioner of Police, Rangoon*, 1950 BLR (SC) 17, 25. From 1948, the published rulings became the Burma Law Reports (BLR). Citations here refer to rulings from the Supreme Court (SC) and the High Court (HC).

[2] Effect had been given to pre-existing laws in the Union of Burma (Continued Observance of Laws) Order, 1948, and the Union Judiciary Act, 8/48.

consequence of modernity.[3] Modern states needed institutions to continue running, and it was profoundly easier to work with the existing 'rickety yet repressive architecture' than to start from scratch.[4]

If Burma's colonial architecture was at once rickety and repressive, it was in part a consequence of design and, in part, of circumstances. Competing political ideals inherent in the technology pulled in different directions with increasing force after independence. Colonial courts had already gone from being sites for turning accused persons into prisoners – as a former magistrate characterised them – to sites of genuine contestation.[5] The contests were not only over the guilt or innocence of an accused but also, in time, over the politics of empire itself. With independence, the contest did not pass away, but evolved into an even fiercer struggle. Democratic life, nationalist spirit, and other factors all contributed to the growth of a rights-based discourse, one that developed and amplified the rule-of-law concept. But the law-and-order concept was also integral to the judicial technology, and deeply ingrained in the thinking of its functionaries. The fight to conciliate law with order took on a new pitch, a new intensity.

This chapter explores that fight through study of the politics of courts in Burma over four decades, from 1948 to 1988. As in the previous chapter, my purpose is not to write a comprehensive history, nor to describe the judiciary from root to branch, but to explore the lineages of law and order and the rule of law in Burma's courts.[6] The chapter begins in the struggle to reconcile new conceptions of substantive rights-based law with the maintenance of order in the early postcolony. It then discusses the interim military government of 1958–1960 and its successor, the Revolutionary Council of 1962 to 1974, which refashioned the state around a mass party designed to suit

[3] Daniel S. Lev, 'The Criminal Regime: Criminal Process in Indonesia', *Figures of Criminality in Indonesia, the Philippines, and Colonial Vietnam*, ed. Vincente L. Rafael, (Ithaca, NY: Cornell University Press, 1999) 178.

[4] Mary P. Callahan, 'State Formation in the Shadow of the Raj: Violence, Warfare and Politics in Colonial Burma', *Southeast Asian Studies* 39.4 (2002): 535.

[5] Maurice Collis, *Trials in Burma* (London: Faber & Faber, 1953) 5.

[6] For a summary of the changing structure and nomenclature of Burma's upper courts see Myint Zan, 'A Comparison of the First and Fiftieth Year of Independent Burma's Law Reports', *Victoria University of Wellington Law Review* 35.2 (2004): 386–87. A chart of courts and reported rulings is available in U Than Maung, 'A Background History of Myanmar Rulings', *Judicial Journal* 1.13 (2002): 54 (article in Burmese; chart in English and Burmese).

the army's purposes. It displaced the rule-of-law idea, insisting on the primacy of policy. While claiming to eliminate the bureaucratisation of the colonial era, it established its own type of highly bureaucratic control, built around a party structure that was in turn based on an assertion of sovereign authority through seizure of political power, the consequences of which continued to reverberate after the party's demise in 1988.

PUBLIC ORDER PRESERVATION

Michael Charney has called the decade preceding Burma's independence 'a long trial run' for the period following it.[7] From 1937 to 1942 as a British colony separated from India, then under Japanese military occupation from 1942 to 1945, and lastly under British tutelage but with significant autonomy in the lead-up to independence, politicians, judges, soldiers, lawyers, police officers, and journalists alike learned their parts amid intense violence and uncertainty. And when the moment of independence arrived, it came with a rush and brought more violence and uncertainty.

The fledgling political elite fell into disarray after gunmen shot dead Aung San, the putative leader of independent Burma, along with five members of his cabinet in July 1947. A special tribunal convicted a rival politician, U Saw, for masterminding the crime.[8] After independence, Saw and his co-accused unsuccessfully appealed the verdict on grounds that the special law passed to establish the tribunal was illegal and the procedures used to obtain confessions were faulty.[9] Of the men left standing, U Nu, also known as Thakin Nu, took up the post of prime minister and the leadership of the Anti-Fascist People's Freedom League, which dominated party politics in Burma for the next decade. An army lieutenant colonel going by the name of Ne Win was in the field at the time of Aung San's murder, tasked with restoring law and order against nefarious armed opponents.[10] He would go on to lead the

[7] Michael W. Charney, *A History of Modern Burma* (Cambridge: Cambridge University Press, 2009) 71.

[8] The trial is narrated in Maung Maung, *A Trial in Burma: The Assassination of Aung San* (The Hague: Martinus Nijhoff, 1962).

[9] *U Saw and 9* v. *Union of Burma*, 1948 BLR (HC) 217.

[10] Maung Maung, *Burma and General Ne Win* (Rangoon: Religious Affairs Dept., 1969) 181. *New Times of Burma*, 10 Mar. 1947, in Hugh Tinker, ed., *Burma: The Struggle for Independence, 1944–1948*, vol. II, 2 vols. (London: HMSO, 1984) 454–55.

army, and as general would become the newly independent state's first military dictator.

Compounding the immense damage caused by the Second World War and postwar intercommunal conflicts, civil war began with the declaration of independence.[11] Burma was awash with weapons and men who knew how to use them. By March 1949, almost twelve thousand military personnel had deserted their posts.[12] An array of separatist and revolutionary groups occupied swathes of the country, seizing towns and cities, and besieging the capital, Rangoon.[13] Some politicians wanted to suspend parliament and declare interim military rule there and then.[14]

Under attack from all quarters, in August 1948 the government proclaimed a state of emergency, citing the efforts of evildoers to destroy law and order, *ngyeinwut-pibyaye*, and endanger the lives and property of law-abiding citizens.[15] Within a few days it announced martial law for Karenni State, 'instructing all law-abiding members of the public to assist in the stability of law and order and public security, and to follow the orders and regulations issued by the military authorities' there.[16] The attorney general did his best to reassure the parliament that martial law did not mean 'no law', and that the substantive protections afforded to citizens distinguished the new exceptional provisions from their predecessors under the British, even if the measures were designed to limit or suspend those protections.[17] Nonetheless, the law-and-order imperative persisted. Exemplifying it was the Public Order (Preservation) Act.

Passed, and amended, in the final year of colonial rule, the Public Order (Preservation) Act had its origin in an expired wartime statute.[18] Its provisions became sites for many early battles between agencies

[11] On the damage caused in this period see Ian Brown, *Burma's Economy in the Twentieth Century* (Cambridge: Cambridge University Press, 2013) 80–96.

[12] Mary P. Callahan, *Making Enemies: War and State Building in Burma* (Ithaca, NY, and London: Cornell University Press, 2003) 135.

[13] As discussed in Martin Smith, *Burma: Insurgency and the Politics of Ethnicity*, 2nd edn. (London and New York: Zed, 1999) 138–40.

[14] Maung Maung, *Burma and General Ne Win* 209–10.

[15] Presidential proclamation in U San Nyein and Daw Myint Kyi, eds., *Burma's Politics 1958–1962*, vol. I, 4 vols. (Yangon: Universities Press, 1991) 253 (in Burmese).

[16] Martial Law Declaration 1, 1948, in San Nyein and Myint Kyi, eds., *Burma's Politics 1958–1962* 254.

[17] Parliamentary proceedings in San Nyein and Myint Kyi, eds., *Burma's Politics 1958–1962* 258–67.

[18] U Hla Aung, 'The Law of Preventive Detention in Burma', *Journal of the International Commission of Jurists* 3.1 (1961): 47.

concerned with the objective of law and order, captured in the statute's title – which reads *ngyeinwut-pibyaye* for 'public order' – and rights-based rule of law. The statute's section 5 permitted the police to arrest without warrant anyone suspected of 'having acted, or acting, or being about to act in any manner calculated to disturb, or to assist a disturbance of the public tranquillity'. One parliamentarian, echoing complaints of his colonial-era predecessors, described it as a section that effectively enabled anyone to be arrested for anything.[19] Judges openly condemned it. Chief Justice U Ba U said it was 'much misused', badly drafted, and in need of urgent amendment.[20] The parliamentary opposition – whose members also became its targets – attempted unsuccessfully to repeal it in 1953.[21] Instead parliament expanded its terms to allow preventive detention of opium dealers and 'economic insurgents'.[22] Ba U's successor, U Myint Thein, described the act's terms as 'counter to the ideas of liberty and freedom enshrined in the Constitution'.[23] Yet not only was the act not annulled; it was to outlast the constitution. It became the instrument of choice for a permanent programme of suppression, one speaking to the persistence of law and order as a political ideal and not merely a response to exigencies of the sort that confronted politicians and officials in the early years after independence.

Nevertheless, the political and legal conditions of the postcolony were not those of the colony. People could assert rights, and courts could entertain their assertions in ways dissimilar to the earlier period, using instruments previously unavailable to them. People could petition the Supreme Court on any violation of fundamental rights contained in chapter two of the 1947 Constitution.[24] Some rights applied only to citizens. The court ruled that others were universal – such as the

[19] Saw Maung Dauk cited in Tekkathoe Myat Thu, *Parliamentary Sights* (Yangon: Sarpay Beikman, 2012) 51 (in Burmese).

[20] *Ma Lone* v. *Commissioner of Police, Rangoon and One*, 1949 BLR (SC) 8, 9.

[21] Hugh Tinker, *The Union of Burma: A Study of the First Years of Independence*, 4th edn. (London: Oxford University Press, 1967) 142.

[22] Govt. of the Union of Burma, *Record of the Chamber of Deputies, Union Parliament* (Rangoon: Govt. of Burma, 1954), 1st session, vol. III, 104–09 (in Burmese). The record contains figures that upwards of ten thousand people had been detained under the act between 1948 and 1952. The figure for 1950 is imprecise, the government stating that it preventively detained 'over 2,700' people.

[23] *Lim Lyan Hwat* (a) *Lim Sway Gaung / Lim Kwin Kee* (a) *Htwa Kong* (a) *Htwa Tong* v. *The Secretary, Ministry of Home Affairs and One*, 1960 BLR (SC) 128, 129.

[24] Art. 25(1), Const. of the Union of Burma, 1947.

right to freedom of movement.[25] The constitution also permitted writ petitions, including for habeas corpus.[26] This writ was the only avenue for appeal against detention under the Public Order (Preservation) Act.[27] By one account, in 1948 and 1949 the habeas corpus petition was the most popularly invoked judicial remedy in the country.[28]

The Supreme Court released people detained under the Public Order (Preservation) Act on a variety of grounds, some of them procedural, but many asserting its role as guardian of citizens' rights.[29] It ordered the release of a man who encouraged workers to strike and acted as a messenger for the Burma Communist Party because both were activities 'within the legitimate rights of a citizen of the Union'.[30] That a detainee happened to be a senior communist party member and influential in effecting strike action was also irrelevant: he had a right to be a communist, and to organise strikes.[31] Possession of a copy of a seditious pamphlet did not prove anything to justify detention.[32] Nor was distribution of pamphlets calling for rebellion a good reason for putting someone in custody: democratic government entitled parties to make political attacks on one another and 'in the language of politicians in these days,' E Maung held, '"rebellion" (*tawhlan-ye*) does not necessarily mean much and no undue importance should, in our opinion, be attached to its use'.[33] A ruling of this sort would have been unthinkable a few years earlier.

The Supreme Court struck down orders under the Public Order (Preservation) Act where it found that police officers and other officials had acted improperly. Police officers could not use the law to punish people where they lacked evidence or inclination to prosecute.[34] One of the authors of a handbill entitled 'Murderer Thakin Nu's fascist government' might have been liable to a charge of

[25] V. E. Rm. N. Rm. *Kasi Viswanathan Chettyar* v. *Official Assignee and One*, 1958 BLR (SC) 74.

[26] Art. 25(2), Const. of the Union of Burma, 1947. See also Nick Cheesman, 'The Incongruous Return of Habeas Corpus to Myanmar', *Ruling Myanmar: From Cyclone Nargis to National Elections*, eds. Nick Cheesman, Monique Skidmore, and Trevor Wilson (Singapore: ISEAS, 2010) 95.

[27] *Bo San Lin* v. *Commissioner of Police and One*, 1948 BLR (SC) 372.

[28] Maung Maung, *Burma's Constitution*, 2nd edn. (The Hague: Martinus Nijhoff, 1961) 99.

[29] As discussed in Winslow Christian, 'Burma's New Constitution and Supreme Court', *Tulane Law Review* 26.1 (1951): 49–56.

[30] *Daw Aye Nyunt* v. *Commissioner of Police, Rangoon and One*, 1949 BLR (SC) 5, 7.

[31] *Pakiya Ammal* v. *Deputy Commissioner, Hanthawaddy and One*, 1949 BLR (SC) 35.

[32] *Ma Mya Khin* v. *Commissioner of Police, Rangoon and One*, 1950 BLR (SC) 8.

[33] *Ma Khin Than* v. *Commissioner of Police, Rangoon and One*, 1949 BLR (SC) 13, 17.

[34] *Ma Than Sint* v. *Commissioner of Police, Rangoon and One*, 1949 BLR (SC) 1.

sedition, but if so the police had to bring evidence to charge him accordingly; they could not hold him under the act.[35] E Maung deplored policemen who in a deliberate attempt to evade the court's authority transferred a detainee to the central prison while the surrounding area was under military administration, owing to insurgency.[36] He also deprecated the practice of ordering indefinite detention under the law, in one case noting the police had apparently forgotten about a man held in custody for over four years.[37] 'We do not desire to make the path of officers entrusted with the preservation of public order and tranquillity difficult,' he explained in one early ruling, 'But the liberty of the citizen and his fundamental right not to be deprived of his personal liberty save in accordance with law are matters of great import.'[38] Over the next decade, E Maung and his successors were to iterate and amplify this message through a variety of statements on fundamental rights.

Courts also kept the procedural wheels of the Benthamite technology turning. The personal liberties of citizens, the Supreme Court stressed, were 'not to be interfered with save in accordance with law and with strict compliance with the procedure prescribed'.[39] Complainants and defendants had equal rights to speak, to know of formal charges in court, and to call and cross-examine witnesses.[40] An alleged foreigner residing illegally in Burma had a right to make a defence in court before deportation.[41] Where an accused pleaded guilty, a judge could not just accept the plea. He had to ensure that the person understood the charge, the facts of the case, and the consequences of admitting guilt.[42] Judges had to record verdicts as required by the Criminal Procedure Code, not just issue them orally.[43] They had to hear cases in open court.[44] Where neither an applicant for review of

[35] *Ma Ahmar* v. *Commissioner of Police, Rangoon and One*, 1949 BLR (SC) 39.
[36] *Bo Aye Ko* v. *Commissioner of Police, Rangoon and 2*, 1950 BLR (SC) 181.
[37] *U Zan* v. *Deputy Commissioner, Insein and Another*, 1951 BLR (SC) 188. See also *Thet Tun* v. *Deputy Commissioner, Shwebo and Another*, 1952 BLR (SC) 33.
[38] *Ah Nywe* v. *Commissioner of Police, Rangoon and Another*, 1948 BLR (SC) 737, 740.
[39] *Lee Kyin Su* (a) *U Su* v. *Commissioner of Excise and 3*, 1957 BLR (SC) 5, 9.
[40] *Maung Ant Bwe and One* v. *Union of Burma*, 1948 BLR (HC) 863; *Union of Burma* v. *Ah Shin and 2*, 1955 BLR (HC) 317; *U Ba Aye and 3* v. *Union of Burma*, 1958 BLR (HC) 548; *Bishu* (a) *Ma Kyin Nu* v. *Union of Burma*, 1953 BLR (HC) 110 (in Burmese).
[41] *Hasan Ali* v. *Secretary, Ministry of Immigration and National Registration and One*, 1959 BLR (SC) 187.
[42] *Sri Sawarmal* v. *Union of Burma (U Thein Maung)*, 1954 BLR (HC) 331.
[43] Courts General Letter 4/1956, 20 Jan. 1956.
[44] *Maung Kyaw Aye* v. *Union of Burma*, 1953 BLR (HC) 114.

a case nor his lawyer appeared, the judge still had a responsibility to go over the record and satisfy himself that the lower court had given the correct order.[45] If a judge made inquiries about a case so as to fill gaps in the prosecutor's argument, rather than simply to understand the facts, his verdict was unlawful.[46] When he purportedly reviewed a case but failed to record any reasoning other than that he was satisfied with the evidence and finding from the lower court, it was void.[47] He could not use the confession of a co-accused or approver to convict, or to fill gaps in missing parts of evidence.[48] If an accused person's statement to the police contained a large number of facts constituting an offence it was a confession, and therefore inadmissible.[49] A preliminary police report prepared after inquiries into a crime had begun was not what it purported to be and was also inadmissible.[50] Where a magistrate was a friend of a government officer in a case before him, sufficient grounds existed to transfer the case, as it created doubt about the impartiality of the judge.[51] Nobody had to prove actual bias. Nor did a person claiming to have confessed because he was afraid of the police have to prove they ill-treated him, only that his fear was justified.[52]

These verdicts need to be kept in perspective. Just as the procedural interstices of the Benthamite technology expanded only so far in the colony, so too in the postcolony the exercise of rights had its limits. Rulings on rights in the higher courts did not necessarily correspond to their active protection in subordinate courts – or provoke action against perpetrators of abuses. Very few police officers or administrators were ever made criminally liable for custodial abuses and other crimes. The government in its early years lacked coercive means to arrest and prosecute its officials, and anyway could not afford to lose more personnel. As in the colonial period, police officers enjoyed a high level of tolerance for their misdeeds. So too did their proxies – proliferating paramilitary units that in many areas were little other than armed thugs, notorious for their cruelty. Only in 1957, under intense public pressure, did the government order inquiries into the litany of illegal

[45] *B. K. Halder* v. *S. Kr. Chelliah Pillay and Others*, 1952 BLR (HC) 340.
[46] *T. S. Mohamed and One* v. *Union of Burma*, 1953 BLR (HC) 107.
[47] *U Ba Din* v. *Union of Burma*, 1956 BLR (HC) 166.
[48] *Khaw Taw and One* v. *Union of Burma*, 1948 BLR (HC) 310; *Maung Aye Maung* v. *Union of Burma*, 1956 BLR (HC) 273.
[49] *Sobika Rahman* v. *Union of Burma*, 1952 BLR (HC) 385.
[50] *Ali Meah* v. *Union of Burma*, 1954 BLR (SC) 65.
[51] *U Ba Khin* v. *Union of Burma*, 1954 BLR (HC) 191.
[52] *Maung Nyi and One* v. *Union of Burma*, 1952 BLR (HC) 282.

arrests and confinement, arson, rape, kidnapping, assault, murder, shooting, and theft of livestock by paramilitary members.[53] The following year a case against some personnel finally came up in the High Court, which found they had committed 'wholesale dacoities [armed robberies] and cold-blooded murders of innocent persons under the cloak of the authority said to have been given to them'.[54] The sheer bloodthirstiness of this case attracted a national outcry.[55] Less egregious abuses remained commonplace.

In many parts of the country, civil administration was practically non-existent, and courts had ceased functioning, for lack of personnel, budget, and security. One senior judicial bureaucrat recalled in his memoirs that he got his first posting as a magistrate while still a student.[56] He objected because the posting was premature, and was told that due to the shortage of personnel he was needed immediately. He also objected because the posting was to his hometown, where he feared getting cases that he could not adjudicate impartially, to which he was told that because insurgents remained active in the area nobody else was willing to go there.

Aside from the practical difficulties associated with protecting people's rights, courts were equivocal and inconsistent in their stated guardianship role. The Supreme Court refused to issue a writ of habeas corpus for a person implicated in the plot to murder Aung San.[57] It dismissed a claim that the police had fabricated the custodial order against him because it had no reason not to believe them or the prosecutor. And although a communist party member organising strike actions had escaped the purview of the Public Order (Preservation) Act, a former policeman who had called for other officers to desert their posts could not. The Supreme Court said his

[53] Daw Myint Kyi and Naw Angeline, eds., *Burma's Politics 1958–1962*, vol. II, 4 vols. (Yangon: Universities Press, 1991) 78–79 (in Burmese).

[54] *Chit Hlaing, Htun Waing, Thein Aung, and 19* v. *Union of Burma*, 1958 BLR (HC) 582, 605. The quote is from Judge U San Maung, writing a concurring opinion in English to the judgement, in Burmese.

[55] The case and its context are discussed in Mary P. Callahan, 'The Sinking Schooner: Murder and the State in Independent Burma, 1948–58', *Gangsters, Democracy, and the State in Southeast Asia*, ed. Carl A. Trocki (New York: Cornell Southeast Asia Program, 1998) 17–38.

[56] U Hse Maung, *My Life as a Public Servant* (Yangon: n.p., 2000) 53 (in Burmese). The autobiography is discussed in Yoshihiro Nakanishi, *Strong Soldiers, Failed Revolution: The State and Military in Burma, 1962–88* (Singapore: National University of Singapore Press; Kyoto: Kyoto University Press, 2013) 147–49.

[57] *Maung Hla Gyaw* v. *Commissioner of Police, Rangoon and One*, 1948 BLR (SC) 764.

was 'undoubtedly a treasonable act'.[58] The court endorsed sections of the law that impinged on the rights of citizens, such as an exemption from the requirement for police officers to take detainees before magistrates after arrest.[59] A group of school students, whom it felt satisfied had secretly contacted insurgents, could also be held under the statute's terms.[60] And the chief justice in 1957 ruled that even where police officers had rearrested a person inside a courthouse immediately after a judge had acquitted him of charges under the Unlawful Associations Act, 1908 and the Emergency Provisions Act, 1950, the custody was lawful. The accused, he found, posed a risk to public order – despite the lack of evidence to convict him of a criminal offence.[61]

That judges continued to issue rulings of this sort speaks to the persistence of the law-and-order ideal in the politics of the period. Under the circumstances, its persistence is hardly surprising. Economic and social life was chaotic. The proponents of law and order had strong grounds to demand that courts facilitate a robust policing response. More noteworthy is the traction obtained by the idea of the rule of law, which was no longer confined to the Benthamite machinery, to the interstices of procedure. Out of the politics of the independence movement, a nascent body of substantive rights had emerged and occupied public space and, with it, much of the space in Burma's courtrooms. Policy makers debated the rule of law in relation to its opposite. The prime minister juxtaposed law and order as a police project in the classical sense – including material and infrastructure development under its auspices – with the rule of law as a legal and political project, one that was concentrated on democratic reform.[62] Granted, the two concepts were also conflated, as in debates where politicians gained mileage by linking demands for emergency powers to the rule of law.[63] And intellectuals grumbled that Burmese political

[58] *Daw Mya Tin* v. *Commissioner of Police, Rangoon and One*, 1949 BLR (SC) 82, 85.

[59] *U Ba Yi and 8* v. *Officer-in-Charge of Jail, Yamethin*, 1950 BLR (SC) 130.

[60] *Maung Kyaw Aye and 6* v. *Taunggoo District Commissioner and Another*, 1957 BLR (SC) 49 (in Burmese).

[61] *Maung Tin Aye* v. *District Commissioner, Pakokku and One*, 1957 BLR (SC) 17 (in Burmese).

[62] U Nu, 'Prime Minister's Address and Instructions at the Meeting on the Four-Year Plan Held on Saturday, 8 June 1957' (Rangoon: Sarpay Beikman, 1957) (in Burmese); *Premier Reports to the People* (Rangoon: Director of Information, Govt. of the Union of Burma, 1957); *We Must Defend Democracy* (Rangoon: n.p., 1959) 42–43, 51.

[63] Maung Maung, *Law and Custom in Burma and the Burmese Family* (The Hague: Martinus Nijhoff, 1963) 25.

elites paid only lip service to the rule-of-law ideal.[64] Nonetheless, the rule-of-law idea was not empty. It was not merely a trope for law and order. Nor was it any longer the colonisers' idea. It was now the rule of law of the independent, sovereign state: the rule of law of a politically active, alert, and rights-claiming citizenry. True, we ought not exaggerate how much the postcolonial rule of law contributed to political change in the decade after 1948, but we should not underestimate it either. The rule of law was a contested concept because it mattered politically, in new and distinctive ways.

'PEACE AND THE RULE OF LAW FIRST'

In 1958, the incumbent ruling party fell apart. Prime Minister U Nu led one faction against a rival group, shut down parliament, and announced fresh elections. Fault lines spread across government, as politicians scrambled to build support among officials and armed groups, including the army, police force, paramilitaries, and surrendered insurgents. Violence flared, with killings on both sides. High-ranking soldiers met Nu in September and told him that parts of the army would soon attempt to grab power. They could not control the situation, they said.[65] Cornered, Nu surrendered power to Ne Win for six months, on condition of a free and fair general election thereafter.[66] Ne Win granted him the condition, but later went to parliament for a constitutional amendment to extend his term in office by a year.[67]

Charney has described this time of caretaker government as a dress rehearsal for the army's takeover in 1962.[68] It was, but the caretaker government was also self-consciously dressed differently from the army-dominated junta that came later: Ne Win's first cabinet was comprised of civilian bureaucrats and the leaders of ethnic minorities, not soldiers. The military worked in the background, consolidating power and getting familiarised with institutional arrangements and personnel.

[64] See, for instance, Maung Maung Gyi, *Burmese Political Values: The Socio-Political Roots of Authoritarianism* (New York: Praeger, 1983) 172–76.

[65] Mary P. Callahan, 'The Origins of Military Rule in Burma', PhD diss., Cornell University, 1996, Ann Arbor: UMI, 1996, 476–77.

[66] U Nu, *U Nu: Saturday's Son*, trans. U Law Yone (New Haven and London: Yale University Press, 1975) 327.

[67] The translated text of his speech to parliament is appended to Govt. of the Union of Burma, *Is Trust Vindicated?* (Rangoon: Director of Information, 1960) 550–54.

[68] Charney, *A History of Modern Burma* 93.

The ousted government for a time played along with the programme. Despite his privately expressed misgivings, Nu publicly described Ne Win as a man who cherished democracy, and reassured people that the country would not go down a path to military administration.[69] Opposition parliamentarians warned otherwise and worried about the consequences of letting the army into government.[70] In 1959, one member openly expressed fears about creeping militarism.[71] Ne Win came to parliament to attack him personally, and he asked rhetorically,

> What is the period when there will be a danger of militarism? As the Honourable Member Bo Khin Maung Kale has said, it is the time when the military itself seizes power, when the military keeps the government on strings, when political organisations use the military to take power.[72]

Too few commentators took heed of this forecast. Instead, journalists tired of years of political turmoil fell over one another in their efforts to lavish praise on Ne Win and his cabinet for uprightness, efficiency, and honesty. They applauded his government's committees for cracking down on crime, and effused at the removal of corrupt bureaucrats and politicos. They cheered on the army for hunting down crooks, which ineffectual policemen and doddery judges could not or would not catch and punish. Marking Ne Win's first year in office, one influential magazine declared that the 'Caretaker Government will go down in the history of the country as the protector not only of parliamentary democracy but also of the Constitution'.[73] Academic writers characterised Ne Win as 'a supporter of constitutional government [whose] . . . record in restoring law and order and giving the country honest elections should come as no surprise'.[74] An American analyst insisted, 'Ne Win is a man dedicated to parliamentary democracy', and the army, 'an effective device for checking and correcting political excesses without

[69] Myat Thu, *Parliamentary Sights* 51.
[70] Govt. of the Union of Burma, *Record of the Chamber of Deputies* (1958), 2nd session, vol. VII, 1332–35.
[71] U Thein Pe Myint, in Govt. of the Union of Burma, *Record of the Chamber of Deputies* (1959), 2nd session, vol. VIII, 788.
[72] *Record of the Chamber of Deputies* (1959), 817.
[73] Editor, 'Parliamentary Democracy', *Guardian* Oct. 1959: 6.
[74] Richard Butwell and Fred von der Mehden, 'The 1960 Election in Burma', *Pacific Affairs* 33.2 (1960): 146.

abusing its power'.[75] The director of the Burma Law Institute lauded Ne Win for showing 'the way of realising our noble objectives, not only by employing legalistic methods, but also by appeal largely to our innate sense of justice and fair-play'.[76] Another author described the rule of law as the interim government's 'greatest administrative success'.[77]

The interim government employed the language of both law and order and the rule of law to describe and pursue its goals. Within a week of taking office, it convened an assembly on 'state law and order', *naingngandaw ngyeinwut-pibyaye*, and established a programme to restore law and order through a hierarchy of military-managed security councils.[78] Simultaneously it ran under the banner, 'Peace and the rule of law first'.[79] By the end of its tenure, it claimed to have restored to courts 'the dignity and prestige which they enjoyed in the pre-war years'.[80] This statement is true only inasmuch as the government pushed back the nascent body of substantive rights that had emerged under the rule-of-law banner after colonial rule, through its takeover of institutional spaces with the language and practices of law and order. It imposed what some parliamentarians had earlier sought but could never achieve because of the nature of democratic government: sweeping powers under a programme of law and order, premised on claims to be bringing back the rule of law.

Policemen and soldiers rounded up thousands of people accused of being underground political activists, opium dealers, gambling brokers, black market traders, loudmouth journalists, illegal Bengalis, pornography peddlers, and whomsoever the government targeted as a threat to law and order. Officials forced some of these people out to distant townships. They sent others to a remote island prison camp under military jurisdiction.[81] One person sent to the island recounted how the arresting officer pulled forth a sheaf of blank warrants, already duly

[75] John Seabury Thompson, Supplement, *The Governance of Modern Burma*, by John S. Furnivall (New York: Institute of Pacific Relations, 1960) 137, 52.

[76] U Hla Aung, 'A Republic and the Rule of Law', *Burma Law Institute Journal* 2.1 (1960): 2.

[77] U Tin, 'The Rule of Law', *Guardian*, June 1960: 31.

[78] Myint Thein, *Changing Myanmar Administrative Systems* (Yangon: Seitguchocho, 2006) 84–87 (in Burmese).

[79] Revolutionary Council, *Burma: Administrative and Social Affairs, 1962–63* (Rangoon: Office of the Director of Information, 1965) 34 (in Burmese).

[80] Govt. of the Union of Burma, *Is Trust Vindicated?* 62.

[81] Ko Ko Lay, *What Is Cocos Island?* (Rangoon: Khin Maung Yi, 1960) 39–43; Maung Chit Yi, *Section Five from Cocos Island* (Rangoon: U Saw Lwin, 1960) 132 (both in Burmese).

signed and authorised, and inserted his details as a substitute for someone the police could not locate.[82] Later the ousted prime minister also alleged widespread illegal arrest and forced confession of his party members.[83]

In the manner of its predecessors, the interim government passed a temporary law to exempt officials from the usual procedural requirements in criminal cases, enabling the police to use confessions taken in their custody as evidence.[84] Encouraged by the use of such methods to stamp out crime, at least one senior administrator suggested that it might be worth thinking about reintroducing colonial-style pacification techniques to stamp out insurgents.[85]

Another temporary measure amended the Emergency Provisions Act. This amendment may account for some of the enthusiasm expressed for the interim government in the media, since it permitted the arrest of anyone who by print or otherwise undermined the discipline or morale of the armed forces or civil service.[86] In a case giving alarming clues to what the country's near future would hold, three army officers in administrative posts testified against a newspaper editor who ran an article criticising a draft bill on labour disputes, which could 'create an impression in the minds of the public that the employment of military officers in civilian departments was undesirable'.[87] This case failed, but the next year another case succeeded that had been brought against a newspaper editor, publisher, and journalist for an article protesting the arrest of a member of parliament.[88]

In 1960, the Nu faction won the election in a landslide, and the interim government stepped down. For a time politicians and judges returned to old habits. Courts reversed orders issued during the previous year-and-a-half, such as those under the Public Order (Preservation)

[82] Chit Yi, *Section Five from Cocos Island* 29.

[83] U Nu, *Address Given by AFPFL (Clean) Chairman U Nu at the 69th May Day Celebration* ([Rangoon]: News and Information Dept., AFPFL [Clean], 1959) 10–20 (in Burmese). Nu's faction was the 'clean' AFPFL. The rival faction was 'stable'.

[84] Criminal Law (Temporary Provisions) Act, 21/58, sec. 2.

[85] Govt. of the Union of Burma, *Excerpts from the Record of the Convention of Security Councils Held at the Defence Services Convocation Hall, Rangoon on April 21, 22 and 23, 1959* (Rangoon: Govt. Printing, 1959) 53 (in Burmese).

[86] Emergency Provisions (Temporary Amendment) Act, 26/58, sec. 5A(1)(b).

[87] *U Yu Maung* v. *Union of Burma*, 1959 BLR (HC) 317, 321.

[88] *U Aung Sein and 2* v. *Union of Burma*, 1960 BLR (HC) 91 (in Burmese).

Act against drug traffickers.[89] But the situation was precarious. In a rare direct statement in court on the concept of the rule of law, Chief Justice Myint Thein noted that the prime minister had called for the Public Order (Preservation) Act not to be used indiscriminately, to which he added that,

> This statement is welcome to all and sundry who cherish liberty and the concept of the Rule of Law, which in passing we would point out, is very different from rule by law promulgated on the plea of necessity to curb the liberty of the individual.[90]

This comment has a keen poignancy, for two reasons. First, in it Myint Thein hints he recognised that the country's democratic future was in serious jeopardy. A willed threat had replaced the authentic threats that the country had faced at the moment of independence. Actual danger was no longer needed for the army to contemplate taking power. Burma's soldiers had learned, as their counterparts in Thailand and Indonesia were also learning, that the survival of the country need not be in peril for them to intervene. They could just as soon act on an imagined threat as on a genuine existential one.

Second, Myint Thein's reference to rule *by* law recalls the distinction made in Chapter 1 between analogous concepts on a rule-of-law continuum, which are different from opposing concepts to the rule of law. The judge's remark suggests that the prospects for a sliding decline in the rule of law troubled him. Perhaps he was reflecting on the experience of constitutional military government or alluding to events in Pakistan, where the superior courts had made the 'plea of necessity' doctrine in order to justify emergency powers.[91]

Another man, who would one day take Myint Thein's place, better apprehended that a second military takeover would not push the country to another point on a rule-of-law continuum, but to somewhere else entirely. Writing during 1959, amid debate about the

[89] As in *Yoe Bun Hwei* (a) *Kek Nek Hwei La* v. *Secretary, Ministry of Home Affairs, Government of the Union of Burma and Others*, 1960 BLR (SC) 175; *Lim Hkwei Ya* (a) *Yaun Ei* v. *Minister of Home Affairs*, 1960 BLR (SC) 189 (both in Burmese).

[90] *Lim Lyan Hwat*, 132.

[91] Tayyab Mahmud, 'Praetorianism and Common Law in Post-Colonial Settings: Judicial Responses to Constitutional Breakdowns in Pakistan', *Utah Law Review* 4 (1993): 1234–42. Paula R. Newberg, *Judging the State: Courts and Constitutional Politics in Pakistan* (Cambridge: Cambridge University Press, 1995) 57–59.

constitutional amendment that allowed Ne Win to stay on as prime minister for a further year, Dr. Maung Maung had suggested that anyone who feared the amendment would be the deathblow to parliamentary democracy in Burma was being melodramatic. And with perhaps unintended prescience he observed, 'If a man is strong and brazen enough to commit a successful *coup* he does not require the support of . . . any section of the Constitution. A *coup* does not obey any law.'[92]

Ne Win proved him right. On the morning of March 2, 1962, army jeeps sped around Rangoon, and soldiers occupied major buildings, pulling politicians, bureaucrats, and other officials out of their houses. In a pathetic scene to mark the end of an era, the elderly chief justice asked troops who came to his residence in the early hours to show a warrant. The men, perhaps uncertain about the new legal space into which their superiors had dispatched them, communicated with their commanding officer. The officer came in person and told the judge that as the armed forces had seized power, they were arresting him under the authority of a military administration.[93] No warrant was required. When the judge tried to telephone the police chief, 'he was politely told that all the telephone lines had been cut'.[94] The former chief justice remained in custody, with hundreds of others, for six years.[95]

The arrest and detention of Burma's chief justice on the morning of the coup is symbolic of the moment when soldiers realised they had no need to obey 'law'. If they wanted, the rule of law for which they had claimed to work as government caretakers could be held in abeyance, indefinitely.

The manner of the judge's arrest also signalled a new political moment, when sovereignty came to reside in 'determining definitively what constitutes public order and security'.[96] The soldiers who came to take him away paused when confronted with the demand for a warrant. They would not pause again. In coming years, when ordered to arrest they would arrest, and when ordered to shoot to hit, as Ne

[92] Maung Maung, 'Section 116 of the Constitution', *Guardian* Mar. 1959: 11, 12.
[93] U Mya Han and U Thein Hlaing, eds., *Burma's Politics 1958–1962*, vol. IV, 4 vols. (Yangon: Universities Press, 1991) 213 (in Burmese).
[94] Myint Zan, 'U Myint Thein MA, LLB, LLD', *Australian Law Journal* 69 (1995): 226.
[95] *WPD* 28 Feb. 1968: 1.
[96] Carl Schmitt, *Political Theology: Four Chapters on the Concept of Sovereignty*, trans. George Schwab (Chicago and London: University of Chicago Press, 1985) 9.

Win threatened in his parting speech in 1988, they would shoot to hit.[97] Controversy would not linger through political debate nor be resolved through courts. A new political order was imminent, one seized with a concern to maintain law and order, not to uphold the rule of law.

SOCIALIST LEGALITY

The day following the 1962 coup, Ne Win dissolved parliament. Over the coming days, his military junta set up new regional administrative bodies in lieu of state governments. It announced that all existing laws would remain in effect and all courts would also continue to exercise enacted authority until otherwise declared.[98] At the end of the month, Ne Win reconstituted the two superior courts into a new apex court, or Chief Court. The bench of the new court was comprised of a chief judge recruited from the Supreme Court, and four former High Court judges as members.[99] Subordinate courts were initially able to carry on with non-political cases as per existing procedures and practices.

A couple of months after the coup, the new government publicly began to set down its ideological bases for the future state. Senior army officers had some ideas about socialism, the political ideology with the most currency at the time, but these ideas did not motivate the takeover. One of the officers later admitted that ideology followed rather than preceded the coup:

> [When] our Revolutionary Council seized power we had no ideology, no political agenda, no design prepared. The General and us leaders – by which I do not mean even all the members of the Revolutionary Council – just wanted to make a socialist-based system. Because the

[97] 'I want the entire people of the country to know that when in future there are crowds making disturbances, if the army shoots it shoots to hit; there is no shooting skywards to frighten.' Ne Win, 'Speech of Burma Socialist Programme Party Chairman U Ne Win', Emergency Party Congress of the Burma Socialist Programme Party (1988) 5 (in Burmese).

[98] U Mya Han, Dr. Daw Khin Hla Han, U Kyaw Nyein, U Than Lwin, and U Sein Myint, eds., *A Period of Change to Myanmar's Political System (1962–1974)*, vol. I, 3 vols. (Yangon: Universities Press, 1993) 57 (in Burmese).

[99] For tabulated details of the heads of apex courts and their changing nomenclature after 1947, see Myint Zan, 'The "New" Supreme Court and Constitutional Tribunal: Marginal Improvement for Judicial Independence or More of the Same?' *Myanmar's Transition: Openings, Obstacles and Opportunities*, eds. Nick Cheesman, Monique Skidmore, and Trevor Wilson (Singapore: ISEAS, 2012) 256–57.

> General said he would go socialist, everyone became socialist. It was like, I have to upstage the other guy at doing whatever I think will please the General.[100]

Consistent with this account, Mary Callahan has written that the new government's move to turn Burma into a socialist country 'was simply a revival of the rhetoric of the anticolonial nationalist movement of the 1930s and 1940s'.[101] By taking up a socialist banner, the new government could situate itself in an historical narrative of anti-imperial and anticapitalist struggle while creating opportunities to target adversaries through new legal and administrative measures couched in ideological terms.

Ne Win cited deteriorating rule of law among the grounds for his takeover.[102] Later he added to the list senior judges' erroneous rulings, self-interested lawyers' scheming, and the use of courts for political ends.[103] He regaled in telling stories about corrupt, inept, and politicised judges and lawyers, asking rhetorically how 'murderers, robbers and people our armed forces had met in battle' could have walked from prison.[104] Mouthpieces of the army's new Burma Socialist Programme Party and its functionaries criticised the old courts and laws as incompatible with Burma's society.[105] Obsequious scholars pointed to the criticisms of former administrators in the colonial government that courts were out of touch with reality and indifferent to the interests and needs of the masses, too expensive and slow, and a cause of crime.[106]

Socialist legality took the place of the rule of law in public language. Some intellectuals and jurists sought to demarcate 'socialist rule of law'

[100] Thakin Aung Gyi, 'The 41-Page Treatise and Collected Writings for Humans' Rights' (Yangon: U Kyi Han, 1990) 14 (in Burmese).

[101] Callahan, *Making Enemies* 209. See also Nakanishi, *Strong Soldiers, Failed Revolution* 91.

[102] U Than Pe Myint, *Historical Records, 62–67* (Rangoon: Sapaung, 1968) 6; Central Organising Committee, *Party Seminar 1965: Speeches of the Chairman and Political Report of the General Secretary* ([Rangoon]: Burma Socialist Programme Party, 1966) 43 (both in Burmese).

[103] Central Organising Committee, *Party Seminar 1969: Speeches of the Chairman and Political Report of the General Secretary* ([Rangoon]: Burma Socialist Programme Party, 1970) 45–70 (in Burmese).

[104] Central Organising Committee, *Party Seminar 1969* 48.

[105] In this chapter, all references to 'the party' and 'one-party legislature' designate the Burma Socialist Programme Party and the legislature that it occupied from 1974 respectively.

[106] Aung Than Tun, 'Law and Lawyer in a Socialist Society', *Guardian* Jan. 1964: 16. U Aung Than Tun, *Legal General Knowledge for Everyone* (Rangoon: Pagan, 1970) 221–22 (in Burmese). Kyaw Yin, 'The Problem of Crime and the Criminal and Its Solution in Socialist Burma', *Journal of the Burma Research Society* 47.1 (1964): 206–07.

from its predecessor.[107] But the rule of law lost its lexical and political force after the coup. The idea of government subordinate to law was inimical to how Ne Win and his team came to power; how they held power; and, the alternative ideology they came to profess. No room existed for the rule-of-law idea, at least not so long as it retained a lexical distinction from law and order. A quarter-century later, when the concepts had collapsed into one another, a successor military government could use the term *taya-ubade-somoye* to signify *ngyeinwut-pibyaye* without anyone's raising an eyebrow. But in the 1960s, with the political lexicon and thought of the prior decade not yet passed away, it would have been inapt for the new government to use the language of the rule of law liberally, so to speak.

Another reason *taya-ubade-somoye* lost lexical force after the coup was that the rule-of-law idea still carried with it the taint of the 'bourgeois' law that socialist legality purported to oppose. Prefixing the rule of law with the adjective 'socialist' was unconvincing. 'The main point of socialist rule of law,' one law professor wrote, 'is that in a socialist country the entire working people obey law that the authorities enact or ratify in accordance with the will of the working people.'[108] 'Socialist rule of law' was supposed to represent 'a higher, more perfect level of the development of the rule of law' than its bourgeois counterpart.[109] In fact, it reduced the rule of law to the process of enacting and enforcing law. Even used in this sense, the expression was oxymoronic, because enacted law did not in any sense rule. The government was responsible not for the rule of law but for the 'preservation of domestic law and order and the working people's rules of law'.[110] The *rules* of law were just expressions of policy.[111] Aung Than Tun, a lawyer writing on the changes at the time observed,

> Laws are passed in a socialist society in order to ... guarantee social justice, and are tools for social engineering. Eminent socialists believed

107 Aung Than Tun, *Legal General Knowledge* 133. Maung Tin Ohn, 'Socialist Rule of Law,' *Myawadi* July 1966: 161–64 (in Burmese).

108 Maung Tin Ohn, A *Miscellany of Legal Knowledge*, 2nd edn. (Rangoon: Minthimun, 1985) 63 (in Burmese).

109 Adam Łopatka, President, Polish Supreme Court cited in Martin Krygier, 'Marxism and the Rule of Law: Reflections after the Collapse of Communism', *Law and Social Inquiry* 15.4 (1990): 638.

110 Instructions appended to Central Committee Headquarters, Burma Socialist Programme Party, Letter 3931/1/SaRa-3(Sa), 1 July 1967, par. 3.

111 The term used was *taya-ubade-siganmya*, where *sigan* signifies discipline, or imposed rules, rather than *somoye* for the rule of law.

> that 'law is only a tool of the State, which in turn is the instrument of the dominant group in society.' . . . Socialist legality and law consolidate and safeguard the social and State system and its economic foundation – the socialist system of economy and socialist property – the rights and freedom of the working people and ensure the development and strengthening of socialist relations in society and call upon the working people to faithfully abide by the laws of the State, without which the socialist system and economy could not be established.[112]

Note the elements in this passage that speak to the movement in thinking away from the rule-of-law ideal and towards a domestic order in which people would be quietened and industrious. First, law is an instrument to effect policy. It is not, to borrow from Douglas Hay, 'a power with its own claims'.[113] It is an instrument for other power – specifically, executive power. Second, because law is an instrument of policy, not independent from it, courts are obligated to help implement policy, not review or question it. Third, because law realises policy for the working people, everyone is morally obliged to abide by it. Anyone who fails to do so risks being accused not merely of breaking the law, but even worse, of intending to damage the emerging socialist society.

The new government's stated aim for the courts was to make government policy a success. From the mid-1960s, when the reconfiguring of courts began in earnest, judges were under express instructions to act on this aim.[114] The project differed decisively from the preceding era. Then, law ideally was independent from policy.[115] The course of justice and the course of public policy were separate. They might coincide, but one could not serve to justify the other. In 1964, by contrast, the new Chief Court rejected a lower court's attempt to interpret the meaning of the 1963 general amnesty order because 'an act of high policy of the Revolutionary Government . . . overrides all existing laws'.[116] Not only could public policy now be an adequate reason for deciding a case, it

112 Aung Than Tun, 'Revolution of Law and Justice', *Guardian* June 1965: 38.

113 Douglas Hay, 'Property, Authority and the Criminal Law', *Albion's Fatal Tree: Crime and Society in Eighteenth-Century England*, eds. Douglas Hay, Peter Linebaugh, John G. Rule, Edward P. Thompson, and Cal Winslow (Middlesex: Penguin, 1975) 33.

114 Courts General Letter 22/1965, 9 Nov. 1965.

115 *Union of Burma* v. *U Chit Swe*, 1950 BLR (HC) 278.

116 *U Ba Kyi* v. *Union of Burma*, 1964 BLR (CC) 306, 308. Citations in the remainder of the chapter refer to rulings issued from 1962 by the Chief Court (CC), from 1974 reconstituted as the Central Court of Justice (CCJ); and, from 1965, the Special Criminal Courts' Appeal Court (SCCAC). All rulings from the Central Court of Justice and SCCAC are in Burmese.

could be a superior one to any offered by law. As the object of trial was to implement policy, the legal view of a case was but one factor in its final outcome: political, economic, social, and administrative viewpoints all had equal relevance.[117]

Because law was an instrument of policy, courts had to have a cooperative relationship with other state agencies. In courtrooms, judges, prosecutors, police officers, and defence lawyers had to cooperate; not be adversarial. All parties to a case would have a shared interest in reaching the correct result, namely, one delivering the best policy outcome. Conflict was to be a thing of the past. Attorneys, defendants, complainants, and witnesses would direct their efforts towards the common end of achieving a socialist economy and society.[118] Judges would no longer adjudicate from the sidelines, but jump into the trial process and use more inquisitorial methods.[119] They would, as Mirjan Damaška has written of policy-implementing legal processes generally, 'join in procedural action whenever necessary to attain the right solution ... duty-bound to seek the correct result entirely apart from the argument that prevails in the forensic contest'.[120]

The subtext of the call for everyone to work cooperatively for the right outcome was that procedure no longer mattered in the way it had previously. Procedure as the spirit of law became anathema when everyone was supposed to be working to give meaning to policy. The whole idea of a procedural regime of law is that it increases the probability of achieving substantively accurate and fair outcomes.[121] Once government directed courts towards substantive outcomes independent from procedure, then doctrines and practices associated with procedure lost relevance. A new socialist doctrine emerged to take their place: the search for authentic truth, *ahmandaya*.[122]

117 *WPD* 16 July 1965: 1, 8.

118 *Ko Khin Maung* v. *Ma Ohn and 2*, 1966 BLR (CC) 572 (in Burmese); *Mister R. S. Bun and 2* v. *Union of Burma*, 1966 BLR (SCCAC) 65; *Maung Chit Htwe and 3* v. *Union of Burma*, 1967 BLR (CC) 69 (in Burmese).

119 U Aung Than Tun, *Four Eras of Burmese Law* (Rangoon: Kalaungpyan, 1968) 414–15; *Union of Burma (Daw Shu Khin)* v. *Maung Mya (a) Mya Oo and 2*, 1971 BLR (CC) 31 (both in Burmese).

120 Mirjan R. Damaška, *The Faces of Justice and State Authority: A Comparative Approach to the Legal Process* (New Haven and London: Yale University Press, 1986) 170.

121 Damaška, *The Faces of Justice and State Authority* 148.

122 *Ahman* is the colloquial term in Burmese for truth or correctness. Here *–daya* is the *taya* of *taya-ubade*, dharma, signifying rightness.

The doctrine's foremost exponent was Dr. Maung Maung, the scholar who wrote that coup makers obey no law. Before the coup, Maung Maung was a keen defender of the rule of law, praising it as 'the foundation of justice in Burma'.[123] After it he became Ne Win's personal jurist, hagiographer, and propagandist.[124] Maung Maung had no prior experience as a judge. Nonetheless, Ne Win appointed him to the apex court in 1962, a few months after the army had seized power. Less than three years later, Ne Win made him chief judge.

Prior to his appointment as chief judge, Maung Maung already had begun dabbling in ideologically oriented rulings. Now he cited a Soviet legal text to introduce the search for authentic truth to jurisprudence in Burma.[125] He explained that according to this text, in the Soviet Union 'courts, government advocates, lawyers for the plaintiffs and defence have to strive cooperatively to uncover the truth' – not the mere *probability* of guilt, but the definitive actual circumstances of each case as it occurred in reality – to which he added, 'this objective corresponds with the criminal jurisprudence of the socialist system'.[126]

Leaving aside the self-evident practical difficulties associated with striving to uncover the actual circumstances of a case as they occurred in reality, the mischief of the truth as foremost object of judicial inquiry is obvious. Emphasis on *the* truth entitles a court to exclude other claims to the collateral purposes of trial, especially any claims to protect individuals from abuses of official power.[127] As the interests of government and those of the public are supposedly in alignment, such claims are superfluous.[128] Because the interests of the politically dominant group and those of the citizenry are ostensibly aligned, the state cannot logically infringe on public interests without infringing on its own.

[123] Maung Maung, *Burma in the Family of Nations*, 2nd edn. (Amsterdam: Djambatan, 1957) 125.

[124] On Maung Maung's chameleon-like qualities, see Myint Zan, 'Comment on Fifty Years of Burmese Law: E Maung and Maung Maung by Andrew Huxley in Law Asia (1996–1997)', *In Camera* 1998: 39–40.

[125] The text cited was Aleksei Trusov, *An Introduction to the Theory of Evidence* (Moscow: Foreign Languages, n.d.).

[126] *Maung Aung Htay Myint* v. *Union of Burma*, 1965 BLR (CC) 397, 404, 05; see also *Daw Si Si* v. *Union of Burma*, 1964 BLR (CC) 876 (both in Burmese).

[127] Mirjan R. Damaška, 'Truth in Adjudication', *Hastings Law Journal* 49.2 (1998): 305.

[128] 'Safeguarding the interests of the socialist state, the court thereby safeguards also the interests of citizens for whom the might of the state is the primary condition essential for their individual well-being.' Andrei Y. Vyshinsky, *The Law of the Soviet State*, trans. Hugh W. Babb (Westport, CT: Greenwood, 1948) 497.

The monopoly claim on the truth was a novel idea for modern government in Burma. No prior government had made such a claim. Nor was the claim confined to the courtroom. It was anchored in a larger claim to hold the monopoly on truth and falsity in all public affairs. The Burma Socialist Programme Party waged campaigns for the authentic truth not only through the prosecution of criminals, but also through the spread of 'true' news, or true information, contrasted with rumours, which were anything the party designated untruthful.[129] The authentic truth of socialist legality, *ahmandaya*, corresponded with the authentic truth of socialist media. Both fell under a transcendent claim to political knowledge of the state that surpassed the incomplete or wrongheaded knowledge of its subjects.

Procedurally, the monopoly claim on truth as *ahmandaya* disbarred considerations of reasonableness and probability. Measures to protect people from arbitrary deprivations of liberty – the requirement for a *prima facie* case prior to going to trial, for the burden of proof placed on the prosecution, and for the accused to have the benefit of the doubt – lost significance. In 1970, a superior court bench summed up the new approach when it held that,

> Legal doctrine ought not be determined by words; what is needed is to stay focused on uncovering just the truth with which to decide. Legal maxims, precedents, etc., are not to be dogmatically applied. One case is different from another. It is necessary to uncover the facts well, from which to decide on right and wrong in keeping with commonsense.[130]

Benthamite technology purported to have scientific foundations of universal applicability and verifiability. The new ideology was also supposed to be scientific and universal. The utilitarians had been satisfied with consistency in making rules and issuing verdicts according to a formula whereby the greatest good would accrue to the greatest number. The new concern was with a joint effort to uncover incontrovertible reality via whatever means and materials available.

[129] As in Central Committee Headquarters, Burma Socialist Programme Party, Letter 3922/1/SaRa-3(Ga), 4 Dec. 1974; Central Organising Committee, 'On Rumours', *Domestic Affairs*, vol. I (Rangoon: Burma Socialist Programme Party, 1966) 141–59 (in Burmese).

[130] *Ma Khin Myint* (a) *Ma Khin Nyunt Kyi* v. *Union of Burma*, 1970 BLR (SCCAC) 1, 5. As discussed in Nick Cheesman, 'How an Authoritarian Regime Used Special Courts to Defeat Judicial Independence in Burma', *Law and Society Review* 45.4 (2011): 815–16.

Insistence on the truth as the legitimate object of inquiry exempted courts from adherence to any particular principles so long as they reached a satisfactory outcome from the facts of the individual case. The truth, although appearing to be a substitute for those doctrines it displaced, was no substitute at all. The doctrine of the search for authentic truth while appearing to establish a general rule enabled decision making that was freed from any specific principle for adjudication. As no two cases were alike, all law could be, as Schmitt insisted, situational law.[131]

On top of these considerations, working people were morally obliged to obey law that was enacted in their interests. Of course, all criminal law obligates obedience. But the nature of the command now differed. Law as an instrument for the delivery of policy in the interests of the working people contained a special moral obligation to comply with policy, not to criticise policy or do anything contrary to it. Departures from party ideology could constitute offences against the people *and* statutory crimes.[132] Ordinary criminal offenders – like black marketeers and thieves of public property – could be prosecuted for intending to damage the socialist economy and undermine public morality.[133] Offences against the body, to use the nomenclature of the Penal Code, could be reinterpreted as offences against the body politic of the working people – since everyone had joined together in a common enterprise for prosperity and well-being. Thus, a police officer who attempted to rape a young woman as she was going to work in the early hours committed an offence not only against her as a private individual but also as a worker who should be entitled to travel safely to and from her place of work for the benefit of the socialist economy.[134] Legal rights and punishments were now determined by the extent that subjects served the interests of the state economically, complied with socialist morality, and were productive in their respective stations.

131 Schmitt, *Political Theology* 13.

132 As in the Law Conferring Authorizations for the Building of a Socialist Economic System, 8/65. Amended by Law 1/68, repealed in 1989 via Law 9/89. The translated title of this law is my own, as are others in this chapter, since between 1962 and 1988 the government issued official versions of laws in Burmese.

133 As in *Maung Than Win* (a) *Tin Aung and 2* v. *Union of Burma*, 1968 BLR (SCCAC) 61; *Maung Chit Hlaing and 6* v. *Union of Burma*, 1966 BLR (SCCAC) 142.

134 *Maung Kyaw Tint* v. *Union of Burma*, 1966 BLR (SCCAC) 41.

PEOPLE'S COURTS, COLONIALISTS' CODES

In his comparative model of the legal process, Damaška has written that when a government develops an appetite to intervene more in social life through courts originally designed to regulate but not direct social and economic interaction 'a dissonance or a tension must now be expected to arise between the legal procedure conceived as a privately controlled contest and the novel objectives of the legal process'.[135] Outwardly, practices may appear to continue as before, but the role of the judge is no longer what it was. Increasingly, courts are forced to depart from procedure to accommodate demands that they comply with policy requirements.

Much of the tension can be resolved by ditching outdated institutions and designing or importing others to suit the state's new objectives, as a revolutionary government did in Vietnam. During the 1940s and 1950s, the communist party there set up special military and civilian courts to bring about dramatic political and economic change in a relatively short time. As the party consolidated and organised new institutions, from 1959 it prohibited the use of French colonial laws and practices, purged old terminology, and eventually imported an entirely new structure from the Soviet Union.[136] Sweeping changes meant that courts ultimately bore little resemblance to their pre-revolutionary counterparts.

Because the project for socialist legality in Burma was animated by the law-and-order ideal, not moved by a spirit of political change emerging from a popular national liberation struggle of the sort found in Vietnam, it was more incremental and less comprehensive than in revolutionary states. The army did not emerge politically as a surrogate for the party movement, as in revolutionary states; it created its own party institutions in parallel with existing bureaucratic and juridical arrangements, which it denigrated and on which it did not want to rely exclusively. Rather than being an instrument of mobilisation for a revolutionary party, the army created and mobilised the party. Beneath its self-styled revolutionary image, the post-1962 government was deeply conservative. It sought to maintain law and order through the continuous attention of authority, and with the continual maintenance of that authority.

[135] Damaška, *The Faces of Justice* 92.

[136] John Gillespie, 'Transplanting Commercial Law Reform: Developing a "Rule of Law" in Vietnam', PhD diss., Australian National University, 2005, 92–95.

The Benthamite pannomion had served essentially the same purpose; however, it also had built into it those procedural interstices that gave the rule-of-law ideal some traction. After 1962 the government retained the criminal codes for continued management and control of the public. Through principles of socialist legality, it could delimit the use of old procedures and doctrines. But judges, lawyers, prosecutors, and other personnel habituated to the old ways would not let go of them easily. So the government embarked on a programme of extensive but gradual change of personnel, aimed at ensuring hierarchical command and military control of courts without doing anything to modify significantly the contents of criminal law on which they ruled. It demolished the boundaries between participants in judicial activities, so that the old professional class could not retain its monopoly over the courtroom, but incongruously retained the technical language associated with legal specialisation, upon which the boundaries had hitherto depended.

Again, Maung Maung led the programme. Shortly after becoming chief judge he began doctrinally by making clear that the separation of powers was inimical to the interests of the working people and socialist society. The executive and judiciary would hereafter work together 'for the people's benefit and in defence of the country's security'.[137] The non-separation of powers was not just an administrative convenience; it was an ideological imperative, as it had been in the early years of colonial rule. Socialist legality opposed the doctrine of separate powers as a matter of principle.[138] Because courts now acted on the wishes of the working people, through policy reflected in law, or overriding law, the notion that courts needed to act as a check on other parts of the state ceased to be relevant.

Paradoxically, non-separation of powers did not mean judicial non-independence. U Kyaw Zeya, a prolific legal writer of orthodox views, explained some years later that even if courts operated under central administrative control, they could still decide independently on the cases before them:

> A socialist economic system is typically constructed by the drawing up of plans. In the domain of planning and implementation, the centre

[137] *U Aung Nyunt* v. *Union of Burma (Sub-Divisional Magistrate, Tachilek)*, 1965 BLR (CC) 578, 582 (in Burmese).

[138] Dr. Tin Aung Aye, 'Three Eras of Change to Burma's Legal System', *Law Magazine* 1978: 25 (in Burmese).

> supervises; however, in the judicial domain, the centre supervises less. . . . [Courts in] ward and village tracts, townships, divisions and states have the authority to adjudicate independently in accordance with their local situations.[139]

Absent from this paragraph is any reference to 'law', *taya-ubade*. When Kyaw Zeya describes courts as independent, he does not refer to the authority of courts to read and interpret law independent from the executive or legislature, but to their freedom to decide *on matters of policy* according to circumstances. The situational jurisprudence of Burma's socialist legality did not inhibit the freedom of judges to decide matters for themselves, so long as their decisions were consonant with the goals of the centre. Within the ambit of socialist policy, in principle judges would still be free to separate right from wrong on a case-by-case basis. Independent adjudication did not require institutional separateness.

The programme to demolish courts' institutional separateness at all levels took about a decade, from shortly after the coup until 1972. The government began by introducing new administrative bodies, which had quasi-judicial functions, to disperse and dilute the courts' authority. Some had special policing units attached, such as tribunals to hear cases of offenders under a statute passed for the building of a socialist economy.[140] The government also established special agencies to decide land and labour disputes, and settle other matters that had previously made their way into the courtroom.

In late 1962, Ne Win signed a statute establishing Special Criminal Courts to hear cases that authorities preferred not to have heard in ordinary courts.[141] The special courts were three-member panels, consisting of serving or retired soldiers, policemen, bureaucrats, judges, and prosecutors.[142] They had wide authority, which narrowed or removed accused persons' ordinary procedural rights. In 1965, a

[139] U Kyaw Zeya, *Lawyer among the People* (Rangoon: Zwe, 1981) 115 (in Burmese). Ward and village tracts, townships, and divisions and states constitute the hierarchy of administrative zones in Burma. Under the Constitution of the Republic of the Union of Myanmar, 2008, divisions became 'regions'.

[140] *WPD* 13 Jan. 1966: 1. Instructions on Procedures for the Taking of Action against Offenders Under the Law Conferring Authorizations for the Building of a Socialist Economic System 1965, Dept. of Home Affairs, Revolutionary Govt., 1965.

[141] Special Criminal Courts Law, 15/62. See further, Cheesman, 'How an Authoritarian Regime Used Special Courts' 808–09.

[142] Records regarding the Special Criminal Courts and Confirming Panels, File 16–20/66, Chief Court, 1966.

final appellate bench comprised of Maung Maung and two army officers from the ruling council began receiving appeals from the tribunals. Because Maung Maung was both a member of the appellate bench and chief judge of the ordinary judiciary, in the new court he used his position to pass rulings unfettered by ordinary legal process or doctrine; he would then cite them in the Chief Court, and issue directives to feed instructions based on these rulings back to the lower judiciary.

The colonial government and early postcolonial governments established special courts and tribunals to exempt their proceedings from the constraints that utilitarian statute imposed, not to alter the work of the mainstream judiciary directly. The superior courts yielded to special tribunals on the pretext that they did not interfere with the work of the apex court, which formally retained its powers as the court of final appeal over all courts in the country, including those set up under special statutes.[143] By contrast, the Special Criminal Courts were not under the authority of the regular judiciary at all. The Chief Court had no jurisdiction over them.[144] Furthermore, with time the appellate bench of the special courts exceeded the Chief Court's authority and became the de facto apex court.[145]

In 1972, the government began to implement a plan to demolish what remained of the colonial-era courts – and the personnel habituated in their ways – and to establish new courts completely integrated with the executive. Administrative boards across the country moved to set up new committees to administer and adjudicate on matters of law in courts at all levels. The committees were comprised of government officials, and those that were higher up also included army officers, bureaucrats, and representatives from the workers' and peasants' councils.[146] Panels took the places of individual judges. Their members included people's representatives with no legal training. Faithful adherence to policy, not knowledge of law, was the key criterion for anyone hoping to sit on the new panels.[147] Court staff, including ousted judges,

143 *Chittambaram* v. *King-Emperor*, (1947) RLR 66 PC; *Union of Burma* v. *U Khin Maung Lat and One*, 1950 BLR (HC) 376; *Khin Maung Myint* v. *Union of Burma*, 1953 BLR (SC) 24.

144 *Daw Aye Tin* v. *Meikhtila District Area People's Court Appeal Court and Another*, 1971 BLR (CC) 17 (in Burmese).

145 *Maung Chit* v. *Union of Burma*, 1972 BLR (CC) 20 (in Burmese). Cheesman, 'How an Authoritarian Regime Used Special Courts' 816–18.

146 Chief Court, *Criminal Justice* (Rangoon: Chief Court, 1973) 11–14 (in Burmese).

147 Burma Socialist Programme Party, *Articles on the Judiciary in the Party Affairs Journal* ([Rangoon:] Burma Socialist Programme Party, 1980) 103 (in Burmese).

offered the panels advice. Although bound to receive the advice, the lay judges did not have to follow it.

In 1974, the government established a one-party parliament and with it a Central Court of Justice consisting of party apparatchiks and military men, which took over from the Chief Court. Together, the judges of the Central Court constituted the Council of People's Justices, through which they reported to the legislature. This council was the supreme judicial body. The party appointed and removed its personnel along with committees of judges at other levels.[148] Chairmen of the peak council and many of its members were former or serving army officers, as were those at the next tier down. The justice ministry ceased to exist. After a while, so too did the Special Criminal Courts, and their appellate bench.[149] People's councils at all levels of the state, consisting of party members, formally took control of all juridical and administrative responsibilities, including matters concerned with 'local security, defence, maintenance of rule of law and order'.[150] The topmost priority was to defend the socialist system, not to uphold justice or even to enforce law.[151]

The collapse of all branches of the state into these omnicompetent councils created a range of predictable difficulties. At the highest levels, officials made examples of accused persons in celebrity show trials in which defendants were formally allowed procedural rights that no longer mattered to the outcome, since the authentic truth, which the state determined, would inevitably prevail.[152] Administrators at lower levels learned how to manipulate court cases so that their personal interests coincided with matters of pressing importance to the state, and the cases could be decided in their favour.

Continued heavy reliance on the colonial-era criminal codes caused a new type of tension between law and order as a political ideal, on one

148 People's Council Law, 8/74, sec. 4, 5, 38, 63–9, 85, 110–16, 132, 157–63; corresponding sections are contained in the Council of People's Justices Law, 13/74.

149 Special Criminal Courts Law Repealing Law, 8/74. Although the repealing law passed on February 28, 1974, the courts continued operating at least until late in the year. Central Court of Justice, File 23–3/74, Jan.–Oct. 1974.

150 Art. 132(c), Const. of the Socialist Republic of the Union of Burma, 1974 (English version).

151 Art. 101(a), Const., 1974.

152 See for instance reports of the trial of army officers who allegedly plotted to kill Ne Win in *WPD* 11 Sept. 1976: 1, 4; 20 Oct. 1976: 1, 4. 1 Dec. 1976: 1, 4; 2 Dec. 1976: 1, 4.

hand, and the stated aspirations of socialist legality, on the other. The (Indian) Penal Code remained the backbone of the criminal law. In addition, courts kept hearing cases under repressive statutes from earlier periods, such as the Unlawful Associations Act and Emergency Provisions Act.[153] And although procedure lost its deeper significance, since the Criminal Procedure Code and Evidence Act continued to serve as the bases for procedure in criminal cases, questions about admissibility and inadmissibility of evidence, trial process, framing of charges, and use of confession under these statutes kept coming up before the courts, as they had since the colonial period. Yet, the Criminal Procedure Code confounded lay judges at the lowest levels.[154] Recognising their difficulties, Maung Maung advised them to think contextually. 'If a case is examined and the facts are brought out well, it is rather like the right decision becomes obvious,' he wrote in a legal primer, adding,

> If the purpose of adjudication is understood, judging is easy. There is no need to get worn out from looking at big thick law books, big and small sections, no need to get confused from reading. Gently put down the books; study the reason that the parties came to court and the cause of their dispute.[155]

Encouraged in this way, lay judges passed situation-specific and policy-based verdicts, disregarding much of what legal advisers suggested.[156] Rulings became more vague, containing generic assertions that a court was satisfied with the guilt of the accused. Former judges serving as advisors struggled to craft legally coherent written judgements out of verdicts based upon purported common sense, or for reasons of bribery, political influence, or other factors.

Yet, colonial-era statutes still chafed lay judges who had been led to believe that they did not need to worry about them greatly. Maung Maung's reassurances that judging is easy encountered resistance every time the police lodged a case under the Penal Code, or defence

[153] As in *Union of Burma* v. *Maung Htun Sein*, 1966 BLR (CC) 1425 (in Burmese); *Saw Bogyu* v. *Union of Burma*, 1967 BLR (SCCAC) 45; *U Tun Aung Tha* v. *Union of Burma*, 1968 BLR (CC) 10; *Maung Tin Maung and 7* v. *Union of Burma*, 1969 BLR (CC) 222 (in Burmese); *U Win Han* v. *Socialist Republic of the Union of Burma*, 1975 BLR (CCJ) 101.

[154] Burma Socialist Programme Party, *Articles on the Judiciary* 124.

[155] Dr. Maung Maung, *Legal General Knowledge*, 3rd edn. (Yangon: Sitthidaw, 2004) 34, 89 (in Burmese).

[156] Kyaw Zeya, *Lawyer among the People* 120–21.

counsel approached the bench with a copy of the Criminal Procedure Code. The persistence of technical language designed to discount, as Pierre Bourdieu has put it, those very 'counsels of common sense' to which lay judges were now encouraged to refer caused confusion and consternation.[157] Party mouthpieces had repeatedly told lay judges that their non-technical, naïve understanding of the facts would suffice, pointing to the day that was supposed to come when people's courts would rule exclusively on people's laws, as in Vietnam. That day never arrived. The colonial statutes remained in perpetuity.

In the early years after the coup, officials and experts explained away the misalignment between new courts and old statute as a result of limited time and resources to make all the necessary changes. Maung Maung Kyi, a registrar and later director of the judicial bureaucracy at the Chief Court, explained,

> Total obliteration of the existing legal system is impossible of achievement at this critical moment of the transition period. It will linger for some time. . . . While awaiting the introduction of new laws, the old laws have perforce to be made use of in cases where they help to protect the gains already obtained by the people and maintain law and order [*ngyeinwut-pibyaye*] against all sorts of anti-social elements.[158]

As time went on, such explanations became less convincing. Some lay judges raised questions as to why they had to enforce colonial-era statutes. The control syndrome inherent in the ideal of law and order showed clearly when such questions came to higher-ups. For superior courts to put policy ahead of law was one thing; for the lower courts to do so, or at least to do so without having received instructions from above, was a different matter. Senior figures resisted the idea of policy as law when the idea came from below. Over time, as the veneer of socialism wore off and the government's underlying conservatism showed through clearly, top officials responded with a renewed insistence on adherence to statute. They even went so far as to reprint and distribute the labyrinthine thirteen-volume Burma Code, consisting of

[157] Pierre Bourdieu, 'The Force of Law: Toward a Sociology of the Juridical Field', *Hastings Law Journal* 38 (1987): 828.

[158] Maung Maung Kyi, A *New Approach to Law and Life in Burma* (Rangoon: n.p., 1967) 101. In Burmese translation, Maung Maung Kyi, *Burmese Law and Life* (Rangoon: Sarpay Beikman, 1975) 131.

the Benthamite pannomion plus 400 other statutes dated to the end of 1954.[159] Maung Maung tried to mollify critics and defend the government's backward-looking views on legal reform:

> Some are inclined to say that the established laws are a legacy of the old colonial-era system, therefore, there is no need to be following those laws and that they can decide as they like. . . . It is true that old laws remain. It is true that some of the old laws' ideas are out of date, also that the writing is convoluted. However, the essential laws have been amended as much as possible. In the Revolutionary Council era, new ideas and precedents were written, a judicial system established, even a new constitution that the people wrote together already enacted. Work must still be done to repeal needless old laws, consider them from a Burmese viewpoint, and write them in Burmese prose. However, that work will have to be coordinated. It has to be discussed and enacted in the legislature. Until these things can be consulted and decided upon in unison, established law must be followed.[160]

Despite the efforts of party bosses to appear as if they were reluctantly applying antiquated law until its final overhaul, the record suggests otherwise. In almost twelve years in power, the Revolutionary Council made only minor adjustments to the Penal Code and Criminal Procedure Code, one time each. The one-party legislature in fourteen years made no changes to either of these statutes, or to other colonial-era criminal law of note.[161] Internal directives to courts likewise reveal a tendency to cling to colonial-era statutes and practice that suited official purposes, such as in the use of exemplary punishment for criminals threatening the political and economic order.[162] And party organs could always blame the new courts' inefficiencies on the colonial codes and the Benthamite technology so long as the codes remained part of how things were done.

At bottom, the tension between colonial codes and socialist legality was not legal but political. One-party government obliged everyone to participate cooperatively so as to serve the state and its interests. It purported to invite opinions from subordinates, but did not have to

[159] *WPD* 27 Mar. 1977: 4. [160] Maung Maung, *Legal General Knowledge* 75–76.

[161] Revolutionary Council, *Concise History of the Revolutionary Council's Activity* (Rangoon: Printing and Publishing, 1974) 615 (in Burmese).

[162] As in Courts General Letter 2/66; 4 July 1966. Council of People's Justices, Instruction 9, 12 July 1975; Council of State, Instruction 5/77, 12 Aug. 1977.

consider them, let alone accommodate them. If the party demanded that courts enforce colonial law, they had to do it. After all, the party had only goodwill for the working people. It would be impertinent to think otherwise – and illegal to say so. Where people talked back to power, for their own good they had to be shouted down. The monopoly on the truth necessitated it.

CONCLUSION

In the first years after Burma's independence, the struggle intensified between forces concerned to maintain law and order and those keen to amplify the rule of law. The government, straining to get minimum effective control over populace, territory, and material resources, acknowledged aspirations for rights while coming to terms with the realities of civil war and economic collapse. It authorised use of draconian law, but did not overtly interfere when courts opposed its interests, and when judges expressed alarm at the misuse of law. The politics of this period fell far short of the rule-of-law ideal, but they also kept it alive.

After the 1962 coup, the rule of law lost salience in public narratives and in state practices. The new government rejected the premises associated with the nascent regime of substantive rights, and also undermined the extant procedural regime through measures aimed at promoting its notion of socialist legality, which emphasised law as a vehicle for policy and subordination of law to policy. It repudiated the rule of law, reshaping the relationship between state and subject according to principles of domination and subordination corresponding with the ideal of law and order, *ngyeinwut-pibyaye*.

The lost significance of procedure meant that the minimal protections against coercive power inherent to the Benthamite technology also lacked the efficacy that they had previously had. Together these developments had the effect of eliminating the bases upon which even a minimal formally conceived rule of law might be established or maintained. Coercive power remained, but the structural defences of rights fell away. The government passed new statutes to institute a socialist economy but did not rewrite or remove the pannomion of codes at the foundation of the pre-existing arrangements. It replaced personnel and institutions but insisted that new courts conform to the strictures of colonial-era statute.

One-party government continued until 1988, when, unable to sustain the monopoly on the truth, it crumbled under the weight of massive nationwide protests. After a few brief moments of optimism that Burma would return to civilian rule, a cabal of soldiers again pushed its way to the forefront of the country's political life. And just as the rule of law was at its nadir, *taya-ubade-somoye* returned to the foreground, no longer as a distinctive concept, but as a trope for law and order.

4

SUBSUMING LAW TO ORDER

When Burma's one-party government collapsed in 1988, the party-based councils at all levels, which horizontally managed courts and other institutions, went with it.[1] A new military junta abolished all existing organs of state power and established new councils with soldiers as chairmen.[2] It named itself, with a nod to its 1958 predecessor, as a council to restore law and order.[3] It established subordinate bodies with the same nomenclature.[4]

1 Many authors have written narratives and analyses of the events in 1988. Some short accounts include Michael W. Charney, *A History of Modern Burma* (Cambridge: Cambridge University Press, 2009) 148–62; Christina Fink, *Living Silence: Burma under Military Rule* (London and New York: Zed, 2001) 50–63; Donald M. Seekins, *State and Society in Modern Rangoon* (London and New York: Routledge, 2011) ch. 7. For more details, see Bertil Lintner, *Outrage: Burma's Struggle for Democracy* (London and Bangkok: White Lotus, 1990); Maung Khine Khant, *Record of the 8888 Uprising* (Yangon: Kyi Hla Maung, 2012) (in Burmese).

2 SLORC Announcement 2/88, 18 Sept. 1988; 5/88, 20 Sept. 1988. All citations of official announcements and orders in this chapter and the remaining chapters refer to Burmese-language texts, unless otherwise stated.

3 The State Law and Order Restoration Council, or *Naingngandaw Ngyeinwut-pibya-hmu Tizauk-ye Apwè*, ran from September 18, 1988 to November 15, 1997, when it reconstituted itself as the State Peace and Development Council, which ran until March 30, 2011. For the sake of simplicity, in this chapter I refer to these two councils without differentiation. For some comments on the limited reconstitution of government between one and the next, see Charney, *A History of Modern Burma* 179–80.

4 Councils at each level under the national level were, in descending order, division/state councils, district councils, township councils, and ward/village tract councils. With the restoration of semi-elected legislative government in 2011, administration continued under essentially the same structure; however, divisions became 'regions', and each region and state got its own legislature. At other levels the councils gave way to officials working under the Department of General Administration, Ministry of Home Affairs.

In the days and weeks before the takeover, senior military officers hinted at their plans, promising concerned citizens that they would help them to maintain law and order, security, and the rule of law.[5] The armed forces commander, General Saw Maung, intimated that the army might act to prevent anarchy and uphold the rule of law, which was 'undeniably' the major public concern.[6] In its inaugural announcement, his military council stated that due to deteriorating conditions the rule of law was the first of its four major tasks.[7] It terminated the people's courts, re-established a Supreme Court, and placed a new chief justice directly under its authority.[8] Eleven days after the takeover, the appointee chief justice, former Central Court registrar U Aung Toe, issued orders making judicial bureaucrats and legal advisors judges, in lieu of the panels of lay judges.[9] To give time for courts to be reconstituted and, it said, so as not to inconvenience litigants, the junta declared all courts closed until the end of March 1989, retrospective to 1 June 1988.[10]

The people's courts were officially a thing of the past. Burma, or rather, Myanmar, had the beginning of a new professional judiciary, one comprising civil servants, arrayed hierarchically under a military council.[11]

The junta indicated that it would stay in power until 1990, when it would conduct a general multiparty election and step down. To prepare for the election it declared martial law and convened military tribunals 'in order to carry out more effectively tasks for security, the rule of law [*taya-ubade-somoye*], and regional peace and tranquillity'.[12] In a series of orders, it withdrew martial law from various parts of the country

[5] *Myanma Alin* 16 Aug. 1988, in Zawana (Agriculture), ed., *Historical Newspaper Accounts from the Democracy Uprising* (Yangon: Zinyadanazaw, 2013) 22–23 (in Burmese).

[6] *Botataung* 13 Sept. 1988, in Win Zaw Latt, ed., *The 8888 Uprising as Told by the Newspapers*, 2nd edn. (Yangon: Toe Myit, 2013) 297 (in Burmese).

[7] SLORC Announcement 1/88. The other three tasks were to provide security for travel and communications; to aid in providing for people's basic needs; and, thereafter to hold multiparty elections.

[8] Judiciary Law, 2/88. Township Law and Order Restoration Councils' Responsibilities and Work Regimen, Office of the State Law and Order Restoration Council, 18 Jan. 1989, appendix B.

[9] SC Notification 2/88, 29 Sept. 1988. The 1988 Judiciary Law established three levels of courts at the apex, division/state, and township levels. District level courts operated under the division/state courts, not as a separate tier. Later, section 12 of the Judiciary Law, 5/2000 established district level courts as a separate tier.

[10] Special Limitations Law, 9/88.

[11] The official change in nomenclature from Burma to Myanmar occurred in mid-1989, as discussed in Gustaaf Houtman, *Mental Culture in Burmese Crisis Politics: Aung San Suu Kyi and the National League for Democracy* (Tokyo: Tokyo University of Foreign Studies, 1999) 44–46.

[12] SLORC Martial Law Order 1/89, 17 July 1989. See also Martial Law Order 2/89, 18 July 1989.

because the rule of law had sufficiently 'improved'.[13] The National League for Democracy overwhelmingly won the May 1990 election, but the military declined to recognise the results as a mandate to govern.[14] Myanmar entered a period of new and protracted repressive rule, culminating in a return to semicivilian legislative government in 2011, over twenty-two years later.

This chapter concentrates on the politics of Myanmar's courts in this period.[15] Unlike the two preceding chapters, it is not chronological. Instead, it tracks political ideas that animate courts and attendant institutions in Myanmar. Subsequent chapters use the same approach.

The chapter sets the scene with the new military government discarding formal ideology. It then turns to a concept I designate 'sovereign *cetana*', a principle of law and order used in Myanmar to qualify, delimit, and withdraw citizens' rights in response to policy imperatives. The exercise of sovereign *cetana* allows for the continued deployment of a language of rights lexically consistent but semantically inconsistent with the rule of law. Rights in this setting have meaning only insofar as they are expedient for the sovereign power. Sovereign *cetana* is a specific instance of law and order having distinctive contents opposed to the rule of law, even as the two terms are conflated.

After explaining how sovereign *cetana* serves as a principle for the politics of law and order in Myanmar, I bring the concept to the problem of the public enemy. In a politically repressive setting, the case against the public enemy is archetypal, because the public enemy is higher in the hierarchy of threats to law and order than other persons. The telos of quietude obliges that the public enemy be immobilised. Even though the number of cases against public enemies may be

[13] SLORC Martial Law Order 3/89, 3 Nov. 1989; and Martial Law Orders 1–12/90, 2 Jan., 11, 15 Mar., 11, 17, 18 Apr., 15, 18, 19, 22, 24, 26 May 1990.

[14] SLORC Announcement 1/90, 27 July 1990. See Charney, *A History of Modern Burma* 173; Derek Tonkin, 'The 1990 Elections in Myanmar: Broken Promises or a Failure of Communication?' *Contemporary Southeast Asia* 29.1 (2007): 33–54.

[15] For commentary on wider political affairs in this period see Charney, *A History of Modern Burma* chs. 8, 9; Nick Cheesman, Nicholas Farrelly, and Trevor Wilson, eds., *Debating Democratization in Myanmar* (Singapore: ISEAS, 2014); Nick Cheesman, Monique Skidmore, and Trevor Wilson, eds., *Ruling Myanmar: From Cyclone Nargis to National Elections* (Singapore: ISEAS, 2010); Monique Skidmore and Trevor Wilson, eds., *Dictatorship, Disorder and Decline in Myanmar* (Canberra: ANU E-Press, 2008); David I. Steinberg, *Burma/Myanmar: What Everyone Needs to Know* (New York: Oxford University Press, 2010). For details of more English-language materials see Andrew Selth, *Burma (Myanmar) since the 1988 Uprising: A Select Bibliography* (Brisbane: Griffith Asia Institute, 2012).

relatively small, they, above all other types of cases, test the mettle of institutions for the maintenance of law and order.

The pursuit of the public enemy through these institutions is not haphazard. It is integrated into their routine workings through paperwork and record keeping, through the examination and cross-examination of lawyers, even if procedures and outcomes are incongruous. Procedure matters in cases against public enemies, precisely because for courts responding to the imperatives of law and order, formal adherence to procedure is all that exists with which to demonstrate aptitude and commitment to ostensibly judicial tasks, to demonstrate that orderliness has been maintained – a theme to which this book returns in each of the remaining chapters.

From this chapter onwards, the book draws primarily on research conducted from 2008 to 2013, which I briefly described in the introduction. The majority of cases come from the years of direct military rule prior to 2011.[16] By 2012, Myanmar had entered a new and distinctive political phase. The military had stepped a little way back from its full frontal role in government – although serving and former army officers took most key positions in the nominally civilian administration formed in 2011.[17] The democracy icon Aung San Suu Kyi had won a seat in the new legislature and was travelling the globe to meet plentiful international supporters and promote her cause. The president had released most political prisoners. Exiled media and political groups had set up offices back in the country. Foreign dignitaries had begun flocking to the new capital, Naypyidaw.[18] A menagerie of international organisations, think tanks, universities, and freelancers had arrived to offer assistance and devise projects for the rule of law.[19] The government announced it would establish rule-of-law centres around the country under a United Nations training project for judges, prosecutors, lawyers, police officers, and bureaucrats.[20]

[16] See appendix for further details.

[17] As discussed in Maung Aung Myoe, 'The Soldier and the State: The Tatmadaw and Political Liberalization in Myanmar since 2011', *South East Asia Research* 22.2 (2014): 233–49.

[18] On the establishment of the new capital, see Dulyapak Preecharushh, *Naypyidaw: The New Capital of Burma* (Bangkok: White Lotus, 2009).

[19] According to one source 'more than 30 separate Myanmar-related rule of law projects' were operative as of October 2013. Robert San Pe, 'Rebuilding Rule of Law in Myanmar: Professional Training and Education for Existing Legal Practitioners' (Parliamentary Committee on Rule of Law [*sic*], 2013) 2.

[20] *Voice Daily* 3 Jan. 2014: 1–2.

In a short time, a lot changed in Myanmar. But experience shows that ideas and practices – once habituated and institutionalised through courts, prosecutorial agencies, and police forces – can prove highly resilient. Around Asia, people still feel the effects of repressive government years after the end of dictatorship. Filipino policemen still torture.[21] Indonesian judges still take bribes.[22] Tectonic shifts in political power can be dramatic and exciting, but shifts in institutional behaviour are protracted and wearisome. For this reason, I treat the following narratives as stories about a continuum of practices running across successive periods, situated in the past, but imbricated in the present.

DOMINATION WITHOUT IDEOLOGY

A new type of political domination came to Myanmar with the collapse of one-party government in 1988. In each prior period discussed in this book, the government of the day had expressed some ideological criteria against which its successes and failures could be measured: utilitarian, liberal, or socialist. The new junta abandoned ideology. It declined to adhere to any coherent set of principles. It conflated the rule of law with the 'law and order' of its title and pronounced this to be its objective. It made no greater attempt at ideological justification. As such, the claim to be upholding the rule of law *as* law and order is the closest thing to a political aspiration against which we can assess two decades of military rule.

In one speech after another, members of the junta iterated their reasons for taking power. Talking to judges in 1994, Lieutenant General Khin Nyunt, then Secretary-One of the ruling council and its intelligence chief, offered a typical account:

> We all know that collapsed rule of law [*taya-ubade-somoye*] and overriding anarchy in the nation was one of the primary reasons that the State Law and Order Restoration Council took over the responsibilities of state. Consequently, the State Law and Order Restoration Council gave special consideration to responsibility for the rule of

[21] Danilo Reyes, 'Torture in Indonesia and the Philippines: A *Jus Cogens* Right with or without Remedy?' LLM diss., University of Hong Kong, 2013.

[22] Simon Butt and Tim Lindsey, 'Judicial Mafia: The Courts and State Illegality in Indonesia', *The State and Illegality in Indonesia*, eds. Edward Aspinall and Gerry van Klinken (Leiden: KITLV Press, 2011) 198.

> law [*taya-ubade-somoye*] and regional peace and tranquility as first among its designated four major tasks.[23]

The new government did not propose to transform society, either through law or policy. Its vision was narrow, its narrative limited. Anarchy prevailed. Law-and-order council took over, and restored the rule of law. In this narrative, the rule of law corresponds with the absence of anarchy – the condition of being kingless, *minmè-zayaik*. The rule of law is just the opposite of anarchy, Hobbes's 'confusion of a disunited multitude'.[24] Its opposition is not found between norms and commands, between one political ideal and another, but merely between the existence of a commander and the absence of one. In this conception, the rule of law is nothing other than the existence of a sovereign, the existence of a sovereign's specific order. To restore law and order through restoration of sovereignty is to restore the rule of law.

The mischief in this formulation lies in its taking certain conditions of political order necessary for both the rule of law and for law and order – the existence of a state, the corresponding absence of anarchy – and imputing that the conditions sufficient to realise one are the same as those to realise the other. The formulation lumps all types of rule making together: as long as somebody is making rules, and people follow them, then the rule of law exists. While referring to norms that transcend the state's specific order, the rule of law takes on the opposite meaning: that the state's specific order transcends any norms of law. Carl Schmitt once insisted, 'The existence of the state is undoubted proof of its superiority over the validity of the legal norm.'[25] Khin Nyunt would have had every reason to agree.

Although the subsuming of law to order throughout official texts of the 1990s and 2000s had a number of characteristics, I will confine my remarks to three. First, it emptied legal principles of significance. Doctrines ceased to attach to any coherent set of ideas that could give them meaning. Second, it levelled out juridical instruments. Injunctions all had approximately the same coercive value. Third, it elevated administrative principles over legal ones.

[23] Khin Nyunt, 'Address at the Work Coordination Meeting of State, Divisional and District Judges and Law Officers', *Supreme Court Rulings, 1994* (Yangon: Myawadi, 1996) n. pag. (in Burmese).

[24] Thomas Hobbes, *Leviathan*, ed. Crawford B. Macpherson (Middlesex: Penguin, 1968) 229.

[25] Carl Schmitt, *Political Theology: Four Chapters on the Concept of Sovereignty*, trans. George Schwab (Chicago and London: University of Chicago Press, 1985) 12.

As discussed in the last chapter, legal doctrine had already taken a beating in the preceding decades. Many criminal legal principles had fallen afoul of the doctrine of the truth and other nominally socialist innovations that courts adopted half-heartedly. But the ideas underpinning the programme had a degree of internal coherence, even if in practice the contradictions between colonial-era statute and the politics of the socialist era caused confusion and disgruntlement.

After 1988, legal principles from prior periods ceased to attach to any particular ideology. This loss of significance did not mean that they fell into disuse. On the contrary, legal principles were as much a part of official language as ever. However, they were no longer anchored to a set of ideas. They floated around, weightless, bumping into one another at random, such as in Khin Nyunt's speech from 1994:

> The laws, procedures and so on are very useful instruments with which to reveal the truth. But in the hands of bad people, legal procedures can be exploited so that which shouldn't happen happens. Once a court's main duty – the revealing of truth – grows dim, the law is separated from one of its arms and playing favourites, playing foul, cheating and lying come to the fore . . . judges in order to have the capability to deliberate and reveal the truth, to enlarge their wisdom and vision, must be honest and also endowed with unblemished morals. . . . Bravely and steadily endeavour without being demoralised to reveal the truth so offenders will fear and respect the law, such that people will trust and rely upon the judiciary.[26]

In 2011, the new chief justice, a former army lieutenant colonel named U Tun Tun Oo, was paraphrased as saying that,

> The main duty of the judiciary is to search for and reveal the truth, that when finding the truth [judges need] to decide fairly in accordance with law, that [they] need to be abreast of judicial affairs and relevant basic facts, that facts and law decide a case, that having resolved to bring out only the authentic truth in the handing down of verdicts one is to act thus, and oneself being free from corrupt practices is to supervise closely at all times to see that corrupt practices also do not occur among one's subordinates.[27]

These statements do not have quite the same meaning as the preceding quote, but they are not far apart. Both speakers fill the spaces ideology once occupied with a jumble of hollowed-out concepts from former

[26] Khin Nyunt, 'Address at the Work Coordination Meeting' n. pag.
[27] *Myanma Alin* 4 Sept. 2011: 1.

periods, brushing against incessant reminders about virtuous public service. The legal rhetoric of the pragmatic state does not reject former doctrines in favour of new ones. It swallows and regurgitates everything – and all of it in the name of the rule of law.

What of the levelling out of injunctions? Of course, different types of injunctions do not literally have the same coercive value. Not every injunction formally carries the same weight or is of the same type. Injunctions must still be functionally differentiated for administrative purposes, at least. But where law is subsumed to order, the difference between a law, a regulation, and an order loses significance. Government establishes an administrative continuum that 'from the general law to the particular measure, makes the public authorities and the injunctions they give one and the same type of principle, according to one and the same type of coercive value'.[28] Laws lose their essential normativity. Statute is merely one type of injunction emanating from a different part of the continuum than directives or notifications.

For over two decades, government in Myanmar procedurally levelled out different types of injunctions. Under military government, the same people, or people working beneath them, issued statutes, orders, and announcements. From 1988 to 2010 the government published statutes in annual volumes with other instruments, not separately, as in prior years.[29] Alongside laws, these volumes included rules, setting out measures to implement laws; executive orders and announcements covering a wide range of topics; and, proclamations appointing and dismissing senior personnel from posts – including judges.[30]

In one speech after another, senior officials also semantically levelled out injunctions. For instance, in 1999 the chief justice said the state had as its goal a 'judicial system on which the entire people can trust and rely, in which judicial tasks are undertaken in accordance with established laws, rules, procedures, orders and instructions, with political views, economic views, social views and administrative views based on the state's policies and aims'.[31] And at the end of 2008 he

28 Michel Foucault, *The Birth of Biopolitics: Lectures at the Collège de France, 1978–1979*, trans. Graham Burchell, ed. Arnold I. Davidson (New York: Picador, 2008) 168–69.

29 I am referring to the Burmese versions of the annual volumes. The English translations contain only statutes.

30 In 1998, the junta sacked five Supreme Court justices via State Peace and Development Council Order 6/98, 14 Nov. 1998.

31 U Aung Toe, 'Judicial Officers Special Refresher Course No. 1 Closing Ceremony Held', *Supreme Court Gazette* 26 Mar. 1999: 11 (in Burmese).

remarked, 'The duty of the judiciary is to search for and reveal the authentic truth, so as to solve grievances in accordance with law. This goal is attainable with the codes of conduct imposed in law, rules, procedures, handbooks, instructions, etc.'[32] These lists are not merely inventories of juridical instruments and other paraphernalia that judges need to have at their disposal. They are inventories of *homogeneous* instruments and paraphernalia. Where order has subsumed law, juridical injunctions all occupy the same semantic plane – whether laws, rules, procedures, orders, or instructions. They all serve the state's interests; all carry much the same rhetorical weight for the senior official admonishing judicial personnel to do their jobs correctly. Furthermore, they all carry approximately the same weight in the courtroom, as internal directives make clear, such as the directive instructing superior judges to investigate whether or not subordinate courts were working 'in accordance with laws, rules and procedures, and the regulations, orders and instructions laid down by the State Law and Order Restoration Council, government and ministries'.[33]

Lastly, where order has subsumed law, administrative principles predominate. These principles are concerned with efficiency and accuracy. They are concerned with the management of subordinates through insistence upon adherence to policies and programmes outlined by the people at the top. And they are concerned with things that can be measured and compared statistically, with evidence of cooperation and coordination among departments, agencies, and personnel.

As discussed in previous chapters, many practices associated with these administrative principles were inculcated in earlier periods. But from the 1990s onwards, lacking any ideological basis for political domination, and gripped by an epistemology in which notoriously unreliable statistical measurement nevertheless determined success, military governments gave administrative principles special emphasis. Both public and internal records demonstrate a constant concern with efficient working procedures, with faster and more accurate sentencing. Throughout, they are preoccupied with methods to count and measure how law is administered – which is to say, how injunctions classed as law are administered. A successful court would not tarry over legal niceties or finer points of a case, but convict often and sentence harshly,

[32] U Aung Toe, 'Chief Justice's Address at Closing Ceremony of Deputy Township Judges Refresher Training No. 6', *Supreme Court Gazette* 14 Nov. 2008: 4 (in Burmese).

[33] SC Letter 5993/Su 14 (Ga) 92/95, 12 Oct. 1995, appendix B, par. 5(b).

as Khin Nyunt again made clear, this time in 2002 on the topic of illicit drugs:

> Everyone is aware that the national government has drawn up a fifteen-year narcotic drugs eradication project and in endeavouring to undertake narcotic drug eradication tasks with vigour it has set up central, state, division, district and township Committees for Drug Abuse Control which are operating widely. In this context, it is necessary for courts to hand down exemplary punishments under the Narcotic Drugs and Psychotropic Substances Law in narcotic drugs-related criminal cases where guilt is established. However, it is observed that some trial courts have not handed down exemplary punishments in cases at first instance, and likewise some upper courts also have handed down light punishments on revision. Therefore, it must be said that it is still necessary for the judicial branch to operate in harmony with the implementing of the state's objectives and projects.[34]

The Supreme Court followed up on such public admonitions by threatening judges in circulars with disciplinary action for failure to convict enough accused persons or to hand out enough exemplary sentences.[35] It also issued warnings against individual judges in its fortnightly gazette, inviting judicial personnel to learn from the mistakes of others, such as a judge in the delta who in 2009 let off drug dealers with light penalties and acquittals:

> At a time that the state is doing projects for the prevention and suppression of narcotic drugs as a national danger, [this] judge who has a responsibility to uphold and implement the state's policy guidelines [turned] a blind eye to the policy guidelines that the state leadership and heads of relevant departments are leaving [*sic*] on exemplary sentencing in criminal cases concerning narcotic drugs.[36]

Closely related to exemplary sentencing, and also a subject of repeated circulars, is speedy handling of cases.[37] Courts across South Asia with substantially the same body of procedural law as Myanmar can take

[34] Khin Nyunt, 'Address on July 9, 2002 at the Institute of Nursing to Supreme Court, Office of the Attorney General and State, Division and District Judges and Law Officers Assembled for Receipt of Advice on Judicial Affairs', *Judicial Journal* 1.14 (2002): 12 (in Burmese).

[35] SC Instruction 4/92, 28 Sept. 1992; 1/99, 5 Jan. 1999; 4/99, 7 July 1999; 1/2001, 2 Feb. 2001. SC Letter 4943/210/94 (LaKaNa), 11 Aug. 1994; 20163/PyitYu/99, 16 Dec. 1999.

[36] SC Order 73/2009, 10 Oct. 2009. Judges issuing lenient sentences or acquittals in cases of gambling, illegal immigration, and theft or damage of state property, among other offences, also risk reproach or worse if their performances are not sufficiently convincing.

[37] As set out in SC Letter 604/Su 11/(7/2007), 13 Feb. 2003.

years or even decades to resolve ordinary criminal cases.[38] In Myanmar, by contrast, the emphasis on efficiency ensures that criminal cases proceed relatively quickly. For an ordinary case to progress from the court of first instance to the top court can take as little as fourteen months. Again, the Supreme Court reprimands individual judges for delays caused by inefficiency.[39] Speedy dispatch improves court statistics, which are tabulated and submitted to higher courts, and reported publicly as evidence of hard work. Judicial bureaucrats incorporate the reports into tables with which to identify and admonish unusually tardy judges. The data contain little with which to evaluate courts' actual performance, but they do help to communicate purported successes to senior figures and, through the media, to the public. Good statistics also help individual judges to dispel allegations of malfeasance, because anticorruption rhetoric associates the acceptance of bribes with delays to cases – a topic revisited in Chapter 6.

SOVEREIGN *CETANA* AND THE CITIZEN

To grasp the concept of sovereign *cetana* and why it matters to the law-and-order ideal in Myanmar, we need to return momentarily to an earlier period, from which I will track this principle in relation to concepts of citizenship and rights.

When Ne Win seized power in 1962 and detained the chief justice, president, and prime minister, among hundreds of others, he asserted through that act that he had the authority to determine the limits of the legal order, and the power to decide where any individual might be placed in relation to it. To reinforce this assertion, his government had to do more than delimit procedures to protect legal rights; it had to delimit and, to an extent, redefine those rights, first to fit within the new mode of government through military domination; and second, to fit its ideological reorientation. Rights all began and ended in the moment of sovereign decision. The state's security, socialist economy, and party programme were all synonyms for the maintenance of the state's specific order as determined from the moment of the coup.

The rights the new government formulated and professed were 'socialist rights', which took the place of 'bourgeois' ones. The

[38] See, for instance, Salar M. Khan, 'Judicial Delays to Criminal Trials in Delhi', *Article 2* 7.2 (2008): 7–60.

[39] For instance, SC Orders 46–7/2003, 31 Mar. 2003.

government deprecated the latter, associating them with the individual freedoms and wealth of the elite it had displaced. The new rights reflected and achieved policy-based goals and outcomes. Expressions of rights contrary to these outcomes ceased to apply, because socialist rights limit the mobility of their bearers, entitling them only to travel in an indicated direction.[40] Mirjan Damaška has explained that this approach to rights is common to states implementing policy through law, or 'activist' states:

> The citizen of the activist state possesses no rights accorded by virtue of his being an end in himself. No right is absolute or abstract. ... Further, because the policies and programs of the activist state are theoretically all-encompassing, broader implications can be detected anywhere: all rights are at least potentially subject to qualification or denial. ... Strictly speaking, then, personal claims based on activist law are mislabeled if characterized as rights ... it would be better to invent new terms – to say that activist decrees accord conditional privileges, create roles, assign tasks, give each their just share, and the like.[41]

Socialist rights did not extend to anyone who dared to demand them without recognising their conditionality, such as the students who protested the government's takeover of university administration in 1962, or workers who went on strike over conditions, pay, and rations at more than a hundred factories, dockyards, rail yards, and sawmills in 1974. In both instances, soldiers and policemen shot dozens, then rounded up and jailed hundreds for attempting to interfere in the building of the socialist state and socialist economy.[42] Rights as conditional privileges could not be exceeded, even if claimed through reference to the same socialist goals of the state. A citizen or citizens who had the audacity to make rights claims beyond those rights the state delimited as conditional privileges could threaten the sovereign.[43] And a citizen had no right to threaten the sovereign because rights

[40] Inga Markovits, 'Socialist vs. Bourgeois Rights: An East-West German Comparison', *University of Chicago Law Review* 45 (1977): 615.

[41] Mirjan R. Damaška, *The Faces of Justice and State Authority: A Comparative Approach to the Legal Process* (New Haven and London: Yale University Press, 1986) 83–84.

[42] On 1962 see Yin Htun, ed., *Record of the 7th July Uprising* (Yangon: Zinyadanazaw, 2013). On 1974, see Kyaw Htet Aung (Shwepyidan), ed., *Popular Opposition Struggles to the BSPP Dictatorship: 74–75–76* (Yangon: Shwepyidan, 2013) 52–172; Poe Kyaw, My *History, Others' History, The Country's History* (Yangon: Thin, 2014) (all in Burmese).

[43] *WPD* 15 Mar. 1979: 1, 4.

extended from the sovereign, not from any other source. Maung Maung made this formulation explicit in 1980 when he said,

> The main *cetana* of the President is that he wants the people to . . . come to have a clear understanding of their rights, and to be able to ask questions and demand their rights if they are in doubt. . . . He wants the kind of law which the people understand and consciously and willingly observe. This is the *cetana* which the President has in making every law.[44]

The term in this passage that the state media translated into English as 'right', *ya-baing-gwin*, denotes a delimited right tied to reciprocal duties.[45] It designates a conditional privilege, not an unfettered right of the sort used to describe fundamental rights, or human rights. Tied to this delimited conception of rights is the reference to presidential *cetana*. A Pali word, in Buddhist teaching *cetana* sometimes translates as 'volition', or 'that which motivates action'. Strictly speaking, its meaning is neutral, and is close to 'intention'; the everyday usage of the word in Thai. In Burmese, it is used in a variety of contexts, religious and secular, and is sometimes translated as 'goodwill'.[46] In political usage, it signifies a positive mental process of someone in authority – a government minister, a judge, or a schoolteacher – especially to bring others together in collective enterprise for some larger purpose. Gustaaf Houtman has written of this type of *cetana*: 'Differences between groups must be set aside, and shared among all must be the intentionality to participate in a benevolent project conceived of in the singular, and contained within the boundaries of the state.'[47] This *cetana* is tied to sovereign authority: the *cetana* of the sovereign depends on his power to realise it. By the same token, enjoyment of rights is contingent upon the recipient acknowledging the *cetana* of the sovereign.

The *cetana* of the sovereign is not aimed at protecting rights generally, but only certain rights for certain people who deserve them because they conform with the sovereign's vision for the community. *Cetana* renders legal rights' efficacy dependent on the goodwill of a higher power. Rights derived from *cetana* are conditional privileges paternalistically bestowed, based on classifications to include some

[44] *WPD* 4 July 1980: 1, 4. [45] *Forward* Aug. 1980: 6.

[46] Nick Cheesman, 'Legitimising the Union of Myanmar through Primary School Textbooks', MEd diss., University of Western Australia, 2002, 219–20.

[47] Houtman, *Mental Culture in Burmese Crisis Politics* 163.

people and exclude others. Implicit in the notion of rights as conditional privileges is the existence of categories of people towards whom rights *do not* accrue. Since all rights are conditional, a person failing to meet the conditions attached to them not only ceases to enjoy those rights but may also be penalised if she attempts to exercise rights that she does not have. Sovereign *cetana* contains within it the means to deny what it claims to deliver.

In modern times, legal rights' linkage to membership in a political community has meant that the most effective way to deny people rights has been to deny them political membership. Inalienable rights founder in the paradox of sovereignty.[48] People can only claim to be protected by law where a sovereign produces law. But the only claim to rights not subject to qualification or withdrawal by a sovereign decision is a claim to a universal or natural right, which exceeds sovereign power and cannot be realised, because no sovereign exists to produce law with which to protect it. Therefore, complete withdrawal of sovereign *cetana* comes through revocation of a person's citizenship. Since all conditional privileges flow from the sovereign towards people designated citizens, withdrawal of citizenship constitutes the withdrawal of those privileges.

Maung Maung's linking of sovereign *cetana* to the rights of subjects was not coincidental. He made his remarks in the context of a speech on a new draft citizenship law. Passed in 1982, the law captured the paradox of inalienable rights. Taking a subsidiary concept of indigenousness from a 1948 antecedent and turning it into the primary basis for citizenship, the law rendered stateless, or potentially stateless, large numbers of people whose ancestors migrated to Burma while it was under British occupation.

In the early to mid-1960s, the government had begun forcing out Indian residents and coercing non-indigenous citizens to leave, some on specific orders, more by measures aimed at making life untenable for them.[49] It accused others, such as 'bloodsucking Chettiar Indians', of

[48] 'The Rights of Man, supposedly inalienable, proved to be unenforceable ... whenever people appeared who were no longer citizens of any sovereign state.' Hannah Arendt, *The Origins of Totalitarianism*, 3rd edn. (London: George Allen & Unwin, 1966) 293.

[49] According to one author, over a hundred thousand people had left the country by September 1964. Robert A. Holmes, 'Burmese Domestic Policy: The Politics of Burmanization', *Asian Survey* 7.3 (1967): 191–92. According to census data for the country, 'The Indian population ... declined from 7.0 percent of the total population in 1931 to 1.9 percent in 1973 ... due largely to emigration'. M. Ismael Khin Maung, 'The Population of Burma: An

financial crimes.[50] In 1968, the government set up a national registration department and committees to scrutinise citizenship applications and records.[51] But the 1982 statute went beyond xenophobic policing actions. It removed the normative basis for some persons' claims to legal rights, on the pretext of protecting the rights of others.

The statute has since denied or significantly delimited the rights of hundreds of thousands of people in Myanmar. Among them are the members of one community that in 2012 attracted extensive international media attention when, not for the first time, over a hundred thousand persons identifying as ethnic Rohingya fled intercommunal violence in western Rakhine State, bordering Bangladesh. Since the mid-1960s, successive governments in Myanmar have refused to acknowledge the existence of the Rohingya, describing them generally as Bengali illegals.[52] A deputy immigration and population minister in 2013 iterated the standard line when he told the national legislature,

> Rohingya have never been an ethnic group of Rakhine State, nor are they among ethnicities recorded in the censuses and records of the colonialist British, or the 1973 and 1983 censuses ... according to which those foreign ethnicities who are not national races are named only as Chinese, Indian, Pakistani, Bengali and Nepalese. Rohingya are also not among the over 100 ethnic groups who are among the national races of Myanmar.[53]

Insofar as the question of citizenship pertains to community identity, it applies to all individuals who identify with a particular community. Under the 1982 law, to identify with a community that officially does not exist is to risk being labelled a foreigner pretending to be a citizen,

Analysis of the 1973 Census', 97, *Papers of the East-West Population Institute* (Honolulu: East-West Center, 1986) 17.

[50] Ministry of Home Affairs, *Ministry of Home Affairs: Historical Record and Achievements* ([Yangon]: Govt. of the Union of Myanmar, 2000) 278–79 (in Burmese).

[51] Khin Maung Kyaw, *Burma: The Problem of Citizens and Foreigners* (Rangoon: San Kyaw Yin, 1971) 217–21 (in Burmese).

[52] Prior governments of independent Burma gave tacit or explicit recognition to Rohingya, as summarised in U Kyaw Min, *A Glimpse into the Hidden Chapters of Arakan History* (Yangon: Daw Khin Ma Cho, 2013) 82–85 (in Burmese).

[53] U Kyaw Kyaw Win in the lower house of the national legislature on February 20, 2013, cited in *People's Age* 20 Mar. 2013: 10. On the concept of national races, see Nick Cheesman, 'Seeing "Karen" in the Union of Myanmar', *Asian Ethnicity* 3.2 (2002): 215–19. See also U Khin Maung Cho, 'The Power to Define "National Races"', parts 1 and 2, *The 1982 Citizenship Law Contradicts the 2008 Constitution, and Selected Articles* (Yangon: Shwethizsa, 2014) 65–72 (in Burmese).

and thereby to incur criminal penalties. It is to identify as a person to whom no sovereign *cetana* accrues.

To illustrate how courts operate to withdraw sovereign *cetana*, in the remainder of this section I will narrate a specific case. Throughout the rest of the book, I will use this method of interrogating political ideas in Myanmar through narratives of contemporary criminal cases. The discussion of ideas would have little merit if isolated from the practices they animate. How law and order is opposed to the rule of law in this setting needs to be understood in praxis. The case of U Kyaw Min is the first of many.

Who is U Kyaw Min, and why is his case useful to explicate the relationship between the exercise of sovereign *cetana* and the rights of the citizen? Kyaw Min graduated from the Institute of Economics and Institute of Education in Yangon. At forty-six he gave up a government job to be elected in 1990 to a seat in the never-to-be-convened parliament, for the National Human Rights Democratic Party, which unofficially identified as a Rohingya party.[54]

Almost two years after the military government nullified the 1990 election results it also outlawed Kyaw Min's party, among eight others, on vague grounds of non-compliance with political party procedures.[55] Officials detained Kyaw Min without charge for three months of the same year. In 2005, he met visiting representatives of the International Labour Organisation and joined with other successful candidates from the 1990 election to call for the military government to allow parliament to sit. One or both of these actions prompted a series of criminal cases against him. Prosecutors charged Kyaw Min and his entire immediate family with falsifying their identities in order to get national registration cards, under section 18 of the 1982 Citizenship Law: that anyone found to have 'acquired citizenship by making a false representation or by concealment' will lose it. According to the prosecution, Kyaw Min and family falsely claimed to belong to national races, when in fact they are Bengali, which is the official descriptor for anyone claiming to be Rohingya.[56] Kyaw Min maintained in court that he and his family are Rohingya, but because the government does not recognise the group's existence, when registering for identity documents they followed the

[54] See NHRDP, *A Short History of Arakan and Rohingya* (Yangon: National Human Rights Democratic Party, 1990) (in Burmese).

[55] SLORC Order 8/92, 19 Mar. 1992.

[56] As noted in ICSVRS, *Report of the Inquiry Commission on the Sectarian Violence in Rakhine State* (Naypyidaw: Republic of the Union of Myanmar, 2013) 7.

advice of officials in putting down some other ethnic details. Despite his explanation, in July 2005 the Yangon Western District Court sentenced him to forty-seven years in prison and his wife, son, and two daughters to seventeen years each – ten years under section 18 and seven for disseminating false news in breach of the Emergency Provisions Act. It convicted Kyaw Min of four separate offences under section 18.[57]

A lawyer took the family's appeals to the Supreme Court. He pointed to the many breaches of law in the cases against his clients, including that the prosecution had framed the charges incorrectly; that the language in the verdicts and pertinent sections of law did not correspond; and that a prosecution witness had submitted evidence via document but the court had not called this witness to be cross-examined.[58] He pointed out that prior to Kyaw Min standing for election in 1990 the authorities had scrutinised his and his wife's backgrounds to determine his eligibility, and had not uncovered any irregularities. He cited numerous procedural errors that should at least have reduced the sentences of the accused. In the Supreme Court, the basic question should have been whether or not the defects in the case vitiated the verdict. The judges did not address this question and simply iterated the facts as set out in the lower courts, disregarding the defence attorney's arguments about errors in law.[59]

The lawyer's arguments were legally relevant, but otherwise pointless, because his clients had ceased to have the conditional privileges necessary to press legal claims. The minutiae of evidence, facts of the case, and their interpretation were relevant only so long as the defendants had legal privileges to make these points stick. Because the law-and-order ideal requires formal compliance with procedure, the attorney could raise an appeal. But because of the withdrawal of sovereign *cetana* from his clients, the procedures that should have given credence to his objections ceased to be operative. They depended on a notion that defence counsel is entitled and obliged to vigorously

[57] *Pol. Maj. Saw Elbert* v. *Kyaw Min (a) Md. Shamsul Anwarul Haque*, 2005 Criminal Case 49, Yangon Western District Court, 29 July 2005. The other three cases under section 18 were decided in Criminal Cases 50–52 of the same court, and the case under section 5(e) of the 1950 Emergency Provisions Act in Criminal Case 55. All verdicts were issued on the same date.

[58] *U Kyaw Min* v. *Union of Myanmar*, 2005 Criminal Appeal 138, Yangon Divisional Court, 9 Dec. 2005; also 2005 Criminal Appeals 139–42; *U Kyaw Min* v. *Union of Myanmar*, 2006 Criminal Revision 144(b), Supreme Court, 3 May 2006; also 2006 Criminal Revisions 145(b), 146(b), 147(b) and 148(b).

[59] *U Kyaw Min* v. *Union of Myanmar*, 2006 Special Criminal Misc. Appeal Application 177, Supreme Court, 23 Aug. 2006; also 2006 Special Criminal Misc. Appeal Applications 178–81.

promote his client's case. The administratively determined status of Kyaw Min and his family as non-citizens, stripped of sovereign *cetana*, rendered these procedures ineffectual.

Kyaw Min's case illustrates how the Citizenship Law authorises government officials in Myanmar to remove the normative basis for claims to legal rights from a person or class of persons by distinguishing between 'a so-to-speak authentic life and a life lacking every political value'.[60] It is the radical differentiator between bearers of the conditional privileges described as rights, and bearers of none. Closely related to it, in its philosophy and practice, is the less precise but no less damaging withdrawal of sovereign *cetana* from the citizen classed as a public enemy.

THE PUBLIC ENEMY

Carl Schmitt thought a great deal about enemies. He took the existence of an enemy to be the defining characteristic of politics.[61] Schmitt, to recall, described the 'normal state' as seeking *total* peace, a perfectly orderly territory, free from conflict or strife.[62] This goal necessitates elimination of internal enemies. But the problem inherent to it is: how is the enemy identified? By what formula can the state isolate the enemy?[63]

My answer to this question is that in Myanmar the public enemy is nobody other than the person from whom sovereign *cetana* has been withdrawn. The public enemy is the person whose attempts to exercise conditional privileges cease to be efficacious, not because the attempts are flawed legally, but because *the person* is flawed politically. No prior, independent formulation for the public enemy exists. To engage in a search for one would not only be futile but would also be to misunderstand the nature of this state. Because the law-and-order state reserves the right to decline to stipulate in advance how it will behave in response to a given situation or case, identification of the public enemy cannot objectively precede action taken against the person. The withdrawal of sovereign *cetana* is not a consequence of prior classification as an adversary. It occurs simultaneously with that classification.

60 Giorgio Agamben, *Homo Sacer: Sovereign Power and Bare Life*, trans. Daniel Heller-Roazen (Stanford: Stanford University Press, 1998) 132.

61 Carl Schmitt, *The Concept of the Political*, trans. George Schwab (Chicago and London: University of Chicago Press, 2007) 26.

62 Schmitt, *The Concept of the Political* 46. 63 Schmitt, *The Concept of the Political* 28.

Bereft of sovereign *cetana*, the public enemy is no longer able to exercise legal privileges as she would ordinarily. She does not cease to be a citizen, but stripped of privileges to participate politically and juridically, she is rendered an object for the orderly performance of administrative practice. The radical distinction between the public enemy and the other criminal accused is that the latter may use vestigial procedural defences. He can also attempt to buy his way out of a case, or out of some aspect of a case, as discussed in Chapter 6. The public enemy can do neither – at least, not without the judge or other court staff putting their jobs, and possibly their own liberty, on the line.[64]

This method of dealing with the public enemy has the added advantage that it strips her of her political potency. A criminalised enemy is still politically dangerous. It is the absence of any distinctive formulation for the public enemy that makes the accused person politically irrelevant. The public enemy is nobody other than any criminal offender, accused and convicted of any criminal offence, and not necessarily an offence with any bearing on the actual reason for her arrest.

The police in Myanmar have long brought cases against public enemies under statutes designed for the purpose, such as the Unlawful Associations Act and Emergency Provisions Act, and particular sections of the Penal Code, such as those concerning sedition and treason. But in the 2000s, they brought cases against public enemies under practically any law, and for all manner of offences – not just those offences that purpose-made injunctions demarcate. They charged a monk who waited outside the court hearing a case against Aung San Suu Kyi during 2009 with insulting religion under section 295(a) of the Penal Code, for allegedly planning to immolate himself – despite the absence of any material evidence to prove the claim.[65] In Pakokku, a young woman arrested for collecting video footage to send abroad went to jail under section 5(1) of the Control of Imports and Exports (Temporary) Act, 1947 for travelling on the back of an illegally imported motorcycle, which the police said she co-owned.[66] She also

[64] In 2007 a judge who tried to make money in a case under the Unlawful Associations Act went to jail for it. SC Order 4/2007, 22 Jan. 2007. A predecessor who did the same also came under investigation. National Intelligence Bureau, Letter 252/ (18–16) 93/MaTaPa 4, 18 Apr. 1995.

[65] *Inspector Zaw Hpone Win* v. *Sandadhika* (a) *Nyi Nyi Lwin* (a) *Nyi Nyi San*, 2009 Criminal Case 507, Bahan Township Court, 2009.

[66] *Inspector Htin Paw* v. *Maung Myint Naing and Another*, 2009 Criminal Case 1763, Pakokku Township Court, 6 Oct. 2009.

got fifteen days under the 1907 Towns Act for failing to register with the local authorities as a visitor at somebody's house. And the police charged a man collecting signatures in Letpadan for a campaign to release political detainees with selling illegal lottery tickets in violation of the Gambling Law, and with assaulting a civil servant under section 353 of the Penal Code.[67] A court convicted another man collecting signatures, who had been arrested separately, of forgery and cheating under sections 420, 465, and 468 of the Penal Code – the police alleged he had filled in the petition with the names of people who had not actually agreed to sign it.[68]

In Nyaungdon, the police prosecuted two men arrested in 2007 for possession of video footage showing the wedding of the gold and diamond-encrusted daughter of the then head of state, Senior General Than Shwe, under the 1996 Television and Video Law. The CD containing the video had not been approved for distribution. They also charged the men under section 505(b) of the Penal Code for upsetting public tranquility, *ngyeinwut-ye*: a generic provision imposing a two-year jail term in cases where accused persons allegedly have threatened public order somehow. In this case, the charge was irrelevant to the alleged offence. By definition, to upset *public* tranquility requires a public act, not the concealment of an offending article. The distance between the charges and the actual reason for the case is clear from the verdict: that the video makers, rather than the two accused, 'had narrated and shot images of ordinary working people's food and interspersed them with the images of dress and food at the wedding of the head of state's daughter, the images of dress and food of the military leaders, and images of the food of the head of state's family [and therefore] that footage caused harm to state law and order and was seditious towards the heads of the state'.[69]

Some public enemies have gone to jail for allegedly giving unregistered tuition classes – a crime carrying a three-year penalty.[70] A court in 2005 sentenced one to the maximum term because he spoke to a group of children on the birthday of the national martyr Aung San, led them in commemorative song, and displayed a T-shirt bearing the image of his daughter, Aung San Suu Kyi. The court verdict makes

67 *Myanma Alin* 10 Oct. 2006: 5. 68 *Myanma Alin* 3 Nov. 2006: 10.

69 *Inspector Kyaw Mya Than* v. *Than Htun and Another*, 2007 Criminal Case 319, Nyaungdon Township Court, 25 Apr. 2007: 5–6. Details of the case are contained in Opinion 7/2008 (8 May 2008) of the UN Working Group on Arbitrary Detention.

70 Tuition Law, 6/84, sec. 22.

clear that the T-shirt constituted evidence of an offence, despite it being irrelevant to the charge of illegal tutoring.[71] Another man went to jail a couple of years later for giving unregistered lessons on human rights.[72] In 2013, he was again charged, this time under section 172 of the Penal Code, for convening classes on political science in defiance of the order of a local administrator.[73] Unlike six years previously, the case against him did not get beyond the township court. By this time his type of political activist no longer automatically passed as a public enemy. Only the administrator with an imperfect sense of the historical moment and his place in it would, in 2013, have pursued such a case without explicit instructions from superiors.

Whereas the types of charges brought against the public enemy assiduously deny her ontology, the *manner* of her trial recognises and addresses it. The public enemy is in effect tried administratively. Despite the term 'trial' still being applied in these cases, what happens is not a trial at all. It is a substitute for one. Rather than calling it a trial, it would be better described as the administrative processing of an accused, in accordance with principles for law and order.

A common procedure applied to cases involving a public enemy that speaks to the administrative processing at work is the closed or 'reserved' courtroom.[74] Reserved courts are not analogous to military tribunals of the sort that the new government set up to try offenders under martial law provisions in 1989. Nor are they like special courts established in preceding eras to exempt trials from ordinary criminal procedure. The juridical space for closed court is located in the ordinary law. Under section 352 of the Criminal Procedure Code, a presiding judge has authority to select the place of hearings and also to issue orders to exclude 'the public generally, or any particular person' from the premises. The provision is grounded in concern for the security of the court.[75] In practice, during the 2000s the Supreme Court, rather than the presiding judges, issued orders to hold closed trials.[76]

[71] *U Sein Lwin* v. *Khin Maung Oo* (a) *U Aung Hpe*, 2005 Criminal Case 210, Twante Township Court, 25 Aug. 2005.

[72] *U Chan Aung* v. *Min Min* (a) *La Min Htun*, 2007 Criminal Case 1874, Pyay Township Court, 30 July 2007.

[73] *U Han Win Zaw (Deputy Departmental Head)* v. *Min Min* (a) *La Min Htun*, 2013 Criminal Case 723, Pyay Township Court.

[74] The courts are not described as closed but as *thi-than*, reserved or separated, usually translated to English as 'special'.

[75] As set out in the Courts Manual, par. 48(1).

[76] As explained by Chief Justice U Tun Tun Oo, in *NLM* 27 Aug. 2011: 7.

Because the ostensible purpose of a court's closure is to ensure the security of its premises, everything else is supposed to go on as normal. In practice, a court once closed is comprehensive in its closure. A judge hearing charges against Phyo Wai Aung, a young man accused of involvement in a fatal April 2010 bombing, refused to allow his lawyer copies of the relevant police records. He also denied the defendant's relatives entry to the courtroom, recording in the court's diary 'that whoever should have permission to enter or leave the courtroom is a matter of no relevance to the court'.[77] According to the judge, the guards, not he, held the keys of authority to the court gates. Phyo Wai Aung's lawyer appealed against this understanding of the judge's authority. In January 2011, a Supreme Court judge ruled that he saw no cause to interfere in the proceedings and dismissed the application. The order for a reserved courtroom was justified because the case was 'not an ordinary criminal case but a well-known case'.[78] The court could not hear the case publicly for the very reason that people would come to look and listen.

Actually, rather than describing these courts as 'closed', we should talk of these cases as being heard in 'enclosed court'. Enclosure takes two forms. One is the enclosure of the court within the penitentiary – or within the juridical perimeter of the penitentiary, even if the court physically sits outside a prison's walls. To describe such a court as reserved or 'separated' is a misnomer. The court is not separated but integrated. It becomes part of the penitentiary, homogenising the defendant's experience of imprisonment and his experience of the juridical process. The enclosed court is in this sense emblematic of how law has been subsumed to order. It best ensures the effective conveyance of the accused through the continuum of administrative activity to his final destination: conveniently, the same place in which the court is itself located.

The enclosed court also encloses the larger institutions of which it is part. Because it remains a part of the hierarchy of courts, the closed court draws ordinary personnel and procedures into a special domain where they maintain the pretence of carrying on with work as usual. Everybody involved is a latent participant in the enclosure. In these

[77] *U Phyo Wai Aung* v. *Union of Myanmar*, 2010 Criminal Revision Application, Yangon Divisional Court, 27 Aug. 2010.

[78] *U Phyo Wai Aung* v. *Union of Myanmar*, 2010 Criminal Revision 495(b), Supreme Court, 14 Jan. 2011: 2.

respects, the enclosed court in Myanmar during the last two decades is again unlike the special courts established under draconian regulations to try rebels against the British colonial government, or the courts established to curtail the procedural rights of defendants during wartime. The whole point of those courts was to impress on all and sundry that exigencies demanded government suspend routine practice and establish a legally anomalous zone where exceptional cases might be dispatched. The use of enclosed courts in the contemporary period, by contrast, conveys a message that nothing abnormal is taking place at all.

The enclosed court also speaks to an administrative principle guiding the work of courts in Myanmar generally – a principle not written into most internal directives and notifications, but on which they are premised – the principle of secrecy. Max Weber once observed that a core principle of bureaucratic administration is to minimise public knowledge of what the administration is doing.[79] And if this principle applies generally, then we might reasonably expect that an autocratic political arrangement will lead to more secrecy than a democratic one.[80] In an authoritarian setting, secrecy is a paramount virtue: something to be cherished and maintained.

Courts in Myanmar have for the last two decades operated on the principle of secrecy, without ever needing to profess it. The principle of secrecy is manifest in the disappearance of the public from the courtroom, in the loss of the unreserved right to treat criminal trials as open. By re-presenting the courthouse as a place of administrative activity, not a place to and from which the public is entitled to come and go freely, officials render courts off limits, demarcating them as places that even professionals may require some skill and aptitude to enter.

The principle of secrecy is also manifest in the disappearance of trials from the public media throughout the 1990s and 2000s. In contrast to the 1950s and even most of the 1960s, when trials were reported by the state and private media alike, by the 1980s news about the work of courts in Myanmar had practically ceased. Judges did not appear on television or in print unless an army officer or the chief justice was

[79] Max Weber, *Economy and Society: An Outline of Interpretive Sociology*, trans. Ephraim Fischoff et al., eds. Guenther Roth and Claus Wittich, vol. III, 3 vols. (Berkeley, Los Angeles and London: University of California Press, 1968) 992.

[80] Robert Barros, 'Secrecy and Dictatorship: Some Problems in the Study of Authoritarian Regimes', *Political Methodology*, 2, Working Paper Series (Mexico City: Committee on Concepts and Methods, 2005) 14–15.

present to lecture them. They appeared as endnotes to articles on the arrest of drug dealers and human traffickers, the sentences they handed down recorded as formalities following the hard work of the police and other officials. Now and then, they participated in a show trial, such as in the 2009 case against Aung San Suu Kyi for alleged violation of the terms of her house arrest.[81] What they stopped doing publicly was to adjudicate.

With the rapid expansion of the private print media from the late 2000s, court officials have found the principle of secrecy increasingly at odds with growing demands that matters of public interest actually be public. More people have begun clamouring to be heard in court, and to have what goes on in court heard outside it. Journalists, previously denied access to courtrooms, have again been able to report on some proceedings under an arrangement for their orderly distribution across court premises, with appropriate cautions about contempt of court.[82] Reporting on some high-profile cases, such as the trial of four journalists and an editor for publishing a story over the alleged construction of a chemical weapons factory, has included detailed narratives of proceedings in court.[83] Still, accounts of criminal cases in the media are as yet dominated by the presence of the policeman – a figure who physically represents the rule of law as law and order far more powerfully than the judge, as discussed in the next chapter.

PAPERWORK AND PLEADERS

Because public enemies have forfeited conditional privileges that would otherwise accrue to them, the residual procedural interstices and other avenues available to the ordinary criminal accused cease to apply in their cases. As long as policemen have done their paperwork, they can submit documents to court consisting of falsehoods, without fear that these records will undermine the case against a public enemy.

On one hand, procedure matters to process an accused public enemy efficiently. Without procedure, the administrative continuum from agency to agency, from officer to officer, cannot be maintained. Paperwork exists to move the defendant from one part of their administrative processing to the next, and to appear to do so in an orderly

[81] *Pol. Lt-Col. Zaw Min Aung* v. *Daw Aung San Suu Kyi and 3*, 2009 Criminal Case 47, Yangon Northern District Court, 11 Aug. 2009.

[82] *Weekly Eleven* 13 Feb. 2013: Supp. A. [83] See, for instance, *Weekly Eleven* 14 July 2014: 5.

fashion. On the other, in the case against the public enemy, procedure does not affect the result. Police officers bringing charges against public enemies need to do their paperwork to facilitate the correct administrative outcome, not to make the case credible. The gap between the two purposes means that in cases of public enemies the contents of paperwork are sometimes disconnected from the facts of the case.

For example, the police charged two public enemies arrested and brought to the central prison from the east of the country in 2008 under the 1947 Foreign Exchange Regulation Act, with illegal possession of United States dollars. Under cross-examination, the investigating officer acknowledged that the purported evidence of an offence, the money, was uncovered at the prison, four days after the two were already taken into custody.[84] His testimony that the police had no evidence of an offence at the time they arrested the couple made no difference to the case outcome, which had been determined before their arrest, by virtue of their prior classification.

In another case, the state media announced the arrest on September 4, 2009, of a man accused of involvement in an antigovernment student group.[85] When the police completed their paperwork, they recorded the date of arrest on the charge sheet as November 12, 2009, two months after the date reported in the newspaper.[86] And in the case of Shwe Gyoe and three others held for approximately half a year for allegedly receiving money from abroad, the cross-examination record shows an investigating officer's replies to a lawyer's questions as follows:

Q. Ko Shwe Gyoe was arrested starting from March 7, 2009?
A. Correct.
Q. This case was submitted for prosecution on September 10, 2009?
A. I see it shown thus before the court.
Q. In your testimony-in-chief you testified that persons in the country connected with Ko Shwe Gyoe alias Mya Soe had accepted financial support, of which I put it to you that you have not been able to submit to the court any supporting evidence, be it receipts or otherwise.
A. Correct.[87]

[84] *Pol. Maj. Ye Nyunt* v. *Khin Moe Aye* (a) *Moe Moe* (a) *Kyidaw Kyi and Another*, 2008 Criminal Case 111, Sanchaung Township Court, Prosecution Witness (PW) 3, 5 June 2008: 2–3.
[85] *NLM* 24 Sept. 2009: 16.
[86] Charge 162/09, Botataung Township Police Station, 10 Dec. 2009.
[87] *Pol. Capt. Myat Kyi* v. *Sein Hlaing and 3*, 2009 Criminal Case 432, Sanchaung Township Court, PW 1, 22 Sept. 2009: 7. In cross-examination records, lawyers' questions are expressed as

Here and elsewhere in the testimony the policeman acknowledges that he has no material evidence to secure a conviction. The lack of evidence does not appear to concern him. He states that the accused did not keep records, and that the facts had 'emerged' in the course of interrogation. His response to the second question, aimed at having him admit to illegal custody of the defendants, is a statement of profound impunity. It constitutes an admission that what the court had on record before it was a false document, as the gap of six months between the date of arrest and date of prosecution was not explained.

Policemen bringing cases against public enemies offer irrelevant, contradictory, inconsistent, and sometimes ridiculous evidence. To prove five accused had visited refugee camps in Thailand, police officers submitted as evidence a map showing the sites of camps along the border taken from a government-issued school textbook.[88] In a related case against five persons accused of setting up an illegal organisation, the prosecution evidence included three innocuous poems authored by one of the accused, and computer equipment and books on computing taken from another, a computing student.[89] The records in this case contain a litany of inconsistencies. The charge sheet recorded the date of arrest of all accused as April 10, 2009, two weeks before charges were lodged in court. Yet, the search-and-seizure records and first information reports all contain dates in January, when the arrests occurred. The defence attorney teased these facts from one of the investigating officers, a member of the police Special Branch.[90] The cross examination ran:

statements suffixed by an expression meaning roughly, 'I put it to you'. For the sake of simplicity in English usage and to avoid repetition, I have expressed some of the questions in the interrogative form, and have inserted Q and A to indicate question and answer.

88 *Pol. Capt. Myo Thant* v. *Nyi Nyi Aung*, 2009 Criminal Case 357, Hlaing Township Court, 22 Oct. 2009. The map is contained in Ministry of Education, *Social Studies: Myanmar History (Basic Education Mid Level)*, vol. II (Yangon: Govt. of the Union of Myanmar, 2001) 52 (in Burmese).

89 *Pol. Capt. Myo Thant* v. *Nyi Nyi Aung and 4*, 2009 Criminal Case 356, Hlaing Township Court, 22 Oct. 2009.

90 'The main duties of the Special Branch are to scrutinise the activities of aboveground and underground subversives, political activities, movements of foreigners, cases brought by military intelligence, investigate emigration and immigration, detect, investigate and prosecute in accordance with law crimes regarding the state, provide security for state ceremonies and VIPs, etc.' Police Manual, par. 18. See also par. 58.

Q. In your capacity as a ranking Special Branch officer searching and seizing material, you searched and seized pursuant to the Criminal Procedure Code?
A. Correct.
Q. You opened a complaint and had authorisation to search and seize in accordance with law?
A. I had a duty to follow orders.
Q. In the current matter of the search, you had a duty to follow said orders from which individual?
A. Police Captain Soe Thein assigned the duty.
Q. Is the date of search on the search form, Evidence Item B, 27 or 28?
A. It is January 28, 2009.
Q. The police charge sheet is (Pa) 156/09?
A. Correct.
Q. On the [police] complaint is written March 26, 2009?
A. Correct.
Q. You were instructed precisely on which items to search for?
A. Correct. My instructions were to search Ko Ne Moe Aung's room, to arrest him if present, and to seize any material infringing the law.
Q. None of the ten varieties of material you seized infringe the law.
A. Incorrect. If you read the poems you can see they infringe it. As regards the remaining items, I don't know exactly.
Q. As you have been a police officer for twenty-four years, you can expertly conduct search and seizure pursuant to the law?
A. [No answer recorded.]
Q. Not being a policeman at an ordinary police station, you can make points [on the record] that are not in accordance with law?
A. I made the seizure in accordance with law.

...

Q. You did not state that you had, nor did you show to Ko Ne Moe Aung a search warrant?
A. Correct. I went and conducted the search without a search warrant. The search was under orders from above.[91]

The lawyer's cross-examination exposes the errors in the arrest and charging of the accused: from the gap between date of arrest and date the police opened the case in court, to the patent lack of evidence. He did not press the police officer's claim that the poems purportedly violated the law, nor was any advantage to be had in doing so. An order from higher up was sufficient for the officer to justify his not

[91] *Pol. Capt. Myo Thant* v. *Nyi Nyi Aung and 4*, PW 2, 2 July 2009: 3–5.

having a warrant to enter and go through the room of the accused, as ordinarily required by section 102(1) of the Criminal Procedure Code.

In any case against a public enemy, officials can reinforce the imperative for law and order and foreclose further questioning via recourse to 'the order' from above. The 'order' once invoked has a lexical superiority to any juridical instrument that may be invoked in favour of the defendant. Not only does the order justify action against the accused, it does not require any explanation. Its origins do not need to be probed. Sometimes, they cannot be probed. When the lawyer for Shwe Gyoe and his co-accused asked the investigating officer who assigned him the case, the officer replied cryptically that it 'was a person with the authority to assign me the duty'.[92] The remainder of his testimony was similarly opaque:

Q. Having testified 'Ko Sein Hlaing was interrogated by me', where was he interrogated?
A. I am unable to say; as my unit is investigating a great many crimes that must be kept secret I am unable to reveal our interrogating places.
Q. You are appearing as a witness to be examined before the court for reason of having been an interrogating officer of Ko Sein Hlaing.
A. Correct.
Q. After arresting Ko Sein Hlaing on March 16, 2009, was the interrogation at the Aungthapyay Camp?
A. I cannot reveal if it was so or not.[93]

Police officers working on cases against public enemies can insist on secrecy for operational reasons and because they are working consistently with administrative principles, as well as with the overarching imperative for law and order. In the case of Kyaw Soe and two other defendants accused of travelling to Thailand illegally in 2006, the complainant officer declined to answer basic questions about how he got information that the accused had committed an offence, on what date he had received the information, or why at least a year had passed between the unspecified date of the alleged offence and his lodgement of a complaint in court.[94] In a related case, another officer said he had investigated some accused as part of a joint operation, but when the

[92] *Pol. Capt. Myat Kyi* v. *Sein Hlaing and 3*, PW 1, 22 Sept. 2009: 10.
[93] *Pol. Capt. Myat Kyi* v. *Sein Hlaing and 3*, PW1: 4.
[94] *Pol. Capt. Myo Thant* v. *Kam Lam Khut* (a) *Kyaw Soe and 2*, 2008 Criminal Case 354, South Dagon Township Court, PW 1, 19 Mar. 2008.

defence attorney asked him to name the other agencies involved, he replied that he was not authorised to reveal details.[95] Quite possibly, one of the other agencies was from the army, which is explicit about the prerogative of secrecy that it enjoys in matters before courts: 'The Armed Forces cannot submit as evidence any secret documentary or telegraphic supporting [evidentiary] material,' a staff member wrote in one earlier case, 'Likewise, Armed Forces informants should not be called to testify, so as not to jeopardise guarantees for their security.'[96]

In sum, efficient pursuit of the public enemy requires that things *not* be done publicly, whether during investigation or during the court process. The record of investigation and courtroom activity exists because the law-and-order imperative requires it. What goes on the record is independent from what the police actually do. To maintain law and order, which is to say, the semblance of orderliness, the factual existence of the record matters more than what it contains.

The records of trials involving public enemies sometimes feature defence lawyers – pleaders or advocates – who persistently and belligerently cross-examine policemen and other prosecution witnesses, as in those cases cited above.[97] Since procedures entitle the accused to have a defence lawyer; since courts are animated by a political ideal in which adherence to procedure matters, and since the presence or absence of a lawyer makes no difference to the outcome to a case, some public enemies have access to lawyers, and some lawyers in Myanmar see themselves as part of a long tradition of defending public enemies.[98] Where present, the defence lawyer can help create a record that starkly reveals the incongruities between how a case is processed and its outcome. But he does not do so always: some public enemies cannot retain legal counsel; some do not want any. And lawyers representing public enemies run the risk of also becoming criminalised adversaries, not just adversaries within the confines of criminal procedure.

Among the small band of lawyers who took up cases on behalf of public enemies in the 2000s, U Aung Thane and U Khin Maung Shein

95 *Pol. Capt. Myo Thant* v. *Kam Lam Khut* (a) *Kyaw Soe and 2*, 2008 Criminal Case 353, South Dagon Township Court, PW 2, 26 Mar. 2008.

96 Dept. of Defence Headquarters (Army), Letter 152/1/Oo 1, 8 July 1994, par. 8.

97 Newly licenced lawyers become 'higher grade pleaders', who can practice in all courts except the Supreme Court. After three years of practice, they may apply to become advocates, and work in the Supreme Court, too (Courts Manual, par. 3). In this book I use the term 'lawyer' for both types.

98 See further, Nick Cheesman and Kyaw Min San, 'Not Just Defending; Advocating for Law in Myanmar', *Wisconsin International Law Journal* 31.3 (2014): 702–33.

in 2008 represented a group of political activists, one of whom verbally informed the court that as they 'no longer had faith in the judiciary' they wished to withdraw power of attorney.[99] According to the lawyers, the judge instructed that the reason for withdrawal of power of attorney be put in writing and submitted through the lawyers. When they followed her instruction, she accused the lawyers of making up the statement that the defendants had lost faith in the judiciary, and lodged a complaint for contempt. Neither lawyer was invited to a hearing. Neither had an opportunity to see the verdict prior to receiving four months' imprisonment. After release, each received a perfunctory notice informing him that the Supreme Court had revoked his licence to practice.[100] Again, neither was offered a chance to make a defence.

The dearth of professional bodies to defend lawyers' interests meant that those lawyers who in the 1990s and 2000s faced accusations of misconduct had little professional support. They also had few avenues for complaint if unfairly judged or if removed for trivial reasons. By law, cases of misconduct should go to the Bar Council, which can inquire by itself or refer the matter to the judiciary. Rules for holding inquiries are set out in the relevant statutes.[101] In the past, the law reports published some cases of lawyers appealing against action by the Bar Council.[102] After 1989, the suspension or dismissal of lawyers went on without information being made public, a matter for judges alone to investigate and decide on. As in other aspects of their work, judges went about this task without making any information public, or even without making their inquiries known to the accused professionals.

U Myat Hla, a retired lawyer, won a seat in the 1990 general election in which he received the most primary votes of any candidate in the country.[103] When parliament was not called, he went back to practice and had a large caseload. In 1992, a client brought a politically motivated complaint against him. Instead of the matter going to the Bar Council for a preliminary inquiry, military intelligence officers

[99] *Daw Naw Than Than Aye v. U Aung Thane and Another*, 2008 Criminal Misc. Revision Application 99, Supreme Court, respondents' rebuttal submission, 6 Nov. 2008: 1.

[100] SC Order 46/2009, 15 May 2009.

[101] Bar Council Act, India Act 38/26, sec. 10–13. Legal Practitioners Act, India Act 18/1879, sec. 13–15.

[102] For example, *In the matter of Messrs. L & T, a firm of advocates*, 1956 BLR (HC) 40; *In the matter of a pleader*, 1960 BLR (HC) 487; *U Thein Lun*, 1972 BLR (CC) 72 (in Burmese); *In the matter of an advocate*, 1985 BLR (CCJ) 81.

[103] *Myanma Alin* Aung Than, ed., *Record of the 1990 Multiparty Democratic General Election* (Yangon: Aungsitthi, 1992) 60 (in Burmese).

investigated and had charges lodged in court. After two years, the lawyer and two co-accused succeeded in getting the case discharged. In the interim, he was suspended. After he was acquitted, he expected the Supreme Court to restore his license. It did not. He was unable to continue practice.

Another lawyer said that in 2007 she wrote complaints to various authorities concerning the arbitrary arrest and physical abuse of a defence witness in a case she represented. She subsequently learned that a senior judge was investigating her complaint. She heard nothing further until 2011, when she read a notice posted at her court that the Supreme Court had suspended her license for one year because she had complained to executive authorities, rather than via an application to a higher court, and that this act constituted a breach of the lawyers' code of conduct.[104] The notice said the Supreme Court had suspended her pursuant to an investigation of the Bar Council, but like Aung Thane and Khin Maung Shein, she was never called for any inquiry.

In November 2011, Aung Thane and Khin Maung Shein were among sixteen deregistered lawyers who submitted a petition to the country's new president asking for their licences back.[105] Happily, both lawyers in 2012 succeeded in having their licences restored. They have since returned to practice, as have many other previously disbarred lawyers, including other signatories to the petition. One who received a six-month jail term *in absentia* for his part in defending public enemies in 2012 returned from exile only to be arrested and jailed.[106] He was released after almost three months in prison through an act of pardon: the topic with which this chapter closes, since it brings the discussion back to the concept of sovereign *cetana*.

A NOTE ON PARDON

In Myanmar, all governments since the colonial period have used pardon for political purposes.[107] In 1963, Ne Win went personally to

[104] See Bar Council, *Lawyers' Code of Conduct, Responsibilities and Rights*, 3rd edn. (Yangon: Office of the Attorney General, 2001) (in Burmese).

[105] 'National Victims of Human Rights Violations', letter, 4 Nov. 2011.

[106] *U Aung Myint Than* v. *Saw Kyaw Kyaw Min*, 2012 Criminal Case 34, Yangon Western District Court, 29 Aug. 2012.

[107] In Burmese, the term used for both pardon and amnesty is *lutngyein-chanthagwin*. Pardon is sometimes distinguished from amnesty by prefixing the term with 'sentence' (*pyitdan*). The three postcolonial constitutions use the term differently: compare Burmese and English versions of article 60 in 1947, article 73(o) in 1974 and article 204 in 2008. The 1947 text

the central prison before he released convicts under a general amnesty order of the same year, telling them to remain quiet when they got out and not 'make more work for us'.[108] Throughout the 1990s and 2000s, military governments also issued pardons. But the distinguishing characteristic of pardons since 2011 is that they have deliberately included public enemies among their recipients.[109]

Far from being a departure from the politics of law and order, the restoration of sovereign *cetana* to the public enemy via pardon is among its essential characteristics. Pardons, like amnesties, are fundamentally political instruments.[110] Rather than being an assurance of the restoration of legality, they constitute its opposite. The accused public enemy who receives a pardon has the *cetana* of the sovereign power restored to him – not via acknowledgement that he is innocent, but via reiteration that he is guilty, with the accompanying acknowledgement that the sovereign is merciful and munificent; that the state has 'loving kindness [*metta*] and *cetana*' for all its citizens.[111] The pardon perfects sovereign *cetana*. It brings the exercise of its withdrawal full circle, by magically restoring something arbitrarily withdrawn, not by correcting the wrongs done to the person, but through dogged insistence that no wrongs have been committed at all – other than by the person pardoned. The pardon thereby reinforces the same political and juridical structure for the denial of rights that led the person to be classed as a public enemy in the first place.[112] It confirms the liberty, not of the pardon's recipient,

is consistent with sections 337–39 of the Criminal Procedure Code, concerning judicial pardon. Presidential clemency is in section 401 of the code termed 'remission' of sentence (*lutngyein-thetthagwin*).

108 Revolutionary Council, *The General Amnesty, and Explanation* ([Rangoon]: Office of the Dept. of Information, 1963) 29 (in Burmese).

109 According to a United Nations report of September 2013, 'Since May 2011, there have been eleven presidential amnesties resulting in the release of 951 prisoners of conscience.' Tomás Ojea Quintana, *Situation of Human Rights in Myanmar* (New York: UN General Assembly, 2013) 3. At the end of 2013, the president issued another order pardoning persons convicted and being prosecuted of certain categories of political crime. Office of the President, Order 51/2013, 30 Dec. 2013.

110 Renée Jeffery, *Amnesties, Accountability, and Human Rights* (Philadelphia: University of Pennsylvania Press, 2014) 31.

111 *Myanma Alin* 13 Jan. 2012: 1.

112 Supreme Court records affirm that findings of guilt stand irrespective of pardon, and remain relevant to other determinations after the person's release from imprisonment. See Letter 1265/170-YaNa (95), 13 Dec. 1995.

but of the sovereign, who arrogates the power to restore arbitrarily something withdrawn arbitrarily.[113]

The pardon is the corollary of the denial of rights through the exercise of sovereign *cetana*, its crowning achievement, and its fulfilment. Through pardon, the risky and undesirable life again becomes deserving.[114] In declaring the danger that the life of the detainee once posed is no longer present, the pardon restores to the individual the delimited rights that she has lost, and extends the sovereign's largesse to the entire body politic, through reassurance that a moment of danger, which the public enemy once represented, has passed. By extending *cetana* to the individual, the sovereign not only restores a life worth living but also reaffirms to all subjects that by virtue of their relationship to the sovereign power their lives too are worthwhile.

CONCLUSION

The new government that seized power in 1988 proposed to do nothing with courts other than use them to enforce its specific order. It would not attempt to shape human society through juridical instruments, as the Benthamites had hoped to do; nor guard the liberties of citizens, as the post-independence courts had professed was their responsibility; nor shape a new economic and moral order of the sort expressed via the post-1962 ideology. It would do no more and no less than maintain its specific order under the rubric of the rule of law.

In this chapter I have looked at two distinctive features of this 'rule of law' as law and order, namely, the exercise of sovereign *cetana* and its corollary, the identification and criminalisation of the public enemy.

In court, the public enemy is an exemplary object for administrative action. The public enemy provides participants in the courtroom process the opportunity to show their commitment to core political ideals, through cooperative efforts to maintain law and order. Participants demonstrate their abilities and willingness to give effect to these ideals through a shared understanding of their respective roles in the administrative continuum. But the case against the public enemy

[113] As discussed in Jacques Derrida, 'Le siecle et le pardon', *Le Monde des Débats* 9 (1999), 10 Aug. 2013 http://hydra.humanities.uci.edu/derrida/siecle.html (in French).

[114] Claudia Aradau, 'Securing Life: Human Trafficking, Biopolitics, and the Sovereign Pardon', *Accumulating Insecurity: Violence and Dispossession in the Making of Everyday Life*, eds. Shelley Feldman, Charles Geisler, and Gayatri A. Menon (Athens: University of Georgia Press, 2011) 168.

also demonstrates the greatest incongruence between official action and declared rule. Expediency demands an outcome that satisfies the imperatives for law and order, independent of declared rules. Consequently, legal rules are emptied of the normative generality that makes them legal.

The juridical framework for the relationship between the sovereign power and the person denied the sovereign's *cetana* has larger implications than those consequences specific to the case of the public enemy. Where the exercise of sovereign *cetana* delimits legal rights, all citizens are put in a new type of relationship with power, in which the notion of citizenship is downgraded generally. From a condition where rights accrue to the individual through a juridical standing that requires no particular demonstration of fidelity to sovereign power, the citizen finds herself in a new relationship, one in which conditional privileges are contingent on her implicit acknowledgement of the sovereign's generosity in granting them. The restoration of sovereign *cetana* to convicts through the act of pardon reinforces this relationship. It assures them that the sovereign is generous, and reminds them that the sovereign is dangerous too.

5

EMBODYING THE LAW AND ORDER IDEAL

The police, Giorgio Agamben has argued, are most proximate to the relationship between violence and right that characterises and preserves the power of the sovereign, because they occupy 'the place where the proximity and the almost constitutive exchange between violence and right that characterizes the figure of the sovereign is shown more nakedly and clearly than anywhere else'.[1] The judge or prosecutor transmits messages as to what constitutes legitimate and illegitimate violence, through interpretive acts.[2] These acts of interpretation are, Pierre Bourdieu has observed, 'designed to determine practical effects'.[3] However, the effects are not instantaneous. The police remain closer in their proximity to sovereign power because they decide and act on the constitutive relationship in the moment, each time they are confronted with an alleged offender.

If the policeman occupies and enlarges an area of indistinction symmetrical to sovereignty where the right of the sovereign to exert violence plays out in the individual case, then in Myanmar this area is further complicated and expanded under conditions in which

[1] Giorgio Agamben, *Means without End: Notes on Politics*, trans. Vincenzo Binetti and Cesare Casarino (Minneapolis and London: University of Minnesota Press, 2000) 104.

[2] Robert Cover, 'Violence and the Word', *Yale Law Journal* 95.8 (1986): 1601–29. See also Austin Sarat and Thomas R. Kearns, 'Making Peace with Violence: Robert Cover on Law and Legal Theory', *Law's Violence*, eds. Austin Sarat and Thomas R. Kearns (Ann Arbor: University of Michigan Press, 1992) 211–50.

[3] Pierre Bourdieu, 'The Force of Law: Toward a Sociology of the Juridical Field', *Hastings Law Journal* 38 (1987): 818.

rationales of public order and security are especially pronounced.[4] In this setting, the policeman is a bearer of political and juridical power that exceeds the formal role assigned to him in criminal procedure. His place is unusually magnified. Consequently, his essential features, his immanent political qualities, are more clearly visible than in other settings, where his role may be less pronounced, his institution obscured by other rationales, institutions, and personnel.

This chapter concentrates on the essentially political quality of the policeman through study of torture to extract confession.[5] In the moment of torture, the sovereign power of the policeman is most clearly manifest. It is, in the language of Walter Benjamin, at once lawmaking and law-preserving: significant in its marriage of both means and ends.[6] Through the act of torture, the policeman exerts power over juridical institutions, as well as over the tortured person.

The chapter's focus on torture to extract confession – as distinct from torture to discipline or punish, or to obtain information, for instance – is deliberately narrow.[7] The quintessence of judicial torture, which is to say, torture referential to a judicial process, is its instrumentality in extracting confession. Another reason for the narrow focus is that torture to extract confessions is possibly the most widespread form of contemporary torture, in Myanmar and worldwide.[8] The focus does not imply that torture for purposes other than obtaining confession is uncommon to Myanmar. However, other uses of torture are not judicial torture because they do not refer directly to the process of trial or to the politics of courts.[9]

4 I refer to the 'policeman' in the singular throughout this chapter to denote an archetype. I refer to him in the masculine because the police force in Myanmar is overwhelmingly male; over 98 percent male, according to Andrew Selth, 'Burma's Police Forces: Continuities and Contradictions', 32, *Regional Outlook Paper* (Brisbane: Griffith Asia Institute, 2011) 9. Furthermore, all of the cases documented here involved male police officers exclusively.

5 By 'essential political quality' I do not mean a quality that is unchanging and stable across time, but rather, those specific attributes of the policeman that speak to his political character and function. On mutable essences, see Ann Laura Stoler, *Along the Archival Grain: Epistemic Anxieties and Colonial Common Sense* (Princeton and Oxford: Princeton University Press, 2009) 4.

6 Walter Benjamin, 'Critique of Violence', *Reflections: Essays, Aphorisms, Autobiographical Writings*, trans. Edmund Jephcott, ed. Peter Demetz (New York: Schocken, 1986) 286–87.

7 For a wide-ranging discussion see Darius Rejali, *Torture and Democracy* (Princeton and Oxford: Princeton University Press, 2007).

8 The 'vast majority of cases' documented by a United Nations expert on torture are of this type. Manfred Nowak, *Study of the Phenomena of Torture, Cruel, Inhuman or Degrading Treatment or Punishment in the World, Including an Assessment of Conditions of Detention* (New York: UN General Assembly, 2010), 19.

9 On torture of convicted prisoners, for instance, see Aung Tha (PPP) and Aung Saw Oo, *The Myanmar Prison System in the Era of Military Dictatorship* (Yangon: Zinyadanazaw, 2013) ch. 5 (in Burmese).

The chapter begins by tracing the lineage of judicial torture to the colonial period, and considers how courts have acquiesced in its use. It then narrates some cases so as to explore how judicial torture binds the tortured to sovereign power, creating a twofold embodiment of the law-and-order ideal, consisting of subject and object – one mobilised, the other perfectly immobilised. Lastly, it explores the inherently transactional quality of judicial torture, which always invites, or demands, an exchange of some sort.[10]

A couple of brief observations remain. First, the politics of the police in Myanmar are partly determined by the close subordinate role of the police force to the military over the last couple of decades. Military commanders have called the police force the 'brother' of the armed forces.[11] The sibling relationship is in part due to how military and policing functions were integrated from the 1960s onward, in part the result of a project in the 1990s to make the police force more responsive to the army's needs and commands. A review of the army-managed police reform project is beyond the scope of this book.[12] However, it is relevant to this discussion insofar as it has broader political implications. By bringing the police force closer to political power, the military privileged the station and role of the police when compared with other juridical institutions. The brother, although having weak corporate power when compared with his sibling, in the courtroom is his representative. And since the military in the 1990s and 2000s claimed sovereign power, and has continued to present itself as the guardian of sovereignty, the policeman, not the judge, is the de facto guardian in the courtroom.[13]

[10] The transactional quality of judicial torture I describe in this chapter approaches theorists' 'economic model' of the phenomenon; however, it does not presume that torturers seek a factual confession or reliable information, as in the literature on 'ticking-bomb' arguments. See J. Jeremy Wisnewski and R. Dillon Emerick, *The Ethics of Torture* (London and New York: Continuum, 2009) ch. 2.

[11] For example, 'The Myanmar Police Force is the brother armed force of the Defence Services and is a key organisation for regional peace and tranquillity and the rule of law.' Senior General Than Shwe speaking on Defence Services Day 1998 cited in Ministry of Home Affairs, *Ministry of Home Affairs: Historical Record and Achievements* ([Yangon]: Govt. of the Union of Myanmar, 2000) 43 (in Burmese).

[12] On the structural reconfigurations of the police force in this period, see Ei Ei Zaw, 'A Study on [*sic*] the Changing Role of [the] Myanmar Police Force (1988–2000)', MRes diss., Yangon University, 2002. See also Andrew Selth, 'Police Reform in Myanmar: Changes "in Essence and Appearance"', *Debating Democratization in Myanmar*, eds. Nick Cheesman, Nicholas Farrelly, and Trevor Wilson (Singapore: ISEAS, 2014) 205–28.

[13] Article 20(e) of the 2008 Constitution reads, 'The primary responsibility to ensure the non-disintegration of the union, non-disintegration of national solidarity and enduring sovereignty lies with the Armed Forces' (my translation).

Second, while this chapter concerns how the law-and-order ideal shapes the relationship between the policeman and court, the presence and practices of the military and the policing functions of a range of other institutions complicate that relationship. Policemen are not the only people to investigate criminal offences and bring cases to court in Myanmar. Others to do so include officials from the immigration and population ministry, municipal authorities in major cities, the Bureau of Special Investigation under the home affairs ministry, and military intelligence. A variety of agencies also take part in routine security and policing operations. Personnel making arrests or searching premises might include firemen, auxiliary firemen, customs officers, education committee members, video scrutiny officers, and religious departmental staff members. Consequently, the notion of the policeman is in some respects amorphous – a point taken up further in Chapter 7, on the management of unauthorised assemblies. Nevertheless, the police as investigators of crimes ordinarily bring cases to court, and they dominate the country's courtrooms. Therefore, the chapter is concerned mainly, but not exclusively, with policemen.

JUDICIAL TORTURE

Torture by the police in Myanmar is a type of judicial torture. To be sure, it is not the judicial torture of history: a formal part of the criminal process, in Europe and in Asia.[14] It is nowadays in most places unofficial – not openly endorsed in policy documents, and informally organised and learned.[15] However, it has instrumental qualities anchored in judicial institutions.[16] The police and others acting on their behalf or together with them torture either for specific judicial purposes – to obtain confession or at least complaisance of the accused when brought to court – or for ancillary purposes, such as to make money via threats that invoke judicial authority, as discussed in Chapter 6. In this sense, it corresponds with classical and early modern

[14] On Europe, see John H. Langbein, *Torture and the Law of Proof: Europe and England in the Ancien Régime* (Chicago and London: University of Chicago Press, 1976). Judicial torture in precolonial Burma is described in U Aung Than Tun, *History of Myanmar Dhammasats*, vol. III, 3 vols. (Yangon: Sarpay Beikman, 2007) 384–91 (in Burmese); Govt. of Burma, *Gazetter of Burma*, vol. I, 2 vols. (New Delhi: Gian, 1987) 478–79.

[15] Piet Van Reenen, 'Routine Police Torture: Towards a Personalistic Analysis and Strategy', *Journal of Human Rights* 1.4 (2002): 542–43.

[16] On the instrumental quality of torture see Paul Kenny, 'The Meaning of Torture', *Polity* 42.2 (2010): 131–55.

conceptions of torture as judicial practice, 'inflicted by a public authority for ostensibly public purposes'.[17]

This chapter is not concerned with torture as punishment, imposed once the judicial process is completed, but with torture occurring as part of the judicial process. Torture in this process is a strategy used in the procedural game, one preceding other parts of the game, which if done properly will yield the required result, just like other procedural steps. The trial or threat of trial hangs over the act of torture, present in the inverted process of interrogation and confession, present also in the promise that the accused will have his day in court once the formalities of the police are completed to their satisfaction.

At the same time, in cases where the police resort to judicial torture, the most important part of the process occurs even before the trial has started. Once the policeman has a confession, he has, in one sense, consummated the criminal inquiry. Everything else happens after the fact of the confession. Torture or threat of torture alludes to the courtroom, but inverts its procedure. The judge must consider evidence so as to assign punishment. The policeman punishes, or threatens to punish, because he needs evidence.[18] An accused may retract the confession and insist he was tortured, but by this point he has already yielded to procedure and has participated in establishing his own guilt. Even if he denies a confession, it remains the centrepiece of the trial, only now the question turns on its veracity. Therefore, the policeman's use of torture to obtain confession is not simply a form of physical abuse. It is an act of tremendous juridical and political power.

The stages in the procedural game that integrates torture require police officers to bring an accused to confess before a magistrate, prohibit a statement given to a policeman from being used as evidence, and also stipulate that any confession apparently taken through inducement, threat, or promise is illegal.[19] The Courts Manual reminds a judge receiving a confession that,

> It is his duty to satisfy himself in every reasonable way that the confession is made voluntarily, and with this end in view he should endeavour to ascertain the exact circumstances leading up to the confession, the length of time during which the accused has been in the custody of the

[17] Edward Peters, *Torture* (Philadelphia: University of Pennsylvania Press, 1996) 3.

[18] Elaine Scarry, *The Body in Pain: The Making and Unmaking of the World* (Oxford: Oxford University Press, 1985) 41.

[19] Criminal Procedure Code, sec. 162–64; Evidence Act, India Act 1/1872, sec. 24–26.

> police and whether any action on the part of the police may have induced the accused to confess. He should, whenever feasible before recording the confession of the accused give him a few hours for reflection in circumstances in which he cannot be influenced by the police.[20]

Superficially, these provisions aim to minimise if not eliminate torture. Against this purpose, I argue that they have the effect of bringing judges into a procedural game for the vindication of torture, by making them complicit in its performance, or the threat of its performance.

To erase law's complicity in the regime of judicial torture, to neutralise the act of torture while effectively endorsing it, judges signal publicly that torture is undesirable. Ever since colonial times, official records and rulings have contained reminders about the need for voluntariness in giving confessions, especially 'in this country, where the Police are so prone to induce prisoners to confess, and where evidence is so frequently manufactured, and sometimes in a skilful and not a clumsy manner'.[21] The apex court in one such case criticised a magistrate and appellate judge for failing to inquire whether or not an accused had voluntarily confessed, recording the latter as in effect having said 'that if a person tells a Magistrate that he is about to make a confession voluntarily there is no intrinsic reason why the Magistrate should disbelieve him', continuing that

> If he were right, that object [to protect persons against forced confession] would be frustrated in every case by the police inducing would-be confessing prisoners to start their statements before a Magistrate with statements similar to the one made before the Magistrate in this case. . . . In view of the propensity of the police to induce prisoners to confess the Legislature has imposed on Magistrates the duty of making a substantial inquiry for themselves as to the voluntary nature of a confession, and unless such enquiry is made, a confession even before a Magistrate is not admissible in evidence.[22]

In a subsequent case, the court made clear that police records of an accused person's words including any incriminating statement would not be admissible evidence.[23] Furthermore, no witness or police officer could be asked in court about what was said during investigation, unless the accused doubted whether a witness statement in court was the same

[20] Courts Manual, par. 602(3). [21] *Shwe Sin and Another* v. *King-Emperor*, 3 LBR 213, 214.

[22] *Thein Maung* v. *King-Emperor*, 3 LBR 173, 174, 75. The 'legislature' here refers to the legislative council that passed the codes in India.

[23] *Mi Ein Tha and Mi O Za* v. *King-Emperor*, 5 LBR 131.

as what he or she said to the police. If so, the accused could ask for the police statement to be put on record, for comparison and cross-examination.[24] Where police induced an accused to confess, even though material evidence corroborated the statement, it was inadmissible.[25] A village headman who told a man that he would not be punished if he had information about a murder had, the court found, induced the defendant, and that evidence too was inadmissible.[26]

Where a colonial policeman or other official proved too savage or inept in his use of violence, he could land in trouble. Colonial judges were at pains to distinguish their regime from what they saw as the arbitrary brutality of the predecessor 'Burmese *régime*'.[27] In one case from Upper Burma that went to trial following the death of the tortured person, a court convicted a police officer of assaulting a woman with a hammer to make her confess to a crime.[28] The police detained her for three days without getting her medical treatment. She died five days after her release. In another case, a police officer on appealing to the court in Mandalay against his sentence for torturing a prisoner to extract a confession had the sentence enhanced as an exemplary punishment to remind the police of their duty to protect, not persecute, members of the public.[29] But such cases were uncommon. They had as their purpose to manage rather than to eliminate the use of torture in criminal procedure. They instructed the police on how to exercise control over the body of the tortured *and* over the criminal process, by obscuring evidence of torture, and keeping routine practices of torture within certain bounds, aimed at achieving specific outcomes.

Colonial courts in many cases disbelieved allegations of torture made as grounds for retracted confession.[30] The tortured body carried the burden of producing evidence to prove the abuse. Where the signs of torture had faded, where the accused was too frightened to show the evidence of abuse, or where the torture did not leave physical evidence, judges dismissed complaints of torture as uncorroborated and unreliable.[31] In any case, a confession once made could stand as evidence, irrespective of whether or not an accused person retracted it

[24] *Bana Singh* v. *King-Emperor*, 6 Ran. 137. [25] *Gaung Gyi* v. *King-Emperor*, 4 LBR 244.

[26] *Nga Kya Thein* v. *King-Emperor*, 8 LBR 94.

[27] *Nga Po Mya* v. *Queen-Empress*, (1897–1901) 1 UBR 320, 322, citing the lower court ruling on the need to stamp out the extorting of confessions.

[28] *Nga Shwe Baw* v. *Queen-Empress*, (1897–1901) 1 UBR 285. [29] *Nga Po Mya*.

[30] For example, *Nga Myat Kyaw* v. *Queen-Empress*, (1897–1901) 1 UBR 41; *Nga Shwe Tat* v. *Queen-Empress*, (1897–1901) 1 UBR 152; *Shwe Yi* v. *Crown*, 1 LBR 336 FB; *Nga Pyan* v. *Crown*, 1 LBR 359; *Shwe Hnit and One* v. *King-Emperor*, 2 LBR 214.

[31] *Maung Tun Hla* v. *Queen-Empress*, (1892–96) 1 UBR 221.

later.[32] Police officers could devote their energies towards getting a detainee to confess with the assurance that a confession would have a good chance of standing up in court. Summing up the scepticism of the superior judiciary towards persons retracting confessions on grounds of abuse, one judge remarked that 'the appellants withdrew their confessions for the most part under the excuse that they were the outcome of force or menace . . . and they tendered no evidence in support of the bare allegation, which is of the kind almost invariably put forward as a last resource'.[33] No doubt the statement contains some truth: people say and do things to try to escape punishment. But by placing the onus on defendants to show evidence of torture, judges could participate with police officers in the procedural game to integrate torture into the judicial process, not remove it, as the colonial statutes and manuals presuppose.

Taylor Sherman describes the use of such violence in the colonial period as 'permitted transgressions' of standing orders on use of force.[34] In my view, this conceptualisation is inadequate. Colonial courts did not just permit transgressions. They participated actively in them. Anupama Rao captures the phenomenon better when she writes that colonial law joined in a regime of torture while also seeking to erase its own complicity through the juridical process.[35] Erasure is exactly the right word. Everything the judge must do in participating in a regime of torture comes after the fact of torture. In this inversion of roles between judge and policeman, the act of torture is potent. The judge does not prevent the policeman from torturing, but must situate his use of torture in the criminal juridical frame. Only where his practices are so egregious or incompetent as to threaten the semblance of orderliness does the judge decline to play this role and instead sanctions the officer or officers involved.[36]

After independence, changed political conditions for a time enlarged the space where people could have complaints of torture and police

32 *Nga Po Kauk and One* v. *King-Emperor*, 4 Ran. 45.

33 *Nga Kain and 11* v. *Queen-Empress*, (1897–1901) 1 UBR 252, 253.

34 Taylor C. Sherman, *State Violence and Punishment in India* (London and New York: Routledge, 2010) 10.

35 Anupama Rao, 'Problems of Violence, States of Terror: Torture in Colonial India', *Interventions: International Journal of Postcolonial Studies* 3.2 (2001): 187.

36 Hence the Courts Manual advises in paragraph 475(1) that although 'allegations of tutoring of witnesses, of the manufacture or suppression of evidence, and of extorting confessions of guilt by threats or inducements, are sometimes adopted as the line of defence . . . for the protection of the police-force . . . judicial comments on such allegations should be carefully weighed'.

abuse heard. Nonetheless, the superior courts stuck to the principle that once a confession was recorded as set down in criminal procedure the judge in a trial was entitled to presume it was genuine.[37] A retracted confession could still stand as proof of a crime if a judge said he believed it was true, and had been made voluntarily. The basic rules of the procedural game remained largely unchanged – namely, that a judge takes confession and that it appears to be given voluntarily. As late as 1959, the year after the first military-run government took power, the Supreme Court issued a notice that it had observed an increased number of convictions in serious criminal cases based on confessions.[38] It said that these convictions would be fatally flawed where, for instance, a judge had failed to check carefully for evidence of torture on the body of the person giving the confession, or where identical confessions were submitted for two accused.

But in the 1991 *Ye Naung* case the Supreme Court changed the rules of the game.[39] Since this case speaks loudly to how courts in Myanmar have evoked the law-and-order ideal, and since it has not previously been the subject of scholarly research, I will set it out briefly before turning to its implications.

Ye Naung was a non-commissioned army officer accused of stealing and selling ammunition from an army base. In 1988, customs officers had caught some other accused persons red-handed. The police opened a case with proof of the munitions found in the men's possession. But no material evidence implicated either Ye Naung or his co-respondent. The evidence against them consisted solely of their retracted confessions, and corroborating confessions of two other accused.

The trouble was that military intelligence had taken Ye Naung's confession.[40] As already noted, statute is explicit that non-judicial officers can neither record nor submit confessions to court. So too

[37] Evidence Act, sec. 80. See *Union of Burma* v. *Ah Hla* (a) *Maung Hla and 2*, 1958 BLR (HC) 29; *Union of Burma* v. *Aung Tun* (a) *Aung Myint*, *Aung Tun* (a) *Aung Myint* v. *Union of Burma*, 1958 BLR (SC) 1.

[38] General Letter 15/59, 15 June 1959.

[39] *Union of Myanmar* v. *U Ye Naung and Another*, 1991 MLR 63. In keeping with the shift in Anglicised nomenclature from Burma to Myanmar in 1989, the citations from this point refer to the Myanmar Law Reports (MLR) of the Supreme Court.

[40] On the history and functions of the intelligence service, see James McAndrew, 'From Combat to Karaoke: Burmese Military Intelligence, 1948–2006', MSc diss., National Defense Intelligence College, Washington, DC, 2007; Andrew Selth, 'Burma's Intelligence Apparatus', *Intelligence and National Security* 13.4 (1998): 33–70.

is case law.[41] Accordingly, a single Supreme Court judge in 1989 acquitted the two accused because the confession was inadmissible. The prosecutor subsequently made a special appeal.

In 1991, the Supreme Court bench overturned the previous order and restored the conviction from a lower court. It achieved this result by avoiding the real issue of whether or not a confession to military intelligence is admissible, restricting its inquiry to whether or not the lower courts in accepting a confession taken by military intelligence personnel had violated section 24 of the Evidence Act, that 'a confession made by an accused person is irrelevant in a criminal proceeding, if the making of the confession appears to the Court to have been caused by any inducement, threat or promise'. To put it another way, rather than ask whether or not it was procedurally correct for the lower court to receive confessions obtained by military intelligence personnel, the superior court only asked if the accused had evidence that military intelligence had tortured them. Finding none, it concluded that 'in the absence of indication that [the confessions] were obtained on account of inducement, threat or promise as stipulated in the Evidence Act, section 24 there is *no reason not to accept* the said interrogation statements given to Armed Forces intelligence personnel'.[42]

According to one practitioner, *Ye Naung* 'shocked' the legal world in Myanmar.[43] Given the shocks this little world had already suffered over the previous decades, his statement ought not be taken lightly. Even by the standards of the time, the ruling was blatant in its endorsement of military impunity and comprehensive in its defeat of legal doctrine. To advance the doctrine of truth, Maung Maung as chief justice had undermined the burden of proof. His successor Aung Toe effectively shifted the burden without offering any explanation at all. As one lawyer in another case pointed out when appealing a decision based on the ruling, *Ye Naung* had unfairly placed the onus on his client to

41 See *Sobika Rahman* v. *Union of Burma*, 1952 BLR (HC) 385; *Maung Tun Tin* v. *Union of Burma*, 1965 BLR (CC) 185; *Maung Thein* v. *Union of Burma*, 1966 BLR (CC) 158 (in Burmese); *Maung Than* v. *Union of Burma*, 1973 BLR (CC) 24 (in Burmese); *U Min* v. *Socialist Republic of the Union of Burma*, 1977 BLR (CCJ) 22; *Maung Ko Ni* v. *Socialist Republic of the Union of Burma*, 1980 BLR (CCJ) 7; *U Sein Tun* v. *Socialist Republic of the Union of Burma*, 1980 BLR (CCJ) 13; *Maung Tint Swe* v. *Socialist Republic of the Union of Burma*, 1980 BLR (CCJ) 20; *Maung Soe Myint* v. *Socialist Republic of the Union of Burma*, 1981 BLR (CCJ) 28.

42 *U Ye Naung*, 69. My italics.

43 Kyaw Min San, 'Critical Issues for the Rule of Law in Myanmar', *Myanmar's Transition: Openings, Obstacles and Opportunities*, eds. Nick Cheesman, Monique Skidmore, and Trevor Wilson (Singapore: ISEAS, 2012) 222.

prove she had *not* been tortured.[44] And the onus was not only reversed in certain types of exceptional cases. The ruling constituted a general repudiation of statute.

The Supreme Court in *Ye Naung* stepped back from its traditional role as a participant in the procedural game associated with judicial torture: not out of concern for its own position or out of repugnance at the practices of military intelligence, but out of acquiescence to the sovereign power embodied in the intelligence officers involved. Hereafter, instead of acting as doorkeepers, ensuring that confessions obtained by torture would comply superficially with the requirements of the procedural game, judges were obligated to leave the door open – at least in those cases that policemen brought at the behest of military intelligence.

Through the open door, cases came. Police officers lodged cases on the back of confessions purportedly taken from political activists by military intelligence, like five men accused of sending a statement to the Voice of America radio station via the United States embassy; three who issued and distributed a statement from a student union without approval, and others accused of having contact with unlawful groups abroad.[45] Public enemies were not the only ones to have confessions taken in military intelligence custody used against them. Police in the country's north, for instance, insisted that a township judge and a lawyer accused of illegality had also confessed to army intelligence personnel, a third accused making his confession 'as per his wish' at the township court.[46] The records of the case offer no explanation as to why a judge and lawyer would confess to soldiers while the third accused enjoyed the opportunity to go before a judge to have his confession recorded.

In 2006, a single Supreme Court judge followed *Ye Naung* but narrowed the ruling somewhat, finding that a confession to military intelligence submitted to court should not be the only evidence on

[44] *Daw Yi Yi Win and 3* v. *Union of Myanmar*, 2006 Special Criminal Appeal Application 19, Supreme Court, 24 Jan. 2006.

[45] *Pol. Capt. Hla Myint* v. *U Aye Kyu* (a) *Monywa Aung Shin and 4*, 2000 Criminal Cases 23–24, Yangon Divisional Court, 14 Dec. 2000; *Pol. Capt. Ye Nyunt* v. *Aung Gyi and 2*, 2003 Criminal Case 1347, South Dagon Township Court (Special), 7 Jan. 2004; *Pol. Capt. Ye Nyunt* v. *Nanda Sit Aung* (a) *Sit Ko Aung and 2*, 2004 Criminal Case 8, Yangon Eastern District Court, 20 Feb. 2004; *Pol. Capt. Ye Nyunt* v. *Yi Yi Win and 3*, 2004 Criminal Cases 74–76, Yangon Western District Court, 23 Sept. 2004. The verdict in each of these cases mentioned *Ye Naung* as the authority for acceptance of a confession or confessions obtained by military intelligence.

[46] Banmaw People's Police Station, Letter 100-KaGaYa/2/Oo 2, 10 Jul. 1994, 6.

which to convict.[47] Whether due to this ruling, new instructions from above, or because the military junta shut down its old intelligence service in 2004, around this time cases seem to have stopped citing *Ye Naung*. But the ruling's spirit, what it represents – the authority of the police to bring cases based on confession possibly obtained by torture or threat of torture – remains integral to the work of the police and courts in Myanmar.

THE POLICEMAN AS SOVEREIGN

In a colonial-era ruling overturning a lower court's sentence of one month's imprisonment for resisting arrest, a superior judge castigated the magistrate for assuming that an arrestee should be handcuffed, even where he resisted a police officer. The judge described the wrongly awarded punishment as grossly excessive, since 'all that is necessary to constitute an arrest is that the arresting officer *shall touch the body of the person to be arrested*. . . . [And] the accused is thereafter in the arresting officer's custody even if that officer does not actually hold or confine him'.[48] Through the policeman, the sovereign reaches out to touch the person. That contact constitutes the full force of law, the coercive power of the state, coming down on the person. It requires him to submit, without obligating the use of physical force. The current of sovereign power electrifies the policeman, binding the person to him, and through him, to the sovereign.

This passage encapsulates how the ideal of law and order through the interventions of a visible power to keep men in awe, to paraphrase Hobbes, secures itself through the contact of two bodies.[49] One is the body of the policeman, who transmits the current of sovereign power, who embodies the sovereign in the moment. The other is the body of the detained, a symmetrical, inverted figure of the sovereign.[50] The policeman's touch is perfectly immobilising: it removes utterly any freedom of movement that the person touched had previously exercised.

The immobilising touch is unlike the interpellating call, which invites the person hailed to submit freely to the policeman by

[47] *U Tin Ngwe, Daw Mya Mya Win* (a) *Daw Than Win* v. *Union of Myanmar*, 2006 MLR 1.

[48] *Tan Sein* (a) *Maung Saing* v. *Crown*, 1 LBR 173, 174. My italics.

[49] Thomas Hobbes, *Leviathan*, ed. Crawford B. Macpherson (Middlesex: Penguin, 1968) 223.

[50] 'In the darkest region of the political field the condemned man represents the symmetrical, inverted figure of the king.' Michel Foucault, *Discipline and Punish: The Birth of the Prison*, trans. Alan Sheridan (London: Allen Lane, 1977) 29.

responding to him.[51] The touch does not recognise the right of the subject to acknowledge his subjectivity of his own accord. The person touched has no alternative but to comply. The policeman may rightfully touch the body of the accused, but the accused has no right to touch the policeman, let alone even to resist his touch. As such, the touch does not preclude the possibility of torture. Instead it precedes it, by establishing a relationship of unilateral power flowing from the policeman as sovereign to the person touched. Far from prohibiting or even inhibiting the use of violence, the jurisprudence of the immobilising touch is intimate with the act of torture.

The policeman as sovereign commits judicial torture using diverse methods, not random ones. Accounts of torture to obtain confession in the narratives of the tortured, their lawyers and family members, letters of complaint about torture submitted to government agencies, and the records of courts from a wide variety of cases speak to routinised and internally regulated practices. Take the case of a man accused of involvement in a bombing during 2010, as told in a letter to higher authorities signed by a relative:

> From the day [he] was arrested and thus detained sixteen police including Inspector Saw Maung interrogated him in pairs on rotation continuously for six days. During the interrogation he was tortured seriously. He was not fed throughout the six days and was given only two handfuls of water per day. [He] was hit in the face and on the cheeks with shoes; was kicked and stomped on the head while his hands were tied with rope at the rear; was forced to kneel on gravel for thirty minutes at a time; had his fingers squeezed together with ball pens between them; had a truncheon pushed into his anus; and, was beaten with truncheons on his back, chest and feet, resulting in serious injuries to his body.[52]

This account contains a number of features of judicial torture in Myanmar. First, teams of police torture detainees: torture is not external to ordinary operating procedure. It is not the work of rogue officers or unusually sadistic individuals; it is ordinary procedure, reinforced through police hierarchy. Second, torture consists of a range of techniques forming a continuum of practices, from the prosaic to

[51] Louis Althusser, 'Ideology and Ideological State Apparatuses (Notes towards an Investigation)', *Louis Althusser Archive*, 2 May 2014, www.marxists.org/reference/archive/althusser/1970/ideology.htm.

[52] In this case and others cited anonymously in the remainder of the book, I have changed the names of persons involved and omitted from the translation any other identifying details. For further discussion on reading and using of sources, see the appendix.

the bizarre. Third, in Myanmar interrogation and confession are largely independent from the question of who committed a crime. In the remainder of this section, I amplify each of these points by narrating a number of cases.

Bombings give rise to cases, like the one described above, involving specialised police agencies staffed with men under pressure who are keen to demonstrate to superiors their ability to apprehend and prosecute culprits quickly. But the police in regular units investigating mundane albeit serious criminal offences also work in teams using similar techniques. Police officers in a rural area of Sagaing in 2010, for instance, detained two men over the rape and murder of a teenage girl. According to a written narrative taken down from one of the men, after a couple of days in the cells without food or water during which time he refused to confess,

> Around 8 p.m. they made me strip naked, handcuffed me behind my back then forced me to kneel for the whole night on a pile of sharp gravel while three police on rotation hit me on my limbs with sticks. . . . Around 10 p.m. Constable Bo Myint came to my right-hand side with the branch of a neem tree about one cubit long, the thickness of a little finger, with which he proceeded to strike my genitals. [Station commander Aung Gyi had told Constable Bo Myint to 'go break off a neem branch with which to hit his balls'.] . . . Around 3 a.m. two police forced me to stretch out my legs and pressed a metal rod on my shins, then ran it up and down with all their might. The insides of my eyes burned like they were on fire. . . . [Two days later] the police forced me to bend my knees, stand on tiptoe and hold the horse-riding pose. My stomach was empty, and meanwhile I was thirsty and suffering unbearable pain from torture wounds. Gritting my teeth I tried to hold the pose but I frequently lost it and fell to the ground, whereupon the police kicked me until I got up.

The man's account continues that the next day policemen strung him up with his arms behind his back for up to an hour, after which they lowered him so his feet could touch the ground and left him upright for the night. A number of other officers later assaulted him and threatened he would not survive beyond ten days if he failed to confess. On another night, three officers came to his cell drunk and forced him to wear the underwear and other garments of the murdered girl that they were keeping as evidence, while they jeered and yelled her name. By this time, the policemen had succeeded in forcing a confession from a co-accused through similar techniques. The other man retracted the confession, but the court held that the evidence sufficed for conviction of both.

In another similar case where police in Mandalay during 2000 detained four men over a murder, accusing two of them of arranging it and the others of carrying it out, the torturers played their victims off against one another. One of the accused said the officers boxed his ears until blood started flowing from one. He became disoriented and frightened and agreed to confess. Then the policemen brought him into the interrogation cells where they continued to torture the other accused. A relatively senior police officer was coming and going from the station to keep an eye on the operation:

> At midday they took me out of my cell to the interrogation room and showed Ko Aye Lwin being interrogated. He was naked and strung up with his arms over his head and chains around his feet, and they were striking him with electrical cables. The concrete floor had blood all over it from the night before when I had heard him faintly crying out. That night I saw the district police commissioner pass my cell in his civvies at some ungodly hour. He didn't open the door of the interrogation room but went into the visiting room, where he watched what was going on via a TV monitor. At that time they took me out of my cell and to the district commissioner. He told me, 'Go tell Aye Lwin, don't make the flesh bear the pain. Make him admit to it.' I went with a policeman into the interrogation room, but when I was in front of Aye Lwin I just stood there not saying anything. He looked at me dazedly. The policeman at my side also said nothing. 'Let's go then!' And with that he took me back to my cell.

Although from his own perspective the narrator is shown the man under torture, the purpose of the visit is not to show *him* anything. Rather, he is on show to the tortured man: he who has already acquiesced to sign whatever document was put in front of him and is now able to stay quietly and without pain. Whether or not he spoke was only incidental to the demonstrative purpose of his visit. In this case, of the four accused, the man whipped with electrical cables was the only one who refused to confess. He later died in prison.

While the severity of torture and urgency of its use seem to correlate with the amount of pressure that the police are under to produce a culprit, and with the relative importance of a case, the techniques used from one type of case to the next, one part of the country to the next, and one unit to the next are familiar, learned, and in a sense, unavoidable. Compare the preceding narrative with a complaint signed by two men that police officers in Yangon illegally detained and tortured them during 2009, one for five days, to admit to the theft of gold from a local businesswoman. According to one:

> They covered my face with a men's sarong, and four or five of them assaulted me. They hit me on the cheeks and punched me in the face. They hit me with truncheons over a hundred times on my ankles, knuckles, elbow joints, shoulder blades and head. They made me stand on my tip-toes then put something sharp and pointy under my feet and made me hold a pose like I was riding a motorcycle, for about two hours. They prodded my back with a truncheon.

The types of torture allegedly practiced in this case, which the other detainee said also included running bamboo up and down his shins, correspond with the descriptions of accused persons in a wide variety of ordinary criminal cases. In 2012, the husband of a sixty-six-year-old woman detained in Yangon as a suspect in the murder of a retired senior police officer's wife made a complaint on her behalf that echoes the preceding account:

> For the two days and nights that police personnel interrogated my wife at the district headquarters they hit her head with a truncheon, put her in shackles and forced her to stand upright throughout the night [as if] riding a motorcycle, boxed her ears repeatedly with open palms and hardback files, neither fed her nor gave water, made her stand and sit while hitting her with a truncheon, hit her with a truncheon on the right side of her body where it is swollen, and so on.

Preliminary methods of judicial torture include beating with fists and blunt objects, kicking, and denial of food and water. More physically violent techniques may follow, such as forcing the person to stand or kneel on sharp gravel, running a roller up and down the shins until skin peels off, suffocation with plastic bags, and injection with unidentified substances. Methods of sexual torture include interrogating the person naked, penetrating the anus, forcing detainees to have simulated or actual sex, and burning, electrocuting, or hitting the genitals.

Because of the prevalence of judicial torture in Myanmar, for some detainees the threat of torture alone is sufficient to make them comply with orders. During 1994, a township judge whom personnel from the Bureau of Special Investigation detained in Sittwe, the capital of Rakhine State, wrote that the investigating officer forced him to confess to taking bribes. The investigator allegedly told the judge that it would be easy to make him suffer, and asked him, 'Are we going to have to hurt you?' The judge reflected on his knowledge of torture practiced in criminal investigations:

> I have heard many people say that in some interrogations if the person questioned won't give the answers they want then they use electric shocks, beat with fists, keep them unfed and in a dark room, and then interrogate them [again]. . . . Rather than suffer such indignity, under inducement and threat I fearfully signed at the bottom of the paper given: I signed afraid that I was going to be tortured.[53]

A judge in 2008 processing a Buddhist monk over his role in protests the year before – the subject of Chapter 7 – asked him why he had retracted a confession. Rather more bluntly than the judge accused of corruption, the monk is said to have pointed to a group of police on one side of the courtroom and replied, 'They said they would do me in the ass if I didn't sign.'[54]

Out of all forms of torture associated with the law-and-order ideal, positional torture constitutes the most literal form of immobilisation. In Myanmar, stress postures include riding a horse or motorcycle on tiptoes, arms outstretched; reading a newspaper standing cross-legged; or driving a car, with one foot on the pedal. The person holding the pose may have to make accompanying noises, imitating the neighing of a horse or the sound of an engine. Beatings occur whenever the person is unable to stay upright or for failing to comply with any other arbitrary instruction, such as not to answer any question in the negative.

In a relatively minor case, if the police can obtain a confession, they need not spend time and effort searching for material evidence or doing real investigative work. If they can get an accused to confess and can gather or manufacture corroborating evidence, they have what they need. They may also be paid to help alter the case outcome in some way, in which case the police are just as likely, perhaps more likely, to use torture.

To illustrate, while researching for this book I followed a case in which a court had convicted two teenage girls of stealing from an employer. The employer had paid the police to charge the girls. As the police had no material evidence, they forced the girls' fingers and hands into stress positions: a simple enough technique on frightened

[53] SC Letter 2315/Su 14 (Ga) 223/94, 18 Apr. 1995, appendix B, 4–5.
[54] Zarganar, *Third, Fourth* ([Yangon]: Ko Thura, 2013) 52 (in Burmese).

teenagers, which took a short time to yield confessions. A lawyer failed in his efforts to get the girls released. After they had served more than half of their sentences – including time deducted spent in remand awaiting trial – he decided to let the case go. He reasoned that if a successful appeal were put up, the employer would learn of it and lodge another false charge. If the girls did their time, the lawyer reluctantly concluded, the employer would leave them be.

In each of the above cases, interrogation and confession have little to do with the question of who committed the crime. Judicial torture in Myanmar is aimed not at getting information but at exercising power to have someone admit guilt. Torture is misunderstood as being associated with information gathering, because the physical act of torture intertwines with the verbal act of interrogation.[55] Interrogation is internal to the structure of torture because it objectifies the act of causing pain in the exercise of power. A policeman who tortures to obtain a confession may have no interest in whether the accused is guilty or innocent. The police treated the men detained over the rape and murder in Sagaing politely when they first detained them, and allegedly told one that they knew he had nothing to do with the crime but had taken him into custody because he had a criminal record and they needed to make a few arrests to look active. The station commander advised him to take it easy and said they would release him after they had made further inquiries and arrests.

In a remarkable testimony to a closed court, Phyo Wai Aung, a survivor of torture whose case I described in the last chapter, recognised this aspect of the juridical process in Myanmar when he said:

> Confession has a use only for the prosecuting agencies. It can have no benefit for anyone else. In my view, it does not even assist in the reduction of crime. In prison, I have met [persons accused of being] thieves who [were convicted] just on the giving of confession. Because of the Myanmar Police Force's inadequate training in the detection of crime, so many accused people facing fabricated charges who do not understand the law and who had nothing to do with anything give confessions in place of the real offenders.[56]

Phyo Wai Aung implicitly recognises in his testimony that confession is desirable not because it distinguishes right from wrong but because it

[55] Scarry, *The Body in Pain* 28–29.

[56] *Inspector Thaung Ngwe* v. *U Phyo Wai Aung*, 2010 Criminal Case 103, Yangon Northern District Court, Defence Witness (DW) 1, 2 Feb. 2012: 10.

represents a form of political and juridical power. The nub of his argument is that police rely on confession because it works for them exclusively. As it can serve only the interests of the sovereign power against the accused, it constitutes acquiescence to sovereign power, and thereby reinforces proper relations of law and order between sovereign and subject. In this setting, torture does not create a political identity for the tortured person anew, as John Parry has put it, but re-creates an existing identity, bound to established political relations.[57] In Phyo Wai Aung's case, this proper reinforcement of relations cost him his life: he died on January 4, 2013, due to the damage caused by torture and imprisonment, shortly after receiving a pardon, in August 2012.[58]

BETWEEN VIOLENCE AND LAW

In the act of torture, the power of the sovereign over the subject is directly expressed through the policeman, insofar as the sovereign 'is the point of indistinction between violence and law, the threshold on which violence passes over into law and law passes over into violence'.[59] Torture is an unruly force of 'law', crossing law's borders untamed.[60] Through torture, the policeman at once moves inside the juridical process and transcends it. He stands above it, invested with political power surpassing the process. He also stands in it, having as his objective the confession that is integral to the procedural games that follow.

For this reason, even in cases where a public enemy is tortured, the police seek a confession, and a judge might hear the accused out when he objects to the confession in court, complaints of torture or other wrongdoing do not affect the court process. As the testimony does not materially alter the result of the case, rather than constituting evidence of guilt or innocence, it just constitutes another stage in the administrative processing of the accused. A court animated by the law-and-order ideal is relatively unconcerned to conceal the violence committed on the body of the public enemy, because it need not do anything about it.

[57] John T. Parry, *Understanding Torture: Law, Violence, and Political Identity* (Ann Arbor: University of Michigan Press, 2010) 207–08.

[58] *Weekly Eleven* 8 Aug. 2012: 1, 25.

[59] Giorgio Agamben, *Homo Sacer: Sovereign Power and Bare Life*, trans. Daniel Heller-Roazen (Stanford: Stanford University Press, 1998) 32.

[60] See Sarat and Kearns, 'Making Peace with Violence' 212–13.

The case that officers from the Yangon Divisional Police Headquarters brought against a young man named Than Myint Aung is indicative. On March 3, 2009, policemen arrested Than Myint Aung and accused him of meeting dissidents in Malaysia during 2007, and of having used the Internet illegally. In court, Than Myint Aung described what happened to him in custody:

> While interrogating they tied a cloth over my face and punched me; I was interrogated while being punched from all sides by on-duty police officers. One of the interrogating police forced my backside onto the floor and made it so that my forehead was on the floor at the same level, then stamped on my spine with boots. . . . I was hit with rubber truncheons and questioned. They hit me like that on the thighs, groin and spine. They also whacked my knuckles with rubber truncheons. They inserted ball pens in between my fingers, grasped them and rotated the ball pens to cause pain, then interrogated more. . . . During that month in interrogation for fifteen days straight I couldn't sleep at all at night. They also didn't feed me or give water. They hit me continuously. They forced me to sit on my haunches. They forced me to stand, and hit me if I sat. . . . Nine days into interrogation, they moved me from upstairs to downstairs and while interrogating me there the duty police hit my head with rubber truncheons to the point of breaking two of them. My head ruptured. They sliced chilli thinly and put it in my mouth. They also stuffed in a bundle of cloth. They stripped my entire body naked and ran rubber truncheons along my shins. A duty policeman stood alongside and pressed down on my thighs so that I couldn't move about. I was hit on the soles of my feet with rubber truncheons and furthermore hit on my back with them also. A duty policeman poured hot water onto my genitals.[61]

In the verdict, the judge reduced this narrative of torture to the following:

> Than Myint Aung (DW-1) testified that ... he was interrogated and assaulted for a month ... that he affixed his signature to three search forms, then after that was sent to Sanchaung Police Station, that as he was unwell he received treatment at the Yangon General Hospital, Emergency and Neurology Departments.[62]

Counsel for the accused unsuccessfully sought to have staff from the hospital appear as witnesses, or at least to obtain their medical records,

[61] *Inspector Thet Naing* v. *Than Myint Aung* (a) *Ko Myo* (a) *Thiha Thura*, 2009 Criminal Case 47, Yangon Western District Court, DW 1, 18 June 2010: 1–3.

[62] *Inspector Thet Naing* v. *Than Myint Aung* (a) *Ko Myo* (a) *Thiha Thura*, 2009 Criminal Case 47, Yangon Western District Court, 15 July 2010.

with which to support the allegations of torture. No reference to these requests or any other aspect of the defence case appears in the judge's summing up, even though after sentencing Than Myint Aung was returned to a medical facility because of the damage sustained to his skull. Similarly, the judge hearing charges against a man accused of going to Thailand to meet opposition groups reduced his lengthy account of torture to a couple of identical lines per judgment before sentencing him to a total of eight years for illegal immigration and contact with unlawful associations.[63] And in 2009 one judge recorded confessions from at least nine different persons charged in at least seven different cases, all of whom retracted their confessions in court, most alleging severe torture at police stations in a number of localities.[64] All were convicted.

In these cases and others like them, the body might serve as a witness to suffering at the hands of the state in narratives among the tortured, as Dhana Hughes has written of torture survivors she met in Sri Lanka; however, it is denied the right to serve that role judicially.[65] It does not speak in court, or it speaks but is not heard, or seen. As a consequence of the withdrawal of sovereign *cetana*, the conditional privileges that accrue ordinarily to citizens cease to have efficacy for public enemies, making the body's evidence irrelevant. The details of torture can be admitted to the court record, but without affecting the outcome of the case.

This situation is true not only of cases where the tortured survive, but also where they die and the body is literally the only thing remaining to testify as to what has occurred. In 2005, for instance, a young woman took a case to court over the death of her husband in custody. Ma Hnin Sanda made a missing person complaint on May 1, the same day unidentified men removed her husband from a public restaurant. On May 10, a lieutenant colonel from military intelligence and some other men came to meet her at her local ward council office. They told her that her husband had died three days earlier, and offered her a hundred thousand Kyat, or about a hundred U.S. dollars, as compensation. When Hnin Sanda said she only wanted her husband's body, the officer

[63] *Inspector Aung Soe Naing* v. *Sithu Zeya*, 2010 Criminal Cases 466–67, Mingalataung-nyunt Township Court, 21 Dec. 2010.

[64] *Pol. Capt. Khin Soe* v. *Myo Min Than and Another*, 2009 Criminal Case 198, Mandalay District Court, 23 Dec. 2009; and Criminal Cases 204–07, 209 and 214.

[65] Dhana Hughes, 'Remembering Sri Lanka's Southern Terror: Narratives of Torture Survivors', *Interventions: International Journal of Postcolonial Studies* 14.2 (2012): 193.

told her that he had already been cremated. She refused the money and lodged an application in court against the lieutenant colonel, two other soldiers, and three police. The application cites officials' testimony in a post-mortem inquiry that the deceased was arrested four days after his wife had already made a missing person complaint. According to them, after being brought to a police station he was transferred to military intelligence, who interrogated him 'only a little' before he was found unconscious in his cell on May 8. He died en route to hospital. The application then quotes the findings of a doctor at the hospital, who examined the body,

> That he saw external injuries in twenty-four places on the body of the plaintiff's husband Ko Aung Hlaing Win; that he saw that left rib no. 4 and right rib no. 4 were each fractured, and that one [other] rib was in one place broken into two pieces ... [and that] the body was dehydrated.[66]

These injuries point to the use of severe torture resulting in the death of this previously reasonably healthy young man. But the doctor found that his death was the result of an enlarged liver, tonsillitis, and pneumonia. The court concluded that as Aung Hlaing Win had died a 'natural' death, Hnin Sanda's complaint was groundless. Applications for revision in higher courts also failed.[67]

Public enemies are not the only persons who struggle to have their bodies seen and heard in court, testifying as witnesses to the torture they have endured. In earlier periods, the relationship between the police and courts was such that a torturer who proved too savage or inept could land in trouble. But the policeman in contemporary Myanmar is resistant to attempts to have him answer for his practices. He may be inconvenienced for killing someone in his custody, but ultimately he is answerable only to his peers and his own institution, not to other parties.[68] Furthermore, he expects cooperation of other agencies in managing the consequences: if policemen beat someone in

[66] *Ma Hnin Sanda* v. *Lt-Col. Min Naing and 5*, 2005 Criminal Case Application, Mayangon Township Court, 1 June 2005: 4.

[67] *Ma Hnin Sanda* v. *State of Myanmar and 6*, 2005 Criminal Revision Application 754, Yangon Western District Court, 1 Sept. 2005. *Ma Hnin Sanda* v. *Union of Myanmar*, 2005 Criminal Revision Application 595, Supreme Court, 11 Oct. 2005.

[68] Like the military, the police reserve the right to decide which personnel are or are not prosecuted for serious crimes: 'A court shall try and sentence [a police officer] ... only in accordance with the instructions and approval of the Myanmar Police Force Headquarters.' Myanmar Police Force Headquarters, Letter No. 100-NaRaGa/2–1/Ye 3 (Ka), 1 Jan. 1996, par. 4.

their custody to death, as they did to a young man in the delta during 2007, the examining doctor's role is to absolve them from blame, not to point the finger.[69]

With political change in Myanmar, prospects have improved that the bodies of at least some deceased victims of torture may soon testify in court and speak back to the power of the policeman. The families of deceased torture victims have more opportunities to use the media and put pressure on the police. Doctors are perhaps more likely to resist demands from police officers, administrators, or maybe even military personnel to resist documenting deaths falsely. In 2013, for instance, a doctor in a rural hospital in Bago, north of Yangon, refused police attempts to have her rush an autopsy on the body of a man the officers claimed had died in custody due to the effects of alcoholism. She insisted on waiting for his relatives to come before examining the deceased. She found that the man's organs were healthy but that he had extensive external bruising and lacerations on practically all parts of his body, including that the left side of his ribcage was fractured and that both shins bore the injuries of a roller run up and down them.[70] Similarly, in 2014 a doctor who examined the body of a middle-aged man who died in police custody told the media plainly that the deceased had been murdered.[71] He described the cause of death as a burst liver due to intense kicking.

Some judges are also taking small steps back towards their historical role of participating actively in the procedural game play of judicial torture. The body of Myo Myint Swe, a teenager detained in mid-2012 over a murder in the suburbs of Yangon, showed extensive signs of torture, including the use of a roller to peel the skin from his shins. The examining doctor recorded cause of death as a heart attack. Despite the finding, a judge wrote in her inquest report that she found it 'difficult to conclude that the death was natural'.[72] The family sought the assistance of a lawyer to pursue the police officers involved. Three police were later dismissed from service, while five

69 The doctor concluded that the young man had died from malaria, rather than from the cranial injuries visible in photographs of the deceased. *Sub Inspector* Myo Min Aung v. *Chan Kun*, 2007 Criminal Misc. Case 3, Pandanaw Township Court, 5 Feb. 2007.

70 Daw Myint Htay, letter citing autopsy report findings, 27 May 2013.

71 *Myanmar Herald* 22 Mar. 2014: 12.

72 *Republic of the Union of Myanmar* v. *Deceased* Myo Myint Swe (a) *Pyi Soe* (a) *Kalagyi*, 2012 Criminal Misc. Case 161, Mayangon Township Court, 9 Nov. 2012: 7.

were demoted.[73] No criminal charges were brought. The police for their part claimed to have obtained a confession from the deceased before he died.[74]

TRANSACTIONS ON A THRESHOLD

Certain transactions are integral to judicial torture, on one side between the torturer and the victim of torture, on the other between the torturer and other officials who will be involved in the case at later stages. Both sides feature in the account of a police investigation into a person accused of involvement in a bombing during 2010, recorded in a letter submitted to higher authorities. According to the complainant, a relative of the accused,

> [The defendant] was arrested at home . . . after midnight and taken to the Aungthapyay interrogation camp for interrogation. [He] explained but could not convince them that he was not among the persons involved in the bombing. Inspector Maung Aye threatened him, 'If you die it's nothing to us', while Police Major Tin Oo threatened him, 'We'll interrogate until you can't take it. We'll bring your family and torture you in front of them.' [He] was forced to stand throughout interrogation for two whole days and nights with his hands cuffed behind his back. He was forced to sit like a jockey and was hit and kicked in the head; stepped on the crook of the knee and hit with a broom; boxed simultaneously on both ears; stripped naked and forced to kneel on gravel with arms raised; burned on his genitals with lit paper; had hot wax dripped onto his genitals; was blindfolded throughout various types of torture; was forced to sit down and stand up repeatedly for over an hour at a time; and was forced to stay seated in a chair for five days without sleeping. There was no order from a court for him to be remanded in custody. [He] was given various promises as inducement, that, 'If you give a confession we'll make the case easy on you'; 'You won't get the death penalty'; 'We'll fix it so that you're out after one or two years'; and, 'If we get another accused, we'll make you a state witness.' As he was afraid for the threats to his life, as he could no longer stand the torture that the police officers unceasingly practiced on rotation; and as he believed the various promises made as inducement, he agreed to give a confession. For three days after he agreed to confess he was fed well and able to sleep well, then the officers made [him] repeat over and over what to say about the bombing. . . . A police inspector made him repeatedly practice his

[73] *Daily Eleven* 11 May 2013: 19. [74] *Biweekly Eleven* 13 July 2012: 9.

> lines until there were no errors, then, 'Just say it like that [in court], and if you say anything wrong it's going to hurt.' . . . He gave a confession at the court due to fear that he would be tortured further.

With a commitment from the detainee to cooperate, the police begin their transactions immediately. They stop torturing him. They feed him and let him rest. These actions indicate to the accused that the police are prepared to make good on their promises, and treat him well if he helps them. But they also show concern for the accused man's performance before the judge who will receive the confession. They help him to remember what he has to say, and warn him not to muck it up.

We ought not mistake the anxiety of the police as concern for the authority of the judge in itself. Their anxiety is not out of fear that the judge might learn of the torture, nor out of concern that the judge might act against them, but over the need for the judge cognisant of torture to cooperate in concluding the process of confession obtained via this route. To this end, they give the judge certain reassurances that the accused can perform well enough to enable his cooperation. Where an accused is unprepared to confess, the police will at least be inconvenienced. They and the judge can be embarrassed publicly, and may suffer some form of punishment. In a rare published Supreme Court ruling referring to use of torture, the prosecution case came apart because the police had to take the accused for confession twice, after making a mess of the first attempt.[75] But nowhere in the judgement is torture condemned, or even commented on. To the contrary, the subtext of the ruling is that the police and judge needed to take more care to ensure the accused was prepared beforehand, so the procedural game would play out as required.

A fully faithful performance is unnecessary. The activity is not aimed at taking a freely given confession, but at satisfying minimum conditions for a semblance of orderliness. In the Mandalay murder case described earlier, the detainee who confessed first was given a number of days to rote learn his lines, but even then he struggled in front of the judge:

> When we arrived at the Maha-aungmyay Township Court, they took me in front of [a judge] and forced me to say what I had been taught, as written. The judge jumped in and helped out with points that I didn't

[75] *Union of Myanmar* v. *Mardin* (a) *Kyi Lwin*, 1996 MLR 129. See also *Union of Myanmar / Toe Yi* v. *Toe Yi / Union of Myanmar*, 1992 MLR 28. A similar case is described in *Maung Pan Zone* v. *Union of Burma*, 1960 BLR (SC) 15 (in Burmese).

> know or had forgotten. I wasn't given any time to think about the confession before I gave it. I was kept handcuffed throughout, and the police didn't keep their distance either. They sat on each side of me.[76]

Sandwiched between his captors and with the judge filling the gaps in his story, he signed a confession that ended with his receiving the death penalty.

Like judges, other officials in the juridical process seek reassurances from the police aimed at protecting their interests. If accused of wrongdoing, they need to show they have played their parts according to procedures. In one case in the central town of Pakokku during 2012, two detainees brought for remand over gold theft had been so badly beaten that a prison officer insisted on taking photographs of them before accepting them into his custody. Family members succeeded in getting photocopies of the pictures. They sent them with a complaint to the new Myanmar National Human Rights Commission.[77] When one of the police officers involved learned that the family had copied the photographs, he came and got them from the prison on a ruse and destroyed them.

On the side of the torturer and the tortured, the most important transaction rests on holding out a promise to end the torture in exchange for a confession. The policeman has the power to commit violence, and he has the power to stop it, if he gets something in return. In a case from 2010, a man testified that policemen tortured him to confess to going to Thailand to meet members of antigovernment groups:

> They told me to admit to having been involved in [a] bombing. As I said that I had not been involved so I could not admit to it, they hit my mouth with a shoe. They said, 'If you don't admit to it, we'll pick up your dad too.' For about four days they tortured me saying like this, didn't feed me or give me water, forced me to stand upright on tiptoes and so on, and then they brought my father's photo. They showed me my father's photo taken with a digital camera. They told me, 'Although you won't admit to the bombing, you'll admit to another case, or your mum will be next.'

[76] The Courts Manual paragraph 602(5) instructs, 'When the confession is being recorded, none of the police who has been concerned in the accused's arrest or in the investigation of the case should be allowed to be within sight or hearing of the accused.'

[77] The government established the Myanmar National Human Rights Commission as a successor to an earlier human rights committee under Notification 34/2011, 5 Sept. 2011. For an outline of its early activities, see Melissa Crouch, 'Asian Legal Transplants and Rule of Law Reform: National Human Rights Commission [*sic*] in Myanmar and Indonesia', *Hague Journal on the Rule of Law* 5.2 (2013): 146–77.

> They made me sign those papers they wrote out about having contact with [the Democratic Voice of Burma] in the adjacent country, and how I would get funds from [DVB]. . . . They said . . . when I would arrive at the court I would have to tell [the details of the documents] in front of the judge, that what the judge asked I was to answer well, and that if I did not then 'you and your dad are going to jail'. Saying that if I spoke well then they would release me from detention, they took me to court. Three police officers took me in front of the judge. At that time, I didn't have a clue about what a confession was. I just said everything that they had told me to say in front of the judge. . . . In reality I had no idea about the meaning of the confession. I said it to get relief from their torture.[78]

The person confessing need not understand what he is doing or why. All he need do is accept the assurance of the police that they have the power to make things better, once the confession is given. Because the policeman as torturer makes promises on a juridical threshold, at a point of indistinction between violence and law, his promises contain no guarantees. He may make false promises to which the tortured clings for want of anything else. Even Phyo Wai Aung said that despite being tortured he still believed the police when they reassured him that he had nothing to worry about if he gave a statement to a judge, and that they had sorted everything out with higher-ups.[79] Only when the police brought him before a court and he heard the charges did he realise that they had duped him.

Here again the policeman as sovereign parallels the sovereign power, which also gives promises to which it cannot be held: offers of leniency through transactions with wayward citizenry, for which people can only take it at its word. Consider the following statement in 2008 from the then police commander, Brigadier General Khin Yi, explaining the state's response to an alleged terrorist conspiracy:

> Among those who attended the trainings to destroy peace and stability, including the explosives training, most did not understand exactly their facts and purpose. . . . As for this sort of innocent and ignorant youth, whose actions constitute a loss for the state and are also for themselves a waste of their lives, I wish to say here with sympathy that if whoever in their circles notifies the responsible persons then our security personnel will treat them with understanding and leniency.[80]

[78] The police did in fact arrest his father and charge him with a number of offences.

[79] *Inspector Thaung Ngwe* v. *U Phyo Wai Aung*, 2010 Criminal Case 103, Yangon Northern District Court, DW 1, 13 Feb. 2012: 7–8.

[80] *Myanma Alin* 8 Sept. 2008: 9. Khin Yi was an army officer appointed to head the police force, hence his military rank.

Khin Yi gives voice to the symmetry of sovereign power found between the state and the society on one hand and between the policeman and the criminal accused on the other. The sovereign is lenient. The person who does wrong but who admits to it, who acts ignorantly but who eventually realises his mistake, may be treated gently. Like the sovereign policeman in the torture chamber, the police commander as sovereign promises to make everything better in exchange for the confession, the admission of guilt, and the acknowledgment of his power through voluntary reporting of the whereabouts of the accused. No principle guarantees anyone fair treatment or a second chance, but pragmatism dictates that some people should get one sometimes.

CONCLUSION

Among personnel in juridical institutions evocative of the ideal of law and order, the policeman occupies a special place, an area of indistinction symmetrical to sovereignty, where the right of the sovereign to exert violence plays out in the individual case. This symmetry is found in the policeman's role everywhere. However, in Myanmar, the space is enlarged by politics in which rationales of law and order have surpassed others. The policeman-sovereign can aggrandise his part and exceed the authority of other personnel in the juridical process.

In this respect, the policeman in Myanmar is structurally differentiated from his counterparts in some other British postcolonies, like India, who engage in comparable practices of torture and who are working according to fundamentally the same criminal codes and colonial traditions, but in dissimilar political conditions. Beatrice Jauregui has written that the police in India are 'situationally hyper-empowered [but] at the same time structurally disempowered'.[81] By this statement she means that the police officer at a given moment may wield authority, but because his corporate interests are structurally subordinated or answerable to the country's fractious and complex politics, multi-layered governments and various other institutional factors, he also frequently encounters challenges to his authority.

By contrast, even if the policeman in Myanmar over the last half century has been subordinated, like other authorities, to the military and its interests, he surpasses the personnel of other juridical

[81] Beatrice Jauregui, 'Beatings, Beacons, and Big Men: Police Disempowerment and Delegitimation in India', *Law and Social Inquiry* 38.3 (2013): 664–65.

institutions. His situation is different from that of his peers in India, and in many other British postcolonies with which it has shared features. When Jauregui writes about 'law and order', like other scholars of postcolonial India, she treats it as a phenomenon, a manifestation, of the police in the uniformed, institutionalised sense.[82] Distinct from that sense of the term, where law and order functions as an encompassing political ideal, asymmetrically opposed to the rule of law, it envelops all institutions, including courts. Where law and order in this larger sense animates the work of juridical institutions, the relationship between the policeman and judge is inverted.

Furthermore, the situational empowerment of the policeman in Myanmar cannot be understated. His ability to decide on the specific moment and the admixture of violence and right in that moment is what makes his presence generally compelling – not just as a threatening figure to the detainee or accused person, but as the embodiment of the law-and-order ideal.

The idiosyncratic structural position of the Burmese policeman means that the essentially political qualities of the violence he practices are more visible than in the case of his counterparts in other British postcolonies. Where law-and-order imperatives override other concerns, as they have done in Myanmar, the political quality of the policeman reveals itself more fully. Far from being a scandal, torture in this setting becomes a form of best practice. Torture's usefulness is in its helping to maintain a well-ordered society, which is to say, one that corresponds with the state's conception of order.[83] Its defence lies 'in its social utility, the "good results" . . . produced in the form of convictions'.[84] Ultimately, not the ends in the individual case but the pervasive ideology of law and order ensure the persistence of judicial torture.

None of the above implies that situations do not arise where individual police officers find themselves at a disadvantage in relation to other people or institutions. Nor does it imply that total impunity comes with the exercise of sovereign power. On the contrary, the semblance of orderliness required of the police obligates them to make amends sometimes, and at least appear responsive to public

[82] Beatrice Jauregui, 'Law and Order: Police Encounter Killings and Routinized Political Violence', *A Companion to the Anthropology of India*, ed. Isabelle Clark-Decès (Oxford: Blackwell, 2011) 371–88.

[83] Peters, *Torture* 7.

[84] Lisa Silverman, *Tortured Subjects: Pain, Truth, and the Body in Early Modern France* (Chicago: University of Chicago Press, 2001) 67.

demands, as well as to the demands of their victims or their families. Policemen who kill people in the course of torturing them may come to offer families hush money and appear contrite. They may fear internal inquiries, demotion, transfer, or dismissal. Policemen who encounter determined complainants can find their careers undermined or ruined. But those officers who fail to hold onto their jobs, posts, or ranks do not fail because of the act of torture itself. They fail because they have demonstrated ineptitude in maintaining the semblance of orderliness on which Myanmar's juridical institutions depend.

6

PERFORMING ORDER, MAKING MONEY

Moneymaking through positions of authority is nothing new in Myanmar. But the sheer scale and audacity with which money is made through courts today compels attention. Writing in 2011, a practicing lawyer recalled how a senior counterpart had told him,

> Bribery and corruption are now prevalent in more than 50 percent of courts in the present legal system. He said it was his opinion that unless a bribe is given, there is no possibility of winning a case. [Another] lawyer said that most of the courts in which he practices take bribes from clients. ... He also added that bribery at the courts was not under the table but that it was on the table, meaning that judges take bribes as if the laws permit it.[1]

The senior lawyer's estimate may be conservative. In an online poll run by a news periodical at the end of 2011, 1,580 out of 2,025 respondents responded that the judicial system is unfair due to bias and corruption.[2] And Aung San Suu Kyi in 2013 speaking on her observations of courts as head of the Rule of Law and Tranquility Committee said:

[1] Kyaw Min San, 'Critical Issues for the Rule of Law in Myanmar', *Myanmar's Transition: Openings, Obstacles and Opportunities*, eds. Nick Cheesman, Monique Skidmore, and Trevor Wilson (Singapore: ISEAS, 2012) 225.

[2] Of the other respondents, 407 said the system was not fair mainly due to weaknesses in laws, and 38, that they were satisfied with the existing system. *Weekly Eleven* 6 Dec. (2011), 11 Dec. 2011 www.weeklyeleven.com.

> Ninety-nine out of a hundred people have no faith in courts. They no longer rely on courts at all. Our observation is that they only rely on money. That shows just how broken our judicial branch has become.[3]

If the level of confidence in Myanmar's courts is as low as Aung San Suu Kyi suggests, and if judges take money as if the law permits it, then the question arises as to why they would bother with keeping up appearances to the contrary. In this chapter, I argue that, as in the case of the policeman who tortures to extract confession, the ideal of law and order compels personnel working in courts to maintain a semblance of orderliness. Law and order puts a higher premium on courts' seeming complaisance with orders than on their application of law. In contrast to the rule of law, law and order is in principle compatible with routine and institutionalised departures from legal rules, provided that courts function to enable political domination through adherence to administrative principles and policies. In short, the court in Myanmar functions as a marketplace where participants buy and sell case outcomes not because judges are underpaid or greedy – or not only for these reasons – but because the logic of law and order makes it possible, and to an extent mandates it.

The chapter begins with a sketch of public language on judicial bribery and corruption. Anti-corruption rhetoric in Myanmar, far from prohibiting moneymaking, establishes guidelines and issues subtextual warnings on suitable and unsuitable methods for earning money, analogous to those laid down for the policeman to obtain confession by torture. It reinforces these messages through sanctions of judges, lawyers, and other judicial personnel who fail to maintain the semblance of orderliness in their undertakings. This chapter illustrates methods of buying and selling criminal cases and case outcomes. These methods reveal how the business of criminal justice in Myanmar is not a simple matter of offering a judge money to acquit or convict someone. It consists of horizontal and vertical arrangements to satisfy all relevant parties, while at the same time accommodating the imperative for a semblance of orderliness.

This chapter draws on material gathered over three phases of research conducted in cooperation with professionals in Myanmar, who between 2009 and 2012 collected data on moneymaking transactions in criminal cases from urban and rural areas around the country.

[3] In *People's Age* 28 Mar. 2013: 21.

The transactions documented contain nuance and local colour; however, in this chapter I will forgo discussion of those details to concentrate on the general characteristics of moneymaking, and on details that speak to how the ideal of law and order animates Myanmar's courts. The material is supplemented by documentary references to Supreme Court records from 1994 to 2010, which validate the findings from research conducted on the ground.[4]

PUBLIC TRANSCRIPTS

The language of counter-corruption in Myanmar goes back to precolonial times, but in its modern form is largely a product of the colonial period. The British initially characterised corruption as residue from earlier power relations based on patronage; a consequence of the presumed inferiority of subject races to Europeans, and a feature of the allegedly arbitrary rule of indigenous monarchs. They portrayed the precolonial state as endemically corrupt, its colonial successor, by contrast, as suffering from subordinate corruption.[5]

In 1940, an official committee acknowledged the extent of practices bracketed as corruption. It described them as widespread because of impunity, secrecy, and superior officers' lack of courage to do anything about it.[6] Like the documents of other state-established commissions of inquiry into ostensibly deviant practices, the committee's report reads in part as a morality tale, in part as a confirmation of what everyone already presumed to know.[7] The committee painted a bleak picture, with police allegedly refusing to record criminal complaints without first receiving money, or recording them incorrectly; taking money from the aggrieved on all sorts of pretexts; and supporting or opposing bail depending on payment of bribes. The committee also estimated that at least half of all judicial officers were receiving gratuities.[8] Combining what Ann Stoler

[4] The records include the *Supreme Court Gazette* for every year in the period covered except 1996, and forty-two files of internal documents from the same period.

[5] Jonathan Saha, *Law, Disorder and the Colonial State: Corruption in Burma, c. 1900* (Basingstoke and New York: Palgrave Macmillan, 2013) 18.

[6] Bribery and Corruption Enquiry Committee, *Report of the Bribery and Corruption Enquiry Committee, 1940* (Rangoon: Govt. Printing, 1941), 44–46.

[7] Ann Laura Stoler, *Along the Archival Grain: Epistemic Anxieties and Colonial Common Sense* (Princeton and Oxford: Princeton University Press, 2009) 141–42.

[8] Bribery and Corruption Enquiry Committee, *Report* 12.

characterises as a 'passion for numbers with ... the pathos of vignette', it cited various examples of how payments were made and monies kept, including cases where judges allegedly took money from both sides but did not return any to the losing side; where the accused was kept in custody and the date for handing down a sentence was repeatedly postponed so that the detainee would pay; and, where trial records were doctored and falsified.[9]

By the late colonial period, officeholders, media reports, and government records uniformly described corruption as a serious phenomenon but generally dismissed it, according to Jonathan Saha, 'as a set of ephemeral, ultimately meaningless acts committed by marginal, errant petty officials'.[10] The speechifying continued and gathered strength following independence with the first prime minister issuing complaints about 'termites' eating at the foundations of state: publicly citing cases of policemen supplying arms to robbers and politicians, and releasing accused criminals on pressure from members of his own political party.[11] He went further than his colonial predecessors in setting up an independent agency to investigate corrupt practices, the Bureau of Special Investigation, but was subsequently forced to defend it against allegations that it was itself corrupt and abusive. The bureau had some successes and for a time was feared among civil servants. After 1962, the military government brought the bureau under the National Intelligence Bureau, and its purpose was defeated – if not its aptitude for exercising violence with impunity.[12]

From 1962, party organs assailed the tactics of capitalists who had used their money to thwart justice. They urged all civil servants, judges, police, lawyers, and citizens to put an end to such practices as soon as possible. Bias, abuses of power, incompetence, and pressures from superiors abounded regardless.[13] Judges became preoccupied with pleasing council officials so as to secure reappointment for reasons

[9] Stoler, *Along the Archival Grain* 142. [10] Saha, *Law, Disorder and the Colonial State* 129.

[11] Thakin Nu, *From Peace to Stability* ([Rangoon]: Ministry of Information, Govt. of Burma, 1951) 63–66, 125.

[12] In 1996, for instance, the chief justice took the unusual step of complaining to the home affairs ministry that the bureau was terrorising a judge, lawyers, and clientele of a township court in Kachin State. SC Letter 7477/Su 14 (Ka) 123/96, 27 Dec. 1996. In 2012, local news media extensively reported on the death of a young woman married to a Japanese businessman who fell from the fifth floor of the bureau's headquarters during a prolonged interrogation.

[13] U Thein Hlaing and Dr. Daw Khin Hla Han, eds., *A Period of Change to Myanmar's Political System (1962–1974)*, vol. III, 3 vols. (Yangon: Universities Press, 1993) 61–62 (in Burmese).

of personal advantage.[14] As economic conditions worsened, party documents privately acknowledged that bribery was endemic and probably uncontrollable through prosecutions.[15] However, when compared with conditions in the 1990s and 2000s, anecdotal accounts suggest that the amounts involved and types of corruption differed. The money economy was smaller, and judges did not aim for ostentatious lifestyles. Payments were often not in cash but in the form of simple, locally manufactured goods that recipients could use or resell – a new sarong, a drum of good-quality cooking oil.

Later governments amplified the rhetoric on corruption, consistent with the lexicon and semantics of law and order. During the 1990s and early 2000s, the intelligence chief Khin Nyunt took centre stage in one performance after another of military officers chastising judges and other personnel for corrupt practices. In 1993, for instance, he said:

> I have time and again ordered that steps be taken to eliminate undesirable things once found around courts, to eradicate malpractice and self-serving behaviour from court environs. However, judicial personnel, including judges, law officers, and People's Police Force personnel at some state, division, district and township courts are colluding and acting as case brokers, saying they will cut short days in detention if a case is prosecuted, will cut the fine, not to hire a lawyer as that would prolong the case, which lawyer to hire, which judge to approach, etc., and that civil servants and lawyers alike are operating fraudulently outside the boundaries of the law. . . . Because of this type of malpractice and self-serving behaviour, the people lack trust in the judicial system, and have a kind of loathsome and fearful attitude towards it.[16]

The following year, Khin Nyunt listed a variety of cases to prove the point; all of them illustrative of routine practices for moneymaking that still continue. They included one where a judge and prosecutor colluded with a defence lawyer to release an accused drug manufacturer; where a judge released three persons accused of counterfeiting banknotes,

[14] Anon., 'Analysis of Myanmar's Legislature, Judiciary and Administration', unpublished paper (2006) 6 (in Burmese). The paper's author was a former public prosecutor.

[15] 'Record of the Party's Position and General Operations Regarding the Involvement of Workers and Students in the Incidents That Occurred During 1974', Central Committee Headquarters, Burma Socialist Programme Party, 30 June 1975, par. 7(b) (in Burmese).

[16] Khin Nyunt, 'Address at the Work Coordination Meeting of State, Divisional and District Judges and Law Officers', *Supreme Court Rulings, 1993* (Yangon: Myawadi, 1995) n. pag. (in Burmese). Prosecutors in Myanmar are officially called 'law officers'. Throughout this book I refer to them by the generic term, 'prosecutors', except in direct citations.

despite ample evidence on which to convict; where another judge altered a charge against timber smugglers from a serious offence to one carrying minor penalties; where a judge imprisoned a person or persons for playing the illegal lottery but released the broker; and where a judge forced the sister of a defendant to have sex with him in his chambers.[17]

The early 1990s was a critical time for rebuilding the law-and-order state, and the language of counter-corruption was especially pronounced. The Supreme Court was busy with a major project to police and punish subordinate wayward judges who until only a few years earlier had been serving as clerks, advisors, and administrators. Khin Nyunt was not making stories up. His tirades reflected the contents of complaints addressed to him personally. They also reflected the contents of internal records during this period, in which top officials warned that despite repeated exhortations to stamp out bribery and other misdeeds, they had ascertained that 'the public remains critical of the continued acceptance of bribes by some civil service organisations'.[18]

Although by the 2000s the superior courts policed and punished their subordinates with less urgency, the narrative on counter-corruption continued. In 2002, for instance, Khin Nyunt warned of possible sanctions for wrongdoing, but as usual stressed the need for judges to be supervised well and to comport themselves appropriately, describing some as being 'notorious for taking bribes'.[19]

In 2004, Khin Nyunt lost his own job, and after he was prosecuted over alleged corruption the home affairs minister placed him under house arrest.[20] His successors continued the moralistic narrative, albeit in a more circumspect manner. In 2007, the then prime minister, General Soe Win, stated that people were commonly discussing the misbehaviour of judges and that all judicial personnel needed to be upstanding in their character and work practices. He added 'that if the

[17] Khin Nyunt, 'Address at the Work Coordination Meeting of State, Divisional and District Judges and Law Officers', *Supreme Court Rulings, 1994* (Yangon: Myawadi, 1996) n. pag. (in Burmese). A case corresponding in description to the last of those listed above is contained in SC Letter 480/Su 14 (Ka) 72/93, 22 Jan. 1994. According to the letter, military intelligence had investigated and concluded that 'irrespective of whether or not the judge committed rape' he had failed to uphold the dignity of his office (par. 3). The Supreme Court dismissed him.

[18] Office of the Council of Government, Letter 1/001-Ka/A-PaYa (6), 25 June 1997.

[19] Khin Nyunt, 'Address on 9 July 2002 at the Institute of Nursing to Supreme Court, Office of the Attorney General and State, Division and District Judges and Law Officers Assembled for Receipt of Advice on Judicial Affairs', *Judicial Journal* 1.14 (2002): 14 (in Burmese).

[20] As discussed in Kyaw Yin Hlaing, 'Myanmar in 2004: Another Year of Uncertainty', *Asian Survey* 45.1 (2005): 175–76; Myat Khine, *Interviews with U Khin Nyunt* (Yangon: Quality, 2013) 41–44 (in Burmese).

weaknesses and flaws are examined, it can be observed that generally they are resulting not from inadequacies and weaknesses in the system, codes of conduct and working procedures, but are flaws and weaknesses of the individual'.[21] In 2009, Prime Minister General Thein Sein, reading from the same script, told assembled judges that the weaknesses were not institutional but ethical; flaws of individuals, not organisations.[22] In March 2011 during his inaugural oratory as president, the former general stressed the importance of the rule of law and avoidance of corrupt practices in order to ensure clean government.[23]

The narrative has continued through a variety of official pronouncements since political change began. For instance, a presidential speech in August 2013 to newly appointed officials warned them 'to keep personal character and integrity, and to avoid dishonesty and corruption' so the country would have the rule of law.[24] The distance between this position and the position of the army officers who until 2011 insisted on holding a monopoly on public discourse is not very great. Since the institutional cause of corruption is supposed to be insufficient money, beyond the question of economics the phenomenon again is reduced to the vices of individuals, and not institutional or ideological factors.

So what is the trouble here? Does not everyone want good, clean government? We would be hard-pressed to find anyone who would ask, at least publicly, for bad, dirty government, but to subscribe to the language of the prime-minister-cum-president and assorted other officials on this basis alone would be to miss the point. The language of counter-corruption does not conceal the dirty linen, but shifts the blame to everyone except people who hold the mantle of authority. Its recurrent theme is that the state is trying its best to eliminate wrongdoing. Corruption is due to human weakness, a result of the rotten apple in the barrel, or in Burmese, a rotten fish in the boat.[25]

Official speechifying on corruption in Myanmar is a distinctive form of what James Scott has described as a public transcript, constituting a '*self*-portrait of dominant elites as they would have themselves seen', which, 'While it is unlikely to be merely a skein of lies and misrepresentations ... is, on the other hand, a highly partisan and

21 *Myanma Alin* 6 Feb. 2007: 6. 22 *Myanma Alin* 13 May 2009: 3, 20.
23 *NLM* 1 Apr. 2011: 1, 7–10.
24 *Eleven Media* 15 Aug. (2013), 15 Aug. 2013 www.elevenmedia.com.
25 'One [rotten] fish makes the whole boat go bad', *Ngagônma tit kaung kyaung, tit hle lôn pôk*, cited in SC Letter 871/Su 12/146/2010, 13 Sept. 2010.

partial narrative.'[26] In the public transcript, benevolent, enlightened men exhort their subordinates to aspire to their own high standards. They do not deny the existence of corruption. On the contrary, they acknowledge it, and, in a sense, they celebrate it. This thing called corruption helps the dominant elite to naturalise its own authority. Its anti-corruption talk affirms that superiors are ethical, subordinates are not; superiors strive for clean and good government, subordinates sully it. The existence of a thing called corruption obliges functionaries to participate in what Lisa Wedeen characterises as the politics of pretence, the politics of 'as if', which 'produces guidelines for acceptable speech and behaviour; ... occasions the enforcement of obedience [and] induces complicity' in techniques for domination.[27] The transcript can be sustained only when an audience tacitly goes along with it. And where the message is delivered to judicial personnel, not only is the audience clearly identifiable; it is also clearly obliged to go along with the performance.

PRETENCE AND PUNISHMENT

Leafing through over a decade of Supreme Court records while researching this book, I came across the following warning in a circular sent to courts around the country:

> Upon examination of the national news on Myanmar Television and the photographs in daily newspapers it is observed that some judicial officers in attendance at the said events are not attired neatly and are not listening attentively to the guidance being delivered.[28]

This warning is a compelling illustration of the ideal of law and order in miniature, of 'the art of the state's splendor as visible order and manifest force'.[29] The state's splendour depends on its personnel maintaining an appropriate image for the cameras. Sloppy, uninterested officials are dangerous. The whole point of such events is that they are occasions to demonstrate obedience, to participate in the politics of pretence.[30]

[26] James C. Scott, *Domination and the Arts of Resistance: Hidden Transcripts* (New Haven and London: Yale University Press, 1990) 18.

[27] Lisa Wedeen, *Ambiguities of Domination: Politics, Rhetoric, and Symbols in Contemporary Syria* (Chicago and London: University of Chicago Press, 1999) 6.

[28] SC Letter 2153/Su 14(8) 36/97, 21 Mar. 1997.

[29] Michel Foucault, *Security, Territory, Population: Lectures at the Collège de France, 1977–1978*, trans. Graham Burchell, ed. Arnold I. Davidson (New York: Picador, 2007) 314.

[30] Wedeen, *Ambiguities of Domination* 19.

Appearances matter entirely. Yawn or doze off when the chief justice is talking, and you will be reprimanded.[31]

The politics of pretence, like the public transcript, require subordinates to produce a credible performance.[32] Where a top official preaches about corruption, it will not do to have a crowd of manifestly uninterested subordinates. Similarly, a judge or judicial bureaucrat must be able to demonstrate an ability to maintain a semblance of orderliness in court. A judge whose court fails to produce reasonably credible performances is a liability. No advantage is had in keeping her employed. By the same token, a judge who when confronted with allegations of wrongdoing can point to a record of orderliness and efficiency stands a good chance of escaping sanction, of mitigating punishment, or of having punishment reviewed. As one removed judge seeking to get his job back put it,

> As judicial work involves deciding between two sides in a dispute, one side will always be dissatisfied. If on account of one of those dissatisfied people a civil servant must suffer a loss, then it is to the state's detriment, just as it is to me, the affected person . . .[33]

Court records show that retention of personnel is as much an institutional concern as is removal of subordinates who are inept at maintaining a semblance of orderliness, if not more so. Hence, despite repeated reprimands, some judges and court staff continue holding office, while others succeed in returning to posts after having been removed, through sufficiently convincing restatements of their commitment to maintain a semblance of orderliness.

Orderliness, for the purpose of this discussion, is both general and specific. Orderliness in dealings with one's superiors, with court staff, and with the public ensures smooth operations of the administrative continuum through courts. This general orderliness encompasses matters of dress, speech, and manner. A judge failing to wear the correct attire, hearing cases in chambers, or having clerks do work that is not their responsibility is failing to do the minimum required. A judge should also be cordial with whoever is in the courtroom, and avoid using impolite, threatening, or abrasive language with peers, superiors, and parties to cases.

[31] As in SC Orders 209–10/2003, 25 Nov. 2003.
[32] Scott, *Domination and the Arts of Resistance* 4.
[33] SC Letter 4066/Su 14 (Ga) 91/95, 6 July 1995, appendix A.

Judges who fail to maintain general orderliness risk their jobs – like one who habitually bickered with his court staff, behaved rudely towards his superiors, and slandered the justices of the Supreme Court.[34] Resentful and annoyed subordinates and peers will look for opportunities to make complaints, as in the case of a township judge who went around saying he would punch a superior trying to find fault with him, and repeated the threat in an official meeting.[35] Regardless of who was really at fault, by failing to maintain appearances, he gave his opponents the material they needed to motivate higher-ups to act on their complaints. Luckily for him, an investigatory tribunal recommended that he be let off with a warning, since the incident amounted to a single infraction and was not part of a pattern of abusive behaviour.[36]

Because of the emphasis on morality in the public transcript, court records also caution judges against drinking heavily, turning up at court drunk, or molesting their counterparts publicly. Sexual liaisons that attract undue attention result in reprimands. The Supreme Court has sacked married judges it has found to be indiscreet in their extramarital affairs.[37] In 2009, it dismissed a judge after he took a second wife when married.[38] The apex court reprimanded another judge after he took one of his clerks to a new posting and cohabited with her.[39] And in 1996 its director general recommended dismissing two judges for having an affair. One was married with children; the other had absconded from her court to be with him.[40]

Public sanctions of women judges for wrongdoing are generally less precise about the nature of the offence, but are more condemnatory in tone. In one, the Supreme Court avoids the details of a judge's relationship with a retired colleague, but pointedly refers to their thirty-year age gap.[41] In another, it vaguely describes a deputy district judge as having engaged in 'abnormal' relations with her senior clerk despite repeated reprimands. The gazetted summary of the case does not spell out the abnormality, but stresses that as a woman judge she had special responsibility to keep her marital affairs in order.[42] The inference is that men

34 SC Letter 468/Su 14 (Ga) 75/92, 25 Jan. 1994.
35 Magway Divisional Court, Letter 122526/8–7/ (94), 14 June 1994.
36 Report of Preliminary Investigation 7/94, 11 Aug. 1994.
37 SC Letter 38/Su 14 (Ka) 166/93, 2 Sept. 1993. Order 97/2006, 17 Nov. 2006.
38 SC Order 70/2009, 28 Aug. 2009. 39 SC Order 100/2006, 29 Nov. 2006.
40 SC Letter 3176/Su 14 (Ga) 134/96, 31 May 1996. 41 SC Order 217/2003, 2 Dec. 2003.
42 SC Order 89/2007, 17 Aug. 2007.

are prone to bad conduct and require supervision, but women should know how to behave. Women set the standard for the menfolk to follow. When a woman fails to maintain the semblance of orderliness, her failure is more damaging than a man's.

Judges can meet with reprimands if for whatever reasons they forget that the ideal to which they are beholden subordinates their institutions to other parts of the state. An orderly judge recognises and accepts his subordinate status; a disorderly one does contrariwise. The Supreme Court chastised a judge who had the nerve not to attend a ceremony organised by the district council nor to send anyone in his stead or offer a reason for non-attendance.[43] It ordered another judge from his post for frequently going out to drink during court sessions; however, it also noted that just three weeks earlier he had 'spoken disrespectfully to the township police commander'.[44]

Court records also narrate cases in which local officials have lodged criminal charges against judges apparently due to interpersonal conflicts.[45] In these cases too, judges may have wrongly estimated the extent of their authority and status relative to office holders in other institutions. And, any judge who has the temerity to rule against a military officer ought to be prepared for repercussions. One judge learned this lesson the hard way after throwing the submission of a local battalion commander over a financial dispute out of court.[46] The outraged soldier sent excoriating complaints to the Supreme Court and his military superiors, demanding the judge's head. Non-judicial personnel, including soldiers, can and do initiate investigations to remove judges from office. Judges come under the same general code of conduct as other civil servants.[47] Anti-corruption statute does not differentiate between judicial and non-judicial personnel when investigating civil servants for malfeasance.[48]

Because the politics of 'as if' are politics of superficial compliance, they also require a specific form of orderliness associated with following orders from above. Any judge or judicial bureaucrat can lose her job for being uncooperative with superiors. A judge in the capital of Mon State

[43] SC Order 105/2002, 18 June 2002. [44] SC Order 99/2006, 29 Nov. 2006.

[45] As in SC Letter 102/Su 14 (Ga) 75/92, 3 Dec. 1993.

[46] SC Letter 484/Su 14 (Ga) 185/92, 21 Oct. 1993, and appendices.

[47] See Office of the Council of State, *Civil Servants Maintenance of Discipline Manual* (Rangoon: Office of the Council of State, 1985) (in Burmese).

[48] Eradication of Corruption Law, 23/2013, which repealed the 1948 Prevention of Corruption Act, 67/48.

ought not to have disregarded orders that as cases involving illegal fishermen were 'policy cases, the [state council] had given direct instructions warning that executive and judicial tasks were to be conducted in harmony'.[49] The state court had ordered subordinate judges to complete these cases as quickly as possible, and to send detailed reports on any matters that might impede the progress of rapid convictions, for instance, where they saw cause to grant bail. The judge in question proceeded to grant bail for legally justifiable reasons, according to ordinary procedure, without recourse to the state court.[50] When lectured for a second time about the orders from above on executive and judicial harmony, she reportedly argued with her supervising judge and persisted in granting bail, leading the state court to take the matter to the Supreme Court.

Orderliness is maintained in moneymaking through tacit advice to personnel on how to go about earning appropriately, and what lines not to cross when profiting from their positions. As in other aspects of professional life, they must follow certain procedures and participate in the politics of 'as if' when making money. For instance, judges ought not socialise with parties, at least not in public. A judge who allegedly enjoyed karaoke with the party to a case he was hearing and slept with a woman who just happened to have come along for the evening could not, for example, be said to have met with this proviso.[51] Nor could two judges seen enjoying regular meals with the defendant in a case at their downtown Yangon court.[52]

Judges also ought not flagrantly or 'excessively' take money from parties to cases.[53] Inflexibility over prices is not good either, unless the price is for a commonplace service and is relatively small and fixed. Judges do need to be willing to take negotiation seriously, and accept less money from parties to cases than they demand, especially where the people paying the money really are at the limit of what they can afford. Some even make a schedule of payments and outcomes so as not to mislead parties into thinking they have made all the payments necessary, when more will be expected later.

[49] Mon State Court, Letter 1/Secret (94), 3 Feb. 1994.

[50] As the accused judge set out in a sixteen-page letter of rebuttal, in SC Letter 4946/Su 14 (Ka) 44/94, 11 Aug. 1994, appendix B.

[51] SC Order 101/2004, 16 Sept. 2004.

[52] Report of the Departmental Investigative Tribunal established per SC Order 4/95, 10 Oct. 1995.

[53] SC Letter 4995/Su 14 (Ka) 86/94, 12 Aug. 1994, par. 1.

Moneymaking ought to be restricted to the routine business of cases in court. A judge who impounded motorcycles parked at the front of his house and demanded money from the owners to get them back went about things the wrong way.[54] He had ample opportunities to make money through routine activities, and should not have been so bold to think that his authority gave him a licence to make money from whomever he liked, or in this instance, disliked, wherever he liked. Another judge – whom an administrative council drafted into a special operation to register unlicensed boats in Myeik, near the southern border with Thailand – joined with a court clerk as well as at least a dozen officials from forestry, transportation, fisheries, revenue, and customs agencies to make a large amount of money off the vessels' owners and operators through extortion. The judge and other personnel involved apparently failed to realise that they would be under more scrutiny than when undertaking routine tasks.[55] A judicial tribunal convened to investigate found that although the clerk and judge should be criminally investigated, none of the evidence pointed to the involvement of the township judicial department head, who 'although he had responsibility for the supervision of his subordinates . . . had carried out his duties thoroughly and without dereliction'.[56] Whether or not the more senior judge was also getting his cut from the moneymaking scheme, he had comported himself correctly. He had proven sufficiently convincing in his performance of orderliness to satisfy the tribunal that he deserved to remain in office.

The admixture of publicity and ambiguity in orders issued against judges and judicial bureaucrats speaks to how the semblance of orderliness is maintained in Myanmar's courts. On one hand, judicial personnel have long been routinely reminded that failure to comply with instructions from above can lead to criminal prosecution. On the other, the lack of clarity about the actual reasons for the dismissal of personnel in many cases and vagueness about what constitutes immoral conduct liable to sanctions mean that nobody can ever be certain that his job and reputation are secure.

Through these subtextual signals judges are reminded that their moneymaking activities are tolerated and to an extent encouraged,

[54] SC Order 86/2006, 11 Oct. 2006.

[55] National Intelligence Bureau, Letter 252/14 (14–24) 93/MaTaPa-4, 28 Feb. 1994.

[56] Report of Preliminary Investigative Tribunal established per SC Letter 1488/Su-14 (Ga) 64/94, 28 Mar. 1994, 10–11.

provided they are orderly. As Lon Fuller has pointed out, this managerial method increases a superior's power over subordinates by allowing him opportunities 'to obtain gratitude and loyalty through the grant of absolutions, at the same time leaving him free to visit the full rigor of the law on those he considers in need of being brought into line'.[57] Obscurity about what constitutes an offence and inconsistency in enforcement of rules are not flaws or oversights. They are essential to maintain practices consonant with the law-and-order ideal.

Moneymaking is made orderly when calibrated through arrangements with other professionals, such as lawyers known as *nèza shene*, who do not move around dealing with cases in different courts, but are intimate with clerks, judges, prosecutors, police officers, and other officials in a single township or district, and are trusted to make deals locally. Sometimes these lawyers are relatives of police officers. The police nominate *nèza shene* to accused persons who do not already have legal counsel and who appear to have the means to pay. In exchange, *nèza shene* give an amount of case fees from nominated clients back to the police as a commission. Judges and court staff can also nominate *nèza shene*, and they also get a percentage of the lawyer's earnings as a commission.

A case broker, who might be a public prosecutor, court clerk, or relative of a judge, is an alternative to *nèza shene*. Official documents and speeches have long recognised the use of brokers. In 2008, the chief justice issued an instruction condemning, not for the first time, the prevalence of brokers in and around court premises. He described them as hanging around waiting for people to offer advice 'from hiring a lawyer, laying charges, applying for bail, submitting evidence, up to who to approach and how to do it to win a case' or how to delay and spoil a case that cannot be won.[58] His words echo those of the 1940 committee report: 'Magistrates and judges not infrequently receive money in person, or through their wives or mistresses, or through friends at clubs; professional touts, clerks, servants, and village headmen are often used as intermediaries'.[59] The language and practices associated with brokerage of criminal cases have evidently remained efficacious throughout the seven-and-a-half decades since.

Lastly, orderliness is maintained while making money through a language of disguise. Brokers, lawyers, prosecutors, and court clerks

[57] Lon L. Fuller, *The Morality of Law* (New Haven and London: Yale University Press, 1969) 213.
[58] SC Instruction 3/2008, 23 Sept. 2008.
[59] Bribery and Corruption Enquiry Committee, *Report* 11.

adopt jargon to discuss openly the buying and selling of cases and case outcomes. Some of it consists of euphemistic, innocuous-sounding exchanges, such as when a judge asks a colleague which hotel he stayed at on a recent trip. This question invites his counterpart to indicate how much money he is making on the side. Some is generic slang, such as the expression 'to water' something as a reference to giving money. If somebody loses a case, his friend may observe, 'You've lost the case! You didn't water it!' Or, a lawyer may advise a client that if she wants to win a case then, 'You'll have to water it well.' Other expressions like 'no oil without beans' are used to stress to a client that without investing in a case, it will not get resolved favourably.

Professionals also use perverted legalese, of which a good example is 'section 870'. A lawyer talking with another in front of the courthouse might suggest section 870 as a means to get the client released from charges. To the passerby unversed in law, it sounds as if they are talking about a technical matter. In fact, section 870 is nowhere to be found in the statutory codes. This section is from a different type of code, for three letters of the alphabet that resemble the Burmese numerals for 8, 7, and 0, which when spelled out mean 'to pay respects', *gayawa pyu*, a euphemism for a payoff. Section 870 inverts the notion of respect for a superior, and respect for the law, by situating both in a moneymaking discourse that feigns legality. It gives the appearance of respectful adherence to law while ridiculing it.

Similarly, personnel refer to 'part four', *a-paing le*. Many forms and documents consist of parts that must be completed for the criminal case to proceed. A police officer or court clerk filling out a form may instruct the defence lawyer that parts one, two, and three are completed, now it is time to do part four. This 'part' is not in the documents. It is word play in which the vowel sounds associated with the words 'part', *a-paing*, and 'four', *le*, are swapped to take on the meaning that it is time to give something, *a-pe laing*, literally, 'giving line'. The numerical reference can also be dropped, the officer requesting payment saying something along the lines of, 'My part is done; only your part is needed.'

The language of negotiation, of coordination, is what Scott calls the language of 'a politics of disguise . . . that takes place in public view but is designed to have a double meaning'.[60] Even as it appears orderly, it mocks courts and also the notion of legality. It inverts and mimics the official narrative, but also makes a concession to the politics of 'as if',

[60] Scott, *Domination and the Arts of Resistance* 19.

acknowledging the necessity for the semblance of orderliness. The purpose of these politics is not, after all, to be believed. They are powerful because they are not believed yet they are compelling.[61] They force participants to speak euphemistically, to maintain an appearance of docility and amiability towards the dominant elite, no matter how much contempt they may feel for them.

CONTROL AND COORDINATION

Every official involved in a criminal case has at least a small amount of control that he can use to get a payment. Control is of different types. In this section, I will discuss just two: one over the physical body of the accused, and another over the material evidence of a crime. The first is a type of control that I looked at in the last chapter with reference to the use of confession and torture, and here will extend to the practices of the marketplace. The second is a type of control over the production of evidence 'whenever and however the law as procedural code demands, rather than as a reality preceding' it.[62]

The most effective means to get control over a person in a criminal case is through control over the body: through confinement or the prospect of confinement. Any government office in Myanmar is a place of latent confinement, a place for the ordinary person to avoid, a place from which one has to struggle to get free. The longer one stays inside, the harder it becomes to leave. As more officials and agencies get involved, everybody wants something to let you go, and the transactions become more complicated and expensive.

Here is one example of a successful effort to get a person out of custody quickly, which also illustrates how practices of control and coordination, or negotiation, start from the moment the police appear on someone's doorstep. The story is from 2005, in a northern town on the border of China, where narcotics are rife and criminal cases for possession of narcotics are common, not just because of the quantities of drugs but also because of the need for high numbers of convictions and exemplary sentencing – as discussed in Chapter 4. According to the brother-in-law of the person arrested, policemen came to a shop where a young man was working and accused him of having illicit

[61] Wedeen, *Ambiguities of Domination* 12.

[62] Beatrice Jauregui, 'Shadows of the State, Subalterns of the State: Police and "Law and Order" in Postcolonial India', PhD diss., University of Chicago, 2010, 307.

drugs. At the time, the brother-in-law asked the police if the accused man would be released. The police inspector leading the arrest replied, 'We'll give you an answer at the station. We'll let you know what needs to be done for our side to settle the case.' The quick-thinking brother-in-law went to get a local official to play the role of broker. The official went to the station with the brother-in-law, and took the inspector to an eatery nearby. After the official went home and the detainee's family came to see him, he reassured them that everything would work out, as retold here in a signed written narrative of the sequence of events:

> 'I have negotiated it. Inspector Myint Kyi asked for twelve lakhs [1.2 million, around USD1,200]. I negotiated for six. So, you look for six. He will come get it in the evening.' Around 3 p.m., my sister-in-law and I took five lakhs to U Maung Maung's house. Inspector Myint Kyi was sitting in the kitchen. 'Will he take five?' my sister-in-law said. U Maung Maung took the money to Myint Kyi in the kitchen. He came back and said, 'He won't take five.' 'My sister-in-law needs to find another lakh. Set a time for it,' I said. 'Give it now,' Myint Kyi said. 'We'll go find it,' we said, and departed. We left the five lakhs. We borrowed a lakh from a neighbour, and went back to U Maung Maung's house. We gave the whole amount, exactly six lakhs. When we gave it, Inspector Myint Kyi threatened us that, 'Make sure news about this doesn't get out. If it gets out, I'll have you in jail.'

The policeman released the detainee from the lockup that day. Having surrendered his control over the body, he had only the threat of impending action to keep the young man and his family from making complaints about the negotiation, or 'coordination' of the release – the word being the same for both, *hnyi-hnaing*.

Sometimes, the police are just looking for opportunities to let a body go, and the coordinating involved is relatively effortless, even if the amounts demanded are not trivial. In a written complaint of mid-2013 to the national human rights commission, for instance, one detainee who alleged that he had already been assaulted at a police station in Mandalay described being railroaded with a co-accused into a transaction for a quick reduction of sentence inside the courthouse:

> The next day [after arrest] the two of us were sent for inquiry at the Chan-aye-thazan Township Court. They did not say anything about what we had been arrested for, or with what section we were charged. A plump policeman came and negotiated [*hnyi-hnaing*] with us that,

> 'If you want the case lightened, pay 170,000 Kyat' [at the time, around USD200]. So I begged my friend for help to pay that policeman. My friend on the very same day paid the amount of money to a uniformed policeman at the Chan-aye-thazan Township Court. After paying the money, other police told us that when the judge asked if I was guilty to admit it.

The defendant learned that his payment had bought him a seven-day prison term for a misdemeanour that could otherwise have carried up to three months in jail. The relatively high amount he was prepared to pay might in part have been due to his confusion and fear of what the police would do if he did not cooperate, and in part due to the location – a lucrative, business-oriented city where the premiums are high. Notably, the police did not offer him an opportunity to get out of the case completely, perhaps from concern to balance the needs of the marketplace with the need for fast and easy convictions to maintain the semblance of orderliness in processing of criminal cases, as discussed further below.

The threat of control over the body is also a source of power for court staff negotiating prices for case outcomes. In a similar scenario to the one above, a judge and court clerk in Yangon allegedly advised a man accused of running an unlicensed bodyworks that if he paid them and pled guilty to a charge then he would get off with a fine, but if he fought the case and lost he would go to jail.[63] He said he watched court personnel divvy up an initial payment, which bought him two weeks to come up with the remaining money. After the time was up and he could produce only one-fifth of the amount, the clerk gave an extension, whereupon he gave most of the amount requested and begged the judge to accept it since he could not find any more.

Control over the body gives its custodians opportunities to earn money, large amounts and small. Wherever people encounter junior custodians, they have to pay little amounts of money for delivery of food and medicines to detainees, and for opportunities to meet with them. Some families also pay superior officers not to torture or mistreat the detainee. They may also pay the crime-reporting officer to put the case to the top of the list that the police will submit to court, and thereby jump the queue for bail.

Wealthy and influential detainees can have a different custodial experience from everyone else. A lawyer recounted one case to me

[63] Ministry of Home Affairs, Letter 4/5 (5–53) 93/Oo 1, 27 Jan. 1994.

about the son of an army officer and a friend in northern Shan State who in 2008 faced charges for the attempted rape of a classmate. As the victim was from a well-known family in her locality, she pressed a complaint with the backing of some officials. The police had little choice but to arrest and open cases against the alleged perpetrators. But once in custody, the two young men did not stay in the cells with other detainees. The station commander put them in a room next to his office normally reserved for playing cards and drinking. Both of the accused reportedly had access to whatever food and alcohol they wanted, as well as to visitors. A court quickly let the officer's son out on remand, due to a supposed medical condition. It later acquitted both men.

Research conducted during 2012 at the main court complexes and township courts in five states revealed patterns in the practices of moneymaking through control over the body. Like the VIP detainees in the abovementioned case, remanded detainees in Loikaw, the capital of Kayah State on the border of Thailand, could avoid being sent to prison by paying from fifty to a hundred thousand Kyat to be kept at a room set aside for the purpose in the police station. The room was not luxurious, but it was better than prison, where remanded detainees feared becoming prey of seasoned inmates.

At many places, police and court officials have a lively trade going for the granting of bail. The Criminal Procedure Code distinguishes between two types of offences, one for which bail should be given automatically and another for which a court order is required under section 497(1). Defendants commonly have to pay for bail in the latter type of case. Complainants can also pay to prevent defendants from going free. During 1996 in a town near Yangon, for instance, a woman whose daughter had eloped with her lover got revenge by paying for the arrest and detention of the young man involved and his four brothers.[64] Foolishly, the judge neglected to shift the charge and denied them bail under a section of the Penal Code for which he should automatically have granted it, giving the detained men strong grounds for complaints against him after they got out.

Going rates for people who want to pay to get out on bail fluctuate from place to place. In Loikaw during 2012 lawyers advised that typically two to three hundred thousand Kyat would do it, with two-thirds of this amount for the judge and a third for the public prosecutor.

[64] SC Letter 2955/Su 14 (Ga) 43/97, 8 May 1997, appendices C and D.

The bench clerk, who can change the sequence of cases posted for hearing and speed up or delay processing of paperwork, would receive ten to twenty thousand Kyat; the police, thirty to fifty thousand.

In Mudon, a town in Mon State further to the south, the bail rates for offences like causing hurt by dangerous weapons under section 326 of the Penal Code or assault on a woman 'with intent to outrage her modesty' under section 354 were about 50 percent more than in Loikaw, although the subsidiary fees of the police and court clerk were roughly the same. The prices in Sittwe, capital of Rakhine State, on the western seaboard, were at least as much as in Mudon; however, lawyers indicated that in cases where an accused was patently innocent or unable to pay, judges and public prosecutors would sometimes settle for less than the standard amount. In Hpa-an, the capital of Karen State, the prices were lower: a minimum of a hundred thousand Kyat for the judge, and around eighty thousand Kyat for the prosecutor, with five to ten thousand Kyat paid to the court clerks and prosecutor's clerk.

Cases are managed and coordinated in similar ways across much of the country, but differ regionally. At a township in Chin State, on the border of India, professionals in 2012 reported that most cases were sorted out through payments in the police station, with relatively few matters going to court. The amounts that the police demanded were also modest – around fifty thousand Kyat to close a vehicle accident case, a bit more if the vehicles involved were unregistered; roughly the same for cattle smuggling; and, twenty to thirty thousand Kyat for minor assault. Professionals attributed the low amounts and tendency of police to keep matters out of court to local customs and fraternal feelings among members of ethnic minority groups there; however, the fact that the region is relatively poor and the money economy still relatively small may be contributing factors.

In certain types of cases where material evidence is unusually important, the control and coordination dynamics differ somewhat from other cases. Narcotics cases may involve chemical analysis of seized drugs or, in the case of users, urine. Under section 15 of the 1993 Narcotic Drugs and Psychotropic Substances Law, a drug user who fails to register voluntarily for rehabilitation can go to jail for three to five years. Police officers collect urine from accused users and send it for chemical analysis. A lab tests the urine and sends a result to the court where the case is posted. Depending on the positive or negative finding, the judge convicts or acquits the accused. In effect, a finding of guilt or innocence in these cases is made at the lab. The judge has limited discretion to decide on the sentence. So in cases lodged against alleged drug users, unlike many others where confession is the best evidence, control over the outcome of the case is contingent on control over the material evidence.

Professionals working on narcotics cases in the late 2000s said that the chemical analysis labs interpreted government policy on deterrence to mean that the default result for urine analysis should be positive. Labs offered negative results in exchange for payment. The 2009–10 starting figure in Kyat for a negative result was around one hundred thousand per urine sample, and a million per sample in the case of seized drugs: at roughly a hundred U.S. dollars and a thousand U.S. dollars respectively, small change for those accused who can afford to pay, including people actually trading in drugs. They are not affordable amounts for anyone with no money, contacts, and knowhow, like an alleged user brought to one station in the north during 2007. A court sentenced him to five years' imprisonment for a positive test result somehow taken from a sample of dirty water that he had provided the police from the toilet bowl at the station, where he was unable to urinate due to an infection.

Chemical analysis plays a part in other types of cases, such as murder, grievous hurt, and rape cases. Lab results are relevant, but trial outcomes do not hinge on them. Judges can also call for expert witnesses, as provided in sections 45 to 49 of the Evidence Act, such as in cases where persons are accused of trafficking items other than narcotics. Some parties pay expert witnesses to provide false evidence, such as to testify that tiger bones found in baggage on a train and apparently being taken to be sold for medicines were bones of another animal; and jade being smuggled illegally was some other, non-valuable, stone. The police also can switch real evidence for fake evidence, either with the complicity of the expert witness or without her knowledge. Township courts generally lack secure arrangements for keeping evidence during trial. Material evidence may be held at the bailiff's quarters on the court premises or at the police station. At either location, police officers and court staff have ample opportunities to damage, misplace, or sell stored items.

When bringing charges of possession, trafficking, and cultivation of narcotics, chemical labs' findings are also relevant, but unlike in users' cases, courts can admit and interpret a range of evidence to reach a verdict. For instance, if a group of people stand accused, a judge can arrange to acquit the ringleaders or real dealers and convict the minor offenders or substitutes. However, in cases where dealers have been caught red-handed with large quantities of narcotics and equipment for its manufacture, like one case in the capital of Shan State in 1994, this method might not be enough to insulate the judge from criticism.[65]

One professional who handles narcotics cases in 2010 said prices vary for acquittal under different offences in the Narcotic Drugs and Psychotropic Substances Law. Many factors affect outcomes, including the severity of the crime, the number of persons involved in the case, and the police units investigating. For example, a township or district judge in the north of the country might be paid anywhere from one to three million for acquittal in cases where the defendant is charged with possession of prohibited materials or implements under section 16(b) of the law, which carries a sentence of five to ten years in jail. In 2009–10 prices, for a charge of possession with intent to sell under section 19(a), which carries a minimum sentence of ten years, an acquittal can cost up to twenty million in payments to judges alone. Thus, narcotics cases contain many meeting points between the semblance of orderliness required of courts and their moneymaking imperative. One does not simply give way to the other. The two intersect and complement one another, communicate with one another, and reinforce each other throughout the business of criminal justice.

THE BUSINESS OF CRIMINAL JUSTICE

Control over the body of an accused criminal, or over the material evidence of a crime, is but one feature of the larger business of criminal justice in Myanmar's courts that pulls in and envelops accuser and accused, demanding something of each at every opportunity. Officials impose 'fees' on the complainant to lodge a case, to have police investigate, to have a superior officer keep a watch on case progress, and to have a public prosecutor handle it properly. The defendant may also pay fees to offset fees the complainant has paid, in addition to fees for release from custody, as discussed in the preceding section.

[65] Ministry of Home Affairs, Letter 4/21 (21–23) 94/Oo 1, 16 Aug. 1994. That the state media reported on this particular drug bust and the apex court expressed an interest in getting updates on it shortly afterward should have sufficed to caution the presiding judge against employing the usual techniques to acquit the primary accused. *Myanma Alin* 26 Oct. 1993: 11. SC Letter 286/11–1 (Pyit-3) 93/Thadin, 13/17 Jan. 1994.

Paperwork is expensive. Both sides pay for documents to be completed, for files to be signed and sealed, and for release and certified copies of records. As in the case of the public enemy, paperwork moves the case along the administrative continuum; only now it passes towards a negotiated outcome. Paperwork is necessary to ensure that everyone handling the case can earn something along the way. Take the cost of paperwork to move a minor criminal case from a township court, for revision at a district court in Mon State during 2012. In the township court, the costs were 2,000 Kyat to get the court bench clerk to release the case file; 1,000 Kyat for another clerk to certify it; 1,000 Kyat to the bailiff; and 100 Kyat per page for another clerk to photocopy it. In the district court, they were 5,000 Kyat to leave the file with the relevant clerk; 2,000 Kyat to the court clerk to issue a summons; and, 5,000 Kyat to deliver it. Optional fees cited for special services include 50,000 Kyat to get the file referred to a preferred judge and 20–30,000 Kyat to get the ruling typed on a computer – a fee worth paying for anyone wanting to have neat, legible records.

Whereas paperwork attracts standardised charges, in negotiation for case outcomes things get more complicated. Coordination of deals to shift charges, acquit, and reduce penalties can also get pricey. In rape cases, defendants like the VIP detainees mentioned above generally aim to pay for acquittal. The threat of a ten-year sentence under section 376 of the Penal Code makes the cost of getting off high; however, professionals say acquittal is relatively easy because as in the colonial period the procedural and attendant obstacles to a successful complaint are formidable. Many judges also seem to share the prejudices of their colonial-era predecessors, such as one described in internal records as having brazenly freed a rapist, while treating the complainant like the suspect.[66] Additionally, the paucity of forensic analysis in Myanmar and the heavy emphasis on witness testimonies, which may be unclear, incomplete, and contradictory, make it easy for a judge to release an accused on receipt of appropriate payments.

In 2010–2011, the cost of acquittal from a single charge of rape in a court of first instance situated in a large town ranged from 1.2 to 3 million Kyat, or about 1,200 to 3,000 U.S. dollars. A professional familiar with rape cases said payments were made approximately as follows: 200–300,000 Kyat to the crime recording officer to process the case quickly, and around the same amount to the prosecutor, paid so

[66] Ministry of Home Affairs, Letter 100/2-KaKa (4) / PaTaYa, 28 Dec. 1994.

as not to examine the case thoroughly in court; half a million to a million for the district judge to acquit; 1,000 Kyat to register the defence counsel's power of attorney with the police station where the defendant is held; 3,000 to 4,000 Kyat to the bench clerk each time the case is posted for hearing, paid to make sure it does get heard at the appointed time; 3,000 Kyat to the police transporting the accused to and from the court each hearing, so as not to assault or abuse the accused; 1,000 Kyat to the police guarding the accused in the court, for the family to meet with him and give food and words of encouragement, and the same amount again for the defence lawyer to meet and discuss the case before each hearing; 1,000 Kyat each time the family takes food to the accused in the lock-up and 3,000 each time the accused is inside prison, or 500 just to see the person for a couple of minutes through the bars, without giving anything. In some instances, the defendant may be advised or expected to pay off officials at the next level up in the hierarchy, to deter any appeal or to ensure an appeal is not successful.

Although rape cases tend towards acquittal through these and other methods, because they also often attract public interest, judges need to be careful to maintain the semblance of orderliness and not deliver a ruling that generates hostility or creates problems higher up. In one case from Yangon during the early 1990s, the uncle of an abducted and raped high school student made complaints against the township judge after she acquitted the accused, despite ample evidence on which to convict. He does not exactly say that the defendant purchased the ruling; however, he is clear enough about what he thinks happened when he writes that the accused 'showed off his people and wealth, bringing lots of individuals unrelated to the case to the courtroom, and driving up in a variety of cars', as well as using 'every other means' available to destroy the case.[67] In another case from a town north of Yangon during the same period, a judge convicted a man of raping a mentally infirm teenage girl but sentenced him to a short prison term, which may have covered the time already spent in remand. The mother wrote to the chief justice: 'At a time that tasks for the rule of law are being prioritised, that educated honourable judges instead of imposing an appropriately heavy punishment for the serious crime of rape ... have imposed a sentence of only six months is wrong in law and also in [the eyes of] society.'[68]

[67] Letter, 25 May 1994, 3, appended to SC Letter 4988/Su 14 (Ga) 143/94, 11 Aug. 1994.
[68] Letter, 17 May 1993, 2.

A deputy director general of the Supreme Court who reviewed the case agreed, and recommended that the judge be disciplined.[69]

Fatal car crashes carry custodial sentences for the negligent driver – or someone put forward as the driver on the real driver's behalf. Professionals say that unlike in rape cases acquittal is not so easily bought. A driver charged under section 304A of the Penal Code with 'doing any rash or negligent act' that causes death faces a maximum of seven years' imprisonment. The section does not stipulate a minimum period. Therefore, negotiations under this charge tend to concentrate on minimising the amount of time to serve. Payments to the judge for reduction of sentence are annualised. In Yangon during 2009–10 they were around one to two hundred thousand Kyat per year.[70]

The negotiations proceed roughly like this: the judge informs the defence lawyer that the accused will be sentenced to six years in prison; the defendant arranges to pay a million Kyat to the judge, and, at a rate of two hundred thousand per year, the sentence is reduced to a single year. The defendant may have been in remand for six months from the time of arrest to the court verdict. When this time is deducted from the sentence, he has to serve only six months before release. If the victim was friendless or her relatives penniless, the court only needs a conviction on paper and can release the accused on the day the verdict is read out in court through the 'sentenced-released' method, *cha-lut*.

Cha-lut is a pithy term referring to a technique enabling judges to maintain a semblance of orderliness while also coordinating (*hnyi-hnaing*) case outcomes. Using this technique, judges convict accused persons but pass sentences less than or equal to the total amount of time the accused has already been in custody awaiting trial, so he is immediately released when the court passes sentence. The accused is happy to go home, the judge and prosecutor make money and get a conviction to add to their statistics, and the defence lawyer has a satisfied client.

An accident where someone does not die but where one party suffers hurt or grievous hurt falls under sections 337 or 338 of the Penal Code. Like section 304A cases, each entails a possibility of imprisonment, for a maximum of two or five years respectively. In the former, an accused

[69] SC Letter 617/Su 14 (Ga) 166/93, 30 Aug. 1993, appendix B.

[70] This process can also work to increase sentences. According to a lawyer familiar with a case in the Supreme Court during 2009–10, an appellant paid ten million Kyat to a judge for the satisfaction of having the respondent imprisoned for five years: the rate of payment in this case too was annualised, at two million, around two thousand U.S. dollars, per year of sentence added.

person can negotiate with the police and with the injured party, to settle the matter without it going any further. If one party is hospitalised with serious injuries, then a duty police officer attached to the hospital should record the case, and it will go into the paperwork. The blameworthy party will then have to pay officials to escape imprisonment. A driver who sped through an intersection near a university campus on the outskirts of Yangon and ran onto the footpath, careening into a group of students, seems to have used this method. The judge acquitted him of section 337/338 offences, reasoning he had swerved to avoid another vehicle, that the injured students had jumped from the footpath and had been hit on the road, and that the police had not presented any evidence to show the defendant had been driving recklessly.[71] Unfortunately for him, the students' complaints to higher authorities had some effect. Police officers from the Criminal Investigation Department reinvestigated.[72] A bureaucrat in the office of the then ruling military council sent instructions to sack and prosecute the judge, prosecutor, and a police officer.[73]

Occasional setbacks for officials notwithstanding, throughout the 1990s and 2000s vehicle accidents remained popular revenue raisers. Here is an example of the expenses for the defence arising from an accident in a northern town during 2009: 50,000 Kyat to be on good terms with the commander of the police station handling the case, the same for the traffic policeman who came to the scene, and the same amount for bail and for the vehicle involved not to be impounded; 500,000 Kyat for the investigating officer, who arranged to resolve the case at a single sitting; 100,000 Kyat for the judicial medical officer recording details of the victim's injuries, to write something favourable for the defence, and another 50,000 Kyat to say something favourable in court; 10,000 Kyat for court clerks; 5,000 Kyat for the prosecutors; 6,000 Kyat for the crime-recording officer at the police station; 20,000 Kyat for the traffic police first on the scene; and, 87,000 Kyat to the

[71] *Sub Inspector Nyunt Swe* v. *Maung Saw Bo Bo Myo*, 1993 Criminal Case 844, Hlaing Township Court, 28 Jul. 1994.

[72] 'The Criminal Investigation Department investigates serious crimes transferred from state/division police forces and additional state/division police forces, compiles information within the purview of the rule of law and community peace and tranquility, investigates and forensically examines narcotics, stores and identifies fingerprints, and carries out other duties.' Police Manual, par. 20. See also par. 57.

[73] Office of the State Law and Order Restoration Council, Letter 302/3 (6) – 2/NaWaTa, 20 Jan. 1995.

injured party as settlement. The total cost of direct payments in this case was around 928,000 Kyat, nearly a thousand U.S. dollars.

The summary of an official investigation into a judge in upper Myanmar provides another good illustration of the opportunities judicial personnel have to make money from car accidents. In this case, from 1994, police charged both drivers of the crashed vehicles – one a light public transport vehicle – with rash driving under section 279 of the Penal Code.[74] The township court opened a case and remanded the two in custody. According to investigators, a court broker advised each side that for 10,000 Kyat – a considerable sum at the time – they could get out of custody with a quick conviction and a fine instead of a prison sentence. The conductor of the public transport vehicle made two payments to the judge directly, totalling 9,000 Kyat, while the owner of the other vehicle paid just 3,000 Kyat.

Another method of conducting the business of criminal justice in Myanmar involves the police initially registering or threatening to register charges under sections carrying heavy penalties and then negotiating downwards to lesser offences, or where possible negotiating to drop the charges altogether. In a car crash resulting in injury, for instance, the accused will seek to shift the charge from grievous hurt under section 338 to ordinary hurt under section 337 and then try to negotiate (*hnyi-hnaing*) to get the charge lifted.

Among other types of cases negotiated in the same manner, particularly in commercial centres such as Yangon and Mandalay, are cases under sections 406 and 420 of the Penal Code. Section 406 is criminal breach of trust. Section 420 is cheating. The legal difference between the two is beyond the scope of this discussion.[75] What matters is that the fine distinction between one and the other enables parties to cases under these sections to enter into a series of negotiating games in which all personnel can make money.

Suppose a businessman has a conflict with another businessman, a former partner, or a competitor; a building contractor, land speculator, or importer-exporter. He goes to the police and pays them to open a case against the other businessman under section 406. This section carries no more than three years' imprisonment. Section 420 carries up

[74] Ministry of Home Affairs, Letter 4/13 (13–46) 93/Oo 1, 28 May 1994.

[75] For a ruling on the difference, see *U Aye Thein* v. *Republic of the Union of Myanmar*, 2012 MLR 77. See also, U Ba Kyaing, 'Section 406? Section 420? Civil Case? How to Differentiate', *Collected Legal Articles*, vol. I (Yangon: Tainglin, 2000) 71–80 (in Burmese).

to seven. On the basis of the punishment alone, section 420 would be the more onerous offence. But complainants lodge cases under section 406 because under this charge an accused does not automatically get bail; under section 420 he does. A defendant taken into custody under section 406 must offer some grounds for release on bail, or get the case shifted to section 420 before proceeding to protracted coordination (*hnyi-hnaing*) to deal with the charge.

A professional who works on commercial criminal cases in Yangon gave the following estimates of costs in 2009–10 for someone lodging a complaint over unlawful possession of a car in a hypothetical section 406–420 case, the car valued at around thirty million Kyat, or a bit more than 30,000 U.S. dollars. To begin, the cost for the complainant to open the case at the police station, paid to the police, would be 500,000–1,000,000 Kyat. Another 200–400,000 Kyat would be paid to the investigating officer to recover the car from the other party as quickly as possible. As the car would initially be impounded, the complainant would have to pay to get it out. Once impounded, not only would the complainant be unable to use it, but it also would either deteriorate sitting in an open compound or have parts go missing, or both.[76] The judge for his part should accept a reasonable amount if offered. He should not sit on a vehicle for too long and cause a disgruntled party to complain elsewhere, as apparently happened in a case in Mandalay over which a judge was removed from office.[77]

With the car out, a further 100–200,000 Kyat would be paid to the crime-recording officer at the police station to submit the case to court promptly. Half a million to one million Kyat would be paid to the prosecutor to give advice for the case to proceed as a criminal case. The judge would get 3–4,000,000 Kyat. Once the case is decided, another 200–500,000 Kyat would be paid to the prosecutor not to take the case to a higher court for revision. And on top of all the above expenses are the pocket monies throughout the trial process: voluntary donations to whatever funds and causes are being promoted at the court and police station; costs of the judge's recreation travel and other leisure activities while the case is being heard; small presents for each of the officials working on the case; and tea and cake monies for the court clerks on each day the case comes up on the docket, which add up to another

[76] As recognised in Committee for the Supervision of Vehicular Discipline, Letter 1419/8/SaSaYa/YaSaKa, 8 Aug. 1994.

[77] SC Order 106/2002, 18 June 2002.

2–3,000,000 Kyat. In total the cost to recover the car, if everything goes to plan, would be from around 7,000 to over 12,100 U.S. dollars, although the amount should not exceed about one-third of the vehicle's market value.

In cases that for one reason or another may attract attention from superiors, more creative techniques may be necessary, but participants in the marketplace still find ways to make money and satisfy demands for a semblance of orderliness. One lucrative technique is 'double cropping' (*nit-thiza*) through the appeal process. The technique has a long pedigree, being mentioned in the 1940 report discussed earlier, whereby a

> Court may deliberately give judgment against the bribe giver, knowing, and explaining to him, that it will be reversed on appeal. Moreover, in many cases the evidence is such that the case be plausibly decided either way. Where this is not so, the Bench may bully the witness so as to get on the record what is desired, or note on the deposition that his demeanour is such that his evidence is to be treated with suspicion, or not record his statement correctly. We have been told of cases where evidence has been re-written afterwards.[78]

Using this technique, which takes its name after cultivation of fertile land twice in a single year, a lower court judge accepts money not to acquit but to impose a lesser sentence on conviction and to arrange for the sentence to be overturned or revised on further payments made on appeal in a higher court. As the court of first instance and the appeal court both make money from the same case, it is a double crop.

In one case during 2007 officials resorted to double cropping to make a tidy profit and because they were worried about public backlash if they acquitted the accused in the court of first instance. A special drug squad swept into a town on the border of China and arrested a dealer in league with the local police. Because of outside agency involvement and the relatively high profile of the case, the judge explained to the defendant's lawyer and prosecutor that he could not acquit. Instead, they agreed he would convict the accused, but prepare a flawed verdict with the connivance of the prosecutor. The judge allowed the defence attorney to ask leading questions; and the prosecutor arranged for witnesses to turn hostile, asked questions that supported the defence, and failed to cross-examine witnesses. The lower court notified the

[78] Bribery and Corruption Enquiry Committee, *Report* 11–12.

appellate judge to look forward to a double crop, and he released the accused because of the flaws in the prior verdict. The prosecutor did not appeal the acquittal. The dealer settled down in another township. He only returned to his hometown after his lower-court sentence had expired, suitably contrite, and also, according to one source, bankrupt due to the heavy costs the double-cropping officials had imposed. In 2012, he was seen running a noodle stand and had reportedly given up on the drug business: an unqualified success for the institutions of law and order, if not for the rule of law.

CONCLUSION

The public transcript on corruption in Myanmar gives the appearance of creating barriers to moneymaking through criminal cases. In fact, it is concerned with the due regulation of moneymaking practices: the provision of guidelines for coordination and control that will work to the advantage of the individual judge or policeman, and the sovereign power. It aims primarily not to address practices identified as corrupt but to affirm the imperative for law and order through a model of probity in which personnel follow orders as required, demonstrate compliance, and maintain an appearance of orderliness.

Rather than prohibiting moneymaking through criminal cases or even papering over what goes on in Myanmar's police stations and courts, the politics of law and order tolerate certain types of disorder, creating 'simulacra' of order through parallel modes of production and profiteering, speaking and doing.[79] Unlike the rule of law, law and order can permit departures from law without damaging its essential qualities, including through practices for the making of money where these maintain a semblance of orderliness.

The politics of law and order have exacerbated and institutionalised moneymaking practices throughout Myanmar's courts, and have honed the skills of practitioners who are keen to maintain a semblance of orderliness and also get ahead financially; however, the lineages of these politics and their attendant practices go back much further than the last few decades. As Saha points out, we have 'good reasons for considering the colonial period onward as a distinct one: a period in

[79] John L., Comaroff and Jean Comaroff, Introduction, *Law and Disorder in the Postcolony*, eds. John L. Comaroff and Jean Comaroff (Chicago and London: University of Chicago Press, 2006) 5.

which corruption has been intrinsic to how the modern state has been seen and performed in its various colonial and post-colonial forms'.[80] And so in parts of neighbouring Bangladesh, a country that shares a colonial institutional and statutory legacy with Myanmar, the business of criminal justice goes on in markedly similar ways, despite the two countries' different postcolonial trajectories.[81] The public transcript too has certain commonalities, with the print media in Bangladesh directing its ire towards members of the subordinate judiciary whom lawyers accuse of being corrupt and engaging 'in irregular practices in the administration of justice'.[82]

Comparisons with other postcolonial states raise further questions about the degree to which moneymaking practices once embedded in juridical institutions are resistant to political change. Research on Indonesia suggests that far from going into decline, the business of criminal justice has thrived with the post-1998 transition to electoral democracy.[83] And in China, repeated and increasingly high-level counter-corruption campaigns have failed to diminish the trade in case outcomes, because the opportunities for moneymaking through courts are – as in Myanmar – well-structured and fully integrated.[84] National politics might evolve, but the practices associated with repressive government are insidious. Those institutions most concerned with these politics are also the most resistant to demands for a new, opposing brand of politics, a brand evocative of the rule-of-law ideal, rather than evoking one or another of its asymmetrical opposites.

80 Saha, *Law, Disorder and the Colonial State* 131.

81 Md. Shariful Islam, *Politics-Corruption Nexus in Bangladesh: An Empirical Study of the Impacts on Judicial Governance* (Hong Kong: Asian Legal Resource Centre, 2010) ch. 3. Muhammad Rafiqul and S.M. Solaiman, 'Torture under Police Remand in Bangladesh: A Culture of Impunity for Gross Violations of Human Rights', *Asia-Pacific Journal on Human Rights and the Law* 4.2 (2003): 8–9.

82 Sarkar Ali Akkas, 'Judicial Independence and Accountability: A Comparative Study of Contemporary Bangladesh Experience', PhD diss., University of Wollongong, 2002, 271.

83 Jacqueline Baker, 'The Rise of Polri: Democratisation and the Political Economy of Security in Indonesia', PhD diss., London School of Economics and Political Science, 2012. Simon Butt and Tim Lindsey, 'Judicial Mafia: The Courts and State Illegality in Indonesia', *The State and Illegality in Indonesia*, eds. Edward Aspinall and Gerry van Klinken (Leiden: KITLV Press, 2011) 189–213.

84 Ling Li, 'The "Production" of Corruption in China's Courts: Judicial Politics and Decision Making in a One-Party State', *Law and Social Inquiry* 37.4 (2012): 848–77.

7

THROUGH DISORDER, LAW AND ORDER

All public assemblies that power holders have not organised or endorsed themselves pose a latent political threat to the dominant group. Political domination contains an implicit assumption that subordinates mobilise only when authorised. Hence, successive governments in Myanmar, and before it, Burma, have been persistently concerned to manage, control, and prohibit public assemblies.

The British colonial government assigned public assembly an inherently criminal quality. The colonial template for its management through courts and police has remained over subsequent decades, but the manner of its application has changed. This chapter explores that change across three events of large-scale protest under successive military governments, in 1974, 1988, and 2007. Concentrating on events during 2007, it discusses how protestors inadvertently crossed a threshold into what Giorgio Agamben describes as a 'zone of anomie', which is neither fully inside nor outside the juridical order, but is a zone where legal determinations are deactivated.[1]

In 2007, two extrajuridical institutions realised the anomic zone that enveloped protestors. A proxy police force, 'the gang', enabled the movement of people into spaces where officials could detain and investigate them without ordinary rules applying. These spaces I designate, reading Agamben, as 'the camp'. Following on from the gang and the

[1] Giorgio Agamben, *State of Exception*, trans. Kevin Attell (Chicago and London: University of Chicago Press, 2005) 23, 50.

camp, courts functioned not to interrogate the work of the police and other personnel, not to determine the guilt or innocence of accused protest leaders brought before them, but to pull the accused back into the formal legal realm, to restore to them the juridical personhood withdrawn from them in the zone of anomie. In closing, I argue that in 2007 unauthorised assembly was criminalised in a highly ambiguous, imprecise manner, in which the juridical and extrajuridical elements of the response were purposefully interwoven throughout.

This chapter is based on the records of eighty criminal cases brought before twenty-eight courts at various levels, interviews, news reports, and other materials collected during research conducted from 2008 to 2011, as well as some collected in the course of events during 2007. I also have drawn on confidential documents concerning the planning and use of the gang to attack and disperse protestors.

The chapter concentrates on events in 2007 because, as in the study of the policeman as torturer, study of the gang-camp-court continuum as an archetype of law and order reveals features of the response to unauthorised public assembly more vividly than in other instances. The chapter also contributes new details and analysis to existing accounts of events in 2007, most of which followed close on the heels of the protests.[2]

UN-AUTHORISING PUBLIC ASSEMBLY

A full chapter of the Penal Code, chapter eight, sets out offences against public tranquility and their punishments. The terms used in

[2] See, for example, Christina Fink, 'The Moment of the Monks: Burma, 2007', *Civil Resistance and Power Politics: The Experience of Non-violent Action from Gandhi to the Present*, eds. Adam Roberts and Timothy Garton Ash (Oxford: Oxford University Press, 2009) 354–70; Richard Horsey, 'The Dramatic Events of 2007 in Myanmar: Domestic and International Implications', *Dictatorship, Disorder and Decline in Myanmar*, eds. Monique Skidmore and Trevor Wilson (Canberra: ANU E-Press, 2008) 13–28; Jeff Kingston, 'Burma's Despair', *Critical Asian Studies* 40.1 (2008): 3–43; Kyaw Yin Hlaing, 'Challenging the Authoritarian State: Buddhist Monks and Peaceful Protests in Burma', *Fletcher Forum of World Affairs* 32.1 (2008): 125–44; Stephen McCarthy, 'Overturning the Alms Bowl: The Price of Survival and the Consequences for Political Legitimacy in Burma', *Australian Journal of International Affairs* 62.3 (2008): 298–314; Andrew Selth, 'Burma's "Saffron Revolution" and the Limits of International Influence', *Australian Journal of International Affairs* 62.3 (2008): 281–97; David I. Steinberg, 'Globalization, Dissent, and Orthodoxy: Burma/Myanmar and the Saffron Revolution', *Georgetown Journal of International Affairs* 9.2 (2008): 51–58.

the code evoke the criminality of unauthorised gatherings: 'criminal force', 'rioting', 'affray'. Here, in the concern with the uncontrolled or potentially uncontrollable mobility of individuals, law gives expression to the fear of the threat that an unauthorised assembly poses to the state – a threat that is framed as a problem of order.

For colonial government, the threat consisted of two types or, rather, posed two challenges: one, when might people mobilise in a manner that could randomly and unintentionally become a latent threat? And two, when might they do so with intent to cause a direct threat?

Colonial government addressed the first of the two challenges via a variety of instruments that prohibited or regulated assemblies deemed potentially threatening, irrespective of whether or not they had any political qualities. The bottom line in most cases was not the nature of the event but the size of the crowd.[3] The larger the number of people assembled, the more likely something might happen without the approval or prior knowledge of the state.

The second of the two challenges was more hazardous. Where people purposefully came together to threaten public tranquility, courts had to establish collective intention.[4] Statements made to the assembly could be used to infer purpose, as could evidence of illegal plans cast as the 'common object' of those assembled.[5] Courts also examined material evidence to support or dispute claims of intention. Simultaneously, they sought to weave narratives into their accounts that for political reasons disavowed or re-ordered the purposes of those assembled. Records from courtroom trials then went on to shape the official narrative of counter-protest and counter-insurgency.[6] Through the official record, the colonial government sought to reassert its control over both the accused and the public domain, and thereby re-establish order.

Political threats posed by public assemblies could be deflected by deliberately blurring rebellious acts with criminal ones and, in particular, with dacoity, or armed robbery by gangs. In his study of rebellion narratives in India, Ranajit Guha has attributed the colonial administration's homogenising of crime and resistance, the amalgamating

[3] As in *King-Emperor* v. *Nga Nyun Bu and 5*, (1897–1901) 1 UBR 370.

[4] As discussed in *Saya Kye and Others* v. *Queen-Empress*, (1892–96) 1 UBR 148.

[5] *Maung Tok and 10* v. *King-Emperor*, 3 Ran. 352.

[6] As discussed in Maitrii Aung-Thwin, *The Return of the Galon King: History, Law and Rebellion in Colonial Burma* (Athens: Ohio University Press; Singapore: National University of Singapore Press, 2011).

and conflating of one type of activity with another, to 'a perception impaled on a single stereotype of rural violence. Unable to distinguish between rebellion and dacoity [colonial government] tended to classify all "rebels" as "dacoits", as if the two words meant the same thing.'[7] Although sympathetic to Guha's argument, I think he oversimplifies matters. The records of administrators in Burma, while at times expressing confusion about violent resistance to British rule, also suggest deliberate misuse of the two concepts. Just as postcolonial governments would later disingenuously decline to recognise the political demands of opponents, preferring to dismiss them as terrorists, saboteurs, and malcontents unwilling to see their compatriots prosper, the colonial government could ignore the grievances and claims of dissidents characterised as bandits.[8] Denying rebels status in public discourse, authorities could assimilate their acts into a category that minimised their political challenge to the state.[9]

By the early 1930s, people in large parts of Burma's countryside were rising up in armed resistance to British rule. As rural unrest spread and solidified, the government moved to amend the criminal law to try a range of Penal Code offences summarily, to detain suspects without trial, and to execute convicted men through special tribunals freed from the evidentiary requirements of regular courts. It also introduced other repressive laws in response to further public events that threatened law and order, such as communal violence in Rangoon during 1938.

Postcolonial governments in Burma and later Myanmar have, as discussed in previous chapters, shown a persistent concern to use juridical and administrative mechanisms of colonial government, adapting them to changing political conditions. However, as time has passed and the narrative of criminalisation associated with certain types of assemblies has persisted, the juridical practices associated with them have diminished in favour of administrative mechanisms, consistent with the politics of law and order. The remainder of this section explores some of the continuities and discontinuities in language and

[7] Ranajit Guha, *Elementary Aspects of Peasant Insurgency in Colonial India* (Durham, NC, and London: Duke University Press, 1999) 101.

[8] As in *Nga Sein* v. *King-Emperor*, 3 LBR 121; *Nga Wa Gyi and 15* v. *King-Emperor*, (1902–03) 1 UBR Evid. 1; *Nga San Nyein and 9* v. *King-Emperor*, (1917–20) UBR 3.

[9] James C. Scott, *Domination and the Arts of Resistance: Hidden Transcripts* (New Haven and London: Yale University Press, 1990) 206.

practices in response to large-scale public protests in 1974 and 1988, before turning in the next section to the events of 2007.[10]

In December 1974, the United Nations returned the body of its deceased former Secretary General, U Thant, to Rangoon for last rites. Students snatched the body and took it to a university campus, where members of the public and the Buddhist clergy, the Sangha, soon joined them. The Council of Ministers later presented a summary of findings on the events:

> What happened was that as U Thant passed away on November 25, 1974, from the time that it was put forward that his remains would be brought to Rangoon, the Rangoon Division People's Council coordinated with U Thant's younger brother U Khant and in accordance with his wishes arranged that the remains could be kept at the Kyaikkasan Ground before obsequies, and the relevant people's councils discussed all aspects of the funeral affairs with concerned departments. Although the Rangoon Division People's Council assisted in all aspects, students, Sangha and some troublemakers forcibly stole U Thant's remains on the day of the obsequies, December 5, 1974, and took them to the university campus. A group of troublemakers, students and Sangha even designated the university campus as a liberated area. Acting in the manner of a rival government, they shouted slogans, gave speeches, distributed documents and generated disturbances for the removal of the state authorities that the working people had elected to office. Although a place was prepared for the obsequies of U Thant's remains in the Kandawmin Park in accordance with the wishes of U Khant and U Thant's family, at 1 p.m. on December 8, 1974 a group of troublemakers opposed the wishes of the majority and entombed the remains on the university campus. Therefore, at 2 a.m. on December 11, 1974 People's Police under direction of the Rangoon Division People's Council, carrying only tear gas canister-firing guns to use as necessary were sent in and cleared the university campus. The Defence Services were sent not far behind as back up to be used only depending on circumstances. It could be clarified that apart from the firing of tear gas canisters, there was no

[10] I am here concerned with the criminalising and un-authorising of these assemblies, not with the events as recorded by eyewitnesses and researchers. For detailed accounts of the December 1974 protests, see Kyaw Htet Aung (Shwepyidan), ed., *Popular Opposition Struggles to the BSPP Dictatorship: 74–75–76* (Yangon: Shwepyidan, 2013) 181–209 (in Burmese); Maung Pan Yi, *Because of the Time that the Mother Peacock's Wings Fell* (Yangon: Zinyadanazaw, 2013) (in Burmese). Andrew Selth, *Death of a Hero: The U Thant Disturbances in Burma, December 1974* (Brisbane: Griffith University, 1989). On 1988, see the first footnote in Chapter 4.

> firing. There was no bloodshed. The people found on the university campus were taken and held for questioning.[11]

I have quoted this passage at length because it captures key features of the public transcript on unauthorised assembly. The protestors engage in violent and unruly action. The government authorities respond with care to ensure events do not get worse. They encourage people caught up in the events by accident to come forth. They try to identify and isolate instigators, both individuals and underground organisations responsible for the spread of protests.[12] And, they use restraint and minimal force to re-secure control.

Accompanying the narrative of unauthorised assembly are the procedural mechanisms to un-authorise it. The procedure followed in 1974 is set out in a government report on the violence after the military had crushed protests at the university:

> Violent disturbances unrelated to the funeral broke out. Starting with the arson of Hino trucks in Kamayut Township, there were simultaneous destructive disturbances in a total of thirteen townships in Rangoon Division. Although the Rangoon Division People's Council promulgated section 144, since it was not possible to bring the situation under control with the People's Police Force, the assistance of the Defence Services was requested. Although the Defence Services gave assistance, since violent agitators were trying to create anarchic conditions, the Council of Ministers submitted to the Council of State that a state of emergency be declared. In accordance with article 76 of the [1974] Constitution, the Council of State designated Rangoon Division as an area under military administration.[13]

In this account, state authorities acted to put an end to the assemblies in a clear sequence. First, they made an attempt at re-establishing control via section 144 of the Criminal Procedure Code, which authorises judges to issue orders for preventive measures to avert disturbances. Second, the civilian authorities called the army to assist in dealing with those demonstrators who did not disperse. Third, when

[11] Govt. of the Socialist Republic of the Union of Burma, *Digest of Undertakings of the First Pyithu Hluttaw* (Rangoon: Office of the Pyithu Hluttaw, n.d.), 246 (in Burmese). In this direct quotation and others I have translated the term for the armed forces, *Tatmadaw*, as Defence Services consistent with official usage.

[12] As stated in Govt. of the Socialist Republic of the Union of Burma, *Digest of Undertakings of the First Pyithu Hluttaw* 276.

[13] Govt. of the Socialist Republic of the Union of Burma, *Digest of Undertakings of the First Pyithu Hluttaw* 246–47.

these measures failed, they followed a constitutional procedure to bring in military administration.

Official accounts of events in 1988, when people around the country protested against the one-party socialist government, describe roughly the same sequence. However, whereas in 1974 the government acknowledged the political nature of the protests, after 1988 it downplayed and obscured this aspect, concentrating instead on the role of instigators and the spread of violence:

> On March 15, 1988, Yangon Institute of Technology students gathered and shouted [slogans and speeches] and also destroyed school furniture. Furthermore, since they posed a danger to the school authorities, schools were temporarily closed. On March 16, due to external political instigations, students spreading the disturbances to Yangon University (Main) marched from Yangon University (Main) to Yangon University (Hlaing Campus). The students reached a place near the White Bridge, when People's Police Force personnel dispersed and contained the assembly. Furthermore, 154 male and female students involved in the disturbance were held for interrogation and it was observed that there were no deaths. However, because of those preventive measures, politicians stoked the flames to increase the intensity of the disturbances.[14]

The narrative establishes the pedigree of the protestors from the beginning, denying them a political programme. They march around destroying things that should be used for their own education: public property, the material stuff of the state. They threaten the school authorities: state officials and representatives of the ruling party. They do everything in an anarchic and aimless way. They are not so much a movement as a contagion. The word used to describe the 'spreading' of disturbances in this passage, *kuzet*, is the same as the word used to describe the spread of an infectious disease – a term found in official narratives denigrating political movements since the colonial period.[15] The idiom of protest as disease conveys a tone of irrationality, a type of madness giving the whole event its virulent, uncontrollable quality.

As in 1974, the public transcript of events in 1988 sets out how the authorities operated with a minimum of force to restore law and order, but despite their best efforts, saboteurs and other troublemakers spread

[14] Govt. of the Union of Myanmar, *Defence Services History*, vol. VI, 8 vols. (Yangon: Office of the Defence Services Historical Museum and Archives, n.d.) 346 (in Burmese).

[15] See Guha, *Elementary Aspects of Peasant Insurgency* 220–22.

the unrest elsewhere. In 1974, the government was at pains to characterise violence around the city as incidental to the events on campus. In 1988, because the government depicted the demonstrators as lacking any authentic political consciousness of their own, it could also blame them directly for the spread of violence:

> On June 21, 1988 ... People's Police Force personnel peacefully and without arms dispersed around 5,000 students and people desirous of violent disturbances who were marching to the Myenigon side of Sanchaung Township, for the purpose of stopping them from going into town. However, violent parties threw stones at the Sanchaung People's Police Station, and making efforts to force their way in through strength of numbers, gave rise to pitched combat with sticks and knives between the people desirous of violence and the People's Police Force personnel. However, since the People's Police Force personnel did not resort to firing, the violent brawlers took advantage and entered and destroyed the police station, stabbing and striking with sticks and knives the People's Police Force personnel they captured, and wickedly committing murder. ... Thus, for the protection of the lives and property of its parents, the people, and for the sake of the rule of law [*taya-ubade-somoye*], the Defence Services came to the assistance of the People's Police Force personnel.[16]

In one incident after another, security personnel beg demonstrators to desist from their destructive path.[17] On each occasion, only when the violence of demonstrators becomes more outrageous, only when the survival of the rule of law – read as law and order – is at stake do the armed forces enter the fray and restore peace, stability, and, of course, the rule of law, with minimum casualties.

Events in 1988 were much more protracted and widespread than in 1974. Official measures to address them followed a similar sequence, but were less clear-cut. Local authorities variously imposed and withdrew section 144 orders in townships around the country. The government also imposed and withdrew orders for military administration sporadically, possibly as part of a strategy to generate disorder that would enable the military to separate the most committed demonstrators from everyone else, and then direct the full force of

[16] Govt. of the Union of Myanmar, *Defence Services History* 350.

[17] See, for instance, *Myanma Alin* 9, 12 Aug. 1988, in Zawana (Agriculture), ed. *Historical Newspaper Accounts from the Democracy Uprising* (Yangon: Zinyadanazaw, 2013) 6–9 (in Burmese).

its response towards the former group.[18] In September, the new military government imposed a nationwide curfew, banned assemblies, and ordered protest camps shut down.[19] With these orders from above, the new era of law and order as the rule of law began, continuing up until 2007, when large unauthorised assemblies again formed around the country. The remainder of the chapter concerns the events of that year.

A CASE STUDY OF AMBIGUOUS CRIMINALISATION

Even when compared to how the police and military handled events in 1988, the official response to events in 2007 was highly ambiguous. The narrative of criminalisation began as usual. In August, small protests started in response to sudden unannounced increases in fuel prices, as reported in the state media:

> Advance information was received that internal and external destructionists not wishing to see the national government's successfully implemented undertakings, and with the sole aim of taking power, have set down and are carrying out a three-point strategy for the downfall of the national government, namely: endeavouring to destroy the National Convention; working for the emergence of a popular uprising like the 88 crisis; and, undertaking of all types of opposition activism within the law. On August 15 the internal and external destructionists, taking advantage of the rise in motor fuel prices as a means to their ends, began making incitements among the people for the success of the three-point strategy.[20]

In official accounts of 1974, the frontline protestors had unacceptable political demands. In 1988, they were the pawns of political manipulators behind the scenes. In 2007, the first protestors onto the streets had the worst qualities of both types from the earlier periods. They were political manipulators and opportunists, bent on national disaster, with unacceptable demands. They had political thoughts and strategies, but their project aimed only at taking power and was destructive, even though they had framed it so as to be 'within the law'. Despite the demonstrators' care not to commit criminal offences, their actions were

[18] Federico Ferrara, 'Why Regimes Create Disorder: Hobbes's Dilemma During a Rangoon Summer', *Journal of Conflict Resolution* 47.3 (2003): 302–25.

[19] SLORC Orders 3–4/89, 27 June and 20 July 1989. SLORC Martial Law Order 2/89.

[20] *Myanma Alin* 22 Aug. 2007: 16.

criminal because they assembled in a manner that inherently threatened law and order.

The catalytic incident for large assemblies was apparently a melee between monks and security forces, which the state media described as follows:

> As information was received that some Sangha from some monasteries in Pakokku town, Magway Division were going to protest, responsible persons went at 2 p.m. on September 5 to keep matters under control; however, the Sangha rejected their supplications and bearing placards with the title of the Sangha Samaggi walked in protest along Bogyoke Road, shouting slogans for the release of arrested protestors and for reduction of commodity prices; that although the responsible persons ... earnestly forbade them, the Sangha refused, and because they pushed over and past the abbot [serving as] Township Sangha Nayaka Chair and protested [further], the abbot and public were in possible danger and so the responsible persons fired three rounds from small arms skywards, frightening the crowd to disperse, at which time around a hundred protesting Sangha fled.[21]

The article continues that the next day officials toured monasteries in the area in an effort to prevent further disturbances, but around fifty monks threw stones at their vehicles and tried to roll them over. The monks allegedly trapped the officials inside a monastery and demanded that the township chairman be brought out to them; when the officials refused to comply, the protesting monks burned the vehicles.

Again, in this scenario the authorities show restraint in the face of provocative unauthorised assembly. As in previous years, the official narrative denied that any monks or citizens had been harmed in the course of these events, despite the reports of foreign news broadcasters to the contrary.[22] It put the blame on the people and monks assembled without authorisation. The reference to the banner of the Sangha Samaggi is also a signifier of intent to upset law and order. The government banned the Sangha Samaggi, or monks' union, in 1990 after it launched a religious boycott of the military.[23] By representing themselves – or being represented – as members of the Sangha Samaggi and pushing over and past the Sangha Nayaka Committee township chair, the monk serving as the official link between religion and state in

[21] *Myanma Alin* 7 Sept. 2007: 16. [22] *Myanma Alin* 8 Sept. 2007: 16, 3.

[23] SLORC Order 6/90, 20 Oct. 1990. The Sangha Sammagi was a leading nationalist anticolonial group established in 1919, from its inception political in character and motives.

the locality, the demonstrators were challenging the state's insistence on the primacy of its authority and on its right to set down rules for maintenance of order, both religious and secular.

The narrative then moved quickly from characterisations of simple defiance into seemingly widespread, random violence. Monks allegedly started leading mobs to attack government buildings in some towns, instigating melees between police officers and members of the public.

The size of protest in 2007 was much smaller than in 1988, yet the official response was more ambiguous. A United Nations independent expert on human rights who visited the country not long after the events said officials informed him that they had responded to the protests by introducing a curfew under section 144 'on 25 September which was made known to the public from 9 p.m. through the towns overnight by thirty-three cars through loud-speakers, advertised on boards at public places and broadcasted by the City FM Radio and advertised in newspapers and journals'.[24] Contrary to this account, the print media do not appear to have referred to section 144 until October 5, ten days after the order took effect. Even then, the news reports mentioned the order in passing. The first formal government statement on October 4 also made no reference to section 144 orders or other measures.[25] Eyewitness reports did describe vehicles driving through affected townships declaring the curfew with loudspeakers, and council officials and other personnel invoking section 144 when instructing people to stay indoors; others indicated that military and police personnel warned people by loudspeaker to disperse under section 144, or be fired on.[26] Notwithstanding, announcements seem to have been issued orally and inexactly.

What is section 144, and why does it matter? The section gives officials formal authority to declare an assembly unlawful and take steps to prevent its continuance or reoccurrence.[27] The moment of an

[24] Paulo Sergio Pinheiro, *Report of the Special Rapporteur on the Situation of Human Rights in Myanmar* (Geneva: UN Human Rights Council, 2007) 26.

[25] Govt. of the Union of Myanmar Announcement 1/2007, 4 Oct. 2007.

[26] HRW, *Crackdown: Repression of the 2007 Popular Protests in Burma* (New York: Human Rights Watch, 2007) 45, 58, 65.

[27] Section 144 of the Criminal Procedure Code is lengthy. Its relevant subsections for this discussion are: '(1) In cases where, in the opinion of a [Magistrate] there is sufficient ground for proceeding under this section and immediate prevention or speedy remedy is desirable, such Magistrate may, by a written order stating the material facts of the case and served in manner provided by section 134, direct any person to abstain from a certain act or to take certain order

assembly's criminalisation is the moment when a section 144 order takes effect. Before the section is invoked, individual acts by members of an assembly may be criminal offences, and the assembly can be dispersed where its members are assembled in order to offend. After it is invoked, the assembly is itself unlawful. How the members of the assembly conduct themselves or the purpose of their gathering no longer matters. Anyone assembled thereafter is committing a crime.

A judge should issue a section 144 order only in response to an exigency of sufficient magnitude that routine arrangements are inadequate to deal with it. The power granted authorities via a section 144 order is, as the Supreme Court of India has ruled, 'not an ordinary power flowing from administration but a power used in a judicial manner and which can stand further judicial scrutiny in the need for the exercise of the power, in its efficacy and in the extent of its application'.[28] For this reason, any person the order affects is entitled to its full text and is further entitled to approach the court that issued it so as to have it revised or rescinded. Therefore, it should be issued in the manner of a summons. A person subject to the order must be notified of its terms in writing. If adequate steps are not taken to notify the person, the order does not stand. In the case of an order regarding the general public, copies should be posted where affected people can read them easily.[29]

In India, judges retain their powers to issue and review orders under section 144. Their counterparts in Burma ceased issuing orders under the section in 1974, when executive councils took the power to do so. In all three periods compared here, administrative officers issued the orders. However, in 1974 the authorities did observe the requirements for publicity and widely reproduced the text of the section 144 order in

with certain property in his possession or under his management, if such Magistrate considers that such direction is likely to prevent, or tends to prevent, obstruction, annoyance or injury, or risk of obstruction, annoyance or injury, to any person lawfully employed, or danger to human life, health or safety, or a disturbance of the public tranquility, or a riot, or an affray. . . . (3) An order under this section may be directed to a particular individual or to the public generally. (4) Any Magistrate may, either on his own motion or on the application of any person aggrieved, rescind or alter any order made under this section by himself or any Magistrate subordinate to him, or by his predecessor in office. (5) Where such an application is received, the Magistrate shall afford to the applicant an early opportunity of appearing before him either in person or by pleader and showing cause against the order and, if the Magistrate rejects the application wholly or in part, he shall record in writing his reasons for so doing'.

28 *Madhu Limaye* v. *Sub-Divisional Magistrate, Monghyr and Others*, 1971 Supreme Court Report [India] (2) 711, 727.

29 Courts Manual, par. 394.

full. In 1988, too, the state media carried official announcements in full with extensive publicity. In 2007, neither the orders themselves nor the issuing authorities appear to have been made known – in full or in writing. In 2007, in contrast to 1974 and 1988, the publicity of the section 144 orders was minimal. The un-authorising of assembly itself went unpublicised.

In 1974 and 1988, the executive openly asserted its authority via orders prohibiting public assembly. In 2007, it did not use the state media to make the text of orders known widely, or completely. The secrecy around the section 144 orders and imprecision of the moment of criminalisation in response to events in 2007 was neither accidental nor incidental. The ambiguity of the criminalising moment also appears throughout the methods used to contain the protests and detain participants, to which this chapter now turns.

THE GANG

In the weeks before the 2007 protests reached their crescendo, residents of Yangon observed Dyna trucks parked near junctions and at other strategic points around the city, with groups of men lounging in or around them. Because the trucks are ubiquitous, they did not immediately attract much attention from passersby. One person told me that he had tried to board one, thinking it had been converted for public transport and was running on his homeward route. When he saw a pile of lumber in the back and one of the men inside growled at him to go away he realised his mistake and followed the instruction quickly.

The Dynas and the gangs of men they carried did not first appear in September 2007. In the prior years and months, gangs of unidentified men apparently operating under orders from officials had set upon public assemblies. In 2003, one allegedly under police and military command attacked a convoy carrying Aung San Suu Kyi and her supporters at Depayin, in the country's north. An eyewitness who fled abroad claimed to have seen members of the group responsible for the attack finishing off wounded victims, after which police cleared the area of any traces of violence, going so far as to scrub the road clean of blood by the following morning.[30] In 2005 and 2006, attacks on people

[30] Burma Lawyers' Council, *Preliminary Report of the Ad Hoc Commission on the Depayin Massacre* (Bangkok: Ad Hoc Commission on the Depayin Massacre, [2003?]) 35–36.

leading gatherings or involved in mobilising people against military rule continued sporadically.

The attacks escalated in 2007, in the lead-up to the events of September. In April, a group of four men engaged in human rights education and documentation in the delta were travelling on two motorcycles when around fifty people assaulted them with sticks, bricks, and slingshots, resulting in two being hospitalised. One wrote later that officials had stood to one side during the attack, with the local secretary of the government's Union Solidarity and Development Association yelling through a loudhailer, 'Hit them! Beat them! Beat them to death!'[31] The state media acknowledged the attack, but justified it as a spontaneous response of villagers to a group of troublemakers.[32]

In May, relatives of twenty-nine persons abducted by another gang as they were on their way to pray for the release of political prisoners wrote,

> Our wives, husbands, children, nephews, nieces, younger brothers and sisters ... were forcibly and illegally taken into custody in violation of universal human rights and not in compliance with domestic law by an unidentified group of so-called 'Pyithu Swunashin' at the Insein-Sule 45 Bus Terminus at the end of Station Street, Sawbwagyigon. ... They are currently being held at an unknown location.

The letter distinctly captures the ambiguity of the gang. It has a name, the Pyithu Swunashin, or generally just Swunashin, but what is it? Who is in it? How does it exist? Why does it exist?

In 2006, the government acknowledged that a new civilian security force was operating alongside official bodies.[33] The first senior official to make direct reference to the group was the police commander Khin Yi. In a press conference, he mentioned that members of a volunteer group had been patrolling with policemen and helping to make arrests. He called the group 'Swunashin', which translates loosely as 'masters of force'. A journalist asked him to explain the meaning of 'Swunashin'. He replied:

> The meaning of Swunashin is that our country's people are the country's 'masters of force'. They are our country's strength. For this reason, when

[31] Ko Myint Naing, letter, 20 Apr. 2007. [32] *Myanma Alin* 23 Apr. 2007: 20, 11.

[33] For an overview of the Swunashin originally published online, later in print, see Moe Ze Nyein, 'What is the Swunashin', *What is the Swunashin and Collected Writings* (Yangon: Nyanekhin, 2014) 9–38 (in Burmese).

> sorting out all of our country's affairs, we are drawing on and using this mighty force, this people's strength. Now, in the various tasks that we are carrying out for the rule of law [*taya-ubade-somoye*], regional peace and tranquility and so on, fire fighters, Red Cross members, PDC [Peace and Development Council] members and the rest are lending assistance with *cetana*, without a penny in payment, and as these individuals are a mighty force, the state chose and designated the word Swunashin with which to honour and refer to them.[34]

Khin Yi's conflation of the gang with agencies assigned routine security tasks like the fire brigade and Red Cross obscures the idiosyncratic purpose of the Swunashin. The other bodies are permanent. They are official groups with large memberships into which the state taps at times of emergency. By contrast, the gang is unofficial, situation-specific and ill defined. Khin Yi does not announce the gang; he simply acknowledges that one day it was there.[35] Recognition of the gang follows from its presence at the site of an arrest. It is not inaugurated or proclaimed with banners and balloons in advance of its factual existence. The gang operates in the open but without any precise frame of reference for people who see it do its work or who become its targets. It operates through the *cetana* of the sovereign and also with the *cetana*, the will or volition, of its individual members.

The Swunashin was a new phenomenon in Myanmar, different from existing state agencies, and also different from the paramilitary forces before it. In the 1950s, the government sought to organise proliferating armed groups into paramilitary levies. At that time, its objective was to secure a modicum of control over parts of the country where it had none. It aimed in the long run to bring irregular forces under its authority, however tenuously. When in the 1960s the government armed and organised villagers into people's militia, it did so under a series of laws and with official guidance of the military; aiming to bring more citizens into the fight against insurgents, as part of a larger ideological project.

The role of the Swunashin was the opposite of paramilitary groups from earlier episodes. It was to create an ambiguous form of state authority that was not integrated into formal structures, unlike the

[34] *Myanma Alin* 3 Nov. 2006: 13.

[35] 'Diels, the head of the Gestapo, could declare, "Neither an order nor an instruction exists for the origin of the [concentration] camps: they were not instituted; one day they were there."' Giorgio Agamben, *Homo Sacer: Sovereign Power and Bare Life*, trans. Daniel Heller-Roazen (Stanford: Stanford University Press, 1998) 169.

other state security forces, which were integrated and formalised, and equipped with formidable resources. No problem of capacity justified the gang. Nor did it serve any conventional security purpose supplementary to the work of official agencies. The Swunashin was not an auxiliary, but a proxy. Its function was not to supplement existing agencies at all, not to lend assistance, but to be a substitute. It was to play the role of the police or military in their stead, and to do so in a manner detached from the ordinary rules and procedures applicable to those agencies.

For these reasons, the gang is not merely antithetical to the rule of law but is also potentially corrosive of the law-and-order ideal. It makes no pretence of adhering to the rules that matter for a semblance of orderliness when uniformed personnel are engaged in violence. Consequently, its corrosive effects had to be neutralised through the administrative function of the court at the end of the continuum from gang to camp, as explained in the section on 'the court', below.

At the time of the protests in 2007, local administrators seem to have been mainly responsible for recruitment to the Swunashin. Lacking precise instructions, and given the ambiguous character of the gang, they performed this task inconsistently. They recruited men belonging to two broad categories: one, a cadre of members who routinely worked with the administrators, police officers, and other officials; and two, short-time muscle hired with the promise of some money, food, and alcohol. The cadre seems to have consisted of men motivated by personal interests, and of conscripts. The former included criminals who could ingratiate themselves with policemen and local government officials, and get protection and contacts through membership. The latter included small businessmen who depended on local officials for licences to operate, men who could ill-afford to decline a request to sign up.[36]

For its part, the muscle seems to have consisted mostly of petty criminals, thugs, and other characters known to the police and local administrators: men making a living from day to day, who would do whatever they were told and not ask questions. According to the published testimony of a man with a criminal record, who was recruited in the days before the protests, an old associate had misled him into

[36] On an undated list of 26 purported township Swunashin heads and deputies in Yangon, 16 are classed occupationally as merchants or vendors, while most others are private professionals and tradesmen. The majority are aged 25 to 40. Moe Ze Nyein, 'What is the Swunashin' 21–29.

thinking they would have some work as part of a vice operation with policemen in the suburbs. Instead, he was taken to a police battalion and kept there for three days, whereupon, 'At about 8 a.m. on [September] 26th, an officer from Police Battalion 1 ordered us to line up. He told us, roughly a hundred in number, "Comrades, now it is necessary for your unit to participate actively and loyally together with we police in crushing an enemy."'[37] Then they boarded trucks, and each man received a bamboo stick. When they arrived at the city centre, the police directed them to assault protestors. The trucks then conveyed detained people to undisclosed locations under control of the police or military.

State news reports gave voice to the ambiguity of this process, often describing persons not as having been arrested formally but as having been 'brought, held, questioned and investigated'. Those responsible for the abductions were 'persons not wanting disturbances'. When cases against abducted persons later came to court, some of their abductors, members of the gang's cadre, appeared as witnesses. A defendant asked one who identified himself as Swunashin whether he came to make an arrest of his own accord or in conjunction with the police. The gang member replied, as scripted,

A. We did not arrest. We just rendered assistance.
Q. To whom did you render assistance?
A. With a mind to avert a disturbance, we rendered assistance. I acted as a member of the public, to avert a disturbance, to avoid disruption of the thoroughfare.[38]

Eyewitnesses with camera phones and other devices captured this 'rendered assistance'. Footage from August 25, for instance, shows a group of unidentified men snatching at the limbs of Htin Kyaw, an activist who had led protests on economic issues earlier in the year. They carry him to an idling Dyna truck on the side of a crowded downtown street, which speeds off into heavy traffic as a small crowd of onlookers gathers. When Htin Kyaw's case came to court, a gang member testified. He said that he and another man 'took hold of [the defendant] between us and brought him to the [township council] office. … I saw that he was then taken by car to the military regional

[37] *Burma Update* 29 Nov. 2007.
[38] *Inspector Soe Naing* v. *U Ohn Than*, 2008 Criminal Case 12, Yangon Western District Court, PW 4, 7 Feb. 2008. For a discussion of this case, see Nick Cheesman, 'Thin Rule of Law or Un-Rule of Law in Myanmar?' *Pacific Affairs* 82.4 (2009): 604–09.

office'.[39] Beginning the witness's cross-examination, the defence attorney picked up on the manner of his client's abduction during the protest in February and again in August:

Q. The Pansodan Police Station is on Konzedan Road in the vicinity of Theindawgyi [where the protest occurred] and the [township council] office is opposite bus stop 105 on Mahabandoola Road.
A. Correct.
Q. Although the police station is on Konzedan Road, on each of these days not a single uniformed police officer was present.
A. I don't know.
Q. Do you know that if there is a demonstration like that, [by law] it must be halted either by an on-duty police officer or judge?
A. I don't know.
Q. On the day[s] during the time when Ko Htin Kyaw demonstrated, neither a judge nor on-duty police officer from the police station was present.
A. Police Officer Myint Swe and Station Commander U Kyaw Tint were present.
Q. On February 22, 2007 Police Captain Myint Swe and Station Commander U Kyaw Tint did not make the arrest. Only civilians were involved.
A. Incorrect.
Q. Who arrested Ko Htin Kyaw?
A. As I have testified, Station Commander U Kyaw Tint and Township Officer U Myint Swe made the arrest . . .
Q. On August 25, 2007 the people who arrested Ko Htin Kyaw were people in civvies from the military region [command].
A. No, Ko Min Min and I made the arrest.
Q. You are not police service personnel and therefore you have no authority to arrest.
A. I don't know.[40]

At night, in a more familiar and longstanding practice, unidentified men moved from the streets and into people's houses. The United Nations human rights expert estimated, 'Between 3,000 and 4,000 people were arrested in September and October. . . . Most of the arrests took place during the crackdown on the demonstrations and the night raids carried out by the security forces and non law enforcement officials'.[41] Daw Win Mya Mya, an organiser of the National League

[39] *Pol. Capt. Myint Swe* v. *Htin Kyaw* (a) *Kyaw Htin*, 2008 Criminal Case 16, Yangon Western District Court, PW 2, 20 Mar. 2008: 2.
[40] *Pol. Capt. Myint Swe* v. *Htin Kyaw* (a) *Kyaw Htin*, PW 2: 2–4.
[41] Pinheiro, *Report of the Special Rapporteur on the Situation of Human Rights in Myanmar* 13.

for Democracy in Mandalay, was among people taken during a night raid. Her brother said on radio:

> A group of about ten Mandalay Division Police in civvies along with the Ward PDC arrived at our house at 12 p.m. They said that they wanted to see Daw Win Mya Mya, that they had some things to ask her. Daw Win Mya Mya asked, 'If that's so, are you taking me to prison? Where are you taking me?' They said that they didn't know.[42]

Even though Win Mya Mya's brother identified the group of officials as policemen, the men removing people from houses at night did not ordinarily make themselves known. They declined to give answers when pressed on their identities. Other people gave similar accounts of men in plain clothes declining to identify themselves, bundling them into vehicles. Sometimes, the men put blindfolds on their captives. The ambiguous identity of men making arrests was necessary for the ambiguity of detention that followed.

THE CAMP

A detainee in 2007 had no idea how long she would be gone, where she would be going, or how she would be treated. In Win Mya Mya's case, the police took her on September 28. The police did not bring charges against her and four colleagues until almost a year later.[43] When the cases came to court, the police recorded the date of arrest of all five persons as August 15, 2008. Lawyers for the accused cross-examined an investigating policeman in court about the gap:

Q. Do you know U Kan Htun was arrested on October 6, 2007 and Daw Win Mya Mya on September 28, 2007?
A. I don't know.
Q. Do you know the date recorded for the arrest of the two accused in the current case as brought before the court is August 15, 2008?
A. I don't know how the investigation was conducted.
Q. Do you know that in almost a year since arrest no bond or bail was given?
A. I don't know how the investigation was conducted.[44]

[42] VOA 29 Sept. 2007.
[43] *Pol. Capt. Win Myint* v. *Daw Win Mya Mya and 4*, 2008 Criminal Case 605, Aungmyay-thazan Township Court, 24 Oct. 2008; and Criminal Cases 608–10.
[44] *Pol. Capt. Thaik Nyunt* v. *Daw Win Mya Mya and Another*, 2008 Criminal Case 608, Aungmyay-thazan Township Court, PW 2, 1 Sept. 2008: 3.

The time between when the police removed Win Mya Mya from her house and the date recorded for her arrest I designate, drawing on Agamben, as 'the camp'.[45] This camp was not a specific place or institution, but an anomalous zone into which people could be forcibly disappeared. Physically, it could be anywhere. In 2007, it encompassed conventional detention facilities and nonconventional ones.

The word used in Burmese to designate 'the camp', *sagan*, is conveniently imprecise. It can variously designate a formal or informal facility: police *sagan*, to refer to a conventional station where a detainee can be held legally; a police or army battalion *sagan*, to refer to a military or paramilitary compound; and, an interrogation *sagan*, to refer to a military intelligence or Special Branch facility. The last of these *sagan* has no basis for its existence in criminal statute or manual. It is not a legal place of detention under the Criminal Procedure Code, nor is it anywhere mentioned in the chapters of the Police Manual concerning police force structure and facilities.[46] Its juridical non-existence makes the *sagan* an essential organ of the camp. More than anywhere else, in its confines the zone of anomie becomes possible – and permanent. The existence of the interrogation camp is undeniable, yet its function as a place of detention and torture must be denied.

In 2007, officials locked up hundreds of people in prisons, but without following ordinary record-keeping procedures. They held other detainees at an interrogation *sagan*, Kyaikkasan; at a technical institute; and at a police battalion *sagan*. A woman released from detention at the technical institute described how,

> They brought us to the Insein teaching school, and put us in this school. I saw people being beaten there, people with head wounds, with broken limbs, this type of thing. We were famished and were prohibited from bathing. They didn't feed us. In the room, there were over 150 women and there was a room to one side for disposal of excrement; we just had to dispose of it in there. As time went on the excrement stank and it was unbearable.[47]

The camp's guardians moved some detainees from place to place. The camp as a body of practices did not require them to hold detainees in a specific location. A university student missing from her family for over six weeks said later she was first kept at Kyaikkasan, then sent to the central prison, at Insein, then sent back to Kyaikkasan, and then to

[45] Agamben, *Homo Sacer* ch. 7. [46] Police Manual, ch. 1, 27. [47] *VOA* 8 Oct. 2007.

Police Battalion 3 before being released.[48] The famous comedian Zarganar, who was freed but charged later, was first taken to Insein, then to the Aungthapyay interrogation camp, then after four days back to the central prison, where he was put in the dog kennels, until a prison officer whom he knew personally intervened and had him moved to one of the buildings.[49] In each case, the locus of the camp was the detainee himself: the camp was wherever the person was suspended.

To ask questions of the camp was pointless. The mother of a seventeen-year-old detainee watched some men take her son on October 10. She waited until the end of the month for news. Police officers came to the house and told the family he was being kept at the central prison, and that they could send food and other items to him, but would not be allowed to meet him. The mother said that when delivering food to her child she asked,

> 'Will it be long? Has he been sentenced?' They said, 'He hasn't been charged. They haven't yet sentenced him. There's no charge.' Then we asked, 'If he hasn't been charged will he be released? Why is he being detained?'[50]

This account captures the essence of the camp. The men taking the boy away said they would be in contact in about three days. The statement has no basis in any law. Why three days? Taken where? Taken for what reason? Inside the camp, such questions ceased to have any significance. Nor did asking them elicit answers. The family was forced to wait until the camp's guardians chose to provide them with information. What else could they do? In the camp, the body of conditional privileges that a person in Myanmar might claim under other circumstances was deactivated, the *cetana* of the sovereign was withdrawn from anyone in its confines.

Nor did 'information' given have to be true. Since those policing the camp were not obliged to say anything at all, they were not obliged to tell the truth. As in the case of the policeman telling his torture victim that everything will be all right if the detainee will just confess, they could say anything they wished to satisfy the questions of an anxious relative, knowing full well that it did not matter whether their answers were correct or not. In the above-mentioned case, contrary to what his mother was told, the seventeen-year-old boy was charged with six other

[48] VOA 27 Nov. 2007.

[49] Zarganar, *Third, Fourth* ([Yangon]: Ko Thura, 2013) 10–21 (in Burmese).

[50] VOA 1 Nov. 2007.

students and jailed for sedition.[51] Relatives of other disappeared people who went to inquire after them at jails were told they were not inside, only to learn later that the opposite was true, sometimes from others who had just been freed.

Many detainees left the camp in a manner as ambiguous as the way they went in, by signing imprecise assurances that they would obey the law in the future. According to state media,

> Up to October 4, 2093 persons had been arrested, brought and questioned in accordance with law for assembling in defiance of section 144. It was found on investigation that among them are persons who were involved in the disturbances, persons who followed and lent support, and persons who unknowingly went along with the assemblies. As the unknowing persons are also violators of the law, up to today 692 have been released by way of a pledge.[52]

This extract suggests that the purpose of suspending people in the camps was to sort them administratively into categories for processing: ringleaders, followers, and the clueless. It also implies that even if everyone in these categories was guilty of a crime, anyone in the third category could be released on signing a pledge.

What were these pledges? A copy of one, which may or may not be representative, contains no reference to any section of law. It does not correspond with any of the conventional forms for release of detainees found in the Police Manual nor with the provisions of criminal procedure, under which a detainee is either released without condition or by posting a bond, which is forfeited if the detainee fails to comply with the terms of release. The pledge has no such provisions. The document's wording is menacing, the detainee signing that:

> I am aware that if I commit the same type of offence in the future, I will be subject to action in accordance with the law. I was arrested because of an offence. I am being released because the state has leniency. I pledge that if summoned, I will come at all times.

As in the cases of persons released through formal pardon, the pledge exercises sovereign *cetana* to give the detainee a gift of conditional freedom. The sovereign power in this instance denies responsibility for how the detainee came to be in custody. But having established that

[51] *Inspector Kyaw Tha Oo* v. *Sithu Maung and* 6, 2008 Criminal Case 9, Yangon Western District Court, Daily Diary, 27 Feb. 2008.

[52] *Myanma Alin* 5 Oct. 2007: 17.

some unstated good reasons must exist for the person's detention, the policeman as sovereign is prepared to exercise *cetana* and release her, if the person will demonstrate compliance, and remain quietened. In other words, while in every respect constituting a denial of the rule of law, the pledge is consistent with the ideal of law and order.

Zarganar, who was held from September 25 to October 17, was among those persons released on a pledge. In June 2008, police officers arrested him after he spoke to the media about conditions in the delta following the cyclone that swept through the region in May of that year. They charged him for offences in connection with the 2007 protests. When his lawyer pointed out that he had been released without charge in 2007, the police officer bringing the case said that he was released after he had signed a pledge that he would comply with the law, having committed criminal offences.[53] Since he had failed to comply with this assurance, the officer explained, they were now bringing those charges against him also.

Police officers could use a breached pledge to justify prosecution, but compliance with a pledge did not guarantee non-prosecution. Khin Sanda Win was released on a pledge on October 25, after being detained illegally from September 29. On November 1, two police officers came to her house and informed her that their station had opened a case against her. The next day the police lodged a charge under the 1878 Arms Act, which the prosecutor changed to attempt to endanger life, under sections 336/511 of the Penal Code. On November 26, the local police station commander testified as a prosecution witness against her. His cross-examination ran:

Q. Do you know . . . among twenty-two detained students [held together], Ma Khin Sanda Win was one of two students released on October 25, 2007, and there is a record that she was released into the guardianship of her parents?

A. I know she was released.

Q. So the Kyauktada Police Station has brought a case against Ma Khin Sanda Win who was released, the security forces having found her not at fault?

A. Our police station brought the charge simply because of a crime [having been committed].[54]

53 *Pol. Maj. Ye Nyunt* v. *Thura* (a) *Zarganar*, 2008 Criminal Case 76, Yangon Western District Court, PW 1, 14 Aug. 2008.

54 *Inspector Soe Naing* v. *Ma Khin Sanda Win*, 2007 Criminal Case 525, Kyauktada Township Court, PW 1, 26 Nov. 2007: 4.

The use of the possessive in the policeman's reply is striking. It introduces a degree of personal responsibility absent from the prior stages of Khin Sanda Win's detention. It marks a lexical break from what came before. The policeman is simultaneously indicating he knows, and is prepared to speak about, what he and his men have done, but whatever happened before is irrelevant to him. His police station works according to law. The moment 'his' station entered into the process was the moment this accused actually became an alleged criminal. It signalled her restoration to the juridical process, the restoration of her juridical personhood, through the re-entry of juridical institutions to the process of investigation and imprisonment; not least among them, the court.

THE COURT

In a collection of accounts about the abduction of people amid massive political violence in Sri Lanka in 1989 and 1990, interviewees describe how their relatives were plucked from near their houses or businesses by white vans without licence plates, went missing from police stations, and were tortured in army camps before disappearing, never to be seen again.[55] The collection's title alludes to the 'exceptional collapse' of the rule of law, discussed in terms of the use of torture, militarisation, and politicisation of the police – phenomena that Sri Lanka and Myanmar have in common.

The collection lacks any considered discussion of the role of courts in response to these events, other than by way of passing references to the inactivity of magistrates who received complaints. Yet, in the role of the court lies the critical difference between the 'exceptional collapse' of institutions for the rule of law in Sri Lanka and the politics of law and order in Myanmar. By integrating the court into the programme of abduction and detention, by making courtroom processing the next step on an administrative continuum from the gang and the camp, the authorities in Myanmar succeed in immobilising people without having to resort to mass killings and permanent disappearances. In Sri Lanka, the military and police framed their response to political threats as

[55] Moon Jeong-ho and Bruce Van Voorhis, *An Exceptional Collapse of the Rule of Law: Told through Stories by Families of the Disappeared in Sri Lanka* (Hong Kong: Asian Legal Resource Centre and Asian Human Rights Commission, 2004). See also Commission of Inquiry into Involuntary Removal and Disappearance of Certain Persons (All Island), *Final Report* (Govt. of Sri Lanka, 2001).

'extralegal action or nothing'.[56] In Myanmar, the legal, or rather, the juridical, deliberately follows the extrajuridical.

In Myanmar during 2007, most disappearances into the camp were not permanent for the very reason that courts were drawn into the programme for processing and punishing of persons held in the camp. Passing through the court, abducted persons had their juridical personhood restored to them. Ironically, the courtroom hearing that followed the gang and camp enabled the survival of accused persons. In so doing, it also enabled the continued political salience of the law-and-order ideal. Through the courtroom, the body of the abducted individual could be brought from the zone of anomie. The court's purpose was not to try the accused, not to establish any kind of guilt or innocence, but to pull her back over the threshold from the anomalous zone in which she had been suspended, and into the ordinary juridical realm – which is to say, back into the continuum of administrative activity on which the law-and-order project depends. The court reactivated the 'juridical' not as a means to make sense of the extrajuridical, but to cancel it out. It did not inquire about the gang or the camp. The court did not have this role at all. Instead, its purpose was to admit whatever ambiguities preceded the appearance of the person in court and to impose an order. Thus, through the courtroom, the body of the abducted person was again rendered worthy of punishment.

Take the case of three men convicted of harbouring a fugitive monk, in which the court heard testimony based on a record from an interrogator whose identity is not made clear in its records. The defence attorney took up this ambiguity when cross-examining one of the policemen who investigated the case:

Q. You have been a policeman for about thirty years and know that a record taken before police is inadmissible [as evidence in court]. . . .
A. I am coming to testify as per the duty assigned to me from above.
Q. Where 'above'?
A. Our Special Branch officer, whose name I am not authorised to reveal. . . .
Q. U Obasa [the fleeing monk] has committed what offence?
A. He participated and demonstrated in the September 2007 events.
Q. In what way did he participate in the said demonstration?

56 Deepika Udgama, Head of Department, Faculty of Law, Colombo University cited in Jane Thomson-Senanayake, *A Sociological Exploration of Disappearances in Sri Lanka* (Hong Kong: Asian Human Rights Commission, 2014) 162.

A. He marched with tens of thousands of people.
Q. Aside from U Obasa being among the many monks who participated, were there other offences?
A. No.
Q. So far as you know, is there a police or court action or warrant pending against U Obasa from which he is absconding?
A. There is no proclamation that he is an absconder.[57]

Practically every aspect of this testimony evokes ambiguity about how the accused were identified, detained, and charged. The persons responsible for ordering that the policeman bring the case to court, and those involved in the investigation, cannot be identified. The fugitive monk's alleged offence is itself elusive. A notice for his arrest has not been issued, and the policeman can say no more than that he marched with thousands of his peers. This admission effectively defeats the prosecution case. Without a declaration that the monk was wanted, the accused could not have known that they were committing an offence, even if they had harboured him. But as the purpose of the hearing was to pull the accused back from the zone of anomie, not to deliberate on the facts, it made no difference to the outcome.

The lack of evidence against persons accused over events in 2007 speaks to the court's strictly administrative function in these cases. The police brought charges against Ma Honey Oo on allegations that she led protestors in Yangon, set up a new student union with a group of friends, and contacted overseas news media. They based all of these charges on 'reliable information'. As cross-examination of one policeman revealed, the nature of that reliable information and its sources could not be disclosed:

Q. Are the persons who gave the reliable information on the list of witnesses [submitted to the court for examination]?
A. They have not been submitted as witnesses.
Q. Can you submit documentary proof regarding your testimony of communications [by the accused] with abroad?
A. I have no documentary proof to submit.
Q. Can you submit documentary proof of the student union of which you testified, together with the membership of the group?
A. I cannot.

[57] *Pol. Capt. Myo Thant* v. *Kyaw Win Chay and 2*, 2008 Criminal Case 356, South Dagon Township Court, PW 2, 26 Mar. 2008: 5–6.

Q. You cannot submit proof of the student union and furthermore you have stated but have no proof that Ma Honey Oo was involved in the student union in the course of which she committed acts to disrupt law and order [*ngyeinwut-pibyaye*] of which you have accused her.

A. It is as per the information received.[58]

Any statement the police officer utters in the case against the criminalised protestor is invested with authenticity. The 'information received' can neither be proven nor refuted. It belongs to a different plane, independent from the authority of the court and everyone in it. Even the police officer bringing the case is just the vessel for this power, bringing it with him into court but not having any possession of it.

Whereas some defendants fought the charges against them, others used hearings to celebrate the events for which they were allegedly criminally responsible. As with the testimonies of torture described in Chapter 5, their statements could be duly recorded without altering the outcome of proceedings. Some defence statements raise ontological problems about the alleged offence that go to the criminalisation of protest itself. In the case of Kyaw Ko Ko, a member of the All Burma Students Union, the judge recorded,

> Defendant-1 Kyaw Ko Ko . . . said in testifying that on September 25, 2007 having marched along Shwedagon Pagoda Road towards the city, on reaching Sule Pagoda Road and the side of the town hall while the crowd was flying the fighting peacock flag he climbed atop a dais and gave a speech . . . that he said in the speech he was an All Burma Students Union leader and that the students had seen the people's difficulties and that they stood for the people; that the students had not given up and had resisted government that had persecuted the people from one era to the next; that he urged the majority of students to fall in behind the Sangha in the current events in order to peacefully send *metta* [loving kindness], to join the battle to confront oppression without fear, and to raise the fighting peacock flag to the heights.[59]

This testimony challenges the notion that the defendant's acts of protest were criminal acts at all. The accused does not deny

[58] *Inspector Hla Thein* v. *Ma Honey Oo* (a) *Honey*, 2008 Criminal Case 30, Yangon Eastern District Court, PW 1, 19 Mar. 2008: 3.

[59] *Sub Inspector Thein Naing* v. *Kyaw Ko Ko* (a) *Rahu* (a) *Klordi*, 2010 Criminal Case 93, Kyauktada Township Court, 11 May 2010: 5–6. The fighting peacock is an emblem that political activists have used since the colonial period, among them the student unions.

involvement in the protests; he rejoices in it. What he denies is that this involvement constitutes a crime. The court for its part put the denial on record and carried on with its responsibility to imprison him.

People also contested charges brought against them for engaging in routine religious practices, which in the context of the protests the police alleged were criminal acts. The police complaint against Thet Zaw, a sports journal editor who had previously been pardoned in a case of high treason, was that on two consecutive days he had purchased twenty rice packets and brought them to the eastern staircase of the Shwedagon Pagoda to distribute to monks. The police insisted that this act of bringing alms to the most revered Buddhist site in the country constituted an attempt to insult religion. The defence attorney asked if Buddhists did not habitually feed monks. A policeman replied that, as per tradition, providing food to monks should be done straightforwardly, implying that the circumstances in which the accused fed the monks constituted an offence. The lawyer argued further that the act of the monks walking on the street chanting verses did not constitute a protest at all. When the police officer rejected his assertion, the lawyer went to the meaning of the word for 'protest' in Burmese, *sanda-pya*, literally, to display one's opinion or desire. A protest, he submitted, would entail some demand. The monks walking on the street to spread *metta* did not constitute such an act. Again the police officer rejected the argument, but he refused to be drawn into what for him would have been a pointless debate about the semantics of protest.[60]

Similarly, the hearings of cases against people who marched in August turned on the alleged illegality of walking on the road because petrol prices had increased. A court recorded the cross-examination of a police officer in one of these hearings:

A. On August 25, 2007 Ko Min Thu led thirty people to demonstrate around wards of Mogok about the increased price of fuel, and while demonstrating presented a letter written by himself to U Kyi Maung, manager of the MPPE government petrol station in Aungnan Ward, for the price of fuel to be reduced to its original level.

Q. The price of fuel did in fact increase.

A. The price of fuel increased as per the government's designation.

Q. So then this was just a presentation for the authorities to know of [the effects of] the increased price of fuel.

60 *Pol. Maj. Ye Nyunt* v. *Thura* (a) *Zarganar and Another*, 2008 Criminal Case 77, Yangon Western District Court, PW 1, 14 Aug. 2008.

A. Incorrect. It was just a protest march to damage the national government by assembling to demonstrate about the increased price of fuel.[61]

While processing Htin Kyaw for sedition following his abduction in August, which I described above, the complainant policeman also had difficulty in identifying what in his protest had constituted a threat to law and order:

Q. On that day, there was no damage to public property.
A. Correct.
Q. He only conducted a solo demonstration.
A. Correct. [But] if it went on for a while, more could have come. If it were not contained in time, a crowd would have come.
Q. That is merely your presumption. In fact, a crowd did not come.
A. It's not a point of view. It was a location where a crowd could come . . .
Q. The writing [on the placard] concerned only commodity prices. There was no seditious content.
A. The writing 'Don't raise commodity prices' is seditious usage.[62]

As in the case of Min Thu, Htin Kyaw's attorney explored the idea that making a demonstration about rising commodity prices could somehow constitute sedition. Cross-examining a civilian witness he asked,

Q. From the time of 1988 to the present time of 2008, commodity prices have risen.
A. Correct.
Q. Among rising commodity prices, food prices have risen.
A. Correct.
Q. Ko Htin Kyaw and party demonstrated for lower commodity prices and twenty-four-hour electricity.
A. Correct.
Q. So commodity prices are rising and therefore it was [simply] a demonstration that commodity prices are rising.
A. Although they demonstrated [about this], on account of the placards they were holding and slogan shouting it was seditious. It also upset national peace and stability and alarmed the public too.
Q. In the writing 'Lower commodity prices', 'Twenty-four-hour electricity' there is not a single seditious word.
A. Incorrect. It was seditious because it could cause unrest.[63]

[61] *Pol. Capt. Win Myint* v. *Min Thu* (a) *Ko Oo*, 2008 Criminal Case 606, Aungmyay-thazan Township Court, PW 1, 22 Aug. 2008: 4–5.
[62] *Pol. Capt. Myint Swe* v. *Htin Kyaw* (a) *Kyaw Htin*, PW 1, 20 Mar. 2008: 2–3.
[63] *Pol. Capt. Myint Swe* v. *Htin Kyaw* (a) *Kyaw Htin*, PW 3, 20 Mar. 2008: 2.

If this witness struggled to explain what in the alleged offence constituted sedition, he was not alone in his difficulty. At least one police officer admitted under cross-examination that although he was investigating cases of sedition, he did not exactly understand what sedition meant.[64] And why should he? Unlike his counterparts in the colonial and early postcolonial periods, he had no narrative of sedition through which to interpret and explain the case, because he had no need for one. All he need do was acknowledge that a person from whom sovereign *cetana* had been withdrawn was liable to have committed the offence. Htin Kyaw's seditious act was consequential to his loss of conditional privileges to make legal claims. His sedition was determined administratively. The question of what constituted sedition ceased to have any meaning for the purposes of criminal inquiry and sentencing. It was a footnote to the assignment of guilt.

Because in 2007 accused persons were usually processed in closed courts, police officers could depart from the public transcript on the protests without fear of being heard to contradict the official narrative. One striking departure is in policemen's descriptions of the rallies that they monitored. Contrary to the state's portrayals of marauding, bogus monks and their dangerous supporters, police officers' accounts in court records give an impression of organised, calm, and non-violent gatherings, and demonstrators at pains to avoid confrontations with officials. An undercover police officer testified how demonstrators grabbed him as he was preparing to take photographs of monks assembling for a march in the north of the country.[65] When they found his police identity card, instead of assaulting or abusing him they took him to a nearby monastery. The monks released him and returned to him his telephone and camera undamaged. He went back to his detachment and rotated duties with another officer.

A policeman responsible for many prosecutions of demonstrators in 2007 admitted he was unable to collect evidence to show that monks had committed violence during the protests.[66] He also accepted that monks walking on the street, chanting verses to send *metta*, did nothing to tarnish the Buddhist religion. A counterpart from Mandalay agreed that in the area where he had been on duty, no monks had done or said

[64] *Inspector Hla Thein* v. *Ma Honey Oo* (a) *Honey*, 2008 Criminal Case 31, PW 1, 19 Mar. 2008: 3.

[65] *Pol. Capt. Win Myint* v. *Win Shwe*, 2008 Criminal Case 612, Aungmyay-thazan Township Court, PW 2, 29 Aug. 2008.

[66] *Pol. Maj. Ye Nyunt* v. *Thura* (a) *Zaganar and Another*, PW 1.

anything to imperil their religion.[67] Nor do any police officers' statements or other court records I have read describe demonstrating monks, or those being prosecuted, as bogus.

Sentencing of persons brought to court over the 2007 protests occurred in two broad phases. In the first phase, in the lead-up to and during the protests, the police brought the accused to courts that handed down sentences with extraordinary efficiency. A defendant who allegedly led a march in Rakhine State on September 19 returned from Yangon to his home in Thandwe on October 13, and policemen arrested him there the same day. For three days, they kept him at the district station, where the police and military intelligence interrogated him. They then brought him to court, where a judge sentenced him on October 17.[68] A lawyer appealed on his behalf. The state court upheld the verdict but reduced the sentence on October 24.[69] The entire process from date of arrest to revision of sentence took under a fortnight.

In another case, policemen in the north arrested Ko Thiha on September 7 and charged him with sedition, and violation of section 505(b) for upsetting public tranquility, after he had gone to collect documents at a photocopy shop, to distribute at demonstrations. On September 14, they brought him to court. A judge heard the case in a single day. On September 17, even before the protests had reached their climax, the judge sentenced Thiha to twenty-two years in prison.[70] In the end, he served over four years and four months for those photocopies, as he was among hundreds of people released through the exercise of presidential pardon on January 13, 2012, along with others whose cases are described in this chapter.

In the second phase of sentencing, many cases against persons detained without charge or hearing, or whose cases had languished, suddenly proceeded in unison. Courts handed down a series of verdicts in October and November 2008, after repeated postponements or long delays. Many cases in this phase dealt with groups of protestors, bundled

[67] *Pol. Maj. Ye Nyunt* v. *Gambhira* (a) *Candobhasa* (a) *Nyi Nyi Lwin* (a) *Hlaing Bwa and 10*, Defence Closing Submission: 4.

[68] *Sub Inspector San Shwe Thein* v. *Min Aung*, 2007 Criminal Cases 28–29, Thandwe District Court, 17 Oct. 2007.

[69] *Min Aung* v. *Union of Myanmar*, 2007 Criminal Appeals 32–33, Rakhine State Court, 24 Oct. 2007.

[70] *Pol. Capt. Win Myint* v. *Ko Thiha*, 2007 Criminal Case 134, Mandalay District Court, 17 Sept. 2007.

together and processed a dozen or more at a time for omnibus offences. For instance, the police charged fourteen persons in a single case for causing hurt to civil servants, endangering life, obscenity, and abetment.[71] Just two of them were visible in the photographs of demonstrators that police officers submitted as evidence. The judge sentenced them all to over three years in jail anyway.

In punishing people accused of involvement in the public demonstrations, the point of reference for sentencing was not the hearing, but the prior criminalisation of the accused. Its purpose was not to affirm guilt, which was taken for granted, but to signify the end of the camp and the beginning of punishment. At the moment of sentencing, the accused became legal persons again. Returned to jail, they were not the same as before. The sentencing concluded a procedure for bringing the accused back across the threshold from the anomalous zone into which they had been thrust, restoring to them the juridical personhood that they had lost in the camp.

CONCLUSION

The juridical response to events in Myanmar during 2007 represented courts' farthest departure from the methods of their progenitors. In cases of unauthorised assembly during the colonial period, officials wrote narratives of criminal opposition to empire. They inserted these narratives into special trials that bypassed ordinary procedure but rhetorically subscribed to the rule of law. In 2007, the courts invented no narratives at all. The official narrative preceded the juridical process. Courts read the narrative into each case of an accused demonstrator or instigator. No narratives were required of them, and none were forthcoming. The imperative to maintain law and order sufficed for everyone involved.

The one-party state and successor military government in 1974 and 1988 resorted to martial law and panels of soldiers to process accused persons. In 2007, no distinct moment of criminalisation occurred. Nor were soldiers required to hear cases personally. Civilian courts functioned as clearing houses for alleged ringleaders brought from the camp. Perversely, by endorsing the extrajuridical treatment of detainees, courts allowed for their return to the juridical process.

[71] Penal Code, sec. 332, 334, 294, and 114. *Pol. Capt. Myint Aung* v. *Kyaw Win and 13*.

The link between the gang and sovereign power was essential for the movement of protestors back and forth across a juridical threshold. Only through its genetic relationship to sovereign power was the gang itself not criminalised. Furthermore, the Swunashin in September 2007 embodied sovereign power in Myanmar more perfectly than any other institution at that moment. It policed the threshold between the juridical and extrajuridical unmediated. Freed from any of the constraints placed on conventional agents of law and order, the Swunashin was the naked manifestation of the sovereign's will to defend the state's specific order. But in its methods and composition the gang also posed a latent threat to that order, hence the necessary correctives through the role of the police, the pledge, and the court.

The zone of anomie from which people in Myanmar were brought back into the juridical realm through the hearing and sentence was in certain respects how Agamben has described the anomalous zone. As I noted at the beginning of this chapter, it was neither fully inside nor outside the juridical order, a zone where the juridical and extrajuridical were blurred. The ambiguity of events in 2007, from the moment of criminalisation to the sentencing of persons accused over the protests, was not incidental. It was indicative of how law and order could be maintained through a continuum of administrative activity even from the extrajuridical back to the juridical. Because nothing in law and order as political ideal obliges adherence to norms secured juridically, people could be moved in and out of this anomalous zone if necessary, to secure the state's particular goals.

However, from study of Myanmar, I do not agree with Agamben that what happens in a place of detention within the zone of anomie depends only 'on the civility and ethical sense of the police who temporarily act as sovereign'.[72] The zone might be outside the ordinary juridical order, but the police-sovereigns make decisions informed by their perceptions of what can and cannot be done through extant institutions. The relationships that the policeman has to other people and agencies place constraints on his exercise of sovereign power. The power of the policeman as sovereign, be it in the camp or in the torture chamber, is not absolute. In Myanmar during 2007, the guardians of the camp made informed decisions concerning the lives and liberties of people in their custody with expectations that they could eventually move them back across the extrajuridical threshold. They made

[72] Agamben, *Homo Sacer* 174.

different decisions from the police-sovereigns in places where no such expectations exist, such as those police and soldiers who patrolled the anomalous zone at a time of collapsed rule of law in Sri Lanka. The arrangements associated with law and order in Myanmar account for why the incidence of custodial abuses is high but the incidence of extrajudicial killing and enforced disappearance outside civil war zones is comparatively low.

8

SPEAKING UP FOR THE RULE OF LAW

A lot of media and academic commentary about Myanmar's political renewal since 2011 has been taken up with the role of elites in negotiating for a more democratic, less repressive future. The players in the country's political transition are characterised as 'regime soft-liners and more pragmatic and flexible leaders of the democratic opposition [who must] come together to agree on new rules'.[1] The storyline of how the soft-liners and pragmatists come together varies, but the characters remain the same: a handful of army officers in mufti, a few others still in uniform; Aung San Suu Kyi plus one or two other notables from her party, and the representatives of some armed groups.

Such a restricted view of politics puts it 'in a realm far from most citizens', Ben Kerkvliet notes, and in so doing 'misses a great deal of what is politically significant'.[2] Absent from an absurdly small cast of characters are untold numbers of people who by talking back to power over successive periods of dictatorship have created politically active, alert, and interested citizens in towns and villages around Myanmar, people eager for new opportunities to participate in public life. These people, who have not needed to wait for new rules on how to engage politically, did not acquiesce to repressive government but spoke against it constantly, many at personal risk, others more cautiously

[1] Larry Diamond, 'The Need for a Political Pact', *Journal of Democracy* 23.4 (2012): 139.
[2] Benedict J. Tria Kerkvliet, 'Everyday Politics in Peasant Societies (and Ours)', *Journal of Peasant Studies* 36.1 (2009): 228–29.

and furtively, spreading 'rumours of rights'.[3] These rumours eroded the notion of law and order, encouraging in its stead the emergence of a new lexicon of citizenship.

This chapter reveals just a few of these people and their traditions of talking back to power, so as to highlight how they have also spoken for the rule of law – not in the sense of law and order, but in other senses entirely. It concentrates on practices of complaint against government officials, because complaints of this sort are the most revealing politically. It also discusses authorities' responses to complaints and political mobilisation arising out of complaints that invoke the rule of law. As with the previous chapter, its purposes are documentary and interpretive. Methods of complaint and resistance practiced in the decades prior to the beginning of political change in 2011 help to account for how people all around Myanmar have begun to mobilise in response to new opportunities, building on existing practices and narratives for rights-based claims.

The chapter is based on a wide variety of sources, including letters, attendant case records, and other materials collected during research from 2008 to 2013.[4] Two case studies of rural activism in defence of agricultural land also draw on interviews conducted with people involved in these events. As in previous chapters, where cases have already been publicised, I have cited them directly. Otherwise, I have referred to them anonymously.

WAYS TO COMPLAIN, MEANS TO SPEAK

Successive governments in Myanmar have invited disgruntled citizens to complain to a given ministry, department, or agency about personnel of that ministry or department. The Supreme Court receives and investigates allegations of wrongdoing among judges or its bureaucrats, the attorney general receives complaints about his own staff, and so on. No single, centralised mechanism invites and receives complaints like, for instance, the Letters and Visits Bureau in China.[5] The government

[3] Julia Eckert, 'Rumours of Rights', *Law Against the State: Ethnographic Forays into Law's Transformations*, eds. Julia Eckert et al. (Cambridge: Cambridge University Press, 2012) 147–70.

[4] See appendix for details.

[5] For short discussions on the bureau, see Dingjian Cai, 'The Development of Constitutionalism in the Transition of Chinese Society', *Columbia Journal of Asian Law* 19.1 (2005): 5; Randall Peerenboom, 'Law and Development of Constitutional Democracy in China: Problem or Paradigm?' *Columbia Journal of Asian Law* 19.1 (2005): 222–23.

in 2004 also permitted the International Labour Organisation, or ILO, to receive complaints of forced labour and, later, recruitment of child soldiers.[6] Many people complained to the ILO even when their complaints did not relate to its mandate – not necessarily because they misunderstood its role, but because the international organisation represented principles associated with the rule of law that were absent from domestic institutions.[7]

Since 2011, the number and diversity of avenues for complainants have increased: so too have the number of complaints made. That year, the Myanmar National Human Rights Commission began its operations and invited complaints.[8] In a little over a year it reported receiving over three thousand letters.[9] A new legislative committee for legal and judicial affairs likewise encouraged people to write to it on specific cases. Its chairman, Thura U Aung Ko, said that in January 2012 alone it had received over three hundred complaints of court cases allegedly decided for reasons of corruption and bias. He said the committee was working with relevant ministries to assess the cases before considering whether to refer them to the courts, adding that the committee needed the assistance of the media 'so as to protect the people with the rule of law'.[10] In 2013, he told an audience at the chamber of commerce that the committee had 'been unable to keep up with the deluge of letters of complaint sent to it by members of the public', now numbering in the thousands.[11]

If Aung Ko was deluged, then his counterpart Aung San Suu Kyi was even more so. Her Rule of Law and Tranquility Committee in its annual report indicated that in 2012–13 it had received over 11,259 submissions of all types, among which, some 3,800 submissions concerned the judiciary; 3,600, the executive; 3,466, confiscation of land, and 393 other matters.[12] The report did not divulge how many complaints the committee had so far examined or what action authorities had taken in response to complaints. However, legislators in 2014

6 As discussed in Richard Horsey, *Ending Forced Labour in Myanmar: Engaging a Pariah Regime* (London and New York: Routledge, 2011).

7 For discussion, see Nick Cheesman, review of *Ending Forced Labour in Myanmar*, by Richard Horsey, *South East Asia Research* 21.2 (2013): 343–47.

8 *NLM* 7 Oct. 2011: 7.

9 Myanmar National Human Rights Commission, Statement 8/2012, 10 Dec. 2012.

10 *Weekly Eleven* 12 Feb. (2012), 17 Feb. 2012 www.weeklyeleven.com.

11 *Mizzima* 4 Feb. (2013), 5 Feb. 2013 www.mizzima.com.

12 Report of the Pyithu Hluttaw Rule of Law and Tranquility Committee, 14 Aug. 2013 (in Burmese).

chastised a newly formed anti-corruption commission after it revealed that it had initiated legal action in only three cases during some five months of operation in which it had received more than 530 complaints.[13] At least two of the three cases involving legal action were brought against judges.[14]

The law-and-order ideal encourages people to perceive and respond to public institutions as an administrative hierarchy staffed by enlightened superiors monitoring the practices of subordinates. Because nobody expects subordinates to act on cases without active monitoring and intervention from above, letter writers often address their complaints to the person at the top, copying them to people who are likely to be the ones to act on them. During the decades of military rule, complainants tended to write to senior military officers. Since 2011, writers have addressed the president or senior ministers, as well as heads of legislative committees. According to a member of the upper house, in 2011 alone the president received 6,660 complaints, many relating to judges, and to all types of cases in courts.[15] This technique of writing to the president or some other senior figure and copying to subordinates aims to put the latter on notice that the complainant has gone over their heads. It carries with it the simple hope that by addressing the letter to the president or some other seemingly important person or persons it will be more efficacious.

Where people allege that officials have committed criminal offences, they can register complaints directly with the police or courts. Some letters of complaint follow initial attempts through these institutions, or proceed in parallel with them. Registering complaints with the police is relatively straightforward and inexpensive, but they are not obligated to investigate. They may also decline to record an allegation where it runs contrary to their interests or has the potential to create unwanted difficulties for them. Lodging complaints in court requires a lawyer and financial means. Again, the court can decline to entertain an allegation or can direct the police to investigate and have them come back with nothing on which to proceed.

The return of habeas corpus writs in 2011 is indicative of the limitations associated with making complaints in courts.[16] In two test cases

[13] *Irrawaddy* 24 Sept. (2014), 26 Oct. 2014 www.irrawaddy.org.

[14] *British Broadcasting Corporation* (*BBC*), 6 Aug. 2014. [15] *BBC*, 23 Feb. 2012.

[16] Articles 296(a)(i) and 378(a)(i) of the 2008 Constitution reintroduced habeas corpus. The Supreme Court started receiving petitions subsequent to the transfer of power from the former military junta to the newly composed state organs in 2011. See further, Melissa Crouch, 'The

the following year, the Supreme Court declined to entertain applications because by the time it heard the applications the army had transferred the detained persons to police custody.[17] The applications did seemingly have the effect of prompting the unit holding the men, both of whom were accused of contact with an unlawful armed group, to pass them on to the police for processing. But the officials' responses to the writ applications and those of the court were consonant with the law-and-order tradition. The whereabouts of the detainees having been identified and the circumstances of their detention resolved, the court turned to the next matter on its docket. Questions as to how the men might have come into military custody, how they were held, and important contested facts – such as the duration of custody prior to their transfer to the police – did not come into it. Where another case involved the abduction and disappearance of a woman, a judge likewise declined to entertain the application on the ground that no evidence existed of her ever being in army custody.[18]

Complainants who want to have their voices heard in public send copies of letters to media outlets, especially to radio broadcasters based abroad. The BBC Burmese Service has a fortnightly programme that features all types of complaints against officials. Other broadcasters, like Voice of America (VOA) and Radio Free Asia (RFA), frequently air interviews with complainants or their representatives. New legislators have mentioned these broadcasts in the legislature. But the radio also had efficacy before 2011, despite the state media lambasting broadcasters publicly as a 'skyful of lies'.[19] A Supreme Court circular in 2010 admitted that 'when news [of government malfeasance] aired on the BBC, VOA, [and] RFA was investigated, it was in all instances found to be genuine, and it is not good that people are going out of their way to complain to the BBC, VOA, [and] RFA because they think it is the only way they will get action taken'.[20]

Common Law and Constitutional Writs: Prospects for Accountability in Myanmar', *Law, Society and Transition in Myanmar*, eds. Melissa Crouch and Tim Lindsey (Oxford: Hart, 2014) 33–58.

[17] *Daw Ma Hkawn* v. *Battalion Commander U Aung Zaw Oo*, 2012 Criminal Misc. Application (Writ) 1, Supreme Court, 1 Mar. 2012; *Daw Marip Hkawn* v. *Battalion Commander U Aung Zaw Oo*, 2012 Criminal Misc. Application (Writ) 2, Supreme Court, 1 Mar. 2012.

[18] *U Dau Lum* v. *Lt-Col. Zaw Myo Htut*, 2012 Criminal Misc. Application (Writ) 3, Supreme Court, 1 Mar. 2012. The case documents are reproduced in U Tin Win, *Writs* (Mandalay: Nwewe, 2012) 43–58 (in Burmese).

[19] As in *NLM* 27 Sept. 2007: 8–9. [20] SC Letter 361/Su 12/84/2010, 29 Mar. 2010.

Some complainants and people working with them also get cases taken up through advocacy groups. Organisations like the Hong Kong–based Asian Human Rights Commission document and issue case-based appeals. Many complainants stand a better chance of getting publicity through intermediaries. Their cases go on to international bodies, like the UN Human Rights Council, sometimes via the Special Rapporteur on human rights in Myanmar, who can put them on the record in international forums and formally request responses from government.

Since 2011, the domestic print media have carried details of more and more complaints. Some publications have pages where they routinely reproduce letters. More enterprising and confident complainants are now also calling press conferences, where they raise specific grievances and name judges and government bureaucrats who they allege have wronged them. And many letters of complaint, case documents, photographs, and other evidence to prove or disprove allegations are making their way onto the Internet. Blogs and Facebook pages host detailed accounts of officials' alleged wrongdoing or ineptitude, sometimes with uploaded images of letters sent to the president or national human rights commission, affidavits, court rulings, and photographic evidence of events and circumstances. The quick circulation of material over the Internet combined with the burgeoning professional media mean that the already well-developed vocabulary of complaint is rapidly expanding. Within it is a lexicon through which people advocate for the rule of law: a lexicon of the citizen as bearer, and wielder, of rights.

A LEXICON OF CITIZENSHIP

In Chapter 4, I argued that the state in Burma during the 1960s, 1970s, and 1980s reconfigured the notion of citizenship and the rights of citizens to correspond to its pragmatic objectives. Henceforth, rights were reconstituted as conditional privileges, which could be extended or withdrawn according to circumstances. No rights existed that could not be delimited if required as a matter of policy, or be subject to a higher imperative.

Contra the official lexicon of qualified rights and reduced citizenship, people in Myanmar have continued to assert rights and to re-invest the lexicon with normative contents that the state denies. This section of the chapter looks at how letter writers have challenged the official idiom by insisting on their rights as citizens – as autonomous holders of rights in a political community, not as the subjects of sovereign *cetana*.

The lexicon of the citizen is not the lexicon of all complainants. Many complainants in Myanmar adopt what I call, following Sheila Fitzpatrick's work on letter writing in Soviet Russia, a supplicatory style:

> The supplicant was implicitly a subject rather than a citizen. He sent his private complaints, requests, petitions and confessions to an authority figure imagined as a benevolent father. . . . Supplicants' letters might ask for justice as well as mercy, but they did not invoke rights. They portrayed their authors as victims and dwelt on their miseries and misfortunes. Supplicants' letters, though sent to public figures and requesting them to act in their official capacity, dealt with private and personal concerns. . . . The citizen was a more 'modern' figure than the supplicant. Citizens wrote letters to the editor or the Politburo to state opinions, criticize policies, suggest improvements, blow the whistle on corrupt officials, point out miscarriages of justice and denounce wrongdoers as their 'duty as a citizen'. They acted, or claimed to act, in the public interest; if they had private motives for writing, they concealed them. They used the language of rights and among the rights they implicitly claimed the right to be heard.[21]

The supplicant endorses and accommodates the public transcript. She hopes to enlist the support of people to whom the complaint is addressed on the basis of her singular eligibility. She aims to demonstrate that she qualifies for the assistance and support of power holders by satisfying certain criteria, which official discourse advises are criteria that if satisfied will help her to have a complaint heard and to have it addressed administratively. She presents her grievance narrowly, concentrating it on her own individual concerns, not wanting to impute into it any larger political implications. She approaches officialdom cautiously, crouched and subdued.

By contrast, the citizen-complainant bothers much less to conceal her true opinions. In making a complaint, she implicitly recognises sovereign will, but she does not bow to it. She asserts her rights independently of the law-and-order ideal. She uses official language provocatively, sometimes inverting or breaking open the meanings of the public transcript in confronting ways, to suit her own interests and

[21] Sheila Fitzpatrick, 'Supplicants and Citizens: Public Letter-Writing in Soviet Russia in the 1930s', *Slavic Review* 55.1 (1996): 103–04.

needs. Moreover, she does so with a view to the interests of the larger political community, to the rights that her fellow citizens share with her. Even when appealing within the administrative parameters provided her, she makes a rights-based claim, a claim that transcends the parameters set for authorised complaint.

Of course, the typology of complaints and complainants is not quite so neat. Sometimes in a series of letters on the same matter, a complainant can shift from supplication to stridency, emerging as a citizen from behind the mask of supplication when attempts at redress fail. In 2006, for example, a woman in the north of the country sent letters to the regional army commander alleging that officers of a police special drug squad manning a roadside checkpoint had stopped her son and two friends, had assaulted him and that he had died in custody. The first letter was a narrow supplication, emphasising the victim's innocence, noting the lack of drugs found in his urine, and concluding with a request for action in accordance with the law. A month later, the case had made no progress, and she found herself under serious threat from the police; in the second letter the citizen's voice can be heard loud and clear:

> These are nothing other than the undignified, lawless and unjust deeds to oppress the people of Special Drug [Inspector Ko Ko] and four police personnel. We the people have become prey for Special Drug Squad members to extort and oppress. Because of these persons' deeds, not only have the people become property-less, homeless and landless, but also they are living lives of misery and poverty. Just as we cannot estimate how many people these persons have in the past arrested on fabricated cases to demand money and put up on narcotics charges, we cannot know how many against whom they will yet lodge narcotics charges, extort and unlawfully assault. . . .
>
> I am a person who respects the integrity of the Defence Services. I believe that [you] regional commander, are a person who will stand truly on the side of the people. I do not accept communications coming from political parties or whichever radio stations abroad. I believe that internal problems should only be solved internally. Accordingly, this complaint is made as a mother and a citizen who respects the integrity of the Defence Services and trusts in [you] father regional commander.

This appeal is a cry for help, but it is not at all like a cry for help from a supplicant. The complainant is a strong and assertive woman, and she lets it be known. Furthermore, she speaks for a wider community: the political community of fellow citizens and rights bearers. The same kind of expression is found in the voice of a young transsexual writing to the police chief in 2014 about abuse suffered while detained in Mandalay, who insists that despite her transgender, she has the same human rights as everyone else. At a time when the national government had prioritized the rule of law, she concludes, action should surely be taken against policemen 'acting lawlessly towards innocent people'. Like the mother before her, this complainant expresses herself through the idiom of 'we the people'. She speaks on behalf of the general political community, rather than as an individual or as a member of a sexual minority.

In a letter sent to the secretary number-one of the ruling council during 2004, another mother describes how her son was sentenced to one year's imprisonment for absconding from the police force. She does not quibble with his offence but explains that the time he spent in custody before the case came to court was not deducted from the sentence. Thereafter, while serving as a prison labourer attached to an army unit in a remote region he died from illness three to four months after the date he should have been released. The mother concludes by stating that she was submitting the complaint 'in order that no mother in the future would feel this type of loss and heart-rending grief, in order that the responsible persons at respective levels not keep anyone in detention beyond date of release – that detainees not lose their entitlements, that each and every responsible person carry out his duties correctly'. As in the letter above, this mother moves from her own personal tragedy to emphasise that she is motivated by a desire to protect the lives of other children. She is concerned to spare other mothers the burden of misery she bears due to the wrongful handling of her child's case.

Another striking feature of the letter quoted at length above is that the author invokes the official narrative of the benevolent, guiding role of the armed forces in national affairs, extolling the virtues of the recipient officer. It seems counter-intuitive for the citizen to quote official rhetoric in this manner. But the reason is not so mysterious. As Kevin O'Brien and Lianjiang Li have observed of China, in a politically repressive setting complainants shape their challenges 'from materials made available by the structure of domination'.[22] Complainants speaking in a politically informed lexicon of rights use

[22] Kevin J. O'Brien and Lianjiang Li, *Rightful Resistance in Rural China* (New York: Cambridge University Press, 2006) 14.

the materials of domination strategically, to advance interests contrary to those of the structures for domination. Thus, in a case during 2010 where police officers arrested a group of men for accusing officials of corruption, relatives complained that subordinates of the regional military commander were undermining his efforts to develop the area. They concluded, 'At this important time that the state and Defence Services leadership are endeavouring for the emergence of a new democratic nation which the people desire, self-seeking persons are causing the national government and Defence Services to suffer lost esteem.' The complainants do their best to align themselves with the interests of the national leadership through affirmations of its policies and objectives, at the same time pointing out that the state's representatives do not share these interests.

Other letters give parts of the public transcript a little twist, such as by playing on the slogan posted or painted at the gates of police stations. In a 2005 letter complaining about police force corruption in a northern town, the author closed with:

> We observe that Myanmar Police Force members ought to be in keeping with the [police] slogan, 'May I help you'. Furthermore, we believe that they must protect the lives and property of law-respecting, law-abiding, non-offending people. Truly, we respectfully submit that action be taken and blame laid against those who instead of being on the side of the law are behaving like licenced bandits, intimidating and extorting money from innocent people.

A letter from relatives of persons arrested in Yangon during 2007 for staying in a locality where they were not registered to reside remarked that they had heard a senior official on television and radio saying 'nobody is above the law', and 'the law does not discriminate', using an idiomatic expression that the law 'does not differentiate the back from the chest'. Evidently, it concluded, this was not true of the unjust local officials, since for them the people with property and money were the chest whereas those without were the back.

When a citizen-complainant characterises the army or administration in glowing terms, her laudatory tone conceals an implicit warning: her acceptance of the army's claims to authority hinges on its capacity to provide her with redress. Imitating the rhetoric of the public transcript, the letter writer puts the onus on the addressee to prove that the rhetoric means something. In a letter sent to the new president in late 2011 on behalf of a detainee whom jailors allegedly assaulted after he was transferred to a remote prison, the author plays up the language of the old government versus the new:

> I have seen and heard that the President's new government is remedying the human rights abuses and acts of impunity committed under the former government. The things that were done to [the detainee] are inhuman, lawless things that should absolutely never have been done. On behalf of all citizens of Myanmar, for the emergence of genuine democracy, the emergence of just law, and the emergence of law to enable the defence of the individual, without malice I respectfully request sanction of the President to prosecute the head wardens of [two prisons] for the violations they have committed and all persons who committed violations in this case.[23]

The letter asserts rights: the right of the victim to justice, the right of the complainant to complain. It also connects these assertions to larger political developments and to the hopes and expectations of the entire political community. The last part, where the writer calls for 'just law', or law with justice, captures the essence of the complaint. The writer does not just want law. She has had enough of plain old 'law'. Her call is for an altogether different type of law from the (law) of 'law and order' as *ngyeinwut-pibyaye*. Superficially, the citizen's letter may make certain concessions. It may even appear to extol the virtues of official ideology by reciting its rhetoric. However, it is a rights-based complaint, using the materials of domination, but not conceding to be dominated. The citizen's complaint is grounded in a notion of *taya-ubade-somoye* as *the rule of law*.

Citizen-complainants invest the language of law with meanings contrary to those of the official narrative. A relative of Phyo Wai Aung, the young man accused in connection with a fatal bombing on whose case I wrote in earlier chapters, in February 2011 admonishes the head of state as the person 'responsible for the rule of law' to take action against jail officials for a variety of unlawful punishments imposed on the prisoner. Superficially going along with the head of state's claims to be a head of a state for which the rule of law matters, the relative is talking back to him of a completely different rule of law, one in which the police and other officials who torture people in their custody are not thereby invested with power, but are themselves subject to punishment.

[23] The letter does not make clear what sanction is required, but presumably it is under section 197(1) of the Criminal Procedure Code, that sanction of the head of state be given before civil servants over a certain level of authority be prosecuted criminally.

Similarly, in 2011 over forty cultivators protesting land confiscation signed a letter as 'farmers together seeking implementation of *just* rule of law'. Their rule of law is not a synonym for law and order: it is the rule of law based on an explicit claim to justice. It implicitly challenges the conflation of the rule of law with law and order, distinguishing it from the rule of law *with justice* that the farmers seek.

With the emergence of new avenues for complaint since 2011, the language of substantive rule of law has become more explicit in some letters. In a complaint submitted to the Rule of Law and Tranquility Committee in February 2013 concerning the torture and death in police custody of a man in a border town adjacent to Thailand the year before, the brother-in-law of the deceased asserts that despite repeated complaints, to his amazement so far no action had been taken against the accused officers. The letter quotes article 5 of the Universal Declaration of Human Rights, on the right not to be tortured, and article 8: 'Everyone has the right to an effective remedy by the competent national tribunals for acts violating the fundamental rights granted him by the constitution or by law.' It continues that the family had previously notified local authorities, their member of the national legislature, the home affairs minister, and the chief minister of the state, all to no avail. It concludes, 'Despite having repeatedly submitted complaints about this loss of human rights, as no action has been taken up to today, it appears that Myanmar's rule of law remains hollow.' The writer ends optimistically that Aung San Suu Kyi's committee will, he trusts, have the ability to give effect to the rule of law where others have failed.

COUNTERING COMPLAINT

Many, probably most, complainants in Myanmar do not suffer repercussions for making complaints. A lot of them are ignored; others meet with officials making inquiries but do not get any satisfaction. A few obtain redress. Some generate quiet resentment among local administrators, who look for routine, petty means to make it known to the complainant that they are holding grudges. But where officials choose to act against complainants, Myanmar's courts and other institutions for law and order offer ready avenues for reprisals. This section looks at some of those avenues.

Use of courts for reprisal against complainants in Myanmar is not novel. It is no coincidence that to this day charges brought against complainants tend to be from sections of the Penal Code. The code's Benthamite designers were keen to ensure that complaints could be received and investigated, but also that anyone presumed to take up government time and money needlessly could be sanctioned. An entire chapter of the code concerns contempt of the lawful authority of civil servants. State officers can also take advantage of a range of other criminal provisions, such as those on defamation, to prosecute complainants. In 2011, for instance, a noncommissioned military intelligence officer brought a case against a complainant for accusing him of selling narcotics, an allegation the police found to be false. The Supreme Court upheld the soldier's right to bring the case, even though he did so independent of his chain of command, finding that the complainant had purposefully sought to undermine the dignity of the individual soldier *and* his unit.[24]

How officials counter complaint depends on the case: who made the complaint, what it is about, the level it reaches, and what the complainant hopes to achieve. Sometimes, reprisals are initiated from high-up levels of government as a matter of policy. A police officer bringing charges in 2008 against a man who had been sending information to the ILO testified that he had received written orders to open the case from the deputy home affairs minister, which he submitted to the court as evidence.[25] More often, counter-complaints are brought at the initiative of low- and medium-level authorities – in urban wards and villages, and at the township level above them.

Occasionally, reprisal for complaint is swift, direct, and brutal. Authorities in 2010 accused six men in Bilin of being insurgent supporters and sympathisers. Their relatives countered that the accusation was motivated by complaints that the men had made about corrupt local officials. Of the six, one was tortured to death, another paid to get out of the case, and a third escaped capture. The remaining three were imprisoned under the Unlawful Associations Act.[26]

In another part of the country affected by protracted armed conflict, during 2013 a father had dared to complain to the national human rights commission that his daughter died in a barrage of poorly aimed

[24] *U Kyaw Thein* v. *Republic of the Union of Myanmar*, 2012 MLR 10.

[25] *Pol. Capt. Thet Tin Htun* v. *U Zaw Htay and Another*, 2008 Criminal Case 53, Magway District Court, Testimony-in-chief of Pol. Capt. Thet Tin Htun, PW 2, 22 Dec. 2008: 2.

[26] *Sub Inspector Chit Swe* v. *Maung Hla Hpone*, 2010 Criminal Case 624, Bilin Township Court, 23 July 2010; *Sub Inspector Chit Swe* v. *U Maung Thein and Another*, 2010 Criminal Case 653, Bilin Township Court, 10 Aug. 2010.

gunfire; an army officer opened a case against him under section 211 of the Penal Code – for bringing false charges with intent to injure.[27] One of the father's letters, sent to the president in September, concluded by asking rhetorically whether 'innocent civilians are the enemy of the Myanmar Defence Services'. It added that as the deceased girl was in her school uniform the army's claim that it had fired mistakenly had no merit. The counter-complaint acknowledged that the girl had died due to military gunfire, but denied that the military had been negligent in its use of weaponry, as the father had alleged.[28]

Countering complaint is often protracted, and consists of a mix of threats and inducements. It sometimes includes offers of money or business opportunities. It may entail partial redress of the complainant's demands, such as transfer, demotion, or dismissal of the wrongdoer. Some complainants and officials reach mutually advantageous agreements: the mother of a worker in a timber mill who in 2006 complained about a group of policemen who had assaulted her son later dropped her complaint reportedly after the police officer who came to negotiate invited her to join an illegal lottery syndicate he was protecting.

Aside from inducements combined with threats of counter legal action or possible violence, local authorities have many other coercive methods to silence a complainant. In a small town or village, state agencies have effective control over practically every part of a person's life. Officials get to know one another professionally and personally, and they do one another favours. Pushing complaints too hard in one place can cause a push-back from another. In cities, the larger number of agencies and more complicated, less intimate relationships between officials make such practices more difficult, but the same general principle applies. Officials study a complainant's affairs and locate points where they can apply pressure to get the complaint withdrawn. They seek to use the coercive instruments of the state at the local level to wear down a complainant who cannot afford, financially or emotionally, to fight for a long time.

To illustrate, I will briefly recount a story that a lawyer explained to me. In 2009, local officials in Yangon brought a charge against his client, whom he says was the victim of assault, not the assailant. The

[27] *Maj. Zarni Min Paik* v. *U Brang Shawng*, 2013 Criminal Case 32, Hpakant Township Court.
[28] Northwestern Regional Command, Frontline Strategic Group 3, Letter 2000/10/Ye/3, 28 Feb. 2013.

story speaks to the complex of factors working against the ordinary complainant from the moment an incident has occurred, and to how only determined complainants can succeed. The case is also indicative of the types of events that take place around Myanmar daily but rarely get attention beyond the immediate vicinity where they occur.

According to affidavits, which the lawyer shared confidentially, the young man who was later charged had gone to his ward council office on a routine matter. When the clerk on duty asked for his identity card, he could not produce it. She ridiculed him and brought him inside the office. There she ridiculed him again in front of the ward chairman and another man. The chairman, who had the stench of alcohol on his breath, also verbally abused the young man. Then he started hitting him. The young man ran for the door. The chairman yelled for his companion to slam it shut, but the youngster got partway through the door before it was closed on him. He fled to the street, where the officials pursued him and continued to beat him up. When onlookers tried to come to his aid, policemen stationed alongside the ward office threatened them to keep back or face the consequences.

When they were done, the officials left the man in the street. Onlookers and relatives revived him and took him to his residence. His outraged mother went back to the ward office, but stated that men at the front drove her out 'like an animal' with warnings that 'we'll have you in the lockup'. She went to complain at the police station. An officer took her to one side and suggested she not proceed, advising that if she did, it would be her son, not the assailants, who would end up in detention. Ignoring his advice, she insisted on making the complaint before taking her son to hospital for treatment. Anticipating where they were going, someone from the council or police station appears to have phoned ahead, because the doctor who conducted the examination wrote at the top of the medical record that the young man said he had sustained his injuries in a fight.

The young man recovered, but his mother kept following up on her complaint. According to the lawyer, she said that her reason for pursuing it was that the chairman had a long history of abusive behaviour. For her, the treatment of her son was the final straw. In other words, she took up the case as a citizen-complainant, concerned to make a rights-based claim in the interests of the larger community, at risk to her own family.

The mother's perseverance paid off: with the help of other locals who had also had enough of the assailant, the chairman and council member lost their jobs. Their removal from office signifies a satisfactory outcome within the law-and-order paradigm. The removal of an unreliable official from the administrative continuum is in the interests of better management. What more could the complainant want? Yet, for this mother it was not enough. She continued to press for a criminal case – again, consistent with the behaviour of the citizen complainant.

Finally the mother got her day in court. About nine months after the incident, a police officer arrived at her house and informed her that her son would be required to appear and present two guarantors to obtain bail. On the designated day, the family and guarantors arrived at court and learned that the two assailants had lodged a Penal Code section 353 case against the young man, for assault or criminal force to deter a civil servant from discharge of his duty. The purpose of this case was to apply pressure and get the case against the former officials dropped, which by this time had been registered for trial under section 325 of the Penal Code, causing grievous hurt.

The two cases went to trial. The same judge heard both. For the judge, they were equally unattractive. On one hand, the case against the former officials was strong, but the officials had already lost their jobs. The basic requirements of law and order had been satisfied. Absent instructions from above that the two former officials be punished criminally, she had no interest in moving on the case against them. On the other hand, the former officials had obviously lodged a fraudulent case against the assault victim as a bargaining chip with which to negotiate for withdrawal of the former case. Therefore, the judge allowed both cases to drag out, giving time to the former officials to further harass and cajole the mother, wearing her down financially and emotionally. Eventually, the mother did what was expected and agreed to drop the case against the assailants in exchange for withdrawal of the case against her son, with the ready assistance of the prosecutor and investigating police, who also saw no personal advantage in either case.

Counter-complaints may be initiated for bargaining purposes, as in this instance. Sometimes they are initiated out of revenge or as warnings to others not to follow the example set by complainants who refused to compromise. In 2005, eight men submitted two written complaints of corruption against local officials in the delta, on behalf of fifty-six farmers. All eight were cultivators, but two held quasi-official positions. One was an executive of the Union Solidarity and Development Association, precursor to the political party that took the lion's share of seats in the legislature during the 2010 elections. The other was a school principal. The township authorities sent a team to investigate their complaint and issued a warning to the council, obliging it to return money to farmers whom it had unfairly taxed. In response, the village tract council went over the township's heads to the district level, where it got approval to lodge a criminal case under section 211 of the Penal Code for bringing a false complaint with intent to injure. The council brought the charge only against the executive and the school principal, perhaps because they were ringleaders, or because they were impertinent in bringing a complaint while holding public offices. A court convicted the two and sentenced them to two years' imprisonment each.[29]

People who bring complaints against judges face peculiar difficulties. Judges can be sanctioned over complaints of wrongdoing, as discussed in Chapter 6. Nonetheless, they also retain a formidable arsenal of legal and institutional defences with which to rebut complaints, and resources with which to carry out reprisals. Aware of these defences and weapons, some aggressive complainants against judges purposefully conceal their identities, like one who launched a tirade against a judge in the delta for alleged corruption, gambling during sitting hours, drunkenness, and socialising at home and outside with parties to cases. Attempts by a special investigator to uncover the identity of the complainant failed, although he surmised from the letter that the complaint's author was 'likely to have been an individual from the court environs'.[30]

Some of the defences judges enjoy are structurally integrated: a consequence of the arrangements for hierarchical oversight and internal policing of the judiciary. The Supreme Court's journal in 2001, for instance, described a case in which a township court sentenced a person to six months in prison under section 182(b) of the Penal Code, for giving false information with intent to cause a civil servant

[29] *U San Shwe* v. *U Win Nyunt and Another*, 2005 Criminal Case 1334, Bogalay Township Court, 2 Dec. 2005.
[30] SC Letter 2323/Su 14 (Ga) 109/94, 19 Apr. 1994, appendix B, 5.

to use his lawful power to the injury of another person.[31] The accused had made complaints to higher authorities that the opposing party in a civil case before the Yangon Additional Divisional Court had conspired with the judges against him. A judge in a township court under the divisional judiciary's supervision heard the case. The presiding judge could hardly be expected to come up with anything other than a guilty verdict, since his future prospects depended on his good relations with his superior. Precisely for this reason, one judge lost his job in 1992 because he had allegedly 'unjustly accused his superiors of corruption', something that, the Supreme Court director general noted disapprovingly, 'should not happen in the world of the civil service'.[32]

In 2007, the Supreme Court convicted a man accused of contempt after he made complaints that three of its judges in Mandalay were taking bribes.[33] The 1926 Contempt of Court Act, under which he was convicted, does not specify what constitutes contempt. Previously, the apex court warned subordinates to use contempt sparingly.[34] Even where finding parties guilty, rulings tended to be short, judges refraining from interpreting the concept at any length.[35] In 1992, the Supreme Court widened the ambit of contempt, ruling that any 'writing, speech or behaviour so as to create an inferior opinion of the court or judge; or constituting interference in the legal uprightness of the court; or amounting to interference in the decision of the court ... and any actions blocking, obstructing or interfering with a legally issued order, summons, warrant, etc., that the court has confirmed are acts of contempt of court'.[36]

In the 2007 case, the Supreme Court found that the complaint was written 'so as to damage the reputation of the Supreme Court, which is supervising each and every court, and to cause trouble for the judiciary'

[31] U Aung Min, 'A Lying Complainant Who Falsely Accused a Judge on Losing a Case Imprisoned for His Crime Upon the Judge Counter-Suing', *Judicial Journal* 1.12 (2001): 56–58 (in Burmese).

[32] SC Letter 941/132-YaNa (94), 31 Aug. 1994, 1–2.

[33] *Daw Than Than Lwin, Assistant Director, Civil Justice Dept., Mandalay* v. *U Thein Kyi (a) Mohamed Muser*, 2007 MLR 112.

[34] *Thakin Myo Nyunt* v. *Thakin Pu*, 1963 BLR (CC) 728.

[35] *Daw Dagon Khin Khin Lay* v. *U Ko Ko Lay and Another*, 1965 BLR (CC) 1065 (in Burmese); *Socialist Republic of the Union of Burma* v. *U Hla Htun*, 1982 BLR (CCJ) 48; *Daw Aye Kyi* v. *U Win Thaung and 3*, 1986 BLR (CCJ) 87.

[36] *U Maung Maung and Another* v. *Daw Kyu Sein and 2*, 1992 MLR 102, 105.

because the complainant was dissatisfied with the outcome of his case.[37] In effect, the ruling held that the higher the position of a judge, the more likely that a complaint against a judge would constitute institutionally oriented criticism. Since superior courts supervise inferior ones, in criticising a superior court the complainant is also criticising the hierarchy of courts it oversees.

The difficulty with this construction is that the complainant should, wherever possible, avoid institutional criticism. For a complaint against a judge to be 'truthful', it should be specific and individualised. But a complaint against a senior judge cannot be individualised, because he is responsible for supervising a hierarchy of subordinates. Any criticism of him constitutes a critique of the whole judiciary. A complainant cannot but make an institutionally oriented complaint against a judge at a higher level. The possibility of individualising the complaint so that it is 'truthful' does not exist.

Official language since 2011 does mark something of a change from before, when bureaucrats described people as complaining because they had lost cases, not because of genuine grievances. The new legislative committee on legal affairs, which I mentioned at the start of the chapter, told journalists in December that out of a hundred complaints of wrongdoing in court proceedings received, it had found clear evidence to support the allegations in sixty-nine, and had sent its findings to relevant courts for review.[38] In the legislature on April 24, 2012, one committee member estimated that 80 percent of allegations about judges were truthful.[39] By 2014, the committee had received in excess of ten thousand complaints, with around 90 percent related to judicial personnel.[40] The most commonly cited grievances were strikingly familiar: receipt of payments to shift charges from more serious to lesser sections of the Penal Code, or to shift from a section under which bail is not automatically attainable to one under which it is; and collusion of police officers and judges for personal advantage.

At the same time, the national legislature passed a new statute for contempt that like its predecessor provides for a six-month jail term.

[37] *Daw Than Than Lwin*, 116.
[38] *Myanmar Times* 9–15 Jan. (2012), 15 Jan. 2012 www.mmtimes.com.
[39] *Weekly Eleven* 29 Apr. (2012), 2 May 2012 www.weeklyeleven.com.
[40] *Daily Eleven* 12 Jan. 2014: 2–3.

Unlike the old law, the new statute includes a definition of contempt in criminal cases. A person, who by oral, written, or visible representation or 'by whatever other means' purposefully disseminates views so as to diminish the authority of a court; to interfere in the delivery of justice; to anticipate the ruling in a trial before it is delivered; or by whatever means acts to undermine public confidence in judicial independence commits a criminal offence.[41] The statute's section 7 attaches a rider to allow criticism in the interest of justice on 'genuine, specific, firm' grounds, yet this provision gives judges more than enough room to threaten potential complainants with contempt where rock-solid proof of wrongdoing is wanting, as is usually the case where bribery or malfeasance is alleged.

Activists in coming years might test the new contempt law by deliberately provoking charges so as to take a stand in court, where they can in writing and speech directly address a judge through the lexicon of rights. Indeed, a feature of reprisal cases against complainants who have asserted rights in the past is that accused complainants have pressed their cases further. Rights-oriented complainants maintain the rightness of their positions in the face of official insistence that they are wrong, and use opportunities that formal procedures offer to reiterate their original complaints, even where they cannot be heard publicly.

In a written argument submitted to court in 2006 on behalf of a farmer facing a charge of making a false accusation against village-level officials, for instance, a lawyer restated in detail the client's original allegations, including that the village chairman and members of the village tract council were smuggling cattle; had sold public land for private profit; and had submitted falsified estimates of summer paddy crop output to the government in order to obtain excess diesel fuel and fertilizer, which they resold instead of distributing at subsidised prices to farmers.[42] The lawyer repeated and expanded on each claim as he proceeded through the document. He then went on to set out how a team sent by the district council to investigate the allegations did not actually investigate. The farmer was convicted but on appeal was released through the *cha-lut* method described in Chapter 6.

[41] Contempt of Courts Law, 17/2013, sec. 2(d).

[42] *U Win Shein* v. *Daw Khin Win*, 2006 Criminal Case 275, Kunchangon Township Court, Defence Closing Submission, 20 Dec. 2006.

Similarly, in 1998 a woman complainant was accused of contempt of court over a letter lambasting a judge for deceit and decrying the judiciary as betraying the legacy of the martyrs for national independence after she declined to apologise when interrogators pressed her to do so.[43] Although she had never attended state school and had obtained a stranger's assistance to write the complaint, she insisted that she fully understood what was in it, that everything was true, and that she had submitted it not expecting justice but to make the facts known as widely as possible.

In court, complainants using the lexicon of rights go beyond the simple presentation of facts necessary for a defence, and try to use the courtroom to spoil the ritual performance of officialdom. In the delta during 2004, for instance, a defence lawyer interrogated a village tract council chairman over whether he had not violated orders prohibiting the use of forced labour, asking if the chairman's own alleged offence was not the real reason for the case against his clients.[44] As the chairman floundered under cross-examination, the prosecutor intervened, and the judge instructed that no further examination of the plaintiff would be allowed.[45]

In another court during 2009, a judge sentenced twelve farmers in Magway to periods of up to five years in prison for criminal trespass and causing damage because they harrowed land that the army had confiscated for a sugar mill.[46] The farmers repeatedly and unanimously referred to a visit by senior officers from the labour ministry and ILO staff in March 2009 as entitling them to use the land. They cross-examined the plaintiffs on the same. They also interrogated the complainants' identities and claims to be cultivators: some of the new occupants described themselves as farmers or peasants, but were actually officials and staff for the army-managed mill that had taken over the fields. As in the case in the delta, although the outcome of the courtroom process was destined to go against them, the defendants used the materials of domination

[43] SC Letter 3683/Su 14 (Ga) 86/98, 9 July 1998, appendices A and B.

[44] Ministry of Home Affairs, Order 1/99, 14 May 1999. Supplementary Order, 27 Oct. 2000.

[45] *U Tin Htun* v. *Ko Ohn Myint and Another*, 2004 Criminal Case 1353, Hinthada Township Court, PW 1, 12 Aug. 2004.

[46] *U Win Htein* v. *U Thein Soe and Another*, 2009 Criminal Case 329, Aunglan Township Court, 16 Oct. 2009; and Criminal Cases 330–33, 336–38. For details of the cases see, ILO, *Developments Concerning the Question of the Observance by the Government of Myanmar of the Forced Labour Convention, 1930 (No. 29) (Gb.306/6)* (Geneva: International Labour Office, Nov. 2009) 3.

made available through the courtroom to rearticulate the rightfulness of their original positions, expose the lies and hypocrisy of their opponents, and in so doing, lay foundations on which to build up rural resistance to the incursions of administrative officers, through a rule-of-law idiom.

RIGHTFUL RESISTANCE

In their work on China, O'Brien and Li have described the struggles of rural villagers to defend rights they believe can be derived from official policies as a form of 'rightful resistance'.[47] Villagers engaging in rightful resistance make rights-based claims referring to the public transcript, claims turning its contents to the claimants' advantage. While I think we ought to be cautious about imputing belief in government policies as the basis for action, we can talk of rightful resistance where people use the materials of domination to represent rights-based demands against political domination.

I am closing the chapter with the topic of rightful resistance, not only because the deployment of the rule-of-law idiom in rural-based political struggles across Myanmar is striking, but also because most of these struggles are concerned with how to defend or regain farmland taken forcibly by the armed forces and its partners without compensation or with compensation at below-market rates. The sheer scale of land confiscation under military government in Myanmar makes the phenomenon unavoidable for anyone concerned with the language of rights and prospects for the rule of law there. The fact that nearly one-third of complaints received by the rule-of-law committee are classed as related to land confiscation speaks to its scale. Even then, this number is but a fraction of the total potential complaints. Estimates that the army has 'confiscated' – a euphemism for stolen – at least a quarter-million acres of land from farmers are probably conservative.[48] The extent of land grabbing over the last quarter century is vast – most of it by the armed forces and people connected with them. It goes well beyond areas of the country where it can be readily documented, into frontier regions where records of tenure and cultivation are scanty or non-existent. Additionally, these figures likely underestimate or do not take into account land confiscated for commercial projects of the sort

[47] O'Brien and Li, *Rightful Resistance in Rural China* xii.
[48] *Irrawaddy* 16 Aug. (2013), 18 Sept. 2013 www.irrawaddy.org.

described in this section, even though many – perhaps most – of these projects have the backing or involvement of the military or its personnel.

In the following two case studies – the first relatively unknown, the second well-known – the army's holding company and a partner firm encroached on farmland that local people had been unwilling to give up. Protracted struggles ensued in the fields, through letters, and in courtrooms. And although the outcomes of each case differ, both speak to the rule-of-law idiom in rightful rural resistance across Myanmar.[49]

In the first case, at the start of 2011 sixty-one farmers in Kanma, central Myanmar, signed a letter protesting the trespasses of the army's Union of Myanmar Economic Holding Limited and its partner firm into areas the farmers were cultivating.[50] On January 27, the local council summoned farmers from affected villages to a meeting. Two retired army majors from the holding company attended. They explained that the project was to construct caustic soda and PVC factories in the locality, was a state project, important for regional development, and that the farmers had to sign the agreements to surrender land. The farmers later testified in court that one of the former army officers told them that whether or not they wanted compensation they had no choice but to sign, and if children – which is to say, the farmers – 'do not listen to the admonitions of their parents then the stick is necessary'.

Instead of getting the farmers to back down, the officials generated more resentment. On February 2, a lawyer submitted complaints from four farmers in the township court against the two retired army officers who had spoken at the January meeting, and against the site manager of the project. The complaints accused the three respondents of illegal trespass, destruction of property, and criminal intimidation. The township magistrate registered four cases, one for each farmer, and instructed the police to investigate. Two weeks later, having received a police report, she found that the complaints were groundless and closed the cases.[51]

[49] For lengthier accounts of both cases, see Nick Cheesman and Kyaw Min San, 'Not Just Defending; Advocating for Law in Myanmar', *Wisconsin International Law Journal* 31.3 (2014); and Nick Cheesman, 'What Does the Rule of Law Have to Do with Democratisation (in Myanmar)?' *South East Asia Research* 22.2 (2014): 221–25.

[50] For details of the company's establishment and its operations, see Maung Aung Myoe, *Building the Tatmadaw: Myanmar Armed Forces since 1948* (Singapore: ISEAS, 2009) 176–80.

[51] *U Than Oo* v. *U Maung Maung Aye and 2*, 2011 Criminal Case 12, Kanma Township Court, 18 Feb. 2011. U Htay, U Aye Cho, and Daw Toke Toke respectively brought the other cases, numbered 13–15, against the same respondents.

The lawyer moved applications to review the matter.[52] In March, the farmers' opponents retaliated by orchestrating an attack on two of the men who had brought the case to court, and three others travelling with them on motorcycle. A group of men from the factory site beat them up and locked them in a room at their office. Shortly thereafter, the police arrested the assault victims and their associates. The prosecutor brought charges against the five men of trespass with intent to cause hurt and endangering public safety, and obscenity and mischief, under sections 452, 336, 294, and 427 of the Penal Code, as well as charges for use and ownership of unregistered motorbikes. A sixth villager was charged over the motorbikes only.

Policemen and security officials came to the courthouse to take photographs and record the details of the people entering and leaving the courtroom. Their activities did not deter farmers from attending the trial. Over a week of hearings when the prosecution presented its case, the court was full of people coming to see and hear the testimonies of company officials, former soldiers, police, and local councillors. With the case receiving so much unwanted attention, the prosecutor had the hearings moved to another township. Thereafter, over a hundred people signed a letter to the country's president to complain about how they had been treated by the police in court. Regarding the transfer of the trial to another township, the letter spoke up for the principle of open court, arguing that 'the intentional creating of difficulties to prevent people from exercising their rights to see and hear the defendants take the stand undermines the authority of the court to adjudicate independently'.

The letter got no reply. On April 27, the defence testimonies began at the new court. Over a hundred villagers travelled by boat and train to attend the trial, along the way talking with other farmers about the case and handing out materials about human rights. Policemen and other personnel again came to the courthouse to photograph and record the identities of people coming to listen. A plain-clothes officer entered the courtroom to take photographs of villagers, but when confronted, he slipped out a side door with the assistance of duty policemen. Local officials also took at least one defence witness to their office, where they allegedly threatened him in order to make him retract his testimony.

[52] *U Than Oo* v. *Union of Myanmar*, 2011 Criminal Revision Application 5, Thayet District Court. The other three litigants brought cases numbered 6–8.

A lawyer for the villagers spoke on radio about the case. The interviewer asked him:

Q. President Thein Sein spoke of the rule of law in his [inaugural] address, and yet within the same month this sort of thing has gone on, so is it that the president's message hasn't filtered down or what?

A. Many villagers have that attitude about this case. I think around 130, 140 signed a letter to President Thein Sein; however, we can see that the same old people are carrying on with this trial in the same old manner as in the past.[53]

On May 19, 2011, a judge convicted the farmers, sentencing them to terms from eight years and six months to twelve years and six months in jail each.[54] On appeal, events took a strange turn. The prosecutor, while insisting on the correctness of the original case acknowledged that the sentences seemed excessive and legally incorrect. To top it off, one of the retired army officers said that as the villagers at the planned location opposed the factory, the project was being moved to an adjacent area. He added that his company just wanted the case resolved amicably and 'held no grudges'. Accordingly, on June 30 the district judge used the *cha-lut* method to uphold the lower court's convictions but reduce the sentences to a few months per offence, thereby releasing the men from prison.[55]

The way that the farmers in this case were released hints at the continuance of practices for the maintenance of law and order through instructions delivered along an administrative continuum. Evidently, the court made its ruling under instructions from higher up. Perhaps the instructions came out of concern that to antagonise the farmers further through continued pursuit of the case and imprisonment of the men was unproductive. Whatever the case, the larger point is that in this relatively small and isolated instance of struggle over land in rural Myanmar, farmers moved to adopt a legal idiom, to communicate through a lexicon of rights and fight with allies through a range of measures speaking to principles underpinning the rule of law.

[53] *Democratic Voice of Burma*, 28 Apr. 2011.

[54] *Maj. Win Myint (retd.)* v. *Than Oo and 4*, 2011 Criminal Case 89, Minhla Township Court, 19 May 2011. This case dealt with the alleged offences under the Penal Code. Three other cases numbered 90–92 brought by a police officer dealt with the unregistered motorcycles that the men were riding.

[55] *U Than Oo and 4* v. *The State [Maj. Win Myint (retd.)]*, 2011 Criminal Appeal 19, Minbu District Court, 30 June 2011. The motorcycle registration cases were revised in case numbers 20, 21, and 23.

The farmers from Kanma also linked up to a larger domestic campaign on rights for cultivators in Myanmar, one aimed at increasing rural citizens' voice through better communication and sharper advocacy.[56] In November 2011, a lawyer and one of the local activists prepared a petition to the president opposing the draft of a new farmland law. By mid-December, more than 3,300 farmers in Magway, including Kanma, had reportedly signed it.[57] In April 2012, the president passed the draft into law anyhow.[58] Despite their failure to stop the law, rural protestors using the idiom of law to fight new political and economic alliances aimed at grabbing and using land for 'state projects' have been vociferous, as the second case discussed here, concerning the demonstrations at the Letpadaung Hills, in Salingyi Township, Sagaing, illustrates.

Unrest in the hills began in mid-2012 after villagers refused to vacate lands that the Union of Myanmar Economic Holding and a Chinese partner forcibly acquired, to expand an existing copper mining operation.[59] The villagers said they were dissatisfied with paltry offers of compensation. People losing homes found that new plots allocated to them to rebuild would be too small. They also did not trust the companies' and local authorities' commitments. Businessmen and officials had already broken promises to give land and money, to build schools or other facilities.

In July 2012, local authorities issued a section 144 order declaring the affected zone off-limits. The villagers applied to the police at least seven times for permits to assemble and protest the land seizure, under a 2011 law that ostensibly gives citizens a right to march peacefully, but that in its substance corresponds with the notion of rights as conditional privileges enjoyed through the exercise of sovereign *cetana*. The conventional English translation of the statute's title, the Peaceful Assembly and Procession Law, 15/2011, misses the critical element in

[56] Tamas Wells and Kyaw Thu Aung, 'Village Networks, Land Law and Myanmar's Democratization', *Debating Democratization in Myanmar*, eds. Nick Cheesman, Nicholas Farrelly, and Trevor Wilson (Singapore: ISEAS, 2014) 75–91.

[57] VOA 13 Dec. 2011. [58] *Myanma Alin* 3 Apr. 2012: 1, 8, 9.

[59] Protests against the mining operation had continued up to 2014. Here I restrict my comments to the period of 2012–13. For details of events in Monywa see Ant Maung, *The Letpadaung Hills: A Grand Finale or Tragic Ending?* (Yangon: Zinyadanazaw, 2013); Thet San Ye (Naypyidaw) et al., eds., *The Letpadaung Chronicle* (Yangon: Thin, 2013) (both in Burmese).

the Burmese title that binds the statute to the discretion of the sovereign: it is the Law Regarding the *Right* to Peaceful Assembly and *Right* to Peaceful Procession; not unfettered rights, but rights subject to officials' decision making – rights delimited by the permission-granting authority of the sovereign's agents. Far from providing any guarantees of free assembly, the new statute requires anyone wishing to assemble to submit details of the intended event to the relevant police station, which can authorise the gathering.[60] In these requirements it does not fill a gap in extant law but adds another layer of provisions on top of chapter five of the 1945 Police Act, 'Maintenance of Law and Order', whereby police officers already have authority to require that demonstrators obtain a licence prior to assembling.[61]

In Salingyi, the police rejected each application to assemble. From August 2012, protests began without permits. By September, the numbers of participants had swelled to thousands, contesting authorities' claims to have the right to decide the future of the Letpadaung Hills; also contesting the philosophy of law and order underpinning the statute obliging them to have their demonstrations authorised. The head of the local administration wrote a letter to subordinates, chastising participants on marches.[62] He said the processions did not look like the work of disgruntled peasants but of other elements bent on causing anarchic conditions. If the farmers had grievances, he wrote, they could go through the proper channels of sending letters expressing their concerns to the army holding company and to authorities at various levels that could assist with negotiations – which is to say, they could proceed through the administrative continuum responsible for the preservation of law and order. He concluded by warning that the law must be enforced, and that anyone responsible for destructive and lawless actions would be prosecuted.

[60] The 2011 law required a permit be issued on scrutiny of the application. The Law Amending the Peaceful Assembly and Procession Law, 26/2014, subsequently softened the provision, so that applicants would require only 'consent' on submitting an application to assemble, rather than a permit.

[61] 'The District Superintendent or any Assistant or Deputy Superintendent [of Police] may also, on being satisfied that it is intended by any persons or class of persons to convene or collect an assembly in any such road, street or thoroughfare, or to form a procession, which would, in his opinion, be likely to cause a breach of the peace if uncontrolled, require by general or special notice that the persons convening or collecting such assembly or directing or promoting such procession shall apply for and obtain a licence.' Police Act, 6/45, sec. 31(2).

[62] Salingyi Township General Administration Dept., Letter 5/43–51/Oo 6 (0697), 14 Sept. 2012.

The gatherings continued throughout September and October. When around eight thousand people converged on a nearby town, local police arrested a number of alleged leaders. Demonstrators gathered at the front of the police station bearing placards reading THE RULE OF LAW and demanding the detainees' release. The police later let a number out without charge, and the remainder on bail, but not before threatening protestors over their actions.[63]

While marching, demonstrators carried signs and banners that responded to and rebutted the legalese of official injunctions by duplicating the contents and imitating the style of government notices. Hundreds of people followed a red and white banner reading, RESPECT THE LAW – the message of the current government and its military predecessors. Under their *own* authority, they erected signboards styled after those of officialdom prohibiting trespassing onto their designated land. The signboards challenged the formal authority of the township administration to declare land off limits through section 144 orders, which invoked the rule of law, *taya-ubade-somoye*, even as they were anchored semantically, as in the past, in law and order.[64]

At the end of November, the home affairs ministry issued a formal warning to demonstrators in the Letpadaung Hills to clear their encampments or face the consequences: the ministry said it would act 'in accordance with law and democratic practice for the rule of law [*taya-ubade-somoye*] and to protect the interests of the state and the public'.[65] Making good on the threat, in the early hours of November 29 policemen raided encamped demonstrators, firing tear gas and an incendiary that inflicted extensive burns on occupants. International news media reported the attack, in part because the majority of the wounded were Buddhist monks.

State media outlets responded to a barrage of criticism from home and abroad by reinforcing the basic message that people who want democracy, not anarchy, obey the law. Newspapers noted that in 2011 the legislature passed its law to permit people to demonstrate.[66] Citizens who respect democratic practices, they continued, would act in accordance with law. The farmers chose to defy lawful orders to clear

[63] *People's Age*, 20 Sept. 2012: 11; *Radio Free Asia*, 11 Sept. 2012.
[64] Salingyi Township General Administration Dept. Orders 13–15/2012, 1 Sept. 2012.
[65] *Weekly Eleven* 29 Nov. (2012), 28 Dec. 2012 www.weeklyeleven.com.
[66] *Myanma Alin* 1 Dec. 2012: 7, 20.

their encampments. The authorities did everything they could to accommodate the demonstrators' wishes, and the president had even set up a commission of inquiry into the copper mine project.

Aung San Suu Kyi headed the commission of inquiry.[67] In a press conference, she said that it would proceed according to rule-of-law principles, and assign guilt only where firm evidence existed.[68] One of the commission's members quickly concluded that the absence of rule of law was the main culprit of the violence that the protestors met in November.[69]

However, when the commission presented its findings in March 2013, it treated the exercise not as an opportunity for dialogue with the affected villagers as substantive political and legal equals, but as a mechanical exercise in which questions of the rule of law were subordinated to technical findings, and the rule of law itself was reduced to the notion in the mandate of Aung San Suu Kyi's rule-of-law committee, that everyone obey enacted law.[70] Far from holding the police and local authorities responsible for the violent attacks on demonstrators, the commission placed the blame on an ignorant population and proposed that administrative agencies needed to put more effort into educating people about the law.[71] The commission also recommended prompt reform of the police force to enable it to perform its 'security and rule-of-law operations' in accordance with the demands of the times.[72]

Erstwhile allies rejected the commission's findings.[73] One lawyers' group objected to 'the omission of actions to be taken in accordance with law [against the police] for the use of incendiaries and excessively violent use of weapons in dispersal' of demonstrators, announcing it would continue to act 'steadfastly and in accordance with civil law, criminal law and international human rights laws for the sake of the

[67] Office of the President, Notification 92/2012, 1 Dec. 2012.

[68] *Weekly Eleven* 6 Dec. (2012), 28 Dec. 2012 www.weeklyeleven.com.

[69] *Mizzima* 5 Dec. (2012), 19 Dec. 2012 www.mizzima.com.

[70] Commission of Inquiry into the Letpadaung Hills Copper Project, 'Final Report of the Commission of Inquiry into the Letpadaung Hills Copper Project' (Naypyidaw: Govt. of the Republic of the Union of Myanmar, 2013) (in Burmese).

[71] Commission of Inquiry into the Letpadaung Hills Copper Project, 'Final Report', par. 93(b)(1).

[72] Commission of Inquiry into the Letpadaung Hills Copper Project, 'Final Report', par. 92(c).

[73] Meikhtila District People's Assistance Network, et al., *Position Statement of Networks, Forces, Unions and Organisations Working in the Public Interest on the Report of the Commission of Inquiry into the Letpadaung Hills Copper Project* (Yangon: National Democracy Network, 2013) (in Burmese).

rule of law'.[74] Its message: if the appointed commission would not hold the police accountable then the rights-bearing citizenry would have to do so instead.

The larger issue here is that in the absence of legal institutionalisation, people with rights claims resort to methods of civil disobedience based on demands for *substantive* legal equality. They transgress positive injunctions described as law in order to exercise rights that should be guaranteed through established institutions. They call attention not only to their specific grievances but also to the failure to institutionalise practices that would enable them to seek redress without having to violate existing law by 'mobilizing law' through political action.[75] They break law in order to generate it.[76]

As in Kanma, the struggles over the Letpadaung Hills went from the fields and into courtrooms. In 2013, a judge processing six activists accused of crimes in connection with the protests, like her counterpart in Kanma, promptly submitted an application for transfer of the trial away from the area of the mine, because the accused were 'members of networks and unions agitating for the destruction of community peace and tranquility and participants in disturbances who if tried in the Salingyi Township Court could give rise to unwanted troubles, riots and unrest'.[77] The request preceded any unrest and was premised on the judge's anticipating crowds at her courthouse. Her problem was not with the prospect of unwanted trouble, but as in earlier years, with the notion of open court itself.[78]

Policemen also arrested people who led marches in urban areas in solidarity with the Letpadaung farmers, charging them for marching without permits or with upsetting public tranquility.[79] One officer

[74] Myanmar Lawyers Network, Announcement 2/2013, 15 Mar. 2013 (in Burmese).

[75] See generally, Frank Munger, Scott L. Cummings, and Louise Trubek, 'Mobilizing Law for Justice in Asia: A Comparative Approach', *Wisconsin International Law Journal* 31.3 (2014): 353–420.

[76] As discussed in Elliott Prasse-Freeman, 'Conceptions of Justice and the Rule of Law', *Myanmar: The Dynamics of an Evolving Polity*, ed. David Steinberg (Boulder: Lynne Rienner, 2014) 89–114.

[77] *Daw Khin Khin Swe* v. *The State and* 6, 2013 Criminal Misc. Application 15, Sagaing Region High Court, 7 May 2013: 2. The Union Judiciary Law, 20/2010 re-established high courts at the region (formerly division) and state levels.

[78] The Courts Manual, paragraph 48 invites a judge to take a range of measures where she might 'apprehend serious disturbances' to trial, short of transferring it to another location, including having members of the public searched before entry to the courthouse, and exclusion of specific persons from the premises.

[79] *Pol. Maj. Khin Maung Kyi* v. *Aung Soe, Thura Tun* (a) *Moe Thwe*, 2012 Criminal Case 525, Bahan Township Court, opened 11 Dec. 2012; *Pol. Capt. Khin Maung Htwe* v. *Daw Shanma*

wrote that two accused who led roughly thirty people to walk with placards in Yangon ought to be prosecuted because 'at a time that the state is undertaking all-round reforms for national development through a democratic system, [they] engaged in dissent to cause loss of public confidence, to smash the administrative machinery, and to undermine community peace and tranquility, and the rule of law [*taya-ubade-somoye*]'.[80]

The language and practices of law and order continue wherever citizens confront powerful people and institutions in Myanmar. In a township north of Yangon during mid-2013, for instance, a young man who repeatedly tried without success to get a permit to march for peasants' rights instead made a placard and demonstrated on the nearby highway alone, having correctly construed that the statute on peaceful assembly clearly applies only to demonstrations involving more than one person.[81] The local administrator and police arrested and charged him nonetheless.[82] His lawyer pointed out to an official in court that his client's solo demonstration, far from constituting a danger to the public, was in the public interest. He met with the straightforward reply that 'It was a demonstration undertaken without permission.'[83] To maintain law and order, mobilisation requires authorisation. The person who mobilises autonomously poses a latent threat to law and order, whether he comes with hundreds of others, or holds his placard aloft alone.

CONCLUSION

For the last half-a-century, successive governments in Myanmar have treated complaint as an essentially administrative problem, one in which the rights of the complainant were ideally delimited by the exercise of sovereign *cetana*. People with complaints resort to a combination of methods, some of them institutional, others based on demands for political and legal equality that transgress the contents of positive injunctions described as law so as to rightfully resist. Recognising the symbolic power of law, their language and methods

and 3, 2012 Criminal Case 373, Pabedan Township Court, opened 27 Nov. 2012; *Pol. Maj. Yu Kyi* v. *Naw Ohn Hla and 9*, 2012 Criminal Case 392, Kyauktada Township Court, opened 27 Nov. 2012.

[80] Submission to Bahan Township Court by Pol. Maj. Khin Maung Kyi, 3 Dec. 2012.

[81] Peaceful Assembly and Procession Law, 15/2011, sec. 2(b)(c).

[82] *U Zaw Lwin* v. *Thant Zin Htet*, 2013 Criminal Case 385, Nattalin Township Court.

[83] *U Zaw Lwin* v. *Thant Zin Htet*, PW 1, 25 June 2013.

of rightful resistance situate them as claimants in an imagined institutional arrangement where they stand alongside and equal with the persons and agencies against whom they make their complaints. Their complaints call attention not only to their specific grievances but also to the failure to institutionalize legally practices that would enable them to seek redress without having to violate existing law. In short, they call attention to the gap between existing practice and the rule-of-law ideal.

Across Myanmar, as the struggles over rights for land have intensified, so too have the struggles to occupy the legal terrain associated with civil rights. In February 2013, villagers in an area near Yangon designated for a new industrial zone carried a banner emphasising their legal rights not to be evicted without a hearing.[84] They pointed out that they had been paying tax on the disputed land since 1997, and by taxing them the authorities had acknowledged their legal right to occupy and use it.

During the same month, hundreds of farmers and police officers fought at Ma-Ubin, in the delta, resulting in the death of a police constable and in charges of murder and unlawful assembly against multiple villagers. Responding to the violence, lawyers again issued a statement calling for an investigation into how the police handled events, so that the rule of law might be respected.[85] A farmer put it more plainly: 'When those people duty-bound to uphold the law don't take any responsibility for it, how can you dare blame us who are facing starvation and have no choice but to act to save our lives if we no longer respect so-called law?'[86] The statement challenges the (law) of law and order as *ngyeinwut-pibyaye*, but also contains within it a challenge to advocates of the rule of law: prove that law deserves the respect of freely thinking and acting bearers of rights; that this political ideal too is not empty.

[84] *Flower News* 12–18 Feb. 2013: Supp. B, D.
[85] Myanmar Lawyers Network, Statement, 27 Feb. 2013 (in Burmese).
[86] Cited in personal communication, 28 Feb. 2013.

9

AGAINST QUIETUDE

This book began with the argument that the rule of law is wrongly conjoined with law and order, and that the two concepts are not analogous, but are opposed. Law and order is, I suggested, a political ideal with its own contents, dissimilar and antithetical to the rule of law, an ideal with quietude as its telos. I also suggested that study of institutions evocative of the law-and-order ideal could facilitate understanding of the rule of law. Therefore, I proposed to study the ideas and practices associated with criminal cases in Myanmar's courts, cases that, I argued, would best reveal the political qualities of these institutions.

I did not choose to study the rule of law through a place where it is absent so as to treat Myanmar as an object of ridicule or cause for dismay. I have not gathered empirical data with which to situate Myanmar somewhere on the low end of a sliding scale for the rule of law. Nor did I pick Myanmar as an easy target to show how the rule of law is subject to abuse, how its name can be misappropriated. On the contrary, my concern throughout has been to explore Myanmar as a complex and paradigmatic case of the asymmetrical relations between the rule of law and an opposing concept, law and order: to take what animates its courts seriously.

As I made clear from the beginning, I am not advocating for law and order as *the* opposing political ideal to the rule of law. To do so would defeat my purpose, by putting the two concepts back into the kind of linear relationship that retards thinking about important political ideas. I *am* advocating for law and order as one among an unspecified number of asymmetrically opposed concepts to the rule of law: a rich plurality of political ideals, rather than an impoverishing singularity. Indeed, my hope is that more study of the rule of law through a plurality of opposed ideas and the practices they animate might encourage a little less hubris in it – a few less hurrahs – and a little more recognition from scholars that what people in different times and places are referring to as the rule of law may not be symmetrical concepts. They might not be the same thing at all.

This conceptual argument has obvious practical implications. If scholars and practitioners use rule-of-law criteria to measure the practices of institutions captured by other ideas, then we are liable to misunderstand and misrepresent them. We hold forms of government to ideals to which they may not subscribe, or to which they may only subscribe rhetorically. We mistake the problem for a gap between principle and practice, between aspiration and reality, to be rectified by better training, laws, and funding, when the problem is of a different nature. Partisans of law and order are not the occupants of low rungs on a ladder to the rule of law; they are climbing a different ladder altogether.[1]

This observation brings me back to Brian Tamanaha's assertion that the rule of law is the pre-eminent legitimating ideal in the world today, despite a lack of agreement on *precisely* what it means.[2] If this is taken simply as a plain fact that governments, political activists, and advocacy groups around the world use terms meaning 'the rule of law' with regularity, then we have cause to agree. But if these terms and their uses are probed, what really are they telling us? How many of these terms signal fundamentally different concepts? Has the rule of law really obtained pre-eminence as a political ideal worldwide? Or is it a convenient amalgam of 'simplified, domesticated, and falsely twinned' words?[3]

Whereas Tamanaha says the reasons that heads of government around the world articulate support for the rule of law vary, it strikes me that *what* they are articulating is probably at more variance than the reasons for articulating it. True, not everywhere is the rule of law

[1] I am grateful to Martin Krygier for this pithy representation of the problem.

[2] Brian Z. Tamanaha, *On the Rule of Law: History, Politics, Theory* (Cambridge: Cambridge University Press, 2004) 4.

[3] Frederic C. Schaffer, 'Thin Descriptions: The Limits of Survey Research on the Meaning of Democracy', *Political Concepts*, 45, Working Paper Series (Mexico City: Committee on Concepts and Methods, 2010) 37.

conflated with its opposition, as it is in Myanmar. However, the rule of law *does* everywhere become embedded in local ideas, language, and practices and takes on meanings that adhere to those settings. More often than not, encounters with other concepts affect its meaning and practices. Among them are hostile concepts, with which the rule of law must share semantic and institutional spaces – concepts like law and order.

Study of kindred terms to *ngyeinwut-pibyaye*, law and order, in non-European languages may help to locate terminology for productive debate about ideas and practices in asymmetrical opposition to the rule of law, as well as to have more meaningful comparative discussion about rule-of-law issues globally. By tracking institutionalised terms like 'the rule of law' and 'law and order' through official narratives, court records, and other texts, researchers can follow strands of meaning and unpick them from the institutions into which they are woven, in order to make more sense of the concepts and those institutions referring to them.

In work on Myanmar's neighbour, Thailand, for instance, some researchers have usefully begun to talk about persistent decisionism and exceptionalism as contrasting sharply with the rule of law.[4] Others have sought to 'disaggregate' the state, thereby showing how competing political ideals and divergent pragmatic interests animate state agencies.[5] David Streckfuss writes that among the 'indeterminate concepts' characterising Thailand's juridical and political practices is a term with echoes of the law-and-order ideal, *khwam sa-ngop riap roi*, or 'peace and order'.[6] This analogous expression to *ngyeinwut-pibyaye* is iterated at moments of perceived danger to the state's specific order in Thailand, such as in the streams of announcements after a military coup in 2006 and unhappily, again in 2014. Any serious study about rule-of-law ideas and practices in Thailand, it seems to me, would have to take *khwam sa-ngop riap roi* into account.

[4] Michael Connors, 'Liberalism, Authoritarianism and the Politics of Decisionism in Thailand', *Pacific Review* 22.3 (2009): 355–73.

[5] Tyrell Haberkorn, *Revolution Interrupted: Farmers, Students, Law, and Violence in Northern Thailand* (Madison: University of Wisconsin Press, 2011). Craig J. Reynolds et al., 'Time's Arrow and the Burden of the Past: A Primer on the Thai Un-State', *Sensate: Journal for Experiments in Critical Media Practice*, May (2012), 17 Sept. 2013 www.sensatejournal.com.

[6] David Streckfuss, *Truth on Trial in Thailand: Defamation, Treason, and Lèse-Majesté* (London and New York: Routledge, 2011) 115.

Nor is the problem of vocabulary only semantic. The fact that the Thai prime minister in 2003 could through a series of directives authorise killing with impunity of probably thousands of people reputed to have committed narcotics offences speaks to the relevance of applying a law-and-order frame to studies of how juridical institutions work in Thailand.[7] Although political opponents of the government blamed the prime minister personally for the killings, only through institutions operating consistently with a political ideal hostile to the rule of law could the killings have been possible. The force of *khwam sa-ngop riap roi* may be such that from time to time it is better to shoot people in their houses and cars than arrest them and put them on trial.

Contra the official narrative of *khwam sa-ngop riap roi*, the rule of law remains an animating idea for political activism in Thailand, as it does in Myanmar. In the contrast between practices to maintain the state's specific order on one hand and the rule of law as a motivator for political mobilisation on the other the distinction between 'peace and order' and the rule of law in Thailand is sharpest. Studying the work of cause lawyers in Thailand, Frank Munger has suggested that the practical meaning of the rule of law lies in its possibilities to open space for ordinary politics by ordinary citizens.[8] His observation goes to the value of the rule of law as a mobilising idea for political resistance and change across Asia. It explains why despite the predominance of *taya-ubade-somoye* as law and order in the public transcript in Myanmar, the rule of law still has resonance for political activists, lawyers, farmers, and human rights defenders. People recognise its normativity. They mobilise around the rule of law for political purposes. But in the process, they re-create its meaning, independent from the dominant law-and-order narrative. They retrieve the rule of law from law-and-order politics and invest it with politics of their own.

Some writers disregard this link between norms and political discourse when they insist that the normative contents of the rule of law

[7] As discussed in Nick Cheesman, 'Murder as Public Policy in Thailand', *Article 2* 2.3 (2003): 29–38.

[8] Frank Munger, 'Globalization, Investing in Law, and the Careers of Lawyers for Social Causes: Taking on Rights in Thailand', *New York Law School Law Review* 53 (2008–09): 747, 799–800; 'Constructing Law from Development: Cause Lawyers, Generational Narratives, and the Rule of Law in Thailand', *Law and Development and the Global Discourses of Legal Transfers*, eds. John Gillespie and Pip Nicholson (Cambridge: Cambridge University Press, 2012) 275.

are, in the words of José María Maravall and Adam Przeworski, 'a figment of the imagination of jurists'.[9] Against this view, I argue the normative contents of the rule of law are not a figment, because they are not made real by jurists, but through political participation and public dialogue, which link an ideal universe of the rule of law to the factual reality of a specific time and place. This participation and dialogue are grounded in, and reinforce, the idea of political equality.

Political equality as a characteristic of discourse on, in, and around courts in Myanmar is not only a response to the fact of inequality that people experience daily, but also a response to the *ideal* of *in*equality inherent in law and order – a concept requiring coercion so as to maintain quietude, to keep people immobilised. The insistence on political equality implicit in demands for the rule of law, versus the inequality of law and order, is part of what gives the rule of law its flavour of universality and its relevance to specific settings, issues, and cases. It is what binds local expressions of political participation to larger debates that transcend specific conditions. This synthesis of the universal and the local makes the rule of law a persistent and powerful animating idea for political activism around the world, everywhere in unique and original ways.

By contrast, institutions enthralled with the law-and-order ideal reject the principle of equality among people subject to their practices. The essentially normative generality of law obliges, ideally, equal treatment of equal cases in a political community bound by law, even if equality is nowhere realised in practice. The particularity of order contains no such element. Institutions evoking the law-and-order ideal may claim factual equality – such as in Carl Schmitt's ominous presupposition that a democratic state rests on the will of a homogenous people – but this account of equality is at best a partial description of reality and at worst a sheer fabrication; one that in Schmitt's time anticipated crimes against humanity.[10] Such claims are not just factually false. They obfuscate the absence of the *principle* of equality, to which the law-and-order ideal stands opposed.

So, although I write against Maravall and Przeworski in defence of the normative contents of the rule of law, I do so out of a shared

[9] José María Maravall and Adam Przeworski, Introduction, *Democracy and the Rule of Law*, eds. José María Maravall and Adam Przeworski (New York: Cambridge University Press, 2003) 1.

[10] Carl Schmitt, *Legality and Legitimacy*, trans. Jeffrey Seitzer (Durham, NC, and London: Duke University Press, 2004) 24.

concern for its political value, not out of reverence for the concept in a pristine originary form of the sort to which they object when they refer to the figments of jurists' imaginations. The rule of law has no unique, original designation. It emerged from historically complex struggles for political power, and continues to evolve through those struggles. Edward Thompson recognised this much when he wrote his famous exposition on the topic, declaring that 'the rule of law itself, the imposing of effective inhibitions upon power and the defence of the citizen from power's all intrusive claims, seems to me to be an unqualified human good'.[11] This statement is sometimes picked up and quoted as if it constitutes an unproblematic endorsement of the rule of law.[12] The contents of Thompson's monograph make plain that nothing could be further from the truth. His is a rule of law bound to the historical, cultural and political conditions from which it emerged, a product of prolonged mobilisation against decisive economic and legal inequality. It is a rule of law rooted in a deep understanding of the circumstances from which it has come, while also having universal qualities that make it politically compelling generally.

Against Thompson's exposition, Morton Horwitz describes the rule of law as 'a conservative doctrine' enabling the shrewd, calculating, and wealthy 'to manipulate its forms to their advantage'.[13] Whether or not this argument can be made of England, America, or Australia, it cannot be made of most countries in the world. In those other countries, the rule-of-law ideal is not a conservative doctrine but a radical one: a doctrine going to the radix, or root, of political power. It is an idea that fundamentally challenges how power has been and continues to be exercised. As Philip Selznick has written, to characterise the rule of law as bourgeois or legalistic is both heartless and naïve.[14] It is heartless because for people who suffer oppression, the rule-of-law ideal represents the possibility of building or rebuilding legal institutions so as to

[11] Edward P. Thompson, *Whigs and Hunters: The Origin of the Black Act* (London: Allen Lane, 1975) 266.

[12] For example, Jeremy Matam Farrall, *United Nations Sanctions and the Rule of Law* (Cambridge: Cambridge University Press, 2007) 24; Frank Upham, 'The Illusory Promise of the Rule of Law', *Human Rights with Modesty: The Problem of Universalism*, ed. András Sajó (Leiden and Boston: Martinus Nijhoff, 2004) 283.

[13] Morton J. Horwitz, 'The Rule of Law: An Unqualified Human Good?' *Yale Law Journal* 86.3 (1977): 566.

[14] Cited in Philip Pettit, *Republicanism: A Theory of Freedom and Government* (Oxford and New York: Oxford University Press, 1997) 177.

resist political manipulation. It is naïve because it fails to appreciate that the rule of law is, as iterated throughout this book, a *political* ideal, around which people can mobilise for all kinds of purposes.

Within South and Southeast Asia, whether in Myanmar or Thailand, Sri Lanka or Bangladesh, the shrewd, calculating, and wealthy enjoy their advantages over other people for want of the rule of law, not because of it. Equality and rights of political participation might be endorsed in constitutions and other framework documents that are convenient for managing complex modern societies, but they are not endorsed in reality. I am here not pointing to the gap, or gulf, between equality as an ideal and inequality as fact. I am referring instead to the contradiction between the ideal of equality expressed in formal documents and the *ideal* of inequality on which the exercise of power is still premised.

My fear is that in our time the triumphant language of the rule of law conceals a general trend away from this ideal, towards law and order, or other concepts opposed to the rule of law. Since the late 1980s, we have heard echoes of William Blackstone's 'due regulation and domestic order' in rule-of-law promotion. Some authors argue that the new global juridical order is one where 'the rule of law' consists of procedures bound to police power and imperial right to create and maintain order.[15] Others echo observations made in Chapter 1 that among many international agencies 'the rule of law has been considered chiefly an aspect of policing and penal powers'.[16]

If seen in relation to these trends – and studied in terms of opposing political ideals, rather than in terms of linear rule-of-law trajectories – then Myanmar becomes an exemplar of how 'the rule of law' can serve as a trope for law and order. The government of Myanmar has understood better than most that if the pre-eminent political ideal of our time is supposed to be the rule of law, then in its surpassing qualities it must itself be subsumed to law and order.

But the rule of law is incompatible with certain values associated with exogenously imposed order. Its normative generality breaks down hierarchical relations to the extent that it formally subjects all people to the same rules. It depends on principles of mutual recognition and

[15] Michael Hardt and Antonio Negri, *Empire* (Cambridge and London: Harvard University Press, 2000) 26.

[16] Hilary Charlesworth, 'Human Rights and the Rule of Law after Conflict', *John Fleming Centre Colloquium* (ANU, Canberra 2008), 5.

respect, not domination and subordination. An association defined by the rule of law is not an association of sovereign *cetana* dispensers and grateful subordinates. To the contrary, it enables people to live their lives as 'active, self-directing *subjects*, not mere objects of sovereign will'.[17] It is a community of people joined in what the Indian polymath and constitutionalist Bhim Rao Ambedkar once described as 'a mode of associated living' through active communication.[18] Ultimately, the rule of law cannot succeed as a project for effective government unless it is based on the reciprocal granting of liberties among members of a political community.

These remarks lead me to conclude that Jürgen Habermas was right to insist on an internal relation between the rule of law and democracy.[19] By communicating and participating in public life, citizens recognise themselves and others as bearers of rights – they engage in a conjoint communicated experience based on an attitude of respect for other members of the community.[20] Each citizen is guaranteed rights to participate and communicate equally and freely. These guarantees of rights ensure order under the rule of law in a democracy. What they do not do is aim to render people immobile in the name of peace, stability, or order. Contrary to the presumption contained in the name of Aung San Suu Kyi's legislative committee on the 'rule of law and tranquility', the rule-of-law ideal does *not* contain within it a guarantee of tranquility.[21] On the contrary, the rule of law entails a certain amount of *dis*quietude, a lack of tranquility necessary for an active and democratic association of equals, in direct opposition to the virtue that the law-and-order ideal claims.

So I conclude by writing against quietude, and for the essential disquietude of the rule of law: a political ideal for our time, if not *the*

[17] Martin Krygier, 'Four Puzzles About the Rule of Law: Why, What, Where? And Who Cares?' *Getting to the Rule of Law*, ed. James E. Fleming, vol. V, Nomos (New York and London: New York University Press, 2011) 80.

[18] Bhim Rao Ambedkar, 'Annihilation of Caste', *The Essential Writings of B. R. Ambedkar*, ed. Valerian Rodrigues (New Delhi: Oxford University Press, 2002) 276.

[19] Jürgen Habermas, 'On the Internal Relation between the Rule of Law and Democracy', *The Inclusion of the Other: Studies in Political Theory*, eds. Ciaran Cronin and Pablo de Greiff (Cambridge: MIT Press, 1998) 253–64; *Between Facts and Norms: Contributions to a Discourse Theory of Law and Democracy*, trans. William Rehg (Cambridge: Polity, 1996) 449.

[20] Ambedkar, 'Annihilation of Caste' 276.

[21] The word used in the committee's title for tranquility, *ti-ngyein-aye-chanye*, contains in its first half two roots for stability, *ti*, and *ngyein*, the condition of stillness shared with law and order.

pre-eminent ideal. The rule of law's symbolic value exceeds the sum of its parts, itemised in lists of formal criteria. It defies attempts to confine it to a particular doctrine or location. It appeals to the global and the local, and invests political struggle with the significance of both. Its merit rests in its being at once deeply contextual and profoundly universal: contextual, because the rule of law signifies the prospects for change to local institutions and practices, the prospects for escape from the past and the prospects for a different future; universal, because it signifies a common struggle for equality, against immobilisation, in the absence of which the rule of law would never have emerged either as an idea or in practice anywhere.

APPENDIX

In 2010, Andrew Selth lamented that research on Myanmar suffered from 'a serious dearth of hard data, little verifiable documentary evidence and relatively few well-informed sources of information about current developments'.[1] Despite new opportunities for scholars of Myanmar since then, the difficulties they encounter are not so peculiar. Researchers of countries with repressive governments generally have difficulty obtaining source materials.[2] However, the tendency of scholars writing on Myanmar in English to rely heavily on English-language sources has enlarged the shortcomings of contemporary work. Coupled with this problem is the tendency to rely, particularly in the study of Myanmar's politics, on a fairly small number of primary sources, and much the same body of secondary literature.

This book departs from both these tendencies by relying heavily on Burmese-language materials, drawn from a variety of primary and secondary sources: most of them written. In this appendix, I supplement the brief sketch of sources in the book's introduction with some additional comments on what I used, how I got it, and how I read it. I begin with an overview of published sources, and then turn to unpublished ones. I close with some remarks on how I have read and cited these sources.

1 Andrew Selth, 'Modern Burma Studies: A Survey of the Field', *Modern Asian Studies* 44.2 (2010): 430.

2 See Robert Barros, 'Secrecy and Dictatorship: Some Problems in the Study of Authoritarian Regimes', *Political Methodology* 2, Working Paper Series (Mexico City: Committee on Concepts and Methods, 2005).

PUBLISHED SOURCES

The introduction briefly sketched some of the published Burmese sources I used when working on this book. Here I expand on that summary for researchers interested to locate and read relevant materials.[3] This outline is not thoroughgoing. It contains references only to some of the more significant bodies of material.

Much of the published material I used is in the National Library of Australia, where I worked as the Burmese collection manager while doing research for this book. Among the library's most valuable acquisitions for my research is a full set of the annual law reports from 1948, housed in the Asian Collections on its third floor. The library also has most of the reports for earlier periods, which are in English, in its main collection. I have included details of the reports' changes in nomenclature, contents, and languages in Chapters 2, 3, and 5.

The library's Burmese collection has a full set of the volumes containing laws, rules, and official notifications from 1989 onwards, an incomplete set from 1974 to 1988, and the three volumes of compiled laws from 1962 to 1974. Additionally, it has an incomplete set of the fortnightly *Supreme Court Gazette* from 1994 to 2010, which contains details about transfers, promotions, retirements, and dismissals of judicial personnel; judicial policy; court administration and inspections; trial delays; budgets; building management; judicial corruption; licensing of lawyers; and awards for good service. Many citations of Supreme Court orders are from this source.

When doing background research, I also copied and read editions of the *Government Gazette*, which the library has in its Burmese collection, too; along with the Hansard for the upper and lower houses of the first, second, and third parliaments, up to 1961. I consulted but have not extensively used published legislative records since 2011, as well as some members' statements available online.

I purchased most reference books in stores and alleyway stalls around Yangon. In addition to monographs, I bought commonly used volumes and compilations of statutes; manuals and handbooks as set out in the bibliography, and a useful guide to legislation and amendments from the colonial era up to 1998, published by the Office

[3] Also see Melissa Crouch and Nick Cheesman, 'A Short Guide to Resources on Myanmar Law', *Law, Society and Transition in Myanmar*, eds. Melissa Crouch and Tim Lindsey (Oxford: Hart, 2014) 21–32.

of the Attorney General. Other items of note include irregularly published volumes of orders, notifications, and announcements of the apex courts covering 1946–2001; compilations of instructions from the executive in various periods, and digests of rulings from the colonial period onwards. Many of these materials are now also available on official websites, as well as via the Online Burma Library. And readers around the world can order print and electronic versions of a large number of publications through the Myanmar Book Centre's website.

UNPUBLISHED SOURCES

To write this book, I consulted four general types of unpublished sources: officially compiled files; court records other than any contained in officially compiled files; letters submitted to government officials other than any contained in court records; and other documentation, typically notes about cases prepared by parties, lawyers, or other people familiar with them, as well as my own notes from meetings with these persons. Here I will concentrate on the preceding three types.

Among the first type of unpublished source, I obtained access to forty-two Supreme Court meeting files from the 1990s, which cover a range of topics similar to those in the gazette, but in more detail, with annexed reports of case proceedings, and documentation from the police force, military intelligence, and government ministries. I also obtained older files from earlier courts, including the Central Court of Justice, the Chief Court, the Special Criminal Courts Appeal Court, and the Supreme Court of the 1950s, but I did not draw greatly on their contents.

As for the second type of source, I examined official records pertaining to 393 criminal cases, spanning over a decade. I assembled this body of material myself, in collaboration with colleagues in Myanmar and abroad, between 2008 and 2013. The distribution of cases by year of registration in court is: 39 in 2013; 23 in 2012; 36 in 2011; 54 in 2010; 69 in 2009; 67 in 2008; 36 in 2007; 24 in 2006; 21 in 2005; 14 in 2004; 4 in 2003; 1 in 2002; and 5 in 2000.

The cases come from 86 courts at all levels. The distribution of cases by level of court in descending order is: Supreme Court, 37; state/regional high courts, subsequent to the 2008 Constitution coming into effect, 15; state/divisional courts, 23; district courts, 150; and township courts, 168. The township courts are courts of first instance. Of the 150 cases at district level, 18 were on appeal, the remainder were at first instance. The cases in the superior courts were all on appeal and revision, except for four habeas corpus writ petitions submitted directly to the Supreme Court under the 2008 Constitution.

Around half of the cases come from in and around Yangon City, and the other half from elsewhere. The geographic distribution of cases by court is as follows, starting with the Supreme Court and then organised in alphabetical order by state or region/division, listing courts in descending order by hierarchy, with the number of cases per court noted parenthetically.[4]

Union level: Supreme Court (37)

Ayeyawady Division/Region:[5] Ayeyawady Divisional Court (4); *District Courts:* Ma-Ubin (5), Pathein (1); *Township Courts:* Bogalay (2), Hinthada (7), Kyaunggon (1), Nyaungdon (1), Pandanaw (1), Pathein (2), Pyapon (1)

Bago Division/Region: Bago Region High Court (2); Bago Divisional Court (5); Pyay District Court (1); *Township Courts:* Daik-U (2), Gyobingauk (1), Htantabin (1), Nattalin (7), Padaung (6), Pyay (4), Thayawady (1)

Chin State: Htantalan Township Court (1)

Kachin State: Hpakant Township Court (1)

Magway Division/Region: Magway Region High Court (1); Magway Divisional Court (2); *District Courts:* Magway (1), Minbu (4), Pakokku (4), Thayet (4); *Township Courts:* Aunglan (10), Kanma (4), Magway (2), Minhla (4), Pakokku (3)

Mandalay Division/Region: *District Courts:* Kyaukse (1), Mandalay (20); *Township Courts:* Aungmyay-thazan (8), Chan-aye-thazan (1), Maha-aungmyay (1), Meikhtila (1), Patheingyi (3)

Mon State: Mon State Court (1); Thaton District Court (1); Bilin Township Court (2)

Naypyidaw Union Territory: Naypyidaw District Court (4)

Rakhine State: Rakhine State High Court (6); *District Courts:* Sittwe (4), Thandwe (2); *Township Courts:* Sittwe (2), Taungup (1)

[4] In 2011 administrative territories previously known as 'divisions' became 'regions'.

[5] Alternative Romanisation for state and region/division names in the same sequence is as follows: Irrawaddy Division/Region, Pegu Division/Region, Chin State, Kachin State, Magwe Division/Region, Mandalay Division/Region, Mon State, Arakan State, Sagaing Division/Region, Shan State, and Rangoon Division/Region.

Sagaing Division/Region: Sagaing Region High Court (1); Monywa District Court (1); *Township Courts:* Monywa (2), Salingyi (1), Shwebo (4)

Shan State: Taunggyi District Court (2); Kalaw Township Court (1)

Yangon Division/Region: Yangon Region High Court (5); Yangon Divisional Court (11); *District Courts:* Yangon Eastern (12), Yangon Northern (14), Yangon Southern (5), Yangon Western (64); *Township Courts:* Ahlone (2), Bahan (4), Botataung (1), Dawbon (2), Hlaing (4), Hlaingthaya (3), Hmawbi (2), Insein (3), Kawhmu (2), Kunchangon (1), Kyauktada (7), Kyimyindaing (3), Mayangon (4), Mingalataung-nyunt (5), North Okkalapa (2), Pabedan (1), Sanchaung (9), Seikkan (6), South Dagon (10), Tamwe (2), Thingangyun (2), Twante (3), Yankin (1)

Many case records include complaint letters that have either deliberately or inadvertently initiated a case; or complaint letters submitted to various authorities in the course of trial or processing of the accused. But a lot of complaint letters do not lead to court or end up in a government file. These letters constitute the third general type of unpublished source material. I read 66 such letters when working on the book. The distribution of these letters by territory where the complainant was residing at time of submitting the letter is as follows: 16 from Ayeyawady Division/Region, 7 from Bago Division/Region, 4 from Kachin State, 2 from Kayah State,[6] 1 from Magway Division/Region, 9 from Mandalay Division/Region, 7 from Mon State, 1 from Rakhine State, 2 from Sagaing Division/Region, and 17 from Yangon Division/Region. The distribution of letters by year of recorded date is as follows: 9 in 2013, 8 in 2012, 7 in 2011, 10 in 2010, 1 in 2009, 3 in 2008, 15 in 2007, 4 in 2006, 3 in 2005, and 6 in 2004. I have not cited these letters directly in the text because none of them are on the official record.

To write Chapter 6, I made a number of research trips between 2009 and 2012, when I met lawyers who gathered data on the buying and selling of cases and case outcomes. They documented practices, and we met on follow-up trips, went over the material together, and planned the next phase. I am solely responsible for presenting and interpreting the material that the lawyers collected, along with everything else in this book. Notwithstanding, as they continue to earn their livelihoods professionally in Myanmar, I have omitted

[6] Alternative Romanisation for Kayah State is Karenni State.

identifying details of them and anyone with whom they spoke. Maybe one day I will acknowledge them publicly. For now a non-specific thank you must suffice: not only for what they contributed to this book, but for all their remarkable unsung achievements; for everything they have done, and for what they continue to do.

READING AND CITING SOURCES

The reading of sources is always, Ann Stoler reminds us, an 'agentive act, one squarely focused on what we know and how we know it'.[7] Knowledge does not spring forth from source materials of its own accord. Rather, it emerges from specific epistemic practices.

Consistent with Stoler's approach, in this book, I have adopted reading strategies that 'stay within the allusive, muddy register' of the source material.[8] I decline to overwrite the records with a neater, more persuasive or comprehensive telling of their contents. In choosing to remain in the midst of things, rather than gaze at them from outside, I have forgone any claim to be able to describe what happens in Myanmar's courts exhaustively. My readings of available evidence are, like the evidence itself, patchy. To pretend otherwise would be to misrepresent not only my findings but also my purpose. And as I wrote in the introduction, it would misrepresent the book's subject matter, too. The records of Myanmar's courts are themselves partial, flawed, and falsified, filled with incomplete and qualified statements of fact. The turgid prose of clerical staff hammering away at worn-out typewriters, the scrawled signatures of judges affixed to hastily scribbled forms, the marginal notations of lawyers to their juniors do not cohere – they pull this way and that.

Consequently, the case narratives in this book have a fragmentary quality. They are fragmentary in the sense evoked by Veena Das: unlike parts of an assemblage that can be put together to make up an image of totality, or a sketch lacking the details of a picture that still contains 'the imagination of the whole, the *fragment* marks the impossibility of such an imagination'.[9] In reading and writing about Myanmar's courts I have tried not only to recognise but also to evince their fragmentary

[7] Ann Laura Stoler, *Along the Archival Grain: Epistemic Anxieties and Colonial Common Sense* (Princeton and Oxford: Princeton University Press, 2009) 45.

[8] Stoler, *Along the Archival Grain* 187.

[9] Veena Das, *Life and Words: Violence and the Descent into the Ordinary* (Berkeley, Los Angeles & London: University of California Press, 2007) 5.

qualities, and the impossibility of the coherent whole that they propose to have us imagine.

The fragmentary quality of the narrative is compounded by unavoidable difficulties in deciding what to put in print, and what to leave out.[10] Like Tyrell Haberkorn in her research on killings of politically active farmers in Thailand, I cannot eliminate the risks associated with making hitherto hidden things public; however, I do aim to limit them.[11] I do not have a fixed set of criteria to that end, but like other researchers sensitive to conditions in Myanmar I have assessed and decided on each case based on my own knowledge, in consultation with informed colleagues.[12] I have entirely omitted stories of some cases that spoke compellingly to the book's contents. Others I have included but have deliberately provided minimal details. I have not footnoted additional comments or references to these cases because the prose contains what information can be shared with the reader. Each anonymous case is mentioned only once, unless I have specifically indicated otherwise. Wherever possible, I have included other relevant details in a citation.

Court records are public documents. Although they may not be readily accessible to an outside researcher, any party to a case or her legal representative can obtain them. A lot of them make their way into media reports, and are reproduced in full on the Internet. I have restricted my direct references to the records of previously published cases. Wherever possible I have consulted parties to cases and their lawyers about the use of these materials, although I have not felt the need to do so in cases of prominent politicians and activists. I have not cited any rape cases directly. I have cited torture cases directly only where the victim has died and the family has fought publicly for justice, or where the survivor has wished it. In narrating details of cases, I have also deliberately concentrated on features of courts and the police in Myanmar relevant to the book's argument, and have limited remarks on the setting and parties.

[10] See Urvashi Butalia, *The Other Side of Silence: Voices from the Partition of India* (New Delhi: Penguin, 1998) 14.

[11] Tyrell Haberkorn, *Revolution Interrupted: Farmers, Students, Law, and Violence in Northern Thailand* (Madison: University of Wisconsin Press, 2011) 25.

[12] See Lisa Brooten and Rosalie Metro, 'Thinking about Ethics in Burma Research', *Journal of Burma Studies* 18.1 (2014): 1–22; Maaike Matelski, 'On Sensitivity and Secrecy: How Foreign Researchers and Their Local Contacts in Myanmar Deal with Risk under Authoritarian Rule', *Journal of Burma Studies* 18.1 (2014): 59–82.

Some documents I read are classified. Among them, publications intended for use within courts and police stations such as the *Supreme Court Gazette* and Police Manual are designated 'restricted'. Despite their classification, these materials are bought and sold openly by street vendors and shopkeepers. Many of the unpublished records containing Supreme Court internal directives, and documents from other agencies, are classed as 'secret'. The documents marked secret that I read came from official files and compilations, which I obtained through secure channels, with the exception of one set of documents that I have not used in writing the book.

For the most part, classified records of courts and the police contain nothing that practicing lawyers, litigants, and the general public in Myanmar do not already know. They do not hide dirty truths or conceal important details. On the contrary, their contents merely validate information obtained through other sources. Their 'secret' status does not signify anything about their specific subject matter.[13] It signals only that the documents earmarked confidential are meant for limited circulation. It demarcates them administratively, and places them in a special relationship with an intended readership. In so doing, it speaks to habits associated with the principle of secrecy that I have described in Chapter 4. Consequently, in dealing with the contents of these records I have throughout the book adopted a principle of disclosure, and have included the reference numbers and dates of files read; however, I have refrained from including any other identifying details out of respect for the privacy of persons named in specific cases.

All of the preceding remarks concern deliberate choices I made about how to read and cite sources, about what to include and what to omit from the book's contents. But in work of this scope and duration, unintended omission and misreading is also inevitable. In particular, I recognise that I will have made mistakes due to my not being a native speaker of Burmese. In thousands of hours of reading and hundreds of hours of conversation, I will have passed over and misinterpreted meanings that a native speaker would not have missed, or have misunderstood. For any such errors and omissions, I alone bear responsibility. Whatever they may be, they will, I hope, not be so great as to alter significantly any of the book's findings.

[13] See Stoler, *Along the Archival Grain* 26–28.

GLOSSARY

ahmandaya	(အမှန်တရား) the truth.
cetana	(စေတနာ) intention, will, goodwill.
cha-lut	(ချလွှတ်) sentenced-released.
hnyi-hnaing	(ညှိနှိုင်း) negotiate, coordinate.
metta	(မေတ္တာ) loving kindness.
minmè-zayaik	(မင်းမဲ့စရိုက်) anarchy.
nèza shene	(နယ်စားရှေ့နေ) lawyer working a single court or locality.
ngyeinwut-pibyaye	(ငြိမ်ဝပ်ပိပြားရေး) law and order.
sagan	(စခန်း) camp, station.
Sangha	(သံဃာ) Buddhist clergy.
Swunashin	(စွမ်းအားရှင်) Masters of Force.
taya-ubade-somoye	(တရားဥပဒေစိုးမိုးရေး) the rule of law.

BIBLIOGRAPHY

BOOKS, ARTICLES AND REPORTS PUBLISHED IN ENGLISH

Abrams, Philip. 'Notes on the Difficulty of Studying the State (1977)'. *Journal of Historical Sociology* 1.1 (1988): 58–89.

Agamben, Giorgio. *Homo Sacer: Sovereign Power and Bare Life*. Trans. Daniel Heller-Roazen. Stanford: Stanford University Press, 1998.

Means without End: Notes on Politics. Trans. Vincenzo Binetti and Cesare Casarino. Minneapolis and London: University of Minnesota Press, 2000.

State of Exception. Trans. Kevin Attell. Chicago and London: University of Chicago Press, 2005.

Althusser, Louis. 'Ideology and Ideological State Apparatuses (Notes towards an Investigation)'. *Louis Althusser Archive*. 2 May 2014. www.marxists.org/reference/archive/althusser/1970/ideology.htm.

Ambedkar, Bhim Rao. 'Annihilation of Caste'. *The Essential Writings of B. R. Ambedkar*. Ed. Valerian Rodrigues. New Delhi: Oxford University Press, 2002. 263–305.

Aradau, Claudia. 'Securing Life: Human Trafficking, Biopolitics, and the Sovereign Pardon'. *Accumulating Insecurity: Violence and Dispossession in the Making of Everyday Life*. Eds. Shelley Feldman, Charles Geisler and Gayatri A. Menon. Athens: University of Georgia Press, 2011. 167–84.

Arendt, Hannah. *On Violence*. New York: Harcourt, 1969.

The Origins of Totalitarianism. 1951. 3rd edn. London: George Allen & Unwin, 1966.

Arnold, David. *Police Power and Colonial Rule: Madras 1859–1947*. Delhi: Oxford University Press, 1986.

Aung Than Tun. 'Law and Lawyer in a Socialist Society'. *Guardian* Jan. 1964: 13–16.
'Revolution of Law and Justice'. *Guardian* June 1965: 38–39.
Aung-Thwin, Maitrii. 'Discourses of Emergency in Colonial and Postcolonial Burma'. *Emergency Powers in Asia: Exploring the Limits of Legality*. Eds. Victor V. Ramraj and Arun K. Thiruvengadam. Cambridge: Cambridge University Press, 2010. 187–212.
The Return of the Galon King: History, Law and Rebellion in Colonial Burma. Athens: Ohio University Press; Singapore: National University of Singapore Press, 2011.
Balasubramaniam, Ratna Reuban. 'Has Rule by Law Killed the Rule of Law in Malaysia?' *Oxford University Commonwealth Law Journal* 8.2 (2008): 211–35.
'Hobbism and the Problem of Authoritarian Rule in Malaysia'. *Hague Journal on the Rule of Law* 4.2 (2012): 211–34.
'Indefinite Detention: Rule by Law or Rule of Law?' *Emergencies and the Limits of Legality*. Ed. Victor V. Ramraj. Cambridge: Cambridge University Press, 2008. 118–41.
'Judicial Politics in Authoritarian Regimes'. *University of Toronto Law Journal* 59.3 (2009): 405–15.
Barber, Nicholas W. 'Must Legalistic Conceptions of the Rule of Law Have a Social Dimension?' *Ratio Juris* 17.4 (2004): 474–88.
'The *Rechtsstaat* and the Rule of Law'. *University of Toronto Law Journal* 53.4 (2003): 443–54.
Barros, Robert. 'Dictatorship and the Rule of Law: Rules and Military Power in Pinochet's Chile'. *Democracy and the Rule of Law*. Eds. José María Maravall and Adam Przeworski. New York: Cambridge University Press, 2003. 188–219.
'Secrecy and Dictatorship: Some Problems in the Study of Authoritarian Regimes'. *Political Methodology*. 2. Working Paper Series. Mexico City: Committee on Concepts and Methods, 2005.
Bedner, Adriaan. 'An Elementary Approach to the Rule of Law'. *Hague Journal on the Rule of Law* 2.1 (2010): 48–74.
Belton, Rachel Kleinfeld. 'Competing Definitions of the Rule of Law: Implications for Practitioners'. 55. *Carnegie Endowment Working Papers*. Washington, DC: Carnegie, 2005.
Benjamin, Walter. 'Critique of Violence'. *Reflections: Essays, Aphorisms, Autobiographical Writings*. 1978. Trans. Edmund Jephcott. Ed. Peter Demetz. New York: Schocken, 1986. 277–300.
Bentham, Jeremy. *The Works of Jeremy Bentham*. 1843. 11 vols. Edinburgh and London: William Tait; Simpkin, Marshall, 1968.
Benton, Lauren A. *Law and Colonial Cultures: Legal Regimes in World History, 1400–1900*. Cambridge: Cambridge University Press, 2002.

Bergling, Per, Erik Wennerström, and Richard Zajac Sannerholm. 'Rule of Law and Security Sector Reform: Casual Assumptions, Unintended Risks and the Need for Norms'. *Hague Journal on the Rule of Law* 4.1 (2012): 98–119.

Bingham, Tom. *The Rule of Law*. London: Penguin, 2010.

Blackstone, William. *Commentaries on the Laws of England*. 1769. Vol. IV. 4 vols. New York: Legal Classics Library, 1983.

Bourdieu, Pierre. 'The Force of Law: Toward a Sociology of the Juridical Field'. *Hastings Law Journal* 38 (1987): 814–53.

'Rethinking the State: Genesis and Structure of the Bureaucratic Field'. Trans. Loïc J. D. Wacquant, and Samar Farage. *State/Culture: State-Formation after the Cultural Turn*. Ed. George Steinmetz. Ithaca, NY, and London: Cornell University Press, 1999. 53–75.

Bribery and Corruption Enquiry Committee. *Report of the Bribery and Corruption Enquiry Committee, 1940*. Rangoon: Govt. Printing, 1941.

Brooks, Rosa. 'The New Imperialism: Violence, Norms, and the "Rule of Law"'. *Michigan Law Review* 101.7 (2003): 2275–340.

Brooten, Lisa, and Rosalie Metro. 'Thinking about Ethics in Burma Research'. *Journal of Burma Studies* 18.1 (2014): 1–22.

Brown, Ian. *Burma's Economy in the Twentieth Century*. Cambridge: Cambridge University Press, 2013.

Brown, Nathan J. 'Law and Imperialism: Egypt in Comparative Perspective'. *Law and Society Review* 29.1 (1995): 103–25.

Brown, R. Grant. *Burma as I Saw It, 1889–1917*. London: Methuen, 1926.

Burma Lawyers' Council. *Preliminary Report of the Ad Hoc Commission on the Depayin Massacre*. Bangkok: Ad Hoc Commission on the Depayin Massacre, [2003?].

Butalia, Urvashi. *The Other Side of Silence: Voices from the Partition of India*. New Delhi: Penguin, 1998.

Butt, Simon, and Tim Lindsey. 'Judicial Mafia: The Courts and State Illegality in Indonesia'. *The State and Illegality in Indonesia*. Eds. Edward Aspinall and Gerry van Klinken. Leiden: KITLV Press, 2011. 189–213.

Butwell, Richard, and Fred von der Mehden. 'The 1960 Election in Burma'. *Pacific Affairs* 33.2 (1960): 144–57.

Cai, Dingjian. 'The Development of Constitutionalism in the Transition of Chinese Society'. *Columbia Journal of Asian Law* 19.1 (2005): 1–29.

Callahan, Mary P. *Making Enemies: War and State Building in Burma*. Ithaca, NY, and London: Cornell University Press, 2003.

'The Origins of Military Rule in Burma'. PhD diss. Cornell University, 1996. Ann Arbor: UMI, 1996.

'The Sinking Schooner: Murder and the State in Independent Burma, 1948–58'. *Gangsters, Democracy, and the State in Southeast Asia*. Ed. Carl A. Trocki. New York: Cornell Southeast Asia Program, 1998. 17–38.

'State Formation in the Shadow of the Raj: Violence, Warfare and Politics in Colonial Burma'. *Southeast Asian Studies* 39.4 (2002): 513–36.

Carothers, Thomas. 'The Rule of Law Revival'. *Foreign Affairs* 77.2 (1998): 95–106.

Chanock, Martin. *Law, Custom and Social Order: The Colonial Experience in Malawi and Zambia*. Cambridge: Cambridge University Press, 1985.

Charney, Michael W. *A History of Modern Burma*. Cambridge: Cambridge University Press, 2009.

Chatterjee, Partha. *The Nation and Its Fragments: Colonial and Postcolonial Histories*. Princeton: Princeton University Press, 1993.

Cheesman, Nick. 'Bodies on the Line in Burma's Criminal Law Reports, 1892–1922'. *Law, Society and Transition in Myanmar*. Eds. Melissa Crouch and Tim Lindsey. Oxford: Hart, 2014. 77–94.

'How an Authoritarian Regime Used Special Courts to Defeat Judicial Independence in Burma'. *Law and Society Review* 45.4 (2011): 801–30.

'The Incongruous Return of Habeas Corpus to Myanmar'. *Ruling Myanmar: From Cyclone Nargis to National Elections*. Eds. Nick Cheesman, Monique Skidmore, and Trevor Wilson. Singapore: ISEAS, 2010. 90–111.

'Law and Order as Asymmetrical Opposite to the Rule of Law'. *Hague Journal on the Rule of Law* 6.1 (2014): 96–114.

'Murder as Public Policy in Thailand'. *Article 2* 2.3 (2003): 29–38.

Rev. of *Ending Forced Labour in Myanmar*, by Richard Horsey. *South East Asia Research* 21.2 (2013): 343–47.

'Seeing "Karen" in the Union of Myanmar'. *Asian Ethnicity* 3.2 (2002): 199–220.

'Thin Rule of Law or Un-Rule of Law in Myanmar?' *Pacific Affairs* 82.4 (2009): 597–613.

'What Does the Rule of Law Have to Do with Democratisation (in Myanmar)?' *South East Asia Research* 22.2 (2014): 213–32.

Cheesman, Nick, and Kyaw Min San. 'Not Just Defending; Advocating for Law in Myanmar'. *Wisconsin International Law Journal* 31.3 (2014): 702–33.

Cheesman, Nick, Nicholas Farrelly, and Trevor Wilson, eds. *Debating Democratization in Myanmar*. Singapore: ISEAS, 2014.

Cheesman, Nick, Monique Skidmore, and Trevor Wilson, eds. *Ruling Myanmar: From Cyclone Nargis to National Elections*. Singapore: ISEAS, 2010.

Christian, Winslow. 'Burma's New Constitution and Supreme Court'. *Tulane Law Review* 26.1 (1951): 47–59.

Colaiaco, James A. *James Fitzjames Stephen and the Crisis of Victorian Thought*. London and Basingstoke: Macmillan, 1983.

Collier, David, Fernando Daniel Hidalgo, and Andra Olivia Maciuceanu. 'Essentially Contested Concepts: Debates and Applications'. *Journal of Political Ideologies* 11.3 (2006): 211–46.

Collis, Maurice. *Trials in Burma*. London: Faber & Faber, 1953.
Comaroff, John L., and Jean Comaroff. Introduction. *Law and Disorder in the Postcolony*. Eds. John L. Comaroff and Jean Comaroff. Chicago and London: University of Chicago Press, 2006. 1–56.
Commission of Inquiry into Involuntary Removal and Disappearance of Certain Persons (All Island). *Final Report*. Govt. of Sri Lanka, 2001.
Connors, Michael. 'Liberalism, Authoritarianism and the Politics of Decisionism in Thailand'. *Pacific Review* 22.3 (2009): 355–73.
Cover, Robert. 'Violence and the Word'. *Yale Law Journal* 95.8 (1986): 1601–29.
Craig, Paul P. 'Formal and Substantive Conceptions of the Rule of Law: An Analytical Framework'. *Public Law* (1997): 467–87.
Crouch, Melissa. 'Asian Legal Transplants and Rule of Law Reform: National Human Rights Commission [*sic*] in Myanmar and Indonesia'. *Hague Journal on the Rule of Law* 5.2 (2013): 146–77.
'The Common Law and Constitutional Writs: Prospects for Accountability in Myanmar'. *Law, Society and Transition in Myanmar*. Eds. Melissa Crouch and Tim Lindsey. Oxford: Hart, 2014. 33–58.
Crouch, Melissa, and Nick Cheesman. 'A Short Guide to Resources on Myanmar Law'. *Law, Society and Transition in Myanmar*. Eds. Melissa Crouch and Tim Lindsey. Oxford: Hart, 2014. 21–32.
d'Entrèves, Alexander Passerin. *The Notion of the State: An Introduction to Political Theory*. Oxford: Oxford University Press, 1967.
Damaška, Mirjan R. *The Faces of Justice and State Authority: A Comparative Approach to the Legal Process*. New Haven and London: Yale University Press, 1986.
'Truth in Adjudication'. *Hastings Law Journal* 49.2 (1998): 289–308.
Darian-Smith, Eve. *Laws and Societies in Global Contexts: Contemporary Approaches*. New York: Cambridge University Press, 2013.
'Precedents of Injustice: Thinking About History in Law and Society Scholarship'. *Studies in Law, Politics, and Society* 41 (2008): 61–81.
Religion, Race, Rights: Landmarks in the History of Modern Anglo-American Law. Oxford and Portland, OR: Hart, 2010.
Das, Veena. *Life and Words: Violence and the Descent into the Ordinary*. Berkeley, Los Angeles, and London: University of California Press, 2007.
Derrida, Jacques. 'Le siecle et le pardon'. *Le Monde des Débats* 9 (Nov. 1999). 10 Aug. 2013 http://hydra.humanities.uci.edu/derrida/siecle.html (in French).
Dharker, C. D., ed. *Lord Macaulay's Legislative Minutes*. London: Oxford University Press, 1946.
Diamond, Larry. 'The Need for a Political Pact'. *Journal of Democracy* 23.4 (2012): 138–49.

Dicey, Albert V. *Introduction to the Study of the Law of the Constitution*. 1885. 8th edn. Indianapolis, IN: Liberty Fund, 1982.
Dietze, Gottfried. *Two Concepts of the Rule of Law*. Indianapolis, IN: Liberty Fund, 1973.
Dressel, Björn. 'Governance, Courts and Politics in Asia'. *Journal of Contemporary Asia* 44.2 (2014): 259–78.
Dulyapak Preecharushh. *Naypyidaw: The New Capital of Burma*. Bangkok: White Lotus, 2009.
Dyzenhaus, David. *The Constitution of Law: Legality in a Time of Emergency*. Cambridge: Cambridge University Press, 2006.
Hard Cases in Wicked Legal Systems: South African Law in the Perspective of Legal Philosophy. Oxford: Clarendon, 1991.
'Recrafting the Rule of Law'. *Recrafting the Rule of Law: The Limits of Legal Order*. Ed. David Dyzenhaus. Oxford and Portland, OR: Hart, 1999. 1–12.
Eckert, Julia. 'Rumours of Rights'. *Law Against the State: Ethnographic Forays into Law's Transformations*. Eds. Julia Eckert et al. Cambridge: Cambridge University Press, 2012. 147–70.
Eckert, Julia, et al. Introduction. *Law Against the State: Ethnographic Forays into Law's Transformations*. Eds. Julia Eckert et al. Cambridge: Cambridge University Press, 2012. 1–22.
Editor. 'Parliamentary Democracy'. *Guardian* Oct. 1959: 6.
Englehart, Neil A. 'Liberal Leviathan or Imperial Outpost? J. S. Furnivall on Colonial Rule in Burma'. *Modern Asian Studies* 45.4 (2011): 759–90.
Fallon, Richard H. '"The Rule of Law" as a Concept in Constitutional Discourse'. *Columbia Law Review* 97.1 (1997): 1–56.
Farrall, Jeremy Matam. *United Nations Sanctions and the Rule of Law*. Cambridge: Cambridge University Press, 2007.
Ferrara, Federico. 'Why Regimes Create Disorder: Hobbes's Dilemma During a Rangoon Summer'. *Journal of Conflict Resolution* 47.3 (2003): 302–25.
Fink, Christina. *Living Silence: Burma under Military Rule*. London and New York: Zed, 2001.
'The Moment of the Monks: Burma, 2007'. *Civil Resistance and Power Politics: The Experience of Non-violent Action from Gandhi to the Present*. Eds. Adam Roberts and Timothy Garton Ash. Oxford: Oxford University Press, 2009. 354–70.
Fitzpatrick, Sheila. 'Supplicants and Citizens: Public Letter-Writing in Soviet Russia in the 1930s'. *Slavic Review* 55.1 (1996): 78–105.
Foucault, Michel. *The Birth of Biopolitics: Lectures at the Collège de France, 1978–1979*. Trans. Graham Burchell. Ed. Arnold I. Davidson. New York: Picador, 2008.
Discipline and Punish: The Birth of the Prison. 1975. Trans. Alan Sheridan. London: Allen Lane, 1977.

'The Political Technology of Individuals'. *Technologies of the Self*. Eds. Luther H. Martin, Huck Gutman, and Patrick H. Hutton. Amherst: University of Massachusetts Press, 1988. 145–62.

Power/Knowledge: Selected Interviews and Other Writings 1972–1977. Trans. Colin Gordon et al. Hemel Hempstead, Hertfordshire: Harvester, 1980.

Security, Territory, Population: Lectures at the Collège de France, 1977–1978. Trans. Graham Burchell. Ed. Arnold I. Davidson. New York: Picador, 2007.

Freitag, Sandria B. 'Crime in the Social Order of Colonial North India'. *Modern Asian Studies* 25.2 (1991): 227–61.

Fuller, Lon L. *The Morality of Law*. 1964. Rev. edn. New Haven and London: Yale University Press, 1969.

Furnivall, John S. 'The Fashioning of Leviathan: The Beginnings of British Rule in Burma'. *Journal of the Burma Research Society* 29.1 (1939): 3–137.

Furnivall, John S., and W. S. Morrison. 'Insein District'. *Burma Gazetteer*. Rangoon: Govt. Printing, 1914. Vol. A.

Ghias, Shoaib A. 'Miscarriage of Chief Justice: Judicial Power and the Legal Complex in Pakistan under Musharraf'. *Law and Social Inquiry* 35.4 (2010): 985–1022.

Ginsburg, Tom. 'The Constitutional Court and the Judicialization of Korean Politics'. *New Courts in Asia*. Eds. Andrew Harding and Penelope Nicholson. London and New York: Routledge, 2010. 145–57.

Gluck, Carol. Introduction. *Words in Motion: Towards a Global Lexicon*. Eds. Carol Gluck and Anna Lowenhaupt Tsing. Durham, NC, and London: Duke University Press, 2009. 3–10.

Goertz, Gary. *Social Science Concepts: A User's Guide*. Princeton and Oxford: Princeton University Press, 2006.

Goertz, Gary, and James Mahoney. *A Tale of Two Cultures: Qualitative and Quantitative Research in the Social Sciences*. Princeton: Princeton University Press, 2012.

Goody, Jack. *The Logic of Writing and the Organization of Society*. Cambridge: Cambridge University Press, 1986.

Govt. of Burma. *Gazetter of Burma*. Vol. I. 2 vols. New Delhi: Gian, 1987.

Govt. of the Union of Burma. *Is Trust Vindicated?* Rangoon: Director of Information, 1960.

Guha, Ranajit. *Dominance without Hegemony: History and Power in Colonial India*. Cambridge and London: Harvard University Press, 1997.

Elementary Aspects of Peasant Insurgency in Colonial India. Durham, NC, and London: Duke University Press, 1999.

'On Torture and Culture'. *Frontier* 23 Jan. 1971: 9–15.

Gupta, Akhil. *Red Tape: Bureaucracy, Structural Violence, and Poverty in India*. Durham, NC, and London: Duke University Press, 2012.

Guyot, James F. 'Bureaucratic Transformation in Burma'. *Asian Bureaucratic Systems Emergent from the British Imperial Tradition*. Ed. Ralph Braibanti. Durham, NC: Duke University Press, 1966. 354–443.

Haberkorn, Tyrell. *Revolution Interrupted: Farmers, Students, Law, and Violence in Northern Thailand*. Madison: University of Wisconsin Press, 2011.

Habermas, Jürgen. *Between Facts and Norms: Contributions to a Discourse Theory of Law and Democracy*. Trans. William Rehg. Cambridge: Polity, 1996.

'On the Internal Relation between the Rule of Law and Democracy'. *The Inclusion of the Other: Studies in Political Theory*. Eds. Ciaran Cronin and Pablo de Greiff. Cambridge: MIT Press, 1998. 253–64.

Haggard, Stephan, and Lydia Tiede. 'The Revival of the Rule of Law in the Wake of Civil War'. *Hague Journal on the Rule of Law* 4.1 (2012): 120–34.

Halliday, Terence C., and Lucien Karpik. 'Political Liberalism in the British Post-Colony: A Theme with Three Variations'. *Fates of Political Liberalism in the British Post-Colony: The Politics of the Legal Complex*. Eds. Terence C. Halliday, Lucien Karpik, and Malcolm M. Feeley. New York: Cambridge University Press, 2012. 3–55.

Hardt, Michael, and Antonio Negri. *Empire*. Cambridge and London: Harvard University Press, 2000.

Harvey, Godfrey E. *British Rule in Burma, 1824–1942*. London: Faber & Faber, 1946.

Hay, Douglas. 'Property, Authority and the Criminal Law'. *Albion's Fatal Tree: Crime and Society in Eighteenth-Century England*. Eds. Douglas Hay et al. Middlesex: Penguin, 1975. 17–63.

Hayek, Friedrich A. *The Constitution of Liberty*. Chicago: University of Chicago Press, 1960.

Law, Legislation and Liberty. London and New York: Routledge, 1982.

The Road to Serfdom. 1944. Chicago: University of Chicago Press, 1994.

Helmke, Gretchen. *Courts under Constraints: Judges, Generals, and Presidents in Argentina*. Cambridge: Cambridge University Press, 2005.

Hilbink, Lisa. *Judges Beyond Politics in Democracy and Dictatorship: Lessons from Chile*. Cambridge and New York: Cambridge University Press, 2007.

Hla Aung, U. 'The Law of Preventive Detention in Burma'. *Journal of the International Commission of Jurists* 3.1 (1961): 47–68.

'A Republic and the Rule of Law'. *Burma Law Institute Journal* 2.1 (1960): 1–2.

Hobbes, Thomas. *Leviathan*. 1651. Ed. Crawford B. Macpherson. Middlesex: Penguin, 1968.

Holliday, Ian. *Burma Redux: Global Justice and the Quest for Political Reform in Myanmar*. New York: Columbia University Press, 2011.

Holmes, Robert A. 'Burmese Domestic Policy: The Politics of Burmanization'. *Asian Survey* 7.3 (1967): 188–97.

Holmes, Stephen. 'Lineages of the Rule of Law'. *Democracy and the Rule of Law*. Eds. José María Maravall and Adam Przeworski. New York: Cambridge University Press, 2003. 19–61.

Horsey, Richard. 'The Dramatic Events of 2007 in Myanmar: Domestic and International Implications'. *Dictatorship, Disorder and Decline in Myanmar*. Eds. Monique Skidmore and Trevor Wilson. Canberra: ANU E-Press, 2008. 13–28.

Ending Forced Labour in Myanmar: Engaging a Pariah Regime. London and New York: Routledge, 2011.

Horwitz, Morton J. 'The Rule of Law: An Unqualified Human Good?' *Yale Law Journal* 86.3 (1977): 561–66.

Horwitz, Paul. 'Democracy as the Rule of Law'. *When Governments Break the Law: The Rule of Law and the Prosecution of the Bush Administration*. Eds. Austin Sarat and Nasser Hussain. New York and London: New York University Press, 2010. 153–81.

Houtman, Gustaaf. *Mental Culture in Burmese Crisis Politics: Aung San Suu Kyi and the National League for Democracy*. Tokyo: Tokyo University of Foreign Studies, 1999.

HRW. *Crackdown: Repression of the 2007 Popular Protests in Burma*. New York: Human Rights Watch, 2007.

Hughes, Dhana. 'Remembering Sri Lanka's Southern Terror: Narratives of Torture Survivors'. *Interventions: International Journal of Postcolonial Studies* 14.2 (2012): 185–210.

Hume, Leonard J. *Bentham and Bureaucracy*. Cambridge: Cambridge University Press, 1981.

Humphreys, Stephen. *Theatre of the Rule of Law: Transnational Legal Intervention in Theory and Practice*. Cambridge: Cambridge University Press, 2010.

Hussain, Nasser. *The Jurisprudence of Emergency: Colonialism and the Rule of Law*. Ann Arbor: University of Michigan Press, 2003.

Huxley, Andrew. 'Positivists and Buddhists: The Rise and Fall of Anglo-Burmese Ecclesiastical Law'. *Law and Social Inquiry* 26.1 (2001): 113–42.

'Pre-Colonial Burmese Law: Conical Hat and Shoulder Bag'. *IIAS Newsletter Online*. 25 (2001). 23 July 2008 www.iias.nl/iiasn.

Ikeya, Chie. *Refiguring Women, Colonialism, and Modernity in Burma*. Honolulu: University of Hawai'i Press, 2011.

ILO. *Developments Concerning the Question of the Observance by the Government of Myanmar of the Forced Labour Convention, 1930 (No. 29) (Gb.306/6)*. Geneva: International Labour Office, Nov. 2009.

Ireland, Alleyne. *The Province of Burma*. 2 vols. Boston and New York: Houghton Mifflin, 1907.

Islam, Md. Shariful. *Politics-Corruption Nexus in Bangladesh: An Empirical Study of the Impacts on Judicial Governance*. Hong Kong: Asian Legal Resource Centre, 2010.

Jauregui, Beatrice. 'Beatings, Beacons, and Big Men: Police Disempowerment and Delegitimation in India'. *Law and Social Inquiry* 38.3 (2013): 643–69.

'Law and Order: Police Encounter Killings and Routinized Political Violence'. *A Companion to the Anthropology of India*. Ed. Isabelle Clark-Decès. Oxford: Blackwell, 2011. 371–88.

Jayasuriya, Kanishka. 'Franz Neumann on the Rule of Law and Capitalism: The East Asian Case'. *Journal of the Asia Pacific Economy* 2.3 (1997): 357–77.

Jeffery, Renée. *Amnesties, Accountability, and Human Rights*. Philadelphia: University of Pennsylvania Press, 2014.

Jones, Seth G., Jeremy M. Wilson, Andrew Rathmell, and K. Jack Riley. *Establishing Law and Order after Conflict*. Santa Monica, CA: RAND, 2005.

Kenny, Paul. 'The Meaning of Torture'. *Polity* 42.2 (2010): 131–55.

Kerkvliet, Benedict J. Tria. 'Everyday Politics in Peasant Societies (and Ours)'. *Journal of Peasant Studies* 36.1 (2009): 227–43.

Khan, Salar M. 'Judicial Delays to Criminal Trials in Delhi'. *Article 2* 7.2 (2008): 7–60.

Khin Maung, M. Ismael. 'The Population of Burma: An Analysis of the 1973 Census'. 97. *Papers of the East-West Population Institute*. Honolulu: East-West Center, 1986.

Kingston, Jeff. 'Burma's Despair'. *Critical Asian Studies* 40.1 (2008): 3–43.

Knemeyer, Franz-Ludwig. 'Polizei'. *Economy and Society* 9.2 (1980): 172–96.

Kolsky, Elizabeth. '"The Body Evidencing the Crime": Rape on Trial in Colonial India, 1860–1947'. *Gender and History* 22.1 (2010): 109–30.

'Codification and the Rule of Colonial Difference: Criminal Procedure in British India'. *Law and History Review* 23.3 (2005): 631–83.

Colonial Justice in British India. Cambridge: Cambridge University Press, 2010.

'A Note on the Study of Indian Legal History'. *Law and History Review* 23.3 (2005): 703–06.

Krygier, Martin. 'Four Puzzles About the Rule of Law: Why, What, Where? And Who Cares?' *Getting to the Rule of Law*. Ed. James E. Fleming. Vol. V. Nomos. New York and London: New York University Press, 2011. 64–104.

'Marxism and the Rule of Law: Reflections after the Collapse of Communism'. *Law and Social Inquiry* 15.4 (1990): 633–63.

'Rule of Law (and Rechtsstaat)'. *International Encyclopedia of the Social and Behavioural Sciences*. 2nd edn., 2015. Forthcoming.

'Still a Rule of Law Guy'. *Recht der Werkelijkheid* 34.1 (2013): 47–55.

Kyaw Min San. 'Critical Issues for the Rule of Law in Myanmar'. *Myanmar's Transition: Openings, Obstacles and Opportunities*. Eds. Nick Cheesman, Monique Skidmore, and Trevor Wilson. Singapore: ISEAS, 2012. 217–30.

Kyaw Yin. 'The Problem of Crime and the Criminal and Its Solution in Socialist Burma'. *Journal of the Burma Research Society* 47.1 (1964): 205–24.

Kyaw Yin Hlaing. 'Challenging the Authoritarian State: Buddhist Monks and Peaceful Protests in Burma'. *Fletcher Forum of World Affairs* 32.1 (2008): 125–44.

'Myanmar in 2004: Another Year of Uncertainty'. *Asian Survey* 45.1 (2005): 174–79.

Langbein, John H. *Torture and the Law of Proof: Europe and England in the Ancien Régime*. Chicago and London: University of Chicago Press, 1976.

Lev, Daniel S. 'Between State and Society: Professional Lawyers and Reform in Indonesia.' *Making Indonesia*. Eds. Daniel S. Lev and Ruth T. McVey. Ithaca, NY: Cornell University Press, 1996. 144–63.

'The Criminal Regime: Criminal Process in Indonesia'. *Figures of Criminality in Indonesia, the Philippines, and Colonial Vietnam*. Ed. Vincente L. Rafael. Ithaca, NY: Cornell University Press, 1999. 175–92.

Levine, Philippa. *Prostitution, Race, and Politics: Policing Venereal Disease in the British Empire*. New York and London: Routledge, 2003.

Li, Ling. 'The "Production" of Corruption in China's Courts: Judicial Politics and Decision Making in a One-Party State'. *Law and Social Inquiry* 37.4 (2012): 848–77.

Lintner, Bertil. *Outrage: Burma's Struggle for Democracy*. London and Bangkok: White Lotus, 1990.

Mahmud, Tayyab. 'Praetorianism and Common Law in Post-Colonial Settings: Judicial Responses to Constitutional Breakdowns in Pakistan'. *Utah Law Review*. 4 (1993): 1225–305.

Maine, Henry. *Dissertations on Early Law and Custom*. London: John Murray, 1883.

Ancient Law. 10th edn. New York: Henry Holt, 1906.

Majeed, Javed. *Ungoverned Imaginings: James Mill's 'The History of British India' and Orientalism*. Oxford: Clarendon, 1992.

Maravall, José María, and Adam Przeworski. Introduction. *Democracy and the Rule of Law*. Eds. José María Maravall and Adam Przeworski. New York: Cambridge University Press, 2003. 1–16.

Margalit, Avishai. *The Decent Society*. Cambridge and London: Harvard University Press, 1996.

Markovits, Inga. 'Socialist vs. Bourgeois Rights: An East-West German Comparison'. *University of Chicago Law Review* 45 (1977): 612–36.

Marmor, Andrei. 'The Rule of Law and Its Limits'. *Law and Philosophy* 23.1 (2004): 1–43.

Mason, Whit. 'Axioms and Unknowns'. *The Rule of Law in Afghanistan: Missing in Inaction*. Ed. Whit Mason. New York: Cambridge University Press, 2011. 319–29.

Massoud, Mark Fathi. *Law's Fragile State: Colonial, Authoritarian, and Humanitarian Legacies in Sudan*. New York: Cambridge University Press, 2013.

Matelski, Maaike. 'On Sensitivity and Secrecy: How Foreign Researchers and Their Local Contacts in Myanmar Deal with Risk under Authoritarian Rule'. *Journal of Burma Studies* 18.1 (2014): 59–82.

Maung Aung Myoe. *Building the Tatmadaw: Myanmar Armed Forces since 1948*. Singapore: ISEAS, 2009.

'The Soldier and the State: The Tatmadaw and Political Liberalization in Myanmar since 2011'. *South East Asia Research* 22.2 (2014): 233–49.

Maung Maung. *Burma and General Ne Win*. Rangoon: Religious Affairs Dept., 1969.

Burma in the Family of Nations. 1956. 2nd edn. Amsterdam: Djambatan, 1957.

Burma's Constitution. 2nd edn. The Hague: Martinus Nijhoff, 1961.

Law and Custom in Burma and the Burmese Family. The Hague: Martinus Nijhoff, 1963.

'Section 116 of the Constitution'. *Guardian* Mar. 1959: 11–12.

A Trial in Burma: The Assassination of Aung San. The Hague: Martinus Nijhoff, 1962.

Maung Maung Gyi. *Burmese Political Values: The Socio-Political Roots of Authoritarianism*. New York: Praeger, 1983.

Maung Maung Kyi. *A New Approach to Law and Life in Burma*. Rangoon: n.p., 1967.

May, Larry. *Global Justice and Due Process*. Cambridge: Cambridge University Press, 2011.

McCarthy, Stephen. 'Overturning the Alms Bowl: The Price of Survival and the Consequences for Political Legitimacy in Burma'. *Australian Journal of International Affairs* 62.3 (2008): 298–314.

Méndez, Juan, Paulo Sergio Pinheiro, and Guillermo O'Donnell. *The (Un) Rule of Law and New Democracies in Latin America*. Notre Dame, IN: University of Notre Dame Press, 1998.

Merry, Sally Engle. 'Law and Colonialism'. *Law and Society Review* 25.4 (1991): 889–922.

'Transnational Human Rights and Local Activism: Mapping the Middle'. *American Anthropologist* 108.1 (2006): 38–51.

Metcalf, Thomas R. *Ideologies of the Raj*. New Cambridge History of India. Ed. Gordon Johnson. Vol. III.4. Cambridge: Cambridge University Press, 1994.

Mill, John Stuart. 'Penal Code for India'. *Writings on India*. Eds. John M. Robson, Martin Moir, and Zawahir Moir. Vol. XXX. Toronto and Buffalo: University of Toronto Press, 1990. 19–30.

Moon Jeong-ho, and Bruce Van Voorhis. *An Exceptional Collapse of the Rule of Law: Told through Stories by Families of the Disappeared in Sri Lanka*. Hong Kong: Asian Legal Resource Centre and Asian Human Rights Commission, 2004.

Moustafa, Tamir. 'Law and Courts in Authoritarian Regimes'. *Annual Review of Law and Social Science* 10 (2014): 281–99.

Moustafa, Tamir, and Tom Ginsburg. Introduction. *Rule by Law: The Politics of Courts in Authoritarian Regimes*. Eds. Tom Ginsburg and Tamir Moustafa. Cambridge and New York: Cambridge University Press, 2008. 1–22.

Munger, Frank. 'Constructing Law from Development: Cause Lawyers, Generational Narratives, and the Rule of Law in Thailand'. *Law and Development and the Global Discourses of Legal Transfers*. Eds. John Gillespie and Pip Nicholson. Cambridge: Cambridge University Press, 2012. 237–76.

'Globalization, Investing in Law, and the Careers of Lawyers for Social Causes: Taking on Rights in Thailand'. *New York Law School Law Review* 53 (2008–09): 745–802.

Munger, Frank, Scott L. Cummings, and Louise Trubek. 'Mobilizing Law for Justice in Asia: A Comparative Approach'. *Wisconsin International Law Journal* 31.3 (2014): 353–420.

Myint Zan. 'Comment on Fifty Years of Burmese Law: E Maung and Maung Maung by Andrew Huxley in Law Asia (1996–1997)'. *In Camera* 1998: 39–40.

'A Comparison of the First and Fiftieth Year of Independent Burma's Law Reports'. *Victoria University of Wellington Law Review* 35.2 (2004): 385–426.

'The "New" Supreme Court and Constitutional Tribunal: Marginal Improvement for Judicial Independence or More of the Same?' *Myanmar's Transition: Openings, Obstacles and Opportunities*. Eds. Nick Cheesman, Monique Skidmore, and Trevor Wilson. Singapore: ISEAS, 2012. 249–68.

'Of Consummation, Matrimonial Promises, Fault, and Parallel Wives: The Role of Original Texts, Interpretation, Ideology and Policy in Pre- and Post-1962 Burmese Case Law'. *Columbia Journal of Asian Law* 14.1 (2000): 153–212.

'Two Divergent Burmese Rulings on Criminal Defendants' Confessions: An "Ideological Analysis"'. *University of Tasmania Law Review* 19.2 (2000): 335–53.

'U Myint Thein MA, LLB, LLD'. *Australian Law Journal* 69 (1995): 225–27.

Nakanishi, Yoshihiro. *Strong Soldiers, Failed Revolution: The State and Military in Burma, 1962–88*. Singapore: National University of Singapore Press; Kyoto: Kyoto University Press, 2013.

Nardi, Dominic, and Lwin Moe. 'Understanding the Myanmar Supreme Court's Docket: An Analysis of Case Topics from 2007 to 2011'. *Law, Society and Transition in Myanmar*. Eds. Melissa Crouch and Tim Lindsey. Oxford: Hart, 2014. 95–116.

Neill, Jeremy. '"This Is a Most Disgusting Case": Imperial Policy, Class and Gender in the "Rangoon Outrage" of 1899'. *Journal of Colonialism and*

Colonial History 12.1 (2011). 18 Aug. 2011 http://muse.jhu.edu/journals/journal_of_colonialism_and_colonial_history.

Neocleous, Mark. 'Policing and Pin-Making: Adam Smith, Police and the State of Prosperity'. *Policing and Society* 8.4 (1998): 425–49.

Newberg, Paula R. *Judging the State: Courts and Constitutional Politics in Pakistan*. Cambridge: Cambridge University Press, 1995.

Nonet, Philippe, and Philip Selznick. *Law and Society in Transition: Toward Responsive Law*. 1978. New Brunswick, NJ, and London: Transaction, 2001.

Nowak, Manfred. *Study of the Phenomena of Torture, Cruel, Inhuman or Degrading Treatment or Punishment in the World, Including an Assessment of Conditions of Detention*. New York: UN General Assembly, 2010.

Nu, Thakin. *From Peace to Stability*. [Rangoon]: Ministry of Information, Govt. of Burma, 1951.

Nu, U. *Premier Reports to the People*. Rangoon: Director of Information, Govt. of the Union of Burma, 1957.

U Nu: Saturday's Son. Trans. U Law Yone. New Haven and London: Yale University Press, 1975.

We Must Defend Democracy. Rangoon: n.p., 1959.

O'Brien, Kevin J., and Lianjiang Li. *Rightful Resistance in Rural China*. New York: Cambridge University Press, 2006.

O'Donnell, Guillermo. 'Why the Rule of Law Matters'. *Journal of Democracy* 15.4 (2004): 32–46.

Oakeshott, Michael. 'The Rule of Law'. *On History, and Other Essays*. 1983. Indianapolis, IN: Liberty Fund, 1999. 129–78.

Office of the Attorney General. 'The Role of the Office of the Attorney General'. Union of Myanmar, 2005. 15.

Ohnesorge, John K. M. 'The Rule of Law'. *Annual Review of Law and Social Science* 3 (2007): 99–114.

Osiel, Mark J. 'Dialogue with Dictators: Judicial Resistance in Argentina and Brazil'. *Law and Social Inquiry* 20.2 (1995): 481–560.

Owens, F. C. 'Pakokku District'. *Burma Gazetteer*. Rangoon: Govt. Printing, 1913. Vol. A.

Palombella, Gianluigi. 'The Rule of Law as an Institutional Ideal'. *Rule of Law and Democracy: Inquiries into Internal and External Issues*. Eds. Leonardo Morlino and Gianluigi Palombella. Leiden and Boston: Brill, 2010. 3–37.

Parker, Kunal M. 'The Historiography of Difference'. *Law and History Review* 23.3 (2005): 685–95.

Parry, John T. *Understanding Torture: Law, Violence, and Political Identity*. Ann Arbor: University of Michigan Press, 2010.

Peerenboom, Randall. 'Law and Development of Constitutional Democracy in China: Problem or Paradigm?' *Columbia Journal of Asian Law* 19.1 (2005): 185–234.

Pereira, Anthony W. *Political (In)Justice: Authoritarianism and the Rule of Law in Brazil, Chile, and Argentina*. Pittsburgh, PA: University of Pittsburgh Press, 2005.

Peters, Edward. *Torture*. Philadelphia: University of Pennsylvania Press, 1996.

Pettit, Philip. *Republicanism: A Theory of Freedom and Government*. Oxford and New York: Oxford University Press, 1997.

Pinheiro, Paulo Sergio. *Report of the Special Rapporteur on the Situation of Human Rights in Myanmar*. Geneva: UN Human Rights Council, 2007.

Pitts, Jennifer. 'Jeremy Bentham: Legislator of the World?' *Utilitarianism and Empire*. Eds. Bart Schultz and Georgios Varouxakis. Lanham, MD: Lexington, 2005. 57–91.

Pompe, Sebastiaan. *The Indonesian Supreme Court: A Study of Institutional Collapse*. Ithaca, NY: Southeast Asia Program, Cornell University, 2005.

Postema, Gerald J. *Bentham and the Common Law Tradition*. Oxford: Clarendon, 1986.

Prasse-Freeman, Elliott. 'Conceptions of Justice and the Rule of Law'. *Myanmar: The Dynamics of an Evolving Polity*. Ed. David Steinberg. Boulder: Lynne Rienner, 2014: 89–114.

Quintana, Tomás Ojea. *Situation of Human Rights in Myanmar*. New York: UN General Assembly, 2013.

Radin, Margaret Jane. 'Reconsidering the Rule of Law'. *Boston University Law Review* 69.4 (1989): 781–819.

Raeff, Marc. *The Well-Ordered Police State: Social and Institutional Change through Law in the Germanies and Russia, 1600–1800*. New Haven and London: Yale University Press, 1983.

Rafiqul, Muhammad, and S. M. Solaiman. 'Torture under Police Remand in Bangladesh: A Culture of Impunity for Gross Violations of Human Rights'. *Asia-Pacific Journal on Human Rights and the Law* 4.2 (2003): 1–27.

Rajah, Jothie. *Authoritarian Rule of Law: Legislation, Discourse and Legitimacy in Singapore*. New York: Cambridge University Press, 2012.

Rao, Anupama. 'Problems of Violence, States of Terror: Torture in Colonial India'. *Interventions: International Journal of Postcolonial Studies* 3.2 (2001): 186–205.

Raz, Joseph. 'The Rule of Law and Its Virtue'. *The Authority of Law: Essays on Law and Morality*. Oxford: Clarendon, 1979. 210–29.

Rejali, Darius. *Torture and Democracy*. Princeton and Oxford: Princeton University Press, 2007.

Reynolds, Craig J., et al. 'Time's Arrow and the Burden of the Past: A Primer on the Thai Un-State'. *Sensate: Journal for Experiments in Critical Media Practice*. May (2012). 17 Sept. 2013 www.sensatejournal.com.

Rogers, John D. *Crime, Justice and Society in Colonial Sri Lanka*. London: Curzon, 1987.
Roque, Ricardo, and Kim A. Wagner. Introduction. *Engaging Colonial Knowledge: Reading European Archives in World History*. Eds. Ricardo Roque and Kim A. Wagner. Basingstoke and New York: Palgrave Macmillan, 2012. 1–32.
Saha, Jonathan. 'Colonization, Criminalization and Complicity: Policing Gambling in Burma c. 1880–1920'. *South East Asia Research* 21.4 (2013): 655–72.
Law, Disorder and the Colonial State: Corruption in Burma, c. 1900. Basingstoke and New York: Palgrave Macmillan, 2013.
'The Male State: Colonialism, Corruption and Rape Investigations in the Irrawaddy Delta c. 1900'. *Indian Economic and Social History Review* 47.3 (2010): 343–76.
Sannerholm, Richard Zajac. 'Looking Back, Moving Forward: UN Peace Operations and Rule of Law Assistance in Africa, 1989–2010'. *Hague Journal on the Rule of Law* 4.2 (2012): 359–73.
Sarat, Austin, and Thomas R. Kearns. 'Making Peace with Violence: Robert Cover on Law and Legal Theory'. *Law's Violence*. Eds. Austin Sarat and Thomas R. Kearns. Ann Arbor: University of Michigan Press, 1992. 211–50.
Sartori, Giovanni. 'Concept Misinformation in Comparative Politics'. *American Political Science Review* 64.4 (1970): 1033–53.
Scarry, Elaine. *The Body in Pain: The Making and Unmaking of the World*. Oxford: Oxford University Press, 1985.
Schaffer, Frederic C. *Democracy in Translation: Understanding Politics in an Unfamiliar Culture*. Ithaca, NY, and London: Cornell University Press, 1998.
'Thin Descriptions: The Limits of Survey Research on the Meaning of Democracy'. *Political Concepts*. 45. Working Paper Series. Mexico City: Committee on Concepts and Methods, 2010.
Schmitt, Carl. *The Concept of the Political*. 1932. Trans. George Schwab. Chicago and London: University of Chicago Press, 2007.
Constitutional Theory. 1928. Trans. Jeffrey Seitzer. Durham, NC, and London: Duke University Press, 2008.
Legality and Legitimacy. 1932. Trans. Jeffrey Seitzer. Durham, NC, and London: Duke University Press, 2004.
Political Theology: Four Chapters on the Concept of Sovereignty. 1922. Trans. George Schwab. Chicago and London: University of Chicago Press, 1985.
Schultze-Kraft, Markus. 'Security and the Rule of Law in Colombia and Guatemala: Priorities, Trade-Offs and Interdependencies'. *Hague Journal on the Rule of Law* 4.1 (2012): 135–57.

Scott, James C. *The Art of Not Being Governed: An Anarchist History of Upland Southeast Asia*. Singapore: National University of Singapore Press, 2010.

Domination and the Arts of Resistance: Hidden Transcripts. New Haven and London: Yale University Press, 1990.

Seekins, Donald M. *State and Society in Modern Rangoon*. London and New York: Routledge, 2011.

Selth, Andrew. *Burma (Myanmar) since the 1988 Uprising: A Select Bibliography*. Brisbane: Griffith Asia Institute, 2012.

'Burma's Intelligence Apparatus'. *Intelligence and National Security* 13.4 (1998): 33–70.

'Burma's Police Forces: Continuities and Contradictions'. 32. *Regional Outlook Paper*. Brisbane: Griffith Asia Institute, 2011.

'Burma's "Saffron Revolution" and the Limits of International Influence'. *Australian Journal of International Affairs* 62.3 (2008): 281–97.

Death of a Hero: The U Thant Disturbances in Burma, December 1974. Brisbane: Griffith University, 1989.

'Modern Burma Studies: A Survey of the Field'. *Modern Asian Studies* 44.2 (2010): 401–40.

'Police Reform in Myanmar: Changes "in Essence and Appearance"'. *Debating Democratization in Myanmar*. Eds. Nick Cheesman, Nicholas Farrelly, and Trevor Wilson. Singapore: ISEAS, 2014. 205–28.

Selznick, Philip. 'Legal Cultures and the Rule of Law'. *The Rule of Law after Communism*. Eds. Martin Krygier and Adam Czarnota. Dartmouth: Ashgate, 1999. 21–38.

TVA and the Grass Roots: A Study in Politics and Organization. 1949. New Orleans: Quid Pro, 2011.

Sevel, Michael. 'Legal Positivism and the Rule of Law'. *Australian Journal of Legal Philosophy* 34 (2009): 53–68.

Shambayati, Hootan. 'Courts in Semi-Democratic/Authoritarian Regimes: The Judicialization of Turkish (and Iranian) Politics'. *Rule by Law: The Politics of Courts in Authoritarian Regimes*. Eds. Tom Ginsburg and Tamir Moustafa. Cambridge and New York: Cambridge University Press, 2008. 283–303.

Sherman, Taylor C. *State Violence and Punishment in India*. London and New York: Routledge, 2010.

Shklar, Judith N. *The Faces of Injustice*. New Haven: Yale University Press, 1990.

Silverman, Lisa. *Tortured Subjects: Pain, Truth, and the Body in Early Modern France*. Chicago: University of Chicago Press, 2001.

Skaaning, Svend-Erik. 'Measuring the Rule of Law'. *Political Concepts*. 29. Working Paper Series. Mexico City: Committee on Concepts and Methods, 2009.

Skidmore, Monique, and Trevor Wilson, eds. *Dictatorship, Disorder and Decline in Myanmar*. Canberra: ANU E-Press, 2008.

Skuy, David. 'Macaulay and the Indian Penal Code of 1862: The Myth of the Inherent Superiority and Modernity of the English Legal System Compared to India's Legal System in the Nineteenth Century'. *Modern Asian Studies* 32.3 (1998): 513–57.

Smith, Martin. *Burma: Insurgency and the Politics of Ethnicity*. 1991. 2nd edn. London and New York: Zed, 1999.

Solum, Lawrence B. 'Equity and the Rule of Law'. *The Rule of Law*. Ed. Ian Shapiro. Vol. XXXVI. Nomos. New York and London: New York University Press, 1994. 120–47.

Stein, Robert. 'Rule of Law: What Does It Mean?' *Minnesota Journal of International Law* 18.2 (2009): 293–303.

Steinberg, David I. *Burma/Myanmar: What Everyone Needs to Know*. New York: Oxford University Press, 2010.

'Globalization, Dissent, and Orthodoxy: Burma/Myanmar and the Saffron Revolution'. *Georgetown Journal of International Affairs* 9.2 (2008): 51–58.

Stephen, James Fitzjames. *A History of the Criminal Law of England*. Vol. III. 3 vols. London: Macmillan, 1883.

Stevenson, Robert C. *Judson's Burmese-English Dictionary*. Rev. edn. Rangoon: Govt. Printing, 1893.

Stewart, Cameron. 'The Rule of Law and the Tinkerbell Effect: Theoretical Considerations, Criticisms and Justifications for the Rule of Law'. *Macquarie Law Journal* 4 (2004): 135–64.

Stokes, Eric. *The English Utilitarians and India*. Oxford: Clarendon, 1959.

Stoler, Ann Laura. *Along the Archival Grain: Epistemic Anxieties and Colonial Common Sense*. Princeton and Oxford: Princeton University Press, 2009.

Streckfuss, David. *Truth on Trial in Thailand: Defamation, Treason, and Lèse-Majesté*. London and New York: Routledge, 2011.

Svolik, Milan W. *The Politics of Authoritarian Rule*. New York: Cambridge University Press, 2012.

Tamanaha, Brian Z. *On the Rule of Law: History, Politics, Theory*. Cambridge: Cambridge University Press, 2004.

Thant Myint-U. *The Making of Modern Burma*. Cambridge: Cambridge University Press, 2001.

Thompson, Edward P. *Whigs and Hunters: The Origin of the Black Act*. London: Allen Lane, 1975.

Thompson, John Seabury. Supplement. *The Governance of Modern Burma*. By John S. Furnivall. New York: Institute of Pacific Relations, 1960. 133–54.

Thomson-Senanayake, Jane. *A Sociological Exploration of Disappearances in Sri Lanka*. Hong Kong: Asian Human Rights Commission, 2014.

Tin, U. 'The Rule of Law'. *Guardian* June 1960: 31–32.

Tinker, Hugh, ed. *Burma: The Struggle for Independence, 1944–1948*. Vol. II. 2 vols. London: HMSO, 1984.

'Structure of the British Imperial Heritage'. *Asian Bureaucratic Systems Emergent from the British Imperial Tradition*. Ed. Ralph Braibanti. Durham, NC: Duke University Press, 1966. 23–86.

The Union of Burma: A Study of the First Years of Independence. 1957. 4th edn. London: Oxford University Press, 1967.

TNI/BCN. *Ethnicity without Meaning, Data without Context: The 2014 Census, Identity and Citizenship in Burma/Myanmar*. Amsterdam: Transnational Institute and Burma Centrum Nederland, February 2014.

Tonkin, Derek. 'The 1990 Elections in Myanmar: Broken Promises or a Failure of Communication?' *Contemporary Southeast Asia* 29.1 (2007): 33–54.

Trusov, Aleksei. *An Introduction to the Theory of Evidence*. Moscow: Foreign Languages, n.d.

Tydd, W. B. 'Sandoway District'. *Burma Gazetteer*. Rangoon: Govt. Printing, 1912. Vol. A.

Upham, Frank. 'The Illusory Promise of the Rule of Law'. *Human Rights with Modesty: The Problem of Universalism*. Ed. András Sajó. Leiden and Boston: Martinus Nijhoff, 2004. 279–313.

'Mythmaking in the Rule of Law Orthodoxy'. 30. *Carnegie Endowment Working Papers*. Washington, DC: Carnegie, 2002.

Van Reenen, Piet. 'Routine Police Torture: Towards a Personalistic Analysis and Strategy'. *Journal of Human Rights* 1.4 (2002): 541–58.

Vern, Wilson Tay Tze. 'The Rule of Law in Myanmar: A Response to Professor [*sic*] Cheesman'. *Comparative and Non-US Constitutional Law eJournal* 8.82 (2013). 10 Oct 2013.

Vyshinsky, Andrei Y. *The Law of the Soviet State*. Trans. Hugh W. Babb. Westport, CT: Greenwood, 1948.

Waldron, Jeremy. 'Is the Rule of Law an Essentially Contested Concept (in Florida)?' *Law and Philosophy* 21.2 (2002): 137–64.

Weber, Max. *Economy and Society: An Outline of Interpretive Sociology*. Trans. Ephraim Fischoff et al. Eds. Guenther Roth and Claus Wittich. Vol. III. 3 vols. Berkeley, Los Angeles, and London: University of California Press, 1968.

Wedeen, Lisa. *Ambiguities of Domination: Politics, Rhetoric, and Symbols in Contemporary Syria*. Chicago and London: University of Chicago Press, 1999.

'Ethnography as Interpretive Enterprise'. *Political Ethnography: What Immersion Contributes to the Study of Power*. Ed. Edward Schatz. Chicago and London: University of Chicago Press, 2009. 75–93.

Peripheral Visions: Publics, Power, and Performance in Yemen. Chicago: University of Chicago Press, 2008.

Wells, Tamas, and Kyaw Thu Aung. 'Village Networks, Land Law and Myanmar's Democratization'. *Debating Democratization in Myanmar*. Eds. Nick Cheesman, Nicholas Farrelly, and Trevor Wilson. Singapore: ISEAS, 2014. 75–91.

Wiener, Martin J. *An Empire on Trial: Race, Murder, and Justice under British Rule, 1870–1935*. Cambridge: Cambridge University Press, 2009.

Williamson, A. 'Shwebo District'. *Burma Gazetteer*. Rangoon: Govt. Printing, 1929. Vol. A.

Wilson, Jon E. *The Domination of Strangers: Modern Governance in Eastern India, 1780–1835*. Basingstoke and New York: Palgrave Macmillan, 2010.

Winston, Kenneth. 'The Internal Morality of Chinese Legalism'. *Singapore Journal of Legal Studies* (2005): 313–47.

Wisnewski, J. Jeremy, and R. Dillon Emerick. *The Ethics of Torture*. London and New York: Continuum, 2009.

Wright, Barry. 'Macaulay's Indian Penal Code: Historical Context and Originating Principles'. *Codification, Macaulay and the Indian Penal Code: The Legacies and Modern Challenges of Criminal Law Reform*. Eds. Wing-cheong Chan, Barry Wright, and Stanley Yeo. Surrey and Burlington, VT: Ashgate, 2011. 19–58.

BOOKS, ARTICLES, REPORTS, AND SPEECHES PUBLISHED IN BURMESE

Ant Maung. *The Letpadaung Hills: A Grand Finale or Tragic Ending?* (အံ့မောင်။ လက်ပံတောင်းတောင်၊ ဇာတ်သိမ်းခန်းလား၊ ဇာတ်ပေါင်းခန်းလား။) Yangon: Zinyadanazaw, 2013.

Aung Gyi, Thakin. 'The 41-Page Treatise and Collected Writings for Humans' Rights'. [သခင်အောင်ကြီး။ လူသားတို့အခွင့်အရေးအတွက် (၄၁) မျက်နှာ စာတမ်းပေါင်းချုပ်။] Yangon: U Kyi Han, 1990.

Aung Min, U. 'A Lying Complainant Who Falsely Accused a Judge on Losing a Case Imprisoned for His Crime Upon the Judge Counter-Suing'. *Judicial Journal* (တရားရေးဂျာနယ်) 1.12 (2001): 56–58.

Aung Tha (PPP), and Aung Saw Oo. *The Myanmar Prison System in the Era of Military Dictatorship*. [အောင်သာ (PPP) နှင့် အောင်စောဦး။ စစ်အာဏာရှင်ခေတ် မြန်မာနိုင်ငံအကျဉ်းထောင်စနစ်။] Yangon: Zinyadanazaw, 2013.

Aung Than, *Myanma Alin*, ed. *Record of the 1990 Multiparty Democratic General Election*. (မြန်မာ့အလင်း အောင်သန်း၊ ပြုစု။ ပါတီစုံဒီမိုကရေစီအထွေထွေရွေးကောက်ပွဲမှတ်တမ်း။) Yangon: Aungsitthi, 1992.

Aung Than Tun, U. *Four Eras of Burmese Law*. (အောင်သန်းထွန်း။ ခေတ်လေးခေတ် မြန်မာ့တရားဥပဒေ။) Rangoon: Kalaungpyan, 1968.

History of Myanmar Dhammasats. (မြန်မာဓမ္မသတ်သမိုင်း။) 3 vols. Yangon: Sarpay Beikman, 2007.

Legal General Knowledge for Everyone. (လူတိုင်းအဖို့ ဥပဒေဗဟုသုတ။) Rangoon: Pagan, 1970.

Aung Toe, U. 'Chief Justice's Address at Closing Ceremony of Deputy Township Judges Refresher Training No. 6'. *Supreme Court Gazette* (တရားရုံးချုပ် ပြန်တမ်း) 14 Nov. 2008: 1–8.

'Judicial Officers Special Refresher Course No. 1 Closing Ceremony Held'. *Supreme Court Gazette* 26 Mar. 1999: 10–19.

Ba Kyaing, U. 'Section 406? Section 420? Civil Case? How to Differentiate'. *Collected Legal Articles*. (ဦးဗကြိုင်။ ဥပဒေဆောင်းပါး ပေါင်းချုပ်။) Vol. I. Yangon: Tainglin, 2000.

Burma Socialist Programme Party. *Articles on the Judiciary in the Party Affairs Journal*. (မြန်မာ့ဆိုရှယ်လစ်လမ်းစဉ်ပါတီ။ ပါတီရေးရာစာစောင်ပါ တရားစီရင်ရေးဆိုင်ရာ ဆောင်းပါးများ။) [Rangoon]: Burma Socialist Programme Party, 1980.

Central Organising Committee. 'On Rumours'. *Domestic Affairs*. (ပါတီစည်းရုံးရေးဗဟိုကော်မတီဌာနချုပ်။ ပြည်တွင်းရေးရာ။) Vol. I. Rangoon: Burma Socialist Programme Party, 1966. 141–59.

Party Seminar 1965: Speeches of the Chairman and Political Report of the General Secretary. (၁၉၆၅ ခုနှစ် ပါတီနှီးနှောဖလှယ်ပွဲ၊ ဥက္ကဋ္ဌကြီး၏ မိန့်ခွန်းများနှင့် အထွေထွေအတွင်းရေးမှူး၏ နိုင်ငံရေးအစီရင်ခံစာ။) [Rangoon]: Burma Socialist Programme Party, 1966.

Party Seminar 1969: Speeches of the Chairman and Political Report of the General Secretary. (၁၉၆၉ ခုနှစ် ပါတီနှီးနှောဖလှယ်ပွဲ၊ ဥက္ကဋ္ဌကြီး၏ မိန့်ခွန်းများနှင့် အထွေထွေအတွင်းရေးမှူး၏ နိုင်ငံရေး အစီရင်ခံစာ။) [Rangoon]: Burma Socialist Programme Party, 1970.

Chief Court. *Criminal Justice*. (တရားရုံးချုပ်။ ရာဇဝတ်တရားစီရင်ရေး။) Rangoon: Chief Court, 1973.

Chit Yi, Maung. *Section Five from Cocos Island*. (မောင်ချစ်ရီ။ ကိုကိုးကျွန်းမှ ပုဒ်မ ငါး။) Rangoon: U Saw Lwin, 1960.

Commission of Inquiry into the Letpadaung Hills Copper Project. 'Final Report of the Commission of Inquiry into the Letpadaung Hills Copper Project'. (လက်ပံတောင်းတောင် ကြေးနီစီမံကိန်း စုံစမ်းစစ်ဆေးရေးကော်မရှင်၏ အပြီးသတ်အစီရင်ခံစာ။) Naypyidaw: Govt. of the Republic of the Union of Myanmar, 2013.

Govt. of the Socialist Republic of the Union of Burma. *Digest of Undertakings of the First Pyithu Hluttaw*. (ပြည်ထောင်စုဆိုရှယ်လစ် သမ္မတမြန်မာနိုင်ငံတော်အစိုးရ။ ပထမအကြိမ် ပြည်သူ့လွှတ်တော်၏

ဆောင်ရွက်ချက်များ အကျဉ်းချုပ်။) Rangoon: Office of the Pyithu Hluttaw, n.d.

Govt. of the Union of Burma. *Excerpts from the Record of the Convention of Security Councils Held at the Defence Services Convocation Hall, Rangoon on April 21, 22 and 23, 1959.* (ပြည်ထောင်စုမြန်မာနိုင်ငံတော်အစိုးရ။ ၁၉၅၉ ခု၊ ဧပြီလ ၂၁၊ ၂၂၊ ၂၃ ရက်နေ့များတွင် ရန်ကုန်မြို့ တပ်မတော်ကပွဲရုံကြီး၌ ကျင်းပသော လုံခြုံရေးကောင်စီများ ညီလာခံကြီး၏ မှတ်တမ်းမှ ကောက်နုတ်ချက်များ။) Rangoon: Govt. Printing, 1959.

Record of the Chamber of Deputies, Union Parliament. (ပြည်သူ့လွှတ်တော် ညီလာခံမှတ်တမ်း။) Rangoon: Govt. of Burma, 1954, 1958, 1959.

Govt. of the Union of Myanmar. *Defence Services History.* (ပြည်ထောင်စုမြန်မာနိုင်ငံတော်အစိုးရ။ တပ်မတော်သမိုင်း။) Vol. VI. 8 vols. Yangon: Office of the Defence Services Historical Museum and Archives, n.d.

Hse Maung, U. My *Life as a Public Servant.* (ဦးဆက်မောင်။ ကျွန်တော်၏ ပြည်သူ့ဝန်ထမ်းဘဝ။) Yangon: n.p., 2000.

ICSVRS. *Report of the Inquiry Commission on the Sectarian Violence in Rakhine State.* (ရခိုင်ပြည်နယ် ပဋိပက္ခများ စုံစမ်းစစ်ဆေးရေးကော်မရှင် အစီရင်ခံစာ။) Naypyidaw: Republic of the Union of Myanmar, 2013.

Khin Maung Cho, U. 'The Power to Define "National Races"'. Parts 1 and 2. *The 1982 Citizenship Law Contradicts the 2008 Constitution, and Selected Articles.* (ဦးခင်မောင်ချို။ ၁၉၈၂ ခုနှစ်၊ မြန်မာနိုင်ငံသားဥပဒေနှင့် လက်ရွေးစင်ဆောင်းပါးများ။) Yangon: Shwethizsa, 2014. 65–72.

Khin Maung Kyaw. *Burma: The Problem of Citizens and Foreigners.* (ခင်မောင်ကျော်။ မြန်မာနိုင်ငံ နိုင်ငံသားများနှင့် နိုင်ငံခြားသားများပြဿနာ။) Rangoon: San Kyaw Yin, 1971.

Khin Nyunt. 'Address at the Work Coordination Meeting of State, Divisional and District Judges and Law Officers'. *Supreme Court Rulings* (တရားရုံးချုပ်၏ စီရင်ချက်များ), *1993*. Yangon: Myawadi, 1995.

'Address at the Work Coordination Meeting of State, Divisional and District Judges and Law Officers'. *Supreme Court Rulings, 1994*. Yangon: Myawadi, 1996.

'Address on July 9, 2002 at the Institute of Nursing to Supreme Court, Office of the Attorney General and State, Division and District Judges and Law Officers Assembled for Receipt of Advice on Judicial Affairs'. *Judicial Journal* 1.14 (2002): 7–20.

Ko Ko Lay. *What Is Cocos Island?* (ကိုကိုလေး။ ဘာလဲဟဲ့ ကိုကိုးကျွန်း။) Rangoon: Khin Maung Yi, 1960.

Kyaw Htet Aung (Shwepyidan), ed. *Popular Opposition Struggles to the BSPP Dictatorship: 74–75–76.* [ကျော်ထက်အောင် (ရွှေပြည်တန်)။ ၇၄-၇၅-၇၆ မ.ဆ.လ. အာဏာရှင်ဆန့်ကျင်ရေး အံတုလှုပ်ရှားမှုများ။] Yangon: Shwepyidan, 2013.

Kyaw Min, U. *A Glimpse into the Hidden Chapters of Arakan History.* (ဦးကျော်မင်း။ ရခိုင်ပြည်နယ်၏ တိမ်မြုပ်နေသောသမိုင်း တစေ့တစောင်း။) Yangon: Daw Khin Ma Cho, 2013.

Kyaw Zeya, U. *Lawyer among the People.* (ဦးကျော်ဇေယျ။ ပြည်သူကြားက ရှေ့နေ။) Rangoon: Zwe, 1981.

Maung Khine Khant. *Record of the 8888 Uprising.* (မောင်ခိုင်ခန့်။ ၈၈၈၈ ဒီမိုကရေစီအရေးတော်ပုံ မှတ်တမ်း။) Yangon: Kyi Hla Maung, 2012.

Maung Maung, Dr. *Legal General Knowledge.* (ဒေါက်တာမောင်မောင်။ တရားဥပဒေ အထွေထွေဗဟုသုတ။) 1974. 3rd edn. Yangon: Sitthidaw, 2004.

Maung Maung Kyi. *Burmese Law and Life.* (မောင်မောင်ကြည်။ မြန်မာ့ဥပဒေနှင့် ဘဝ။) Rangoon: Sarpay Beikman, 1975.

Maung Pan Yi. *Because of the Time That the Mother Peacock's Wings Fell.* (မောင်ပန်းရည်။ ဒေါင်းမိခင် တောင်ပံကျချိန်မို့။) Yangon: Zinyadanazaw, 2013.

Meikhtila District People's Assistance Network, et al. *Position Statement of Networks, Forces, Unions and Organisations Working in the Public Interest on the Report of the Commission of Inquiry into the Letpadaung Hills Copper Project.* (မိတ္ထီလာခရိုင် ပြည်သူ့အကျိုးဆောင်ကွန်ရက် နှင့် အခြားအဖွဲ့များ။ လက်ပံတောင်းတောင် ကြေးနီစီမံကိန်း စုံစမ်းစစ်ဆေးရေးကော်မရှင်အစီရင်ခံအပေါ် ထားရှိသည့် နိုင်ငံလူထုအကျိုးပြု ကွန်ရက်၊ အင်အားစု၊ သမဂ္ဂ၊ အဖွဲ့များ၏ သဘောထားကြေညာချက်။) Yangon: National Democracy Network, 2013.

Ministry of Education. *Social Studies: Myanmar History (Basic Education Mid Level).* [ပညာရေးဝန်ကြီးဌာန။ လူမှုရေးဘာသာ၊ မြန်မာ့သမိုင်း (အခြေခံပညာ အလယ်တန်းအဆင့်)။] Vol. II. [Yangon]: Govt. of the Union of Myanmar, 2001.

Ministry of Home Affairs. *Ministry of Home Affairs: Historical Record and Achievements.* (ပြည်ထဲရေးဝန်ကြီးဌာန။ ပြည်ထဲရေးဝန်ကြီးဌာန၊ သမိုင်းမှတ်တမ်းနှင့် စွမ်းဆောင်ချက်များ။) [Yangon]: Govt. of the Union of Myanmar, 2000.

Moe Ze Nyein. 'What is the Swunashin'. *What is the Swunashin and Collected Writings.* (မိုးဇေညိမ်း။ ဘာလဲဟဲ့ စွမ်းအားရှင်နှင့် အခြားစာစုများ။) Yangon: Nyanekhin, 2014. 9–38.

Mya Han, U, et al., eds. *A Period of Change to Myanmar's Political System (1962–1974)*. [ဦးမြဟန် နှင့် အခြားသူများ၊ ပြုစု။ မြန်မာ့နိုင်ငံရေးစနစ်ပြောင်းကာလ (၁၉၆၂-၁၉၇၄)။] Vol. I. 3 vols. Yangon: Universities Press, 1993.

Mya Han, U, and U Thein Hlaing, eds. *Burma's Politics 1958–1962*. (ဦးမြဟန် နှင့် ဦးသိန်းလှိုင်၊ ပြုစု။ ၁၉၅၈-၁၉၆၂ မြန်မာ့နိုင်ငံရေး။) Vol. IV. 4 vols. Yangon: Universities Press, 1991.

Myat Khine. *Interviews with U Khin Nyunt*. (မြတ်ခိုင်။ ဦးခင်ညွန့်နှင့် အင်တာဗျူး။) Yangon: Quality, 2013.

Myat Thu, Tekkathoe. *Parliamentary Sights*. (တက္ကသိုလ်မြတ်သူ။ ပါလီမန်မြင်ကွင်း။) Yangon: Sarpay Beikman, 2012.

Myint Kyi, Daw, and Naw Angeline, eds. *Burma's Politics 1958–1962*. (ဒေါ်မြင့်ကြည် နှင့် နော်အင်ဂျလင်း၊ ပြုစု။ ၁၉၅၈-၁၉၆၂ မြန်မာ့နိုင်ငံရေး။) Vol. II. 4 vols. Yangon: Universities Press, 1991.

Myint Thein. *Changing Myanmar Administrative Systems*. (မြင့်သိန်း။ ပြောင်းလဲလာသော မြန်မာနိုင်ငံ အုပ်ချုပ်ပုံစနစ်များ။) Yangon: Seitguchocho, 2006.

NHRDP. *A Short History of Arakan and Rohingya*. (ရခိုင်ပြည်နှင့် ရိုဟင်ဂျာလူမျိုး သမိုင်းအကျဉ်းချုပ်။) Yangon: National Human Rights Democratic Party, 1990.

Nu, U. *Address Given by AFPFL (Clean) Chairman U Nu at the 69th May Day Celebration*. [ဦးနု။ ၆၉ ကြိမ်မြောက် မေဒေးနေ့အခမ်းအနားတွင် ဖ၊ဆ၊ပ၊လ (သန့်ရှင်း) အဖွဲ့ချုပ် ဥက္ကဋ္ဌကြီး ဦးနု ပြောကြားသည့် မိန့်ခွန်း။] [Rangoon]: News and Information Dept., AFPFL (Clean), 1959.

'Prime Minister's Address and Instructions at the Meeting on the Four-Year Plan Held on Saturday, 8 June 1957'. (၁၉၅၇ ဇွန်လ ၈ ရက် စနေနေ့တွင် ကျင်းပသော လေးနှစ်စီမံကိန်း ဆွေးနွေးပွဲကြီးတွင် မြွက်ကြားသည့် နိုင်ငံတော်ဝန်ကြီးချုပ်၏ မိန့်ခွန်းနှင့် ညွှန်ကြားချက်များ။) Rangoon: Sarpay Beikman, 1957. 33.

Poe Kyaw. *My History, Others' History, The Country's History*. (ဖိုးကျော့။ ကိုယ့်သမိုင်း သူ့သမိုင်း နိုင်ငံသမိုင်း။) Yangon: Thin, 2014.

Pyithu Hluttaw. Report of the Pyithu Hluttaw Rule of Law and Tranquility Committee. (တရားဥပဒေစိုးမိုးရေးနှင့် တည်ငြိမ်အေးချမ်းရေးကော်မတီ၏ အစီရင်ခံစာ။) 14 August 2013.

'Rule of Law and Tranquility Committee'. (ပြည်သူ့လွှတ်တော်။ တရားဥပဒေစိုးမိုးရေးနှင့် တည်ငြိမ်အေးချမ်းရေးကော်မတီ။) Naypyidaw, 2012. 25 Nov. 2012. www.pyithuhluttaw.gov.mm.

Revolutionary Council. *Burma: Administrative and Social Affairs, 1962–63.* (တော်လှန်ရေးကောင်စီ။ မြန်မာနိုင်ငံ၊ အုပ်ချုပ်ရေးနှင့်လူမှုရေး ၁၉၆၂-၆၃။) Rangoon: Office of the Director of Information, 1965.

Concise History of the Revolutionary Council's Activity. (တော်လှန်ရေးကောင်စီ၏ လုပ်ဆောင်ချက် သမိုင်းအကျဉ်းချုပ်။) Rangoon: Printing and Publishing, 1974.

The General Amnesty, and Explanation. (အထွေထွေလွတ်ငြိမ်းချမ်းသာခွင့်နှင့် ရှင်းလင်းကြေညာချက်။) [Rangoon]: Office of the Dept. of Information, 1963.

San Nyein, U, and Daw Myint Kyi, eds. *Burma's Politics 1958–1962.* (ဦးစံငြိမ်း နှင့် ဒေါ်မြင့်ကြည်၊ ပြုစု။ ၁၉၅၈-၁၉၆၂ မြန်မာ့နိုင်ငံရေး။) Vol. I. 4 vols. Yangon: Universities Press, 1991.

Than Maung, U. 'A Background History of Myanmar Rulings'. *Judicial Journal* 1.13 (2002): 48–58.

Than Pe Myint, U. *Historical Records, 62–67.* (ဦးသန်းဖေမြင့်။ ၆၂-၆၇ သမိုင်းဝင်မှတ်တမ်းများ။) Rangoon: Sapaung, 1968.

Thein Hlaing, U, and Dr. Daw Khin Hla Han, eds. A *Period of Change to Myanmar's Political System (1962–1974).* [ဦးသိန်းလှိုင် နှင့် ဒေါက်တာ ဒေါ်ခင်လှဟန်၊ ပြုစု။ မြန်မာ့နိုင်ငံရေးစနစ်ပြောင်းကာလ (၁၉၆၂-၁၉၇၄)။] Vol. III. 3 vols. Yangon: Universities Press, 1993.

Thet San Ye (Naypyidaw) et al., eds. *The Letpadaung Chronicle.* [သက်စမ်းရေ (နေပြည်တော်) နှင့် အခြားသူများ၊ ပြုစု။ လက်ပံတောင်းမော်ကွန်း။] Yangon: Thin, 2013.

Tin Aung Aye, Dr. 'Three Eras of Change to Burma's Legal System'. *Law Magazine* (ဥပဒေမဂ္ဂဇင်း) 1978: 22–25.

Tin Ohn, Maung. *A Miscellany of Legal Knowledge.* (မောင်တင်အုံး။ သုတဥပဒေအထွေထွေ။) 1977. 2nd edn. Rangoon: Minthimun, 1985.

'Socialist Rule of Law.' *Myawadi* (မြဝတီ) July 1966: 161–64.

Tin Win, U. *Writs.* (ဦးတင်ဝင်း။ စာချွန်တော်။) Mandalay: Nwewe, 2012.

Win Zaw Latt, ed. *The 8888 Uprising as Told by the Newspapers.* (ဝင်းဇော်လတ်။ သတင်းစာတွေ ပြောတဲ့ ၈၈၈၈ အရေးတော်ပုံ။) 2nd edn. Yangon: Toe Myit, 2013.

Yin Htun, ed. *Record of the 7th July Uprising.* (ယဉ်ထွန်း၊ ပြုစု။ 7th July အရေးတော်ပုံမှတ်တမ်း။) Yangon: Zinyadanazaw, 2013.

Zarganar. *Third, Fourth.* (ဇာဂနာ။ တတိယ၊ စတုတ္ထ။) [Yangon]: Ko Thura, 2013.

Zawana (Agriculture), ed. *Historical Newspaper Accounts from the Democracy Uprising.* [ဇဝန (စိုက်ပျိုးရေး)။ ဒီမိုကရေစီအရေးတော်ပုံမှ ပြောသော သတင်းစာသမိုင်း။] Yangon: Zinyadanazaw, 2013.

UNPUBLISHED SOURCES

Akkas, Sarkar Ali. 'Judicial Independence and Accountability: A Comparative Study of Contemporary Bangladesh Experience'. PhD diss. University of Wollongong, 2002.

Anon. 'Analysis of Myanmar's Legislature, Judiciary and Administration.' Unpublished paper, 2006. 6 (in Burmese).

Baker, Jacqueline. 'The Rise of Polri: Democratisation and the Political Economy of Security in Indonesia'. PhD diss. London School of Economics and Political Science, 2012.

Balasubramaniam, Ratna Reuban. 'Rule by Law as Juridical Pathology'. Unpublished paper, 2009. 39.

Callahan, Mary, Christoph LeFranc, and Nancy Stiegler. Documentation of Risk Mitigation Report: 2013 Pilot Census, Myanmar. n.p.: UNFPA, 2013.

Charlesworth, Hilary. 'Human Rights and the Rule of Law after Conflict'. *John Fleming Centre Colloquium*. Australian National University, Canberra, 2008.

Cheesman, Nick. 'Legitimising the Union of Myanmar through Primary School Textbooks'. MEd diss. University of Western Australia, 2002.

Ei Ei Zaw. 'A Study on [*sic*] the Changing Role of [the] Myanmar Police Force (1988–2000)'. MRes diss. Yangon University, 2002.

Gillespie, John. 'Transplanting Commercial Law Reform: Developing a "Rule of Law" in Vietnam'. PhD diss. Australian National University, 2005.

Jauregui, Beatrice. 'Shadows of the State, Subalterns of the State: Police and "Law and Order" in Postcolonial India'. PhD diss. University of Chicago, 2010.

McAndrew, James. 'From Combat to Karaoke: Burmese Military Intelligence, 1948–2006'. MSc diss. National Defense Intelligence College, Washington, DC, 2007.

Ne Win. 'Speech of Burma Socialist Programme Party Chairman U Ne Win'. (မြန်မာ့ဆိုရှယ်လစ်လမ်းစဉ်ပါတီ ဥက္ကဋ္ဌကြီး ဦးနေဝင်း၏ မိန့်ခွန်း။) Emergency Party Congress of the Burma Socialist Programme Party. 1988.

Reyes, Danilo. 'Torture in Indonesia and the Philippines: A *Jus Cogens* Right with or without Remedy?' LLM diss. University of Hong Kong, 2013.

San Pe, Robert. 'Rebuilding Rule of Law in Myanmar: Professional Training and Education for Existing Legal Practitioners'. Parliamentary Committee on Rule of Law [*sic*], 2013.

RULINGS REPORTED IN ENGLISH

Abdul Rahman v. *King-Emperor*, 5 Ran. [Rangoon Series, Indian Law Reports] 53 PC [Privy Council].

Ah Nywe v. *Commissioner of Police, Rangoon and Another*, 1948 BLR (SC) [Burma Law Reports (Supreme Court)] 737.

Ah Shee and 22 v. *King-Emperor*, 3 LBR [Lower Burma Rulings] 229.
Ali Meah v. *Union of Burma*, 1954 BLR (SC) 65.
B. K. Halder v. *S. Kr. Chelliah Pillay and Others*, 1952 BLR (HC) [High Court] 340.
Ba Yin and One v. *King-Emperor*, 7 Ran. 759.
Bana Singh v. *King-Emperor*, 6 Ran. 137.
Bo Aye Ko v. *Commissioner of Police, Rangoon and 2*, 1950 BLR (SC) 181.
Bo San Lin v. *Commissioner of Police and One*, 1948 BLR (SC) 372.
Chit Tun and 4 v. *Crown*, 1 LBR 238.
Chittambaram v. *King-Emperor*, (1947) RLR [Rangoon Law Reports] 66 PC.
Chwa Hum Htive and Another v. *King-Emperor*, 11 Ran. 107.
Crown v. *Majun and 12*, 1 LBR 120.
Crown v. *Nga Kyauk Lon*, 1 LBR 75.
Crown v. *Nga Nyein*, 1 LBR 90.
Daw Aye Nyunt v. *Commissioner of Police, Rangoon and One*, 1949 BLR (SC) 5.
Daw Mya Tin v. *Commissioner of Police, Rangoon and One*, 1949 BLR (SC) 82.
E. E. Mayeth v. *King-Emperor*, 3 Ran. 612.
G. C. Siricar v. *King-Emperor*, 3 Ran. 68.
Gaung Gyi v. *King-Emperor*, 4 LBR 244.
H. M. Eusoof and Abdul Khudus v. *King-Emperor*, 11 LBR 73.
Hasan Ali v. *Secretary, Ministry of Immigration and National Registration and One*, 1959 BLR (SC) 187.
Hnin Yin (King-Emperor) v. *Than Pe*, 9 LBR 92.
In the matter of a pleader, 1960 BLR (HC) 487.
In the matter of Messrs. *L & T, a firm of advocates*, 1956 BLR (HC) 40.
K. M. Subbaya Naidu v. *King-Emperor*, 7 Ran. 470.
Kha Hlaw and Poo Sa v. *King-Emperor*, 4 LBR 116.
Khaw Taw and One v. *Union of Burma*, 1948 BLR (HC) 310.
Khin Maung Myint v. *Union of Burma*, 1953 BLR (SC) 24.
King-Emperor v. *Channing Arnold*, 6 LBR 129 FB [Full Bench].
King-Emperor v. *Kwe Haw and 16*, 4 LBR 213 FB.
King-Emperor v. *Kyan Baw*, 2 LBR 239.
King-Emperor v. *Maung Cho and Others*, 2 LBR 43.
King-Emperor v. *Mi Wa*, 8 LBR 534.
King-Emperor v. *Myat Aung*, 4 LBR 135.
King-Emperor v. *Nga Khaing and One*, 6 Ran. 531.
King-Emperor v. *Nga Lun Thuong*, 13 Ran. 570 FB.
King-Emperor v. *Nga Nyun Bu and 5*, (1897–1901) 1 UBR [Upper Burma Rulings] 370.
King-Emperor v. *Nga Po*, 5 LBR 72 FB.
King-Emperor v. *Nga Po Min*, 10 Ran. 511 FB.
King-Emperor v. *Po Ba*, 8 LBR 143.
King-Emperor v. *Po Gyi*, 3 LBR 114.
King-Emperor v. *Po Ni and Others*, 3 LBR 116.

King-Emperor v. *Po Thin*, 7 LBR 62.
King-Emperor v. *Po Thin Gyi*, 7 Ran. 96.
King-Emperor v. *Ramara*, 4 LBR 103.
King-Emperor v. *Taik Pyu and Nga Thaik*, 5 LBR 21.
Lee Kyin Su (a) *U Su* v. *Commissioner of Excise and 3*, 1957 BLR (SC) 5.
Lim Lyan Hwat (a) *Lim Sway Gaung / Lim Kwin Kee* (a) *Htwa Kong* (a) *Htwa Tong* v. *The Secretary, Ministry of Home Affairs and One* 1960 BLR (SC) 128.
Ma Ahmar v. *Commissioner of Police, Rangoon and One*, 1949 BLR (SC) 39.
Ma Khin Than v. *Commissioner of Police, Rangoon and One*, 1949 BLR (SC) 13.
Ma Lone v. *Commissioner of Police, Rangoon and One*, 1949 BLR (SC) 8.
Ma Mya Khin v. *Commissioner of Police, Rangoon and One*, 1950 BLR (SC) 8.
Ma Than Sint v. *Commissioner of Police, Rangoon and One*, 1949 BLR (SC) 1.
Madhu Limaye v. *Sub-Divisional Magistrate, Monghyr and Others*, 1971 Supreme Court Report [India] (2) 711.
Maung Ant Bwe and One v. *Union of Burma*, 1948 BLR (HC) 863.
Maung Aye Maung v. *Union of Burma*, 1956 BLR (HC) 273.
Maung Hla Gyaw v. *Commissioner of Police, Rangoon and One*, 1948 BLR (SC) 764.
Maung Kyaw Aye v. *Union of Burma*, 1953 BLR (HC) 114.
Maung Nyi and One v. *Union of Burma*, 1952 BLR (HC) 282.
Maung Pu v. *Maung Chit Pyu*, 5 Ran. 129.
Maung San Myin v. *King-Emperor*, 7 Ran. 771.
Maung Thwe v. *King-Emperor*, 3 Ran. 74.
Maung Tok and 10 v. *King-Emperor*, 3 Ran. 352.
Maung Tun Hla v. *Queen-Empress*, (1892–96) 1 UBR 221.
Mawzanagyi v. *King-Emperor*, 8 Ran. 511.
Mi Ein Tha and Mi O Za v. *King-Emperor*, 5 LBR 131.
Mi Hauk v. *King-Emperor*, 4 LBR 121.
Mohamed Hayet Mulla v. *King-Emperor*, 7 Ran. 370.
Mohamed Ismail v. *King-Emperor*, 13 Ran. 754.
Nga Aung Dwe v. *Queen-Empress*, (1892–96) 1 UBR 229.
Nga Hla U v. *King-Emperor*, 3 Ran. 139.
Nga Kain and 11 v. *Queen-Empress*, (1897–1901) 1 UBR 252.
Nga Kya Thein v. *King-Emperor*, 8 LBR 94.
Nga Myat Kyaw v. *Queen-Empress*, (1897–1901) 1 UBR 41.
Nga Po Chon v. *King-Emperor*, 4 Ran. 356.
Nga Po Gaung v. *King-Emperor*, (1897–1901) 1 UBR 96.
Nga Po Kauk and One v. *King-Emperor*, 4 Ran. 45.
Nga Po Hmi v. *Queen-Empress*, (1897–1901) 1 UBR 29.
Nga Po Kyaw and 3 v. *King-Emperor*, (1902–03) 1 UBR Pen. Co. 1.
Nga Po Mya v. *Queen-Empress*, (1897–1901) 1 UBR 320.
Nga Po Nyun v. *King-Emperor*, 2 LBR 76.
Nga Po Shein and 2 v. *King-Emperor*, (1910–13) UBR 152.

Nga Po Tein v. *King-Emperor*, (1910–13) UBR 149.
Nga Po Tha and 2 v. *King-Emperor*, (1917–20) UBR 54.
Nga Po Than v. *King-Emperor*, 3 Ran. 156.
Nga Po Thaw v. *King-Emperor*, (1910–13) UBR 155.
Nga Po Thet v. *Queen-Empress*, 1 LBR 29.
Nga Pyan v. *Crown*, 1 LBR 359.
Nga San Myin v. *King-Emperor*, (1910–13) UBR 123.
Nga San Nyein and 9 v. *King-Emperor*, (1917–20) UBR 3.
Nga Sein v. *King-Emperor*, 3 LBR 121.
Nga Shwe Baw v. *Queen-Empress*, (1897–1901) 1 UBR 285.
Nga Shwe Tat v. *Queen-Empress*, (1897–1901) 1 UBR 152.
Nga Shwe Ywe v. *Crown*, 1 LBR 71.
Nga Thet U v. *King-Emperor*, 2 LBR 115.
Nga U Khine and Others v. *King-Emperor*, 13 Ran. 1.
Nga Wa Gyi and 15 v. *King-Emperor*, (1902–03) 1 UBR Evid. 1.
Pakiya Ammal v. *Deputy Commissioner, Hanthawaddy and One*, 1949 BLR (SC) 35.
Po Hla v. *King-Emperor*, 8 LBR 357.
Queen-Empress v. *Nga Chit Kyu*, (1897–1901) 1 UBR 325.
Queen-Empress v. *Nga Han Shin*, (1892–96) 1 UBR 50.
Queen-Empress v. *Nga Lu Gyi and 7*, 1 LBR 49.
Saya Kye and Others v. *Queen-Empress*, (1892–96) 1 UBR 148.
Shwe Bwin v. *King-Emperor*, 2 LBR 270.
Shwe Hnit and One v. *King-Emperor*, 2 LBR 214.
Shwe Sin and Another v. *King-Emperor*, 3 LBR 213.
Shwe Yi v. *Crown*, 1 LBR 336 FB.
Sobika Rahman v. *Union of Burma*, 1952 BLR (HC) 385.
Sri Sawarmal v. *Union of Burma (U Thein Maung)*, 1954 BLR (HC) 331.
T. S. Mohamed and One v. *Union of Burma*, 1953 BLR (HC) 107.
Tambi v. *Appalsawmy (King-Emperor)*, 9 LBR 208.
Tan Sein (a) *Maung Saing* v. *Crown*, 1 LBR 173.
Tha Hmu v. *King-Emperor*, 2 LBR 206.
Thakin Myo Nyunt v. *Thakin Pu*, 1963 BLR (CC) 728.
Thein Maung v. *King-Emperor*, 3 LBR 173.
Thet Tun v. *Deputy Commissioner, Shwebo and Another*, 1952 BLR (SC) 33.
Ti Ya and 6 v. *King-Emperor*, 8 LBR 38 FB.
Tinsa Maw Naing v. *Commissioner of Police, Rangoon*, 1950 BLR (SC) 17.
U Ba Aye and 3 v. *Union of Burma*, 1958 BLR (HC) 548.
U Ba Din v. *Union of Burma*, 1956 BLR (HC) 166.
U Ba Khin v. *Union of Burma*, 1954 BLR (HC) 191.
U Ba Kyi v. *Union of Burma*, 1964 BLR (CC) 306.
U Ba Thein and Another v. *King-Emperor*, 8 Ran. 372.
U Ba Yi and 8 v. *Officer-in-Charge of Jail, Yamethin*, 1950 BLR (SC) 130.

U Saw and 9 v. *Union of Burma*, 1948 BLR (HC) 217.
U Tun Aung Tha v. *Union of Burma*, 1968 BLR (CC) 10.
U Yu Maung v. *Union of Burma*, 1959 BLR (HC) 317.
U Zan v. *Deputy Commissioner, Insein and Another*, 1951 BLR (SC) 188.
Union of Burma v. *Ah Hla* (a) *Maung Hla and 2*, 1958 BLR (HC) 29.
Union of Burma v. *Ah Shin and 2*, 1955 BLR (HC) 317.
Union of Burma v. *Aung Tun* (a) *Aung Myint, Aung Tun* (a) *Aung Myint* v. *Union of Burma*, 1958 BLR (SC) 1.
Union of Burma v. *U Chit Swe*, 1950 BLR (HC) 278.
Union of Burma v. *U Khin Maung Lat and One*, 1950 BLR (HC) 376.
V. E. Rm. N. Rm. Kasi Viswanathan Chettyar v. *Official Assignee and One*, 1958 BLR (SC) 74.
V. S. M. Moideen Brothers v. *Eng Thaung and Co.*, 9 LBR 45.

RULINGS REPORTED IN BURMESE

Bishu (a) *Ma Kyin Nu* v. *Union of Burma*, 1953 BLR (HC) [Burma Law Reports (High Court) (မြန်မာနိုင်ငံ တရားစီရင်ထုံးများ၊ တရားလွှတ်တော်)] 110.
Chit Hlaing, Htun Waing, Thein Aung and 19 v. *Union of Burma*, 1958 BLR (HC) 582.
Daw Aye Kyi v. *U Win Thaung and 3*, 1986 BLR (CCJ) [Central Court of Justice (ဗဟိုတရားရုံး)] 87.
Daw Aye Tin v. *Meikhtila District Area People's Court Appeal Court and Another*, 1971 BLR (CC) [Chief Court (တရားရုံးချုပ်)] 17.
Daw Dagon Khin Khin Lay v. *U Ko Ko Lay and Another*, 1965 BLR (CC) 1065.
Daw Si Si v. *Union of Burma*, 1964 BLR (CC) 876.
Daw Than Than Lwin, Assistant Director, Civil Justice Dept., Mandalay v. *U Thein Kyi* (a) *Mohamed Muser*, 2007 MLR [Myanmar Law Reports (မြန်မာနိုင်ငံတော် တရားစီရင်ထုံးများ)] 112.
In the matter of an advocate, 1985 BLR (CCJ) 81.
Ko Khin Maung v. *Ma Ohn and 2*, 1966 BLR (CC) 572.
Lim Hkwei Ya (a) *Yaun Ei* v. *Minister of Home Affairs*, 1960 BLR (SC) [Supreme Court (တရားလွှတ်တော်ချုပ်)] 189.
Ma Khin Myint (a) *Ma Khin Nyunt Kyi* v. *Union of Burma*, 1970 BLR (SCCAC) [Special Criminal Courts' Appeal Court (အထူးရာဇဝတ်ရုံး အယူခံအဖွဲ့)] 1.
Maung Aung Htay Myint v. *Union of Burma*, 1965 BLR (CC) 397.
Maung Chit v. *Union of Burma*, 1972 BLR (CC) 20.
Maung Chit Hlaing and 6 v. *Union of Burma*, 1966 BLR (SCCAC) 142.
Maung Chit Htwe and 3 v. *Union of Burma*, 1967 BLR (CC) 69.
Maung Ko Ni v. *Socialist Republic of the Union of Burma*, 1980 BLR (CCJ) 7.

Maung Kyaw Aye and 6 v. *Taunggoo District Commissioner and Another*, 1957 BLR (SC) 49.
Maung Kyaw Tint v. *Union of Burma*, 1966 BLR (SCCAC) 41.
Maung Pan Zone v. *Union of Burma*, 1960 BLR (SC) 15.
Maung Soe Myint v. *Socialist Republic of the Union of Burma*, 1981 BLR (CCJ) 28.
Maung Than v. *Union of Burma*, 1973 BLR (CC) 24.
Maung Than Win (a) *Tin Aung and 2* v. *Union of Burma*, 1968 BLR (SCCAC) 61.
Maung Thein v. *Union of Burma*, 1966 BLR (CC) 158.
Maung Tin Aye v. *District Commissioner, Pakokku and One*, 1957 BLR (SC) 17.
Maung Tin Maung and 7 v. *Union of Burma*, 1969 BLR (CC) 222.
Maung Tint Swe v. *Socialist Republic of the Union of Burma*, 1980 BLR (CCJ) 20.
Maung Tun Tin v. *Union of Burma*, 1965 BLR (CC) 185.
Mister R. S. Bun and 2 v. *Union of Burma*, 1966 BLR (SCCAC) 65.
Saw Bogyu v. *Union of Burma*, 1967 BLR (SCCAC) 45.
Socialist Republic of the Union of Burma v. *U Hla Htun*, 1982 BLR (CCJ) 48.
U Aung Nyunt v. *Union of Burma (Sub-Divisional Magistrate, Tachilek)*, 1965 BLR (CC) 578.
U Aung Sein and 2 v. *Union of Burma*, 1960 BLR (HC) 91.
U Aye Thein v. *Republic of the Union of Myanmar*, 2012 MLR 77.
U Kyaw Thein v. *Republic of the Union of Myanmar*, 2012 MLR 10.
U Maung Maung and Another v. *Daw Kyu Sein and 2*, 1992 MLR 102.
U Min v. *Socialist Republic of the Union of Burma*, 1977 BLR (CCJ) 22.
U Sein Tun v. *Socialist Republic of the Union of Burma*, 1980 BLR (CCJ) 13.
U Thein Lun, 1972 BLR (CC) 72.
U Tin Ngwe, Daw Mya Mya Win (a) *Daw Than Win* v. *Union of Myanmar*, 2006 MLR 1.
U Win Han v. *Socialist Republic of the Union of Burma*, 1975 BLR (CCJ) 101.
Union of Burma v. *Maung Htun Sein*, 1966 BLR (CC) 1425.
Union of Burma (Daw Shu Khin) v. *Maung Mya* (a) *Mya Oo and 2*, 1971 BLR (CC) 31.
Union of Myanmar v. *Mardin* (a) *Kyi Lwin*, 1996 MLR 129.
Union of Myanmar v. *U Ye Naung and Another*, 1991 MLR 63.
Union of Myanmar / Toe Yi v. *Toe Yi / Union of Myanmar*, 1992 MLR 28.
Yoe Bun Hwei (a) *Kek Nek Hwei La* v. *Secretary, Ministry of Home Affairs, Government of the Union of Burma and Others*, 1960 BLR (SC) 175.

OFFICIAL MANUALS

Bar Council. *Lawyers' Code of Conduct, Responsibilities and Rights.* (တရားရုံးချုပ်ရှေ့နေများ ကောင်စီ။ ရှေ့နေရှေ့ရပ်များ၏ ကျင့်ဝတ်သိက္ခာများ၊ တာဝန်များနှင့် အခွင့်အရေးများ။) 3rd edn. Yangon: Office of the Attorney General, 2001.

Myanmar Police Force Headquarters. *Union of Myanmar Police Manual.* (မြန်မာနိုင်ငံ ရဲတပ်ဖွဲ့ဌာနချုပ်။ ပြည်ထောင်စုမြန်မာနိုင်ငံတော် ရဲလက်စွဲ။) Vol. I, II. 4 vols. Yangon: Myanmar Police Force Headquarters, 2000.

Office of the Council of State. *Civil Servants Maintenance of Discipline Manual.* (နိုင်ငံတော်ကောင်စီရုံး။ ဝန်ထမ်း စည်းကမ်းထိန်းသိမ်းရေးလက်စွဲ။) Rangoon: Office of the Council of State, 1985.

Supreme Court. *Courts Manual.* (တရားရုံးချုပ်။ တရားရုံးလက်စွဲ။) 4th edn. Vol. I. Yangon: Supreme Court, 1999. (In English and Burmese.)

STATUTES

Arms Act, India Act 11/1878

Bar Council Act, India Act 38/26

Citizenship Law, 2/82 (မြန်မာနိုင်ငံသား ဥပဒေ၊ ၂/၈၂)

Constitution of the Republic of the Union of Myanmar, 2008

Constitution of the Socialist Republic of the Union of Burma, 1974

Constitution of the Union of Burma, 1947

Contempt of Court Act, India Act 12/26

Contempt of Courts Law, 17/2013 (တရားရုံးများကို မထီမဲ့မြင်ပြုမှု ဥပဒေ၊ ၁၇/၂၀၁၃)

Control of Imports and Exports (Temporary) Act, 56/47

Council of People's Justices Law, 13/74 (ပြည်သူ့တရားသူကြီးအဖွဲ့ ဥပဒေ၊ ၁၃/၇၄)

Criminal Law (Temporary Provisions) Act, 21/58

Criminal Procedure Code [or, Code of Criminal Procedure], India Act 5/1898

Electronic Transactions Law, 5/2004 (အီလက်ထရောနစ် ဆက်သွယ်ဆောင်ရွက်ရေး ဥပဒေ၊ ၅/၂၀၀၄)

Emergency Provisions Act, 17/50 (အရေးပေါ်စီမံမှု အက်ဥပဒေ၊ ၁၇/၅၀)

Emergency Provisions (Temporary Amendment) Act, 26/58 [အရေးပေါ်စီမံမှု (ယာယီပြင်ဆင်ချက်) အက်ဥပဒေ၊ ၂၆/၅၈]

Eradication of Corruption Law, 23/2013 (အဂတိလိုက်စားမှု တိုက်ဖျက်ရေး ဥပဒေ၊ ၂၃/၂၀၁၃)

Evidence Act, India Act 1/1872

Foreign Exchange Regulation Act, 44/47

Gambling Law, 6/86 (လောင်းကစား ဥပဒေ၊ ၆/၈၆)

Judiciary Law, 2/88 (တရားစီရင်ရေး ဥပဒေ၊ ၂/၈၈)

Judiciary Law, 5/2000 (တရားစီရင်ရေး ဥပဒေ၊ ၅/၂၀၀၀)
Law Amending the Peaceful Assembly and Procession Law, 26/2014 (ငြိမ်းချမ်းစွာ စုဝေးခွင့်နှင့် ငြိမ်းချမ်းစွာ စီတန်းလှည့်လည်ခွင့်ဆိုင်ရာ ဥပဒေကို ပြင်ဆင်သည့်ဥပဒေ၊ ၂၆/၂၀၁၄)
Law Conferring Authorizations for the Building of a Socialist Economic System, 8/65 (ဆိုရှယ်လစ်စီးပွားရေးစနစ် တည်ဆောက်မှုအတွက် လုပ်ပိုင်ခွင့်များ အပ်နှင်းသည့် ဥပဒေ၊ ၈/၆၅)
Law on Registration of Organisations, 31/2014 (အသင်းအဖွဲ့များ မှတ်ပုံတင်ခြင်းဆိုင်ရာ ဥပဒေ၊ ၃၁/၂၀၁၄)
Legal Practitioners Act, India Act 18/1879
Narcotic Drugs and Psychotropic Substances Law, 1/93 (မူးယစ်ဆေးဝါးနှင့် စိတ်ကိုပြောင်းလဲစေသော ဆေးဝါးများဆိုင်ရာ ဥပဒေ၊ ၁/၉၃)
Organisation Law, 6/88 (အသင်းအဖွဲ့များ ဖွဲ့စည်းခြင်းဆိုင်ရာ ဥပဒေ၊ ၆/၈၈)
Peaceful Assembly and Procession Law, 15/2011 (ငြိမ်းချမ်းစွာ စုဝေးခွင့်နှင့် ငြိမ်းချမ်းစွာ စီတန်းလှည့်လည်ခွင့်ဆိုင်ရာ ဥပဒေ၊ ၁၅/၂၀၁၁)
Penal Code, India Act 45/1860
People's Council Law, 8/74 (ပြည်သူ့ကောင်စီ ဥပဒေ၊ ဂ/၇၄)
Police Act, 6/45
Prevention of Corruption Act, 67/48 (အဂတိလိုက်စားမှု တားမြစ်ရေး အက်ဥပဒေ၊ ၆၇/၄၈)
Public Order (Preservation) Act, 16/47
Special Criminal Courts Law, 15/62 (အထူးရာဇဝတ်ရုံး ဥပဒေ၊ ၁၅/၆၂)
Special Criminal Courts Law Repealing Law, 8/74 (အထူးရာဇဝတ်ရုံး ဥပဒေကို ရုပ်သိမ်းသည့် ဥပဒေ၊ ၈/၇၄)
Special Limitations Law, 9/88
Television and Video Law, 8/96 (ရုပ်မြင်သံကြားနှင့်ဗီဒီယို ဥပဒေ၊ ၈/၉၆)
Towns Act, 3/07
Tuition Law, 6/84 (ဘာသာရပ်သင် ကိုယ်ပိုင်သင်တန်း ဥပဒေ၊ ၆/၈၄)
Union Judiciary Act, 8/48
Union Judiciary Law, 20/2010 (ပြည်ထောင်စုတရားစီရင်ရေး ဥပဒေ၊ ၂၀/၂၀၀၀)
Unlawful Associations Act, India Act 14/08

NEWS MEDIA

Asia Sentinel
Biweekly Eleven (in Burmese)
Botataung (ဗိုလ်တထောင်)
British Broadcasting Corporation (*BBC*) (Burmese Service)
Burma Update (in Burmese)
CNN
Daily Eleven (in Burmese)
Democratic Voice of Burma (Burmese Service)
Eleven Media (in Burmese)
Flower News (in Burmese)
Forward (ရှေ့သို့)
Irrawaddy
KQED
Mizzima
Myanma Alin (မြန်မာ့အလင်း)
Myanmar Herald (မြန်မာသံတော်ဆင့်)
Myanmar Times
New Light of Myanmar (*NLM*)
People's Age (ပြည်သူ့ခေတ်)
Radio Free Asia (Burmese Service)
Voice Daily (in Burmese)
Voice of America (*VOA*) (Burmese Service)
Weekly Eleven (in Burmese)
Working People's Daily (*WPD*)
Yale News

INDEX

Books in the Series

Diseases of the Will
Mariana Valverde

The Politics of Truth and Reconciliation in South Africa: Legitimizing the Post-Apartheid State
Richard A. Wilson

Modernism and the Grounds of Law
Peter Fitzpatrick

Unemployment and Government: Genealogies of the Social
William Walters

Autonomy and Ethnicity: Negotiating Competing Claims in Multi-Ethnic States
Yash Ghai

Constituting Democracy: Law, Globalism and South Africa's Political Reconstruction
Heinz Klug

The Ritual of Rights in Japan: Law, Society, and Health Policy
Eric A. Feldman

The Invention of the Passport: Surveillance, Citizenship and the State
John Torpey

Governing Morals: A Social History of Moral Regulation
Alan Hunt

The Colonies of Law: Colonialism, Zionism and Law in Early Mandate Palestine
Ronen Shamir

Law and Nature
David Delaney

Social Citizenship and Workfare in the United States and Western Europe: The Paradox of Inclusion
Joel F. Handler

Law, Anthropology and the Constitution of the Social: Making Persons and Things
Edited by Alain Pottage and Martha Mundy

Judicial Review and Bureaucratic Impact: International and Interdisciplinary Perspectives
Edited by Marc Hertogh and Simon Halliday

Immigrants at the Margins: Law, Race, and Exclusion in Southern Europe
Kitty Calavita

Lawyers and Regulation: The Politics of the Administrative Process
Patrick Schmidt

Law and Globalization from Below: Toward a Cosmopolitan Legality
Edited by Boaventura de Sousa Santos and Cesar A. Rodriguez-Garavito

Public Accountability: Designs, Dilemmas and Experiences
Edited by Michael W. Dowdle

Law, Violence and Sovereignty among West Bank Palestinians
Tobias Kelly

Legal Reform and Administrative Detention Powers in China
Sarah Biddulph

The Practice of Human Rights: Tracking Law between the Global and the Local
Edited by Mark Goodale and Sally Engle Merry

Judges Beyond Politics in Democracy and Dictatorship: Lessons from Chile
Lisa Hilbink

Paths to International Justice: Social and Legal Perspectives
Edited by Marie-Bénédicte Dembour and Tobias Kelly

Law and Society in Vietnam: The Transition from Socialism in Comparative Perspective
Mark Sidel

Constitutionalizing Economic Globalization: Investment Rules and Democracy's Promise
David Schneiderman

The New World Trade Organization Knowledge Agreements. Second Edition
Christopher Arup

Justice and Reconciliation in Post-Apartheid South Africa
Edited by François du Bois and Antje du Bois-Pedain

Militarization and Violence against Women in Conflict Zones in the Middle East: A Palestinian Case-Study
Nadera Shalhoub-Kevorkian

Child Pornography and Sexual Grooming: Legal and Societal Responses
Suzanne Ost

Darfur and the Crime of Genocide
John Hagan and Wenona Rymond-Richmond

Fictions of Justice: The International Criminal Court and the Challenge of Legal Pluralism in Sub-Saharan Africa
Kamari Maxine Clarke

Conducting Law and Society Research: Reflections on Methods and Practices
Simon Halliday and Patrick Schmidt

Planted Flags: Trees, Land, and Law in Israel/Palestine
Irus Braverman

Culture under Cross-Examination: International Justice and the Special Court for Sierra Leone
Tim Kelsall

Cultures of Legality: Judicialization and Political Activism in Latin America
Edited by Javier Couso, Alexandra Huneeus, Rachel Sieder

Courting Democracy in Bosnia and Herzegovina: The Hague Tribunal's Impact in a Postwar State
Lara J. Nettelfield

The Gacaca Courts and Post-Genocide Justice and Reconciliation in Rwanda: Justice without Lawyers
Phil Clark

Law, Society, and History: Themes in the Legal Sociology and Legal History of Lawrence M. Friedman
Robert W. Gordon and Morton J. Horwitz

After Abu Ghraib: Exploring Human Rights in America and the Middle East
Shadi Mokhtari

Adjudication in Religious Family Laws: Cultural Accommodation: Legal Pluralism, and Gender Equality in India
Gopika Solanki

Water On Tap: Rights and Regulation in the Transnational Governance of Urban Water Services
Bronwen Morgan

Elements of Moral Cognition: Rawls' Linguistic Analogy and the Cognitive Science of Moral and Legal Judgment
John Mikhail

A Sociology of Constitutions: Constitutions and State Legitimacy in Historical-Sociological Perspective
Chris Thornhill

Mitigation and Aggravation at Sentencing
Edited by Julian Roberts

Institutional Inequality and the Mobilization of the Family and Medical Leave Act: Rights on Leave
Catherine R. Albiston

Authoritarian Rule of Law: Legislation, Discourse and Legitimacy in Singapore
Jothie Rajah

Law and Development and the Global Discourses of Legal Transfers
Edited by John Gillespie and Pip Nicholson

Law against the State: Ethnographic Forays into Law's Transformations
Edited by Julia Eckert, Brian Donahoe, Christian Strümpell, and Zerrin Özlem Biner

Environmental Litigation in China: A Study in Political Ambivalence
Rachel E. Stern

Law, Society, and History: Themes in the Legal Sociology and Legal History of Lawrence M. Friedman
Robert W. Gordon and Morton J. Horwitz

Transnational Legal Ordering and State Change
Gregory C. Shaffer

Legal Mobilization under Authoritarianism: The Case of Post-Colonial Hong Kong
Waikeung Tam

Complementarity in the Line of Fire: The Catalysing Effect of the International Criminal Court in Uganda and Sudan
Sarah M. H. Nouwen

Political and Legal Transformations of an Indonesian Polity: The Nagari from Colonisation to Decentralisation
Franz von Benda-Beckmann and Keebet von Benda-Beckmann

Pakistan's Experience with Formal Law: An Alien Justice
Osama Siddique

Human Rights under State-Enforced Religious Family Laws in Israel, Egypt, and India
Yüksel Sezgin

Why Prison?
Edited by David Scott

Law's Fragile State: Colonial, Authoritarian, and Humanitarian Legacies in Sudan
Mark Fathi Massoud

Rights for Others: The Slow Home-Coming of Human Rights in the Netherlands
Barbara Oomen

European States and their Muslim Citizens: The Impact of Institutions on Perceptions and Boundaries
Edited by John R. Bowen, Christophe Bertossi, Jan Willem Duyvendak, and Mona Lena Krook

Religion, Law and Society
Russell Sandberg

The Experiences of Face Veil Wearers in Europe and the Law
Edited by Eva Brems

The Contentious History of the International Bill of Human Rights
Christopher N. J. Roberts

Transnational Legal Orders
Edited by Terence C. Halliday and Gregory Shaffer

Lost in China? Law, Culture and Identity in Post-1997 Hong Kong
Carol A. G. Jones

Security Theology, Surveillance and the Politics of Fear
Nadera Shalhoub-Kevorkian

Opposing the Rule of Law: How Myanmar's Courts Make Law and Order
Nick Cheesman

Indigeneity and Legal Pluralism in India: Claims, Histories, Meanings
Pooja Parmar

The Clinic and the Court: Law, Medicine and Anthropology
Ian Harper, Tobias Kelly, and Akshay Khanna

Iraq and the Crimes of Aggressive War: The Legal Cynicism of Criminal Militarism
John Hagan, Joshua Kaiser, and Anna Hanson

The Quiet Power of Indicators: Measuring Development, Corruption, and the Rule of Law
Sally Engle Merry, Kevin Davis, and Benedict Kingsbury

Lightning Source UK Ltd.
Milton Keynes UK
UKOW06n2130100315

247656UK00003B/41/P